Mass Communication Research:
On Problems
and Policies
The Art of Asking
the Right Questions

In Honor of
James D. Halloran

Mass Communication Research:
On Problems and Policies

The Art of Asking the Right Questions

In Honor of
James D. Halloran

Edited by
Cees J. Hamelink
Olga Linné

Ablex Publishing Corporation
Norwood, New Jersey

Copyright © 1994 by Ablex Publishing

Printed in the United States of America

Library of Congress Cataloging-in-Publication Data

Mass communication research : on problems and policies : "the art of
  asking the right questions" / Cees J. Hamelink, Olga Linné editors.
      p.   cm.—(Communication and information science series)
   Festschrift in honor of James D. Halloran.
   Includes bibliographical references and index.
   ISBN 0-89391-738-9.—ISBN 0-89391-951-9 (pbk.)
   1. Mass media—Research.   I. Hamelink, Cees J., 1940–
II. Linné, Olga, 1941–   III. Halloran, James, D. (James Dermot)
IV. Series.
P91.3.M367 1994
302.23—dc20   93-46341
                                                          CIP

Ablex Publishing Company
355 Chestnut Street
Norwood, New Jersey 07648

Contents

Part VI   On Media Education

Part VII   On Communication Technology

Part VIII   On International Issues

About the Authors

Paul A.V. Ansah was Professor and Director, School of Journalism and Communication at the University of Ghana, Legon, Ghana. Dr. Ansah died in 1993. He was the president of the African Council on Communication Education and worked as a consultant with various international agencies.

Nelly de Camargo (Professor at the Multimedia Department, UNI-CAMP, Sao Paulo, Brazil.) Dr. De Camargo teaches communication theory and policy applied to development. She has been Unesco's regional advisor for communication in Latin America.

Brenda Dervin (Professor and Ameritech Fellow at the Department of Communication, Ohio State University, Columbus, Ohio, U.S.A.) Her publications include *Rethinking Communication* (edited with Lawrence Grossberg, Barbara O'Keefe, and Ellen Wartella), two volumes (1989).

K.E. Eapen (Professor Emeritus, former Dean, Faculty of Communication, Bangalore University, Bangalore, India.) Dr. Eapen is an honorary member of the International Association Mass Communication Research and has published widely in the area of communication and development. His books include *The Media and Development* (1973).

Cecilia von Feilitzen (Research fellow at the Department of Journalism, Media and Communication, Unit of Media and Cultural Theory, Stockholm University, and at the Audience and Programme Research Department, Swedish Broadcasting Corporation.) Dr. Von Feilitzen is also former head of the Association of Swedish Mass Communication Researchers and co-editor of several international media journals.

George Gerbner (Professor of Communications and former dean, Annenberg School of Communications, University of Pennsylvania, Philadelphia, U.S.A.) Dr. Gerbner is editor of the *Journal of Communication*. His publications include *World Communications: A Handbook* (edited with Marsha Siefert) (1984).

Todd Gitlin (Professor of Sociology and director of the mass communications program at the University of California, Berkeley, U.S.A.) Among his books are *The Whole World Is Watching, Inside Prime Time,* and *The Sixties: Years of Hope, Days of Rage.*

Cees J. Hamelink (Professor of Communication at the University of Amsterdam, the Netherlands.) Dr. Hamelink is president of the International Association for Mass Communication Research. His publications include *Global Communications and Cultural Autonomy* (1983), *Finance and Information* (1983), *Transnational Data in the Information Age* (1984), and *The Technology Gamble* (1988).

Alan Hancock Between 1983 and 1993 Dr. Hancock coordinated Unesco's research program in communications before becoming director of the new division of communication development and free flow of international, which grouped together Unesco's operational and research functions. He has recently been appointed Director of the Unesco Programme for Central and Eastern European Development. His publications include *Planning and Educational Mass Media* (1977) and *Communication Planning for Development* (1980).

Anders Hansen (Lecturer at the Centre for Mass Communication Research at the University of Leicester, England. Convenor of the Working Group on Environmental Issues and the Mass Media of the International Association for Mass Communication Research.) Currently Anders Hansen directs a research project on the production and presentation of science in the British press and broadcast media.

Olof Hultén (Lecturer at the University of Gothenburg for Media and Communication Studies.) Dr. Hulten has worked for the Swedish Broadcasting Corporation in audience research (1969–1974) and strategic planning and policy analysis (1976–Present). He was for several years the Treasurer of the International Association for Mass Communication Research.

Keval Joe Kumar (Reader in the Department of Communication and Journalism at the University of Poona, India. Former coordinator of media education at the Centre for the Study of Communication and Culture, London.) Dr. Kumar's publications include *Mass Comunication in India* (1989), *Business Communication: A Management Perspective* (1990), and *Advertising* (1990).

Gladys Lang and Kurt Lang (Professors of Sociology and Political Science at the School of Communication, University of Washington, Seattle, Washington, U.S.A.) Prolific authors in such fields as the sociology of communication and public opinion research. Among their important publications is *The Battle for Public Opinion: The President, The Press and the Polls During Watergate* (1983).

Olga Linné (Senior research fellow at the Centre for Mass Communication Research, University of Leicester, England.) Dr. Linné is Vice-President of the International Association for Mass Communication Research. Her publications include *Mass Communication Theories* (with Cecilia von Feilitzen) (1972) and *Why Do Female Professionals Produce Male Messages?* (1986).

Len Masterman (Lecturer at Nottingham University, England, and consultant to UNESCO and the Council of Europe.) His publications include *Teaching about Television* (1980), *Teaching the Media* (1985), and *Television Mythologies* (1985).

Denis McQuail (Professor of Communication at the University of Amsterdam, the Netherlands.) His major publications include *Towards a Sociology of Mass Communication* (1968), *Sociology of Mass Communications* (editor, 1972), *Analysis of Newspaper Content* (1977), and *Mass Communication Theory* (1984), and *Media Performance* (1992).

David Morrison (Director and Head of Media, Research International, London) has held posts at the Centre for Mass Communication Research at the University of Leicester; the City University, London; and the Broadcasting Research Unit, London.

Hamid Mowland (Professor of International Relations and founding director of the International Communication Program at the School of International Service, the American University, Washington, D.C.) Dr. Mowlana is President-Elect of the International Association for Mass Communication Research. His most recent publications include *Global Information and World Communication: New Frontiers in International Relations* (1986), *Communication Technology and Development* (1988), and *The Passing of Modernity: Communication and the Transformation of Society* (1990).

Graham Murdock (Senior lecturer at the University of Lough-
borough, England.) For many years Graham Murdock was a research fellow at the Centre for Mass Communication Research,
University of Leicester, England. His publications include *Mass
Media and the Secondary School* (with Guy Phelps) (1973), *Demonstrations and Communication* (with James D. Halloran and
Philip Elliott) (1970), and *Televising "Terrorism"* (with Philip Elliott
and Philip Schlesinger) (1984).

Elisabeth Noelle-Neumann (Founder and director of the Institut
für Demoskopie Allensbach, West Germany. Professor of Mass
Communication Research and founder of the Institut für Publizistik at the University of Mainz.) Dr. Noelle-Neumanns major
publications focus on methods of survey research, international
comparative analysis of value systems, public opinion theory, and
the effects of the mass media.

Kaarle Nordenstreng (Professor of Journalism and Mass Communication at the University of Tampere, Finland and past president of the International Organization of Journalists.) His
publications include (with H.I. Schiller, Eds.) *National Sovereignty
and International Communication* (1979); and *The Mass Media
Declaration of UNESCO* (1984). Dr. Nordenstreng is president of the
IAMCR Section on Professional Education.

Gertrude Robinson (Professor of Communication and former director of the Graduate Program in Communications, McGill University, Montreal, Canada.) Dr. Robinson has published widely on
international and Canadian communications issues, disciplinary
history, television news, and the media and feminism. She is
currently editor of the *Canadian Journal of Communication* and
Treasurer of the International Association for Mass Communication Research.

Rafael Roncagliolo (Director of the Center on Transnational Culture of the Instituto Para America Latina (IPAL). Founder member
of the Peruvian Association of Communication Researchers and the
Latin American Association of Communication Researchers (AL-
AIC).) His publications include *Iglesia, Prensa y Militares* (1978),
Trampas de la Informacion y Neocolonialismo (1979), and *Politicas de television en los Paises and Andinos* (1987).

Herbert I. Schiller (Professor Emeritus at the University of California, San Diego, U.S.A.) His numerous publications include *The
Mind Managers* (1973), *Communications and Cultural Domination* (1976), *Who Knows: Information in the Age of the Fortune 500*

(1981), *Information and the Crisis Economy* (1984), and *Culture Inc.: The Corporate Takeover of Public Expression* (1989).

Colin Seymour-Ure (Professor of Government and former Dean of Social Sciences at the University of Kent at the Centerbury.) He has published widely in the field of political communications and mass media and has recently compiled a short history of the British press and broadcasting since 1945.

Tamas Szecskö (Former Director of the Hungarian Institute for Public Opinion Research, Budapest, Hungary.) Dr. Szecskö has published widely in various areas of mass communication research. He was for many years the Secretary General of the International Association for Mass Communication Research. He has also served Unesco in various capacities.

Howard Tumber (Director of Communication Policy Studies, City University, London.) Together with Philip Schlesinger, he is writing a book on media politics of crime and criminal justice.

Robert A. White (Director of the Centro Interdisciplinare sulla Comunicazione, Georgian University, Rome, Italy.) Former research director of the London-based Centre for the Study of Communication and Culture, Dr. White is coeditor of the book series *Communications and Human Values*, published by Sage.

Preface

The chapters in this book are written to pay a special tribute to Professor James D. Halloran, Director of the Centre for Mass Communication Research at the University of Leicester, England. This tribute has been occasioned by his retirement after 18 years as President of the International Association for Mass Communication Research. The contributions to this book were not meant as mere praise but instead as scholarly inputs in teaching and learning in the field of mass communication.

The three decades or so in which Halloran has been involved in communication research have seen a massive growth and development of the field. Halloran has been instrumental in this expansion, and because he has been involved in research on a variety of topics he has managed to stay in touch with a wide range of contemporary developments. It seems most appropriate, therefore, that this book is organized into sections that reflect Halloran's research interests.

On Mass Communication Research and Policy Making

A crucial source for the attention to communication policy and planning was the meeting of experts on mass communication and society held at Montreal in 1969. The report of that meeting, which clearly bears Halloran's imprint, discusses the contribution of mass communication research to policy making. This passage sets the agenda for much that was to follow:

> There is a need for research into the goals of mass communication systems and their possible future goals. Such "goal" research might help to clarify policies and objectives in relation to any given society, suggest to policy makers and practitioners new bases for mass media

performance, and stimulate more comprehensive theories with regard to mass communication in general.

On Mass Media Effects

Many students of communication will have come across Halloran's work primarily through his research on media effects. The first mark of his contribution to these perennial questions of media research came with a working paper from the Television Research Committee, *The Effects of Mass Communication*. This was 1964, and the foreword states that the working paper had been written by Mr. J.D. Halloran, a sociologist. It was evident from the content of the working paper that this was a sociologist with a critical perspective on his trade, critical of the social scientist who

> may have helped to create confusion, cynicism and pessimism, for not only has he failed to give definite answers, but he may also be accused of doing something worse, namely of providing evidence in partial support of every view.

On Violence

Halloran has also paid considerable attention to the focal point of much media effects research: violence and aggression. Already in 1966 he proposed that research in this area would have to encompass "studies of repeated exposure, examinations of links with personality variables and, in particular, extensions of the work to non-laboratory settings so that consequences can be observed in more natural conditions in order for this research to be socially relevant." This is an area of abiding interest to him and is one in which he has been especially keen to spell out of the role of the critical researcher. In 1989 he wrote

> The dominant and still prevailing approach has been psychologistic and over-centered on the media, and this has led to the media being studied in isolation without appropriate reference to other institutions....Our task is to see whether the media are related to violence in any way , and not just in the simple, direct casual ways of popular speculation.

On Journalism and Society

The broad sociological perspective that Halloran has promoted throughout his work could hardly bypass the analysis of the message producer. Written in collaboration with his colleagues Philip Elliott and Graham Murdock, the book *Demonstrations and Communication: A Case Study* (1970) was a pioneering study that laid the basis for much of our understanding about the selection and production of news. It has become a classic and frequently quoted work.

On Communication and Development

Halloran encountered the communication and development issue through work in several different contexts: through the affiliation with Unesco, the many Third World students enrolling in the M.A. and Ph.D. programs at Leicester, and, of course, through IAMCR. In 1973, at an international seminar called to provide guidance on the question of mass communication research and developing countries, Halloran contributed to the debate on the export of research models from the North to the South, commenting

> What we're doing is exporting bad research models. It is not so much that we are exporting Western models, although that is true: the relevant factor is that we are exporting inadequate research designs that are inadequate everywhere.

On Media Education

It would fit the repeated emphasis on the processual approach that the public understanding of the communication process also would receive Halloran's attention. Here the research interest was particularly focused on the improvement of the public's capacity to cope with the media environment. Guidance for research to capacitate the audience was provided in his inaugural lecture at the University of Leicester by such questions as:

> Is it not time that the media were demystified, and that we began to question the restrictions and the possible tyranny of professionalism? Must we always have the few talking about the many to the many?"

On Communication Technology

In recent years, as interest in the analysis of the role of advanced communication technology in society grew, Halloran pleaded once again for the broad, critical, and processual approach. Drawing up a research agenda in 1986, he argued:

The implications of technological innovations in communication can only be studied within the appropriate historical, economic and sociological contexts, and due attention must be given to other non-communication institutions, processes, and trends.

On International Issues

The long-time affiliation with the IAMCR made an interest in the international dimensions of communications almost inevitable. In this line by duty Halloran advised the MacBride commission and called for

a clearer articulation of the proposed relationship between the New International Economic Order and the New International Information Order.

This book is subtitled *The Art of Asking the Right Questions*. This points to a continuing theme in Halloran's work. He has consistently reminded us of the need to define problems adequately and the need to ask the right questions. If we don't ask the right questions, Halloran seems to have been saying, we are unlikely to receive sensible answers. This may be a truism, but it is one that bears repeating. It is to be hoped that the spirit of this, perhaps Halloran's central research principle, is reflected in the chapters that follow.

Many distinguished individuals from all over the world have been involved in the production of this book. This in itself is testimony to the significance of Halloran's work and is a measure of the respect and appreciation his colleagues hold for him.

We are, first of all, therefore, very grateful to all our fellow authors, who took time from overloaded schedules to contribute original articles. We are also grateful to Brenda Dervin for her support of the entire project on behalf of the publishers. At the Ablex Publishing Corporation, particularly Joanne Palmer needs to be thanked for her good and professional advice. Thanks are also due to David Morrison, who provided significant help by introducing several additional contributors to us. We must thank our colleague Roger Dickinson for helping us to edit and prepare the final manuscript for publication. At the Institute of Social Studies in the Hague, Aïda Jesurun gave valuable assistance in text processing.

Cees J. Hamelink and Olga Linné.
Amsterdam and Leicester, December 1993.

PART

I

On Mass Communication Research and Policy Making

CHAPTER

The Unesco Expert Panel with the Benefit of Hindsight

KAARLE NORDENSTRENG

It was the famous year of 1968 (with the Prague spring, the Paris riots, etc.) that started the process whereby a new chapter was to be written in the world history of communication research. That year, in November 1968, the General Conference of Unesco (15th session) authorized the organization "to promote and undertake studies and research on the role, present state and effects of the media of mass communication in modern society."

By chance, it was the same year, 1968, that brought this author into contact with James D. Halloran. It happened in Salzburg in early September, at a reception of a Council of Europe symposium on "Human Rights and Mass Communications," where I brought to him fresh impressions from another symposium on "Mass Media and International Understanding," held some days earlier in Ljubljana under the auspices of the IAMCR (for the latter, see Osolnik, Pavlic, Vreg, & Lrimsek, 1969). This point of contact led to an intensive cooperation between us—and to Jim Halloran's real entry to the IAMCR.[1]

---

[1] James D. Halloran gives himself the following testimony of his first contacts with the IAMCR (in private communication with the present author in September 1990):

> I first heard about IAMCR in 1964 in the USA from Leo Bogart and George Gerbner and became a member in 1965. At that time the only UK member I was aware of was a man called Simpson from Cardiff University

THE PRELUDE IN MONTREAL

As the first step toward materializing the 1968 Unesco mandate, a meeting was convened in Montreal in June 1969. An extensive working paper for this "Meeting of Experts on Mass Communication and Society" was commissioned from the Director of a newly established Centre for Mass Communication Research at the University of Leicester—Halloran's first assignment with Unesco. The working paper (amended and expanded by its author) and the formal report of the Montreal meeting (prepared by the Secretariat through Pierre Navaux and Lakshmana Rao) were published under the title "Mass Media in Society: The Need of Research" (Unesco, 1970).

The Montreal meeting was attended by 20 participants from all over the world (7 from Europe, among them Halloran and myself), as well as observers from various media organizations.[2] This representative group emphatically endorsed the Unesco mandate to launch an international research program in the media field and it outlined—guided by the working paper—the approach to be taken, in terms of both research philosophy and topics to be covered. It also recommended that regional centers be made the focal points in organizing research and training—a boost for centers such as CIESPAL in Quito and AMIC in Singapore, gradually leading to the formation of COMNET.

The approach advocated by the meeting was clearly a critical one against what is known as administrative research. Not surprisingly, Dallas Smythe was outspoken with the point that science is not value-free and that empiricism has biased the academic community to accept only what is countable as worth researching ("counting mania"). A critical approach was amplified by perspectives of the developing countries, such as those voiced by a

---

who if I remember right was a Media Education man. He was on one of the governing bodies of the IAMCR and around 1967–8 he approached me with a view to having a conference in England—Oxford was suggested, but nothing came of it and I never actually met him.

The next "point of contact," apart from receiving the usual material from Bourquin, was Salzburg, and you are familiar with that and what happened thereafter. My first attendance at any meeting was Constance 1970.

[2] The Unesco Secretariat consulted Halloran about whom to invite, and he recommended, among others, the present author. (After this first meeting in Salzburg, Halloran and I stayed in close touch by correspondence; among other things I commented on the manuscript for *Demonstrations and Communication* by Halloran, Elliott, and Murdock).

Lebanese participant in terms of "new imperialism," "consumption ideology," and alternative news values of "what is important for our own people." Halloran—along with most Western participants— emphasized in the discussion that at issue was theory, social relevance, and even ideology—not only research techniques.[3] Besides, Halloran reminded the meeting, "head counting" service research gets as much as 60 times more money than social research, and thus it was natural that one of the summary points for discussion in his working paper was the following:

> The needs for commercial and administrative research are recognized, but the primary need is for independent, basic social scientific research into mass media as social institutions and mass communication as a social process. This work is ideally suited to universities. It could either fall within the framework of existing departments of sociology or psychology or lead to the formation of new specialised departments of mass media studies, or centres of mass communication research.

This point—as well as most that were raised in the working paper— was included in the collective final report, although sometime watered down and written in "Unescese." One aspect not clearly reflected in the report was the point, made particularly by myself and Ulf Himmelstrand from Sweden, that the goals and policies of the media should be submitted to critical investigation so as to make the underlying values explicit. (During the meeting we even wrote a joint paper, "The Need for Goal-Research Regarding Mass Communications.") My intervention voiced the point that "not only commercial head counters but also academic social scientists have been good servants of the status quo Establishment since they have not critically questioned the goals of the game." It was an unusual point coming from the head of research in a national broadcasting corporation, but it was logical given the particular conditions of the Finnish Broadcasting experiment at the time (Nordenstreng, 1972, 1973a; Pietilä, Malmberg, & Nordenstreng, 1990) and given my assessment of U.S. communication research (Nordenstreng, 1968).

In one respect, however, goals and policies were given high attention in the Montreal report: the proposed program "should be

---

[3] The observations on and quotes from the proceedings of this meeting, as well as of subsequent panel sessions, are mainly based on unpublished working documents and personal notes taken and stored by the present author. I am indebted to Cees Hamelink for inspiring me to utilize this unique documentation for outlining an interesting passage of history.

designed to identify the ways in which the mass media can best serve the needs of present and future societies." Thus research was conceived as part and parcel of communication policies. But it is not quite clear whether this was understood to mean that research is an instrument—a kind of technical means—employed to identify the ways that lead to maximize the needs of societies, or whether research was taken as mental ferment in distilling the values that lie behind the words "best serve the needs."

The overall outcome of the Montreal meeting was welcomed by Unesco's next (16th) General Conference in 1970, which authorized the organization "to promote research within the framework of an international programme on the effects of mass communication on society." In other words, the mandate was essentially the same as 2 years earlier, but now—after Montreal—the case was tested by an expert hearing.

THE MAKING OF A CLASSIC

The Secretariat of Unesco (at this stage mainly Gunnar Naesselund and John Willings) decided to continue the process with the assistance of a panel of consultants. The letter of invitation from February 1971 laid down the task as follows:

> As part of its programme in the field of mass communication, Unesco intends to promote an international programme of research on the effects of communication on relations between changing societies and social groups. In order to plan this programme, we are convening an international panel of ten consultants to help the Secretariat in defining broad research themes of national and international importance and, secondly, indicating the multidisciplinary studies which are required within those themes to provide the fullest possible inquiry into the complete spectrum of communication. Thirdly, the panel will assist in establishing common criteria and methodology for conducting the studies in order to ensure the comparability of their results.

Among those invited were four (Halloran, myself, Smythe, and Rao, who in the meantime had moved from Unesco to AMIC) who had also attended the Montreal meeting, while the rest were "new faces" from Latin America (Luis Ramiro Beltran), Africa (S.O. Biobaku), the Middle East (Nabil Dajani), and Europe (Tomo Martelanc, Walery Pisarek, Pierre Schaeffer, and Elisabeth Noelle-Neumann as rapporteur). The first workshop meeting in Paris in April 1971 produced a document entitled "Proposals for an International Programme of Communication Research" (Unesco, 1971).

This document, better known by its Unesco code "COM/MD/20," was put together by the Secretariat from a number of draft chapters written by the panelists—not least Halloran—during the week-long meeting (without much work left for the rapporteur). The document ran to less than 30 pages, but it was given a record distribution with altogether 7,000 copies in various languages. COM/MD/20 received more professional and political attention than the Montreal document ever did, so much so that it is justified to call it Unesco's classic in the field of communication research.

Yet its intellectual substance remains more or less the same as that put forward in Montreal, with an overall social and critical approach. It contained more concrete and operational proposals, but its philosophical theme was merely a variation of what was already proposed in the Montreal prelude. Still there were two subthemes that received particular emphasis in the new blueprint: first, the need for a holistic approach ("research that covers all aspects of the communication process...within the wider social, political and economic setting"); and second, the need for a policy orientation ("need for theoretical sophistication is recognized...but the main emphasis must be that the research is directed towards the solution of social problems").

The relation to communication policies is spelled out in the one-sentence summary of COM/MD/20:

It stresses the urgent need for concentrated and co-ordinated research into the mass media and their functions in society in order to fully understand the communication process, its relationship to economic, social and cultural development, and to be a fundamental tool in the establishment of national and international communication policies and strategies.

The role of research is here as ambiguous as it was in the Montreal report: promoting critical awareness of communication on the one hand, and providing instruments for social engineering on the other. It is revealing that the authors were not afraid of calling research "a fundamental tool" for policies and strategies. Likewise, the introductory chapter, under the subtitle "Why do we need research?," makes the point that "we need the knowledge that only research can provide before we can develop adequate communication policies" (p. 4), and it elaborates:

> Once a government possesses such data it can refine very considerably its national policies and it can adjust its development plans and operations far more closely than it can possibly do today. Efficient research can assist governments in setting proper priorities, in using efficient strategies, in reducing frustrations, by developing and employing its communication resources in optimally productive ways. Scientifically acquired knowledge can facilitate the formulation of appropriate communication policies and the development of institutions and practices directly related to the development needs. (p. 5)

Such paragraphs were obviously written with a view to selling the idea of research—to ensuring resources—but all the same they expose a fairly naive approach to the research–policy relationship. It was natural that the panel rejected a distinction between "pure" research into the processes of communication in society and "applied" research into communication in development policies and planning—a distinction that was built into an annotated agenda for the meeting by the Secretariat and that was immediately dismissed by Halloran as a "false dichotomy." At the same time, however, the panel failed to be alert to the risk of turning a holistic and critical approach into a neopositivistic and technocratic approach. As a matter of fact, today we can see how the panel was a child of its time, with a naive trust in rational management by society, and in the universal validity of scientifically based policies and planning.

To be sure, it was not the panel that transmitted this grand idea to Unesco; it entered the corridors and documents of Unesco from all directions at that time. A parallel Unesco program even convened another expert meeting and produced another landmark document specifically on communication policies and planning (Unesco, 1972).[4] And one of the projects in which Unesco took special pride in those years was a "total program" for a national communication policy for Afghanistan—in today's perspective not only a failure but also an irony!

Notwithstanding such (auto)critical reflections, there is no reason to underrate the significance of COM/MD/20, either. It was and remains a classic—in good and bad. If anything, one has to wonder how it was possible that a group of individuals, most of whom did not know each other at all, could come up with such a substantial outcome during a one-week meeting. No doubt the ideas did not

---

[4] This meeting was attended by 22 experts, three of them from among the panelists (Beltran, Dajani, and me) and two who would join the panel later (Opubor and Szecsko). I was elected chairman of the meeting.

need much elaboration, since they were "in the air" at that time, but still a great role was played by personalities with persuasive power and writing skills—above all Halloran, but also Smythe and Beltran.

Moreover, at this stage there was a perfect understanding between the panel and the Secretariat, and therefore the Unesco bureaucracy did not place any obstacles in the way of the intellectual performance of the experts. As a matter of fact, the marriage was so close that two concrete project proposals written into the document were immediately commissioned from the panelists: a survey on the international flow of TV materials proposed by me and my Finnish colleague Tapio Varis (Unesco, 1974) and a case study on external radio broadcasting from Tomo Martelanc and his Yugoslav colleagues (Unesco, 1977).

OPERATIONALIZING THE CLASSIC

The panel met again at the IAMCR conference in Buenos Aires in September 1972 (Alfred Opubor now replacing his Vice-Chancellor Biobaku). This was a brief session to follow up reactions to COM/MD/20 and to outline a further concretization of the program—as well as to facilitate the panelists' participation at the Buenos Aires conference (where Halloran became President).

The proper second meeting of the Panel was convened in Paris in October 1973—after another Unesco General Conference had mandated the program to continue and the panel to be an instrument for the Secretariat. At this stage Dallas Smythe was replaced by the research director of the Canadian Broadcasting Corporation (Arthur Laird), Pierre Schaeffer was replaced by a French scholar (Jean Cazeneuve), and Walery Pisarek of Poland was replaced by Tamas Szecskö of Hungary. These changes in the panel's composition were explained as normal rotation, but at least in the case of Smythe it is arguable that the replacement was politically motivated.

In opening the October 1973 meeting, the Assistant Director General for Communication (A. Obligado) said:

Mainly as a result of the first meeting of your panel, Unesco's sector of Communication has changed its structure. We now have a new Division of Communication Research and Planning. This has been a great step forward. The need for communication research has been endorsed by our General Conference, together with the need for objective information upon which national governments can formulate their communication policies and plan strategies for the realistic development of communication systems which serve social needs. This is true not only in the developing areas of the world, but has lately become a primary concern also within Europe and within North America.

Accordingly, the panel and its classic had been instrumental in promoting and even institutionalizing communication research within Unesco. At the same time research became more and more connected with policies and planning—with an administrative rather than a critical bias. Unesco's Programme and Budget for 1973–1974, as well as the Medium—Term Plan for 1973–1978, included the implementation of all major proposals of COM/MD/20. The task of the panel—now called the "International Advisory Panel of Communication Research"—was to advise the Secretariat on how to proceed in practice—how to further operationalize the classic.

The panel did not, however, jump straight into practical advice. It first exercised general assessment, both in the light of replies to a questionnaire sent from Unesco to governments and thousands of institutions concerning their reactions to COM/MD/20, and in the light of the panel's own "critical reappraisal" of the document.

In this discussion Halloran singled out two disadvantages of the document in the form of rhetorical questions: "Does it make research less administrative? Does it help the independence of social science?" He reminded the panel that "70 per cent of research supports the status quo," but all the same he admitted—in accordance with the classical social-democratic formula—that "we must work within the present structures." My own point—consistent since Montreal—was that "critical research does not help unless backed by social forces (political parties)." And whereas Halloran did not hide his uneasiness to serve the nation and his displeasure about Unesco's separate program of national communication policies, I pointed out that "policy research (even state controlled) explicates mass communications and thus helps criticism." Tamas Szecskö, for his part, reflected on such contradictions in the document as long-term recommendations vs. short-term proposals, or the fact that it addressed policy makers in social-science language. In general, there was a feeling that the document had not paid enough attention to the "how" while it concentrated on the "what" and "why."

Thus there were mixed opinions of the classic among its authors, but nevertheless all agreed that "the document, as it was written

2½ years ago, was still very relevant and projected the needs of communication researchers and policy makers both realistically and idealistically." If anything, the developments around the world had made the document "relatively more important." Therefore the panel decided "that COM/MD/20 should stand as it is...that the document itself need not be either rewritten nor need it be elaborated but what was perhaps needed was for it to be somewhat simplified in its totality and somewhat expanded by...more specific proposals."

The panel worked out several proposals during the 5 days of its meeting in Paris, and it also held a hearing with relevant nongovernmental organizations in order to help coordinate various initiatives. Apart from IAMCR, the 1-day hearing was attended by the International Film and Television Council, the International Broadcast Institute (IBI; later IIC), and the World Association for Christian Communication (WACC) jointly with the Lutheran World Federation.[5]

The hearing was remarkable for the absence of any notable conflicts—such as emerged later in the 1970s and especially in the 1980s around Unesco's work in communication. All parties seemed to be content with the new emphasis on communication research, and few raised doubts even about communication policies in this connection. The panel itself was also quite unanimous, and its relationship with the Secretariat—mostly represented by John Willings—was very smooth.

Among the panel's proposals was a new blueprint of "Mass Media and Man's View of Society" (one of the main chapters of COM/MD/20). Instead of laying down ready-made research projects (largely borrowed from the Leicester pipeline), as was the case with the original document, this proposal—again written by Halloran—pointed out three vital topics for comparative studies: on media policies (not far from the Montreal paper by Himmelstrand and myself), on information needs, and on communication in the community. The first two did not lead to any notable follow-up, but the third led to a "model project" jointly carried out by the panelists and their national teams (Unesco, 1982).

As far as the area "International Flow of Media Materials" is concerned, the panel also proposed three main topics: (a) the flow of

---

[5] The two last mentioned were represented by Cees Hamelink, who at that time was in charge of the communication research desk of LWF and carried out a study on "Media and Ethics."

news, (b) the economics of the international flow of cultural materials, and (c) the cultural contents of the international flow. In addition, a fourth focal point was proposed to be an overall "philosophical analysis" of the free flow concept by bringing together "a multidisciplinary and multinational group of experts to produce a thorough theoretical account on the subject, relating the empirical realities of international flows with a firm conceptual framework." This proposal no doubt is to be seen as a follow-up to the "Tampere study," which culminated in May 1973 in an international symposium, with Finland's President Kekkonen questioning the free flow doctrine (Unesco, 1974). Little, if anything, of these operationalizations was ever implemented by Unesco, but as ideas by the panel, all this is important in itself.

Proposals concerning the "mechanics" of further work included the promotion of the "Inventory of Basic Data" (annex to COM/MD/20). This did not lead to any major project at Unesco, although national model inventories were inspired notably by Noelle-Neumann in West Germany and myself in Finland. It is obvious, however, that the panel and its classic did give a boost to Unesco's regular compilation of communication statistics, in particular the standardization of radio and TV statistics achieved in the mid-1970s.[6]

Another area where the panel had an indirect but significant contribution was the creation of a network of documentation centers. In fact, the panel's meeting in Paris was followed by a 2-day consultation of directors of those centers, including several of the panelists. The working paper that came out of this consultation, as well as an overview of what later became to be known as "COMNET," is included in my chapter in the biannual IAMCR publication prepared before the 1976 Leicester conference (Nordenstreng, 1976).

All in all, the 1973 meeting can be seen as a climax of the momentum that began in 1968. Obviously COM/MD/20 in 1971 was brought about in such swing that even the panelists themselves did not at that time possess a comprehensive understanding of what was being done. It was only now, more than 2 years later, that the

---

[6] The standardization of Unesco's radio and TV statistics was proposed by a meeting of Governmental Experts in June 1976. The present author represented Finland (in his capacity as member of the Finnish National Commission for Unesco and head of its Communication Section) and was elected Chairman of the meeting. The outcome of the meeting was adopted by the General Conference of Unesco in Nairobi later in 1976.

full dimensions of the classic were digested. At least this was so in my own case, as shown by my paper for the first Nordic conference on mass communication research in Oslo in June 1973 (Nordenstreng, 1973b) as well as by subsequent reviews on "European communication theory" (Nordenstreng, 1975, 1977).

It took 2 more years before the panel was convened at its third proper meeting in 1975. Meanwhile, two workshops were organized (and financed by Unesco) in order to implement the "model project" on communication and community, which grew out of the COM/MD/20 chapter "Mass Media and Man's View of Society." One of them took place during the 1974 IAMCR conference in Leipzig and the other at Unesco in January 1975.

It turned out to be much more difficult to carry out research in practice, as a comparative international venture, than to generate ideas about research policy. As is well exposed by Halloran's introductory chapter to the final report of this exercise (Unesco, 1982), it was a research process that produced—instead of the euphoria experienced by the panel until 1973—complications and frustrations both at the theoretical-paradigmatic level and at the practical-managerial level. Contradictions also surfaced between the panelists and their paradigms—even between myself and Halloran. No wonder the outcome was far from exciting and inspiring; viewed against its ambitious starting point, it can even be classified as a failure. Indeed, the less encouraging experience of the community project was one of the factors that makes it justified to conclude that the panel and its classic began to lose momentum after 1973.

THE MOMENTUM LOST

The panel's third main meeting was an intensive 4-day workshop at Unesco in October 1975. (Wolfgang Seeger was now the main officer at the Secretariat.) Its composition was very much the same as in 1973; all except Beltran were present.

At the outset, the panel seemed to play an extraordinary role on this occasion, since the Secretariat shared with it the first draft for the communication chapter of Unesco's Medium-Term Plan for 1977–1982 (under preparation for the 19th General Conference in 1976). The panel examined the draft and provided a number of comments and proposals, some of which were included in the final draft. Notably not included were proposed studies on the image of foreign countries as presented by the mass media and as reflected in public opinion, as well as on the philosophy and international politics of the doctrine "free flow of information."

A central point of discussion was the future of the panel itself. The Secretariat's draft no longer included a standing advisory panel; what was envisaged, instead, was a number of ad hoc expert groups on various topics, including those emanating from COM/MD/20. Also foreseen was a central role for the IAMCR, which, as put by Pierre Navaux, "once renovated can serve the advisory capacities." This would follow the pattern set by other Unesco Sectors such as science, where representative NGOs play a similar role. An inconclusive discussion pointed both to the need for flexibility and rotation, and to the advantage of a "fixed core" (Martelanc's phrase) or a "pool" (Szecskö). All seemed to agree on the IAMCR occupying the role of the panel if the latter were to be discontinued.

At the end of its meeting the nine panelists signed a letter addressed to Director-General M'Bow concerning the "possible reorganization of Unesco's Secretariat whereby the present status of the Communication Sector might be changed...by incorporating it in another Sector of Unesco's activities." The panel pointed out that such a move would "not be regarded as a purely technical matter but may be reflected in the national policy of many Member States where downgrading of the Communication Sector would be contrary to all Unesco's efforts to this date to stress the overall importance of communication in national development." The concluding paragraphs of the two-page letter read as follows:

> In the Panel's opinion, the Department of the Free Flow of Information and Development of Communication, has been successful in maintaining the multi-disciplinary nature of communication in its programme. Particularly during the last few years its innovativeness has been widely recognised in professional as well as academic communities as it has pioneered in advocating new directions in communication research and policies. In this context the Panel strongly wants to emphasize that, in the area of communication, research and policies should be understood as an inseparable whole, an idea that indeed has been the core of the Panel's advice and the Department's programme.
>
> The wide recognition that communication has achieved, thanks largely to Unesco's own initiatives in this regard, both as a field of study and as a crucial component of all developmental efforts, makes it imperative that the Department continues to retain separate identity and pursue its leadership role.

This letter did not stop the Director-General from merging Culture and Communication into one large sector, placed under a single Assistant Director-General. However, the merger caused no reduction in the resources allocated to communication, including communication research, and the Department and its divisions (for communication research and policies, on the one side, and development of communication systems, on the other) retained their bureaucratic structures without any real loss of profile or prestige. (A radical cut in communication occurred at Unesco only a decade later.) So the alarm voiced by the panel was largely premature—obviously inspired by those working in the Communication Sector and concerned about their bureaucratic integrity. Still the letter may have contributed to a general recognition of the importance of communication, while Unesco's medium-term strategies were under a fundamental review with the leadership of a new Director-General.

Consequently, there were no real threats on the panel's horizon in late October 1975. The ideas launched in Montreal and highlighted in COM/MD/20 were still alive, moving in several channels within and outside Unesco. The panel and the Secretariat people (all those mentioned above, plus Lloyd Summerland) continued to play together in perfect harmony. And yet it turned out to be the last tango in Paris.

THE PANEL IN PERSPECTIVE

Today—with the benefit of hindsight—it is easy to see that the panel was running out of steam around 1975 and the momentum for the classic had gone. What is more important, this loss of momentum in the middle of the 1970s coincided with the entering of communication issues on the agendas of high politics in both East–West and North–South relations. After all, it was 1975 when the Final Act of the Conference on Security and Co-operation in Europe, with its "third basket," was signed in Helsinki (see Nordenstreng & Schiller, 1976). It was also the same year that gave birth to the Non-Aligned News Agencies Pool, after the 1973 Algiers Summit of Non-Aligned countries launched a program for cultural and informational decolonization (see Nordenstreng, 1984, p. 9).

These broader developments toward a new international order in the field of information and mass communication were by no means at variance with the panel's approach and proposals. On the contrary, the new wave of critically and globally oriented communication research, with such landmarks as the Montreal meeting and the panel itself, enters as an essential passage in any comprehensive review of the new information order movement (see, e.g., Nordenstreng, 1984, p. 12).

Accordingly, we are faced with a paradoxical situation: The panel was withering away at the very point when its message was being picked up and further promoted by the most determining forces of the international community. How can we explain this? A determinist view of the history of ideas would simply suggest that the panel was no longer needed now that the same ideas were in the hands of real political actors such as the Non-Aligned Movement. But this would not be a sufficient explanation, although it no doubt makes an important point. A better explanation is provided by the fact that most of the issues involved became more and more openly politicized and thus more and more controversial, as a consequence of mobilization of conflicting forces (Western private enterprise vs. socialist and developing countries). In practice, this led to a gradual reduction of the space for independent scientific encounter. In this perspective we could say that the panel and its message became a hostage of high politics.

It is indeed another paradox that the same policy orientation, with a holistic and critical approach, that originally inspired the panel's antipositivistic philosophy, lost its momentum after it became openly sponsored by vital political forces. In other words, what had been welcomed since the late 1960s as healthy social relevance and an openly normative emphasis, in contrast to the prevailing esoteric tradition, had by the late 1970s often turned into excessive politicization, which, for the researcher, became a burden rather than an inspiration. Earlier it was vital for research to have a feel for politics, but later too much politics even had a paralyzing effect.

To be sure, the panel did not go through such a dilemma of overpoliticization; it was discontinued—perhaps mercifully—before entering that stage. But it is not difficult to see that there was little space left for research at Unesco—in the sense advocated by the panel—once things became so politicized, as was the case by the time of Unesco's General Conference in Nairobi in late 1976 (for details, see Nordenstreng, 1984, pp. 94–113).

The MacBride Commission, appointed after Nairobi and resulting in the famous MacBride Report (Unesco, 1980), was a perfect example of a predominantly political exercise, with research input, in a situation that was politically too heated for such a rational research approach as advocated by the panel. No wonder, then, that a collection of essays on the MacBride Report, written by a number of IAMCR colleagues, including several panelists (Hamelink, 1980), had quite a critical approach—mainly because the report was seen to represent political compromise rather than scientific reflection.

The lesson to be learned from this issue of overpoliticization is twofold. Firstly, overpoliticization tends to reduce the intellectual potential of research unless the latter is protected by some kind of ivory tower that allows for free and critical reflection. In this respect the present author wishes to complement his above-quoted point— that critical research does not help unless backed by social forces (political parties)—by another point: that critical research does not survive if it is dominated by politics. Secondly, in addition to this intellectual aspect there is an institutional one: overpoliticization makes intergovernmental structures such as Unesco nonconducive—sometimes even repressive—for a truly scientific approach. An illuminating example in this respect is the story of a symposium on the Mass Media Declaration of Unesco (Nordenstreng, 1993).

Returning to the panel and its significance, it certainly serves as an instructive case to demonstrate the dialectical relationship between science and politics: to show how timely research initiatives can meet a momentum and indeed make a difference, but also to show how the same research can be quickly dismissed by a tide of political history.

No doubt the panel and its products had a universal impact— how significant, and how independent from other parallel factors, remains to be determined. While it is obvious that an impact was there, and that writings of such U.S. scholars as Herbert Schiller and John Lent further amplified a certain impulse from the research community to the political sphere,[7] it would be incorrect to exhibit this as a case in point where philosophers operating in their forum of intellectual reflection (Unesco, IAMCR, etc.) gave crucial directions to politics and thus in fact changed the world (instead of just explaining it). The impact was by no means direct; indeed it is

---

[7] One direct input from critical scholars to the Non-Aligned Movement was channeled by me: I sent to the Tunisian organizers of the Non-Aligned Symposium on Information in early 1976 a package of texts by Schiller, Lent, and others (including the above-mentioned speech by Finland's President Kekkonen of 1973). These texts served as a source of inspiration—in some cases even wording—for the organizers in preparing the speeches and draft documents for the Tunis Symposium, which was to become a landmark forum in launching the movement toward a New International Information Order (in fact the very phrase surfaced there for the first time). I attended the Tunis Symposium as an invited guest, representing the Government of Finland.

even misleading to think in terms of an impact, since ultimately both the intellectual and the political movements were part and parcel of the same overall sociohistorical process.

Moreover, in a broader historical perspective, the panel proves to be less a unique phenomenon in the global development of communication research than it would seem if one just looked at the period since the late 1960s. After all, there were at least two earlier major initiatives to mobilize and reorientate this field, with Unesco playing a central role. First of all, there was the project to set up an "International Institute of Press and Information" to follow up the many moves made at the United Nations Conference on Freedom of Information in 1948 and also to pool together the emerging scientific know-how in the field (Unesco, 1948–1949). The momentum of this project was killed by the Cold War—by an overpoliticization of the time. The second international wave of mobilizing the field occurred around 1956 to 1957, at a time when the worst of the Cold War was over and various kinds of initiatives were floated to bring détente and unity to the deeply divided world of journalism and mass communication (see Nordenstreng & Kubka, 1988, pp. 60–65). And this time there was a concrete outcome: the establishment of the IAMCR.

REFERENCES

Hamelink, C. (Ed.). (1980). *Communication in the eighties: A reader on the "MacBride Report"*. Rome: IDOC International. (Reprinted in D.C. Whitney, E. Wartella & S. Windahl (Eds.), *Mass Communication Review Yearbook* (Vol. 3, pp. 236–287). Beverly Hills: Sage.

Nordenstreng, K. (1968). Communicative research in the United States: A critical perspective. *Gazette, 14,* 207–216.

Nordenstreng, K. (1972). Policy for news transmission. In D. McQuail (Ed.), *Sociology of mass communications* (pp. 386–405). Harmondsworth, UK: Penguin.

Nordenstreng, K. (Ed.). (1973a). *Informational mass communication.* Helsinki: Tammi.

Nordenstreng, K. (1973b, June). *Normative directions for mass communication research.* Paper presented at the first Nordic Conference on Mass Communication Research, Oslo, Norway. (Published in proceedings "Mediaforskning: Kommunikasjon og samfundsansvar," Institute for Press Research, University of Oslo, Report No. 29/1973, pp. 45–55.)

Nordenstreng, K. (1975). Recent developments in European communications theory. *Diogenes, 92,* 104–115. (Also in B.D. Ruben (Ed.), *Communication Yearbook I* (1977, pp. 73–78). New Brunswick, NJ: International Communication Association & Transaction Books.)

Nordenstreng, K. (1976). Towards a global system of documentation and information centres. In J.D. Halloran (Ed.), *Mass media and socialization* (pp. 117–130). Leicester, UK: IAMCR.

Nordenstreng, K. (1977). From mass media to mass consciousness. In G. Gerbner (Ed.), *Mass media policies in changing cultures* (pp. 269–283). New York: Wiley.

Nordenstreng, K. (1993). The story and lesson of a symposium. In G. Gerbner, H. Mowlana, & K. Nordenstreng (Eds.), *The global media debate: Its rise, fall and renewal* (pp. 99–107). Norwood, NJ: Ablex Publishing Corp.

Nordenstreng, K., with Hannikainen, L. (1984). *The Mass Media Declaration of UNESCO*. Norwood, NJ: Ablex Publishing Corp.

Nordenstreng, K. & Kubka, J. (Eds.). (1988). *Useful recollections: Excursion into the history of the international movement of journalists (Part II)*. Prague: International Organization of Journalists.

Nordenstreng, K. & Schiller, H. (1976). Helsinki: The new equation. *Journal of Communication, 26*, 130–134. (Reprinted in K. Nordenstreng & H. Schiller (Eds.), *National sovereignty and international communication* (1979, 238–243). Norwood, NJ: Ablex Publishing Corp.

Osolnik, B., Pavlic, B., Vreg, F. & Lrimsek, P. (Eds.). (1969). *Mass media and international understanding*. Ljubljana: School of Sociology, Political Science and Journalism.

Pietilä, V., Malmberg, T., & Nordenstreng, K. (1990). Theoretical convergencies and contrasts: A view from Finland. *European Journal of Communication, 5*, 165–185.

Unesco. (1948–1949). *Draft project for the establishment of an international institute of press and information,* (MC/2, 4 August 1948; MC/3, 29 April 1949). Reprinted in *Historical Documents on the Mass Media* (Dossier No. 4/1987, 172–238). Prague: International Journalism Institute.

Unesco. (1970). Mass media in society: The need of research. *Reports and papers on mass communication* (No. 59). Paris.

Unesco. (1971). *Proposals for an international programme of communication research* (COM/MD/20). Paris (10 September 1971).

Unesco. (1972). *Report of the Meeting of Experts on Communication Policies and Planning* (COM/MD/24). Paris (1 December 1972).

Unesco. (1974). *Television traffic—A one-way street?* Reports and papers on mass communication (No. 70). Paris.

Unesco. (1977). External radio broadcasting and international understanding. *Reports and papers on mass communication* (No. 81). Paris.

Unesco. (1980). *Many voices, one world: Report by the International Commission for the Study of Communication Problems*. Paris (London: Kogan Press; New York; Unipub).

Unesco. (1982). Communication in the community. *Reports and papers on mass communication* (No. 87). Paris.

CHAPTER

Communication Policies, Planning, and Research in Unesco: From the Seventies to the Nineties

ALAN HANCOCK

INTRODUCTION

I am using the first person in this article for two reasons. First, I want to make it clear to the reader (and to remind myself) that this is a personal view of events, not necessarily one that would be endorsed by Unesco. Second, I have been a participant observer in this process, and in recent years more participant than observer. My account, therefore, has both the advantages and the limitations of direct involvement.

In writing, I have made use of the tried, and understandably contested, tradition of placing events in cycles. However, I hope it is clear that I have done so not to impose an artificial order upon events, but rather to have it serve as an analytical tool to help organize and present a mass of data.

The article was begun shortly before the 25th Session of Unesco's General Conference, opened in October 1989, and it was completed in the few days following the conference. So, while it takes account of that very critical meeting, by the time that it is read its predictions for the future may already have been put to the test.

UNESCO

Unesco is both an intensely private and an intensely public organization. It has its own codes, its own language (at times impenetrable to the outsider), and often seems to be obsessed with its own agenda, to the extent of appearing to be a virtually closed system. It has a complex decision-making machinery, working through the approval, by biennial conferences, of elaborate programs in each of its fields of competence. Many of its decisions (especially consensus decisions, which are the product of a negotiating process) are ambiguously formulated. It does not have the simplicity and directness that would make its activities easily accessible to the journalist, or to the general public.

At the same time, what happens inside the organization is never unrelated to the outside world. Within its mandate for education, science, and culture, Unesco's programs interact with, and are a reflection of, external priorities and patterns of thought (sometimes admittedly of hindsight and reaction, rather than perspective). From this perspective, therefore, Unesco is both microcosm and analogue of intellectual trends on an international scale.

Communication does not always dovetail too easily into this pattern. It is not as discrete as other parts of Unesco's mandate, made up as it is of many disciplines and methodologies drawn from the human and social sciences, the natural sciences, and technology. Although communication functions ("the free flow of word and image") and communication means ("of mass communication") are written into its constitution, the very intersectorality and cross-disciplinarity of the field have produced an uneven record throughout the organization's history. Even its role within the UN system is ambiguous, since, while it has always been ascribed a principal coordinating role, other agencies are concerned with particular aspects of communication (a telecommunications perspective within the ITU, sectoral applications within FAO and WHO).

In the early days, Unesco activities were confined to professional training and to communication applications (notably to education). At times communication has been a sector in its own right; at other times (as today) it has shared its identity with culture. This hesitant track record has not been helped by the prominence with which the organization, especially in the eighties, came into the public eye, mostly through the controversy associated with a new world information and communication order. In many ways, this publicity took the organization by surprise, and it has not found it easy to adjust to a mass media spotlight. Perhaps for this reason, communication activities have not been boosted as much as might have been expected in view of the growing significance of the information agenda. Communication has been perceived at times as a service sector, at other times as an independent field of action and research, but these shifts have reflected internal preoccupations or political divides as much as an objective evaluation of the field.

THE SEVENTIES: UNESCO AS SUBJECT

This assessment of Unesco's standing may seem both too long and too internalized, but I believe it is important in disentangling many recent trends. In moving to the historical record, the most convenient starting point is probably the meeting of experts on mass communication and society held in Montreal in August 1969. It was at this meeting that the tone of Unesco's future program was set, captured in these sentences drawn from its final report:

> More comprehensive, system-oriented research into mass communication is needed at all levels and in all areas. This includes the analysis of media organization, ownership and financial support, the decision-making process in media production ethics, the actual value systems of communications, and their perception of their role in society...It may also be useful inquire into whether it would be advisable to bring about change, where indicated, in production and information structures to allow for a wider participation in management and decision-making processes on the part of the professional working elements of media units. (Unesco, 1970, p. 27)

Unesco's involvement in communication research up to this point had been somewhat marginal. Until Montreal, interest in the media was essentially for educational applications; Schramm's (1964) *Mass Media and National Development* was focused on educational media, based on the program of the International Institute for Educational Planning. The mass communication department worked mostly on production training, screen education, and project development; its research interests throughout the sixties lay in adult and nonformal education. Typical research meetings, projects, and publications of the time were devoted to rural radio and farm forums, educational media, television and the social education of women, satellites for education and development, and the book development program. While a main concern of the communication department was to reach developing country audiences, its program was based not so much on development research (which was more the preserve of the social science sector) as on professional antecedents.

Consequently, when the Montreal meeting took place, the research tradition of the communication sector was mostly confined to the positivist U.S. research tradition of the time (and especially to the work of Schramm, Lerner, and Rogers). As a result, when an international panel of consultants was formed two years later, and put forward a set of "Proposals for an International Programme of Communication Research" in 1971, it was working in relatively unexplored territory.

The Montreal meeting was anxious to extend research into communication and development, and drew as far as possible upon what was then an embryonic Third World research constituency. But the research panel also had other characteristics. It went well outside the traditional U.S. research community; it had a strong socialist country representation; and it was quite Eurocentric, with a strong influence from James Halloran and the Leicester Centre. The association of the IAMCR with this program was also unequivocally expressed in the composition of the panel, which was headed by Halloran and included Luis Ramiro Beltran, Nabil Dajani, Tomo Martelanc, Kaarle Nordenstreng, Walery Pisarek, Dallas Smythe, Lakshmana Rao, and Elizabeth Noelle-Neumann.

The program that emerged was, in keeping with its time, engaged, and socially activist. The report of the panel stated "If something is socially significant, it should be self-evident that we need to know something about it.... In short we need the knowledge that only research can provide before we can develop adequate communication policies. Ideally such policies should be based on 'total' knowledge (i.e. on the operation of the media in the wider social-economic-political setting) and on 'public' needs rather than on 'partial' knowledge and 'private' needs as is so often the case at present."

The orientation proposed by the panel was therefore of a specific kind. Broadly speaking, communication research has had four main axes. One has been concerned with media and society, emphasizing the political and socioeconomic environment of mass media. A second has been devoted to media organizations and occupations, drawing substantially on organization theory. A third has focused on messages and media content, while a fourth has investigated media uses, effects, and audience impact.

The interest of the panel was mostly in the first and fourth strands, with a sidelong glance at media professions and institutions (in itself derivative of the societal focus). In turn, this interest was translated into a research framework that dominated Unesco's work in the following decade: a committed, interventionist program that culminated in the publication of the MacBride Report, *Many Voices, One World*, in 1980, and the 21st Session of the Unesco General Conference in Belgrade. It had strands of communication and planned social change, mass media and the human view of society, and research into international communication structures. There was very little, if anything, to be found on semiology, the social psychology of media, institutional analysis, or the development of microresearch methods. The program was pitched at a macro level, and was more concerned with issues than methods.

Over the period from 1969 to 1981, Unesco was a principal actor in a rising international communication debate, many of whose features stemmed from the proposals of the International Panel. The underlying debate on information flow, for example, was first fed by the pioneer work carried out at the University of Tampere by Kaarle Nordenstreng and Tapio Varis (1974), which led to the summary report *Television Traffic—A One-Way Street?* The series of regional intergovernmental conferences on communication policies largely spanned this period, beginning with the Latin American and Caribbean conference in Costa Rica in 1976, and continuing with the Asia conference (ASIACOM) held in Kuala Lumpur in 1979, and AFRICOM in Yaounde in 1980. The International Commission for the Study of Communication Problems followed much the same research agenda (if not always consciously) when it was set up after Unesco's 19th General Conference in Nairobi in 1976.

The debate was not, of course, confined to Unesco—it quickly became part of an international political agenda. The issue of transfrontier broadcasting, for example, and especially the implications of direct broadcasting satellites, originated in Unesco but moved to the United Nations in 1972, where it led to an historic vote (102–1) against the U.S. position. It was in the seventies that the United Nations became a major forum for the political discussion of communication, largely through the activities of its Information Committee.

It should also be remembered that the new world information and communication order, now identified almost exclusively with Unesco, did not originate there. It began with the Non-Aligned Movement, where in 1974 the idea of a New International Information Order was first approved by the Fourth Conference of Heads of State.

Nevertheless the focal point of the debate remained Unesco, and apart from the continuing thread of NWICO there were two other specific points of interest: the 1978 Declaration on the Media, and the work of the MacBride Commission.

In the years from 1972 to 1978, various drafts of the *Declaration on the Media* were being considered, often in an atmosphere of conflict, though the adoption of the *Declaration* in 1978 finally was unanimous. Another issue that came into prominence in these years, and also evoked vehement reactions, was the debate on the protection of journalists.

The influence of the 1971 international panel continued to be strong for several years, until the creation of the MacBride Commission reduced its influence. (The members of the commission represented a rather different international constituency, though there were inevitably some overlaps of interest and focus.) But the normative approach adopted by the panel foreshadowed the commission's interest in dependency theory, the concept of cultural imperialism, and selected sociocultural or politico-economic perspectives.

I do not intend to add more than a few paragraphs about the International Commission for the Study of Communication Problems, since it has also been extensively reported. There has always been some ambiguity as to how much the work of the commission was a part of, or independent of, Unesco's research program; it is often emphasized today that it was an independent commission, reporting only to Unesco. Certainly, while it was serviced by a Unesco Secretariat, the members of this unit were mostly not drawn from the communication sector itself, and there was a genuine separation of roles and responsibilities. Much of the interest of the MacBride Commission really lay outside the final published text (although this is often accused of being overlong, it represents only a fraction of the material made available). Many background documents and research compilations were produced; there were many parallel seminars and debates. Unfortunately, most of these have never been published.

Nevertheless, a resolution of the 21st Session of Unesco's General Conference in Belgrade did endorse the report in emphatic terms, and in the same resolution the basic premises of a new world information and communication order were articulated (Resolution 21/C 4.19 Item 14). This summary of the principles underlying the NWICO remains to this day the most concrete expression of the new order concept, and it reflects a mix of approaches: endorsing pluralism, press freedom, and respect for human rights alongside the elimination of the negative effects of monopolies, the responsibility of media professionals, respect for cultural identity, and so on.

It is because of this mixed approach that I would like to return to the underlying questions of media theory to which I referred when introducing the work of the international panel. They seem to me to be fundamental to the debate on Unesco (even if this has not often been traced back to its theoretical origins).

Unesco's mandate for communication goes back to its constitution, which speaks explicitly of "advancing the mutual knowledge and understanding of peoples, through all means of mass communication, and to that end recommend[ing] such international agreements as may be necessary to promote the free flow of ideas by word and image." Over the years, it has added to the concept of free flow a parallel concept of the "wider and better balanced dissemination of information." The core of the controversy lies in different understandings of that second concept—in particular, its practical implications. How is a "wider and better balance" to be secured? Through enlarging freedoms (and capacities) that are undernourished? Or by restraining those who are most vocal under the status quo?

This is, of course, the classic dilemma of individual freedom and social restraint, which dominates political theory. But if confined to communication, the twin concepts of the free flow of information and of its wider and better balanced dissemination may also be related directly to media theory.

A good deal of this body of theory, particularly if it has a methodological bias, is relatively neutral: uses-gratifications theory, communication process models, and techniques of content analysis can be applied in most cultural settings. However, many research traditions are more directly derivative from their sociopolitical setting. Free press, libertarian theory, and theories of liberal pluralism have inbuilt assumptions; they originate in a view of social conviction that focuses on an unrestricted flow of information. Conversely, theories of hegemony, neo-marxist approaches, dependency theory, and culturalist approaches are rooted in a world view where improvements in information balance and dissemination are particularly highlighted.

It would be simplistic to insist too much upon this relationship— the twin concepts of free flow and balance are not watertight separations. (Indeed, the recent 25th session of Unesco's General Conference was at pains to relate them more organically than in the past, in order to clarify what had become a contentious opposition between the two.) In general terms, however, the work of the original international panel was mostly focused on the concept of a wider and better balanced dissemination of information, and the body of theory that sustains it. This focus was to a considerable extent reinforced by the work of the MacBride Commission, which had its roots in the same tradition. However, the commission conducted its work in public, and was subject to many external forces: The Belgrade Conference at which the report was received was even more susceptible to such pressures. Consequently, the statement of principles underlying a new world information and communication order was, not surprisingly, a mixture of positions, some of which may appear to be incompatible: it has all the hallmarks of a negotiated consensus. Such accommodations are quite normal, of course, in most international organizations, and they are equally possible in pluralist societies, particularly if a distinction is made between domestic activities and activities oriented externally. For example, the United States, while strongly endorsing pluralist models of media organization at home, has found no real difficulty in accommodating interventionist programs in its development operations in the Third World, where programs harnessing the mass media to developmental goals are regularly financed and approved.

THE EIGHTIES: UNESCO AS OBJECT

I said at the beginning of this chapter that the device of treating history in cycles is an analytical tool, not a precise demarcation. Consequently, when I characterize the next cycle, from 1981 to 1988, as a passive period in Unesco's communication history, I am only pointing to a general trend (the watershed being, essentially, the publication of the MacBride Report). Unesco came into public prominence for the first time in the eighties as an object of attack, leading to the U.S. withdrawal at the end of 1984, and that of the United Kingdom a year later. The controversy has continued, with occasional lulls, up to the present day.

As always, this general characterization needs some qualification. Watershed or not, the activist programs did not all terminate with the publication of *Many Voices, One World* (nor was the earlier cycle as unidimensional as I may have suggested). Moreover, the eighties provided an opportunity, particularly in their later years, for a much-needed evaluation of the achievements of the seventies.

Nevertheless, what the outside world was seeing in the eighties was a Unesco attempting to reconcile itself with diametrically

COMMUNICATION POLICIES, PLANNING, AND RESEARCH IN UNESCO 29

opposed interests. The debate on a new world information and communication order became an almost exclusively political debate: Consensus was achieved through a series of linguistic gymnastics (the use of lower casing, the introduction of an indefinite article, the addition of a qualifying phrase "seen as an evolving and continuous process"). Alternative formulations were deemed acceptable or unacceptable in different contexts, so that what was permissible in the United Nations was not so in Unesco, necessitating a bewildering series of cross references. The perception of NWICO became at least as important—if not more so—than the reality. To many Western journalists, it stood for state control, the licensing of journalists, the denial of media independence. To many developing countries, it was an affirmation of the right to cultural identity.

Could the situation be resolved? While hostilities were still being engaged over NWICO, there was little hope of more than short-term political accommodations, but other less public approaches were at least being tried.

The first was an attempt to move away from the political arena into one of consolidated action: to concentrate upon building up infrastructures in the developing world and improving human resources. Its most significant feature was the emergence of the International Programme for the Development of Communication (IPDC).

The IPDC was conceived as an alternative to the new world information and communication order concept: originally proposed (by a U.S. representative) as a mechanism for coordinating both multilateral and bilateral aid, this role was redefined at the conference (DEVCOM, 1980) that established ground rules for its existence. At this conference, two propositions were on the table, each the work of a different constituency. One proposal (from the United States) was for the coordinating mechanism described above; the second, drawn from the MacBride Report and advocated by one of the commission's members, saw the IPDC almost as an alternative to Unesco's own communication sector: it envisaged a research, training, and operational institute for communication.

The DEVCOM conference finally produced a mechanism that was very much founded on compromise. It had autonomy from Unesco (in the shape of a 35-member Intergovernmental Council), but its director and secretariat were to be appointed by Unesco's Director General; the execution of its program lay largely in Unesco hands. It was denied a fund but allowed a special account, which could receive financial contributions.

Over the following decade, many of the imperfections of the IPDC's conception surfaced concretely, to a point at which the program itself decided to take matters in hand and embark upon a streamlining process. Its first problem was one of resources. The guiding principle of the IPDC, and one passionately maintained by its first president, Gunnar Garbo, was that it should be a professional forum, which would solicit funds for its special account, receive project proposals, evaluate these proposals during its annual meeting, and then decide upon an apportionment of finance. However, while the level of contributions to the IPDC remained stable over the years (the main contributor, providing 50 per cent of special account resources, being Norway) the number of projects submitted increased dramatically after the first few years. Unfortunately, the ability of the Council to discriminate between projects never fully matured; allocations were made according to block and regional quotas; and few projects were ever refused. In consequence, the average sums assigned per project became so small (down at one stage to $42,000) that genuine projects could hardly surface. At the same time, the council—for many years an oasis free of the political concerns of Unesco—itself became politicized, in part over the production of *World Communication Report,* a summary of recent developments in communication that some agencies feared would be another MacBride Report. In 1986, this led to the phenomenon of a roll call vote being taken within the IPDC Intergovernmental Council to evaluate a summary of contents of the Report.

From 1987 onwards, this position changed. *World Communication Report* was produced in a pilot version and finally welcomed even by some of its detractors. Second, the resources of the IPDC were increasingly enlarged by funds-in-trust contributions (made on an individual basis to specific projects in specific countries). This formula, of course, did nothing to improve the resource level of the special account, the basis of the IPDC's original creation (funds-in-trust arrangements have existed in Unesco for many years). But at the same time, a reform process had already resulted in a considerable reduction of the number of projects approved for financing under the special account, and the average level of project financing was raised to $88,000.

Apart from the IPDC, three other strategies were also tried. The first was the extension of a tradition that had its roots in the seventies, linked to planning. Communication planning had a place in the original recommendations of the international panel, but in a rather prosaic manner. The panel did not include any professional planners, and its recommendations on the subject reflected conventional, linear planning theory. Throughout the seventies and eighties, however, Unesco attempted to develop new planning methodologies, including participatory approaches that sought to reconcile the classic problem of freedom and constraint. These drew upon methods and techniques evolved in other fields, especially those of development planning. Within the communication research tradition, they also looked to messaged-centered theory and organization theory for stimulus. The program included case study research, the development and evaluation of training materials (including simulations), and research into concrete problems such as technology transfer. It was divorced from the Unesco controversy in part because it was based not in the research division but in an operational section. (Unesco was guilty for many years of divorcing its theoretical from its operational programs; it was not until the late eighties that the two functions were merged in an attempt to force greater interaction.)

The second strategic alternative affected research. The research studies carried out in the seventies (and to a lesser extent in the early eighties) had been carefully planned, methodologically exact, and sought genuine comparability through a common methodological framework. At the same time they were underfinanced (an endemic problem for Unesco's poorly endowed Regular Programme), and had to cope with widely ranging standards of research experience, institutional support, and political acceptance. The studies that were undertaken—for example, on television flow, or a 29-country study of the media's portrayal of foreign images, conducted under an IAMCR umbrella—experienced many frustrations and reflected many compromises.

In the eighties, therefore, some rather different research approaches, which were more realistic in their appreciation of budgetary and methodological constraints, were tried out. The long-running research program into the sociocultural impact of the new communication technologies, which began with an international symposium held in Rome in December 1983 and eventually involved 50 institutions across 20 studies, was based on different assumptions. It recognized that funding was limited, and that genuine comparability, involving strict adherence to a highly structured research design, was not truly possible within Unesco. Instead, it sought to catalyze and network ongoing or proposed studies of the new technologies and to provide greater contact among researchers and thus encourage a cooperative research process without making too many claims for methodological exactness.

In a bid to enlarge the range and variety of data, especially in developing countries, particular emphasis was placed upon case study research upon which other researchers could draw (and upon which planning approaches might be based). Perhaps the best index of this gradual change is found in the titles of the Unesco house series "Reports and Papers on Mass Communication." Begun in 1956, this series has always been of academic interest, in that it affords a showcase for research efforts that are unlikely (because they are too specialized or minority) to find a place in book publications. While, in the mid-seventies, this series concentrated on comparative studies (for example, of information flow) based on original, policy-related research and on ethical studies, by the mid-eighties other kinds of title had begun to predominate: research summaries and syntheses (for example, of the relationship between violence and media), communication in relation to technology, development-focused activities, and case studies of the news media (on freedom of information).

A third approach lay in evaluating the products of the communication policy and research program—not so much the research findings as the mechanisms and practical proposals that the international panel had originally recommended. These included the formation of national policy councils, the launching of communication policy conferences, and the development of communication policy statements at a national level, to be used as a basis for planning.

In the event, these proposals did not prove to be as dynamic as their sponsors had hoped. Few national communication policy councils were formed (and even fewer survived). Research conducted under the planning program revealed that the idea of communication policy statements, which would precede strategic communication planning, was ingenuous; it is more usually the planning process itself that leads to the emergence of a policy statement as an outcome of coordination and negotiation, and this is essentially iterative, far less clear-cut than the linear process originally envisaged. But perhaps the main results of evaluation concerned the highly publicized intergovernmental conferences on communication policy were evaluated. In the main, these were carried out before 1981 (ARABCOM in 1987 was an exception, as it had been long delayed). An as-yet-unpublished impact evaluation carried out for Unesco's Executive Board by Cees Hamelink concluded that these promotional activities, which had received the greatest financing, had in fact had a lesser impact than more concrete but less well resourced activities, such as training and curriculum development. Many reasons were advanced to explain this finding, but one of the principal conclusions was that communication policy was not really on the decision makers' agenda, so that policy makers were not fully aware of what they were being asked to discuss. Few of the major recommendations (such as the formulation of national policy councils) were ever put into practice; many recommendations were primarily directed towards Unesco's own institutional agenda, with a strong element of legitimization.

Too much investment had been made in the conference series for them to be overtly repudiated; they had long been a lynchpin of the Unesco philosophy (and not purely for communication). Moreover, they should not be dismissed out of hand simply because they did not fulfill very concrete objectives. Unesco's evaluation strategies (made explicit only in recent years) have been rather Western in concentration, tied to material or behavioral objectives that are quantified wherever possible. If the policy conferences had an impact, this is far more likely to have been in gradual sensitization—the attribution of status to the communication field. In any case, with a new focus on operational approaches, they were quietly and gradually downplayed and did not feature in the plan for the 1990s.

INTO THE NINETIES

The arguments in this final section are more speculative, as the cycle has barely begun. Its starting point, however, must be the aftermath of the 24th Session of Unesco's General Conference, held in Paris in 1987, at which a new Director-General, Federico Mayor, was appointed.

During the election campaign, Mr. Mayor pledged himself publicly to defend the free flow of information, and his first appearances in his new role were before professional media audiences. By this time, the main outlines of the debate, and of the polemic, had been focused on one main issue: the free flow of information, as set against its wider and better balanced dissemination.

The Western industrialized countries regarded the concept of free flow as something that could not, by definition, be limited; they were therefore opposed to any mention of balance, which to them suggested the imposition of an artificial equilibrium. The developing and the socialist countries were equally adamant in insisting upon the balanced formulation, in one of its many variants, as a recognition of existing inequalities and disparities and of the need to redress them.

It must be remembered that, by this time, we were no longer dealing with pure concepts or simple terminology; each of the component phrases of the information flow debate had a long history, and each new juxtaposition of language was judged against its origins. The perception of events was quite as important as the reality, and in this process the symbolic center of the debate, and of its opposing factions, was the new world information and communication order.

The main vehicle for the debate was now the preparation of Unesco's Third Medium Term Plan, in which the fourth Major Programme Area was entitled Communication in the Service of Humanity. It was at this stage that Unesco's Executive Board, reviewing the draft of the Third Medium Term Plan, took a stand that was at the time little recognized: it decided to set aside the terminology of NWICO, without prejudice to the merits of the concept, but in the knowledge that it had become counterproductive.

It was this decision, taken at the 29th session of the Executive Board in May 1988, that afforded the first opportunity in many years to break through the straightjacket of debate, and after a protracted dialogue, conducted largely through the pages of the media, allowed the 25th Session of the General Conference, in 1989, to contain the controversy, through the so-called "new strategy" of the Third Medium Term Plan.

The core of the new strategy, apart from its avoidance of references to NWICO, was to be the acceptance of a new equation between free flow and wider and better balanced dissemination. In the first place, the two were separated by some textual distance, in a formula that read "the free flow of information, at international as well as national levels, and its wider and better balanced dissemination." More concretely, the relationship between the two was differently expressed. On the one hand, free flow was seen as an absolute concept, something that (as the presentation of an ideal objective) could not be delimited. Secondly, the idea of improved dissemination was positively associated with reinforcement of communication infrastructures in the developing world, which should, when fully mature, ensure a dialogue on equal terms with the industrialized countries, an exchange among partners.

This new construction was presented by Unesco's Director-General as a two pillar approach: the first pillar being an unequivocal acceptance of the free flow of information, and the second envisaging a causal link between balanced dissemination and the creation of adequate means in the developing countries. It was not, however, accepted as such by the General Conference, and the working group, which met over three days to hammer out a common position, had three components that came, on occasion, close to foundering. In the end a three-part accommodation was reached. The free flow formulation was retained without ambiguity. The wider and better balanced formulation was also retained, but linked to freedom of expression (in order to avoid any suggestion of censorship). The third strand, emphasizing infrastructures, was also retained from the original formula, but without any direct linkage being made explicit in the text. So the final formula adopted was as follows: "to ensure a free flow of information at international as well as national levels, and its wider and better balanced dissemination, without any obstacle to freedom of expression, and to strengthen communication capacities in the developing countries, so that they can participate more actively in the communication process."

As many speakers in the debate pointed out, the language was far from elegant, but it was more imperative at this stage to find a community of opinion than to observe the niceties of language. This was the price to be paid to avoid the divisive vocabulary of NWICO. (Also implicit in the agreement was enhanced funding for the IPDC).

While this was certainly a new departure in Unesco's political approach to communication, nonetheless the contents of the Third Medium Term Plan continued traditions that had existed for many years. The new plan was intended to be more user friendly: working through professional and organizational networks, as a facilitator, broker and catalyst, and the charged language of the plan itself and of its accompanying Resolutions, did not finally affect the activities of the work plan.

Part of the program was to be devoted to improving information flow (through exchanges, co-productions, for example) and to measuring its progress. Changing needs and methodologies for audience research were included, as well as the involvement of new actors (the collection of data on media freedom by independent organizations was the one specific activity extensively discussed during the political debate). Database and documentation services were emphasized; the long-neglected COMNET network of communication documentation centers, for example, should become more functional, using a modernized communication thesaurus.

A second part focused on operational programs, in particular through a reinforced and streamlined IPDC. This component also included methodological work in the area of planning and better coordination with other UN agencies.

However, there was also a third strand that emerged partly from the consensus debate, but that was also a major focus of the times: the new communication technologies, their impact, and their implications for audiences. The debate upon the NCTs has assumed an importance in international communication that goes way beyond its technical worth. From the viewpoint of development theory, the perceived advantages of the NCTs have produced what might well be considered a revival of the original modernization approach to development: the potential of instant access and individualized service evoked the same degree of enthusiasm as did the mass media in the fifties (symbolized by Schramm's *Mass Media and National Development*).

This has also fed into the political debate. While the view of the NCTs is not universally positive, and both their affirmative and negative consequences are discussed as an agenda item, they have become very much a consensus issue. The third strand of the current Unesco program is focused on these technologies—their sociocultural impact, their developmental potential, their relevance to Unesco's spheres of competence, and the need for users and audiences to become media-literate. The program on media education (the education of users), which began its life as a pedagogic activity linked to media education in the schools, assumed a much greater significance once it was directly associated with the ability of the user to master the new technologies and to acquire the skills to defend his or her interests. However, one underlying reason why the string of new communication technologies has been entrenched as the main research item in the new Medium Term Plan is probably because it seems to be sufficiently technocratic to avoid the pitfalls of a NWICO debate.

How problematic is this new accommodation? And can it last?

In many ways, the low-key profile of the new program has an advantage—it can give the communication subsector time to re-group, to reinforce elements (of methodology, data processing and dissemination) that have inevitably been neglected during the long political debate. Concentration on building up developing country infrastructures is also productive in other than material ways: It helps to develop strengths in planning theory or evaluation design.

In my opinion, however, it cannot last over the longer term. Sooner or later, the new technologies will either have to measure up to their expectations or suffer a backlash if they do not do so (for whatever reason—overoptimism, inadequate assimilation, over-complexity). Eventually, the euphoria is bound to subside.

Even more important is the fact that, at present (and quite deliberately, in the interest of maintaining a consensus position), many of the right questions are not being asked. The impetus is to build up infrastructures, to educate and train, to improve endogenous production, but there is very little questioning of the kinds of infrastructure that are being developed, the character and contents of training, the relevance and ethnicity of endogenous production. If we were to enquire too closely into the capacity of many of the new infrastructures (often assisted by the IPDC) to enhance media freedom, or to enlarge the free flow of information, the present accord might be far less widely accepted. What would be the reaction if we were to ask more of training than that it should be practical and skills oriented (and therefore, apparently, content free)? If endogenous production were to be exposed to criteria of quality, audience involvement, and technical excellence, its results might be less generally applauded.

The consensus, like most of its kind, seems to be once again a matter of temporary accommodation to secure a breathing space—it does not really resolve the fundamental concerns of freedom and constraint, to which there are no easy answers. The old questions will eventually resurface, and then the pendulum may swing back with renewed vigor. In the meantime, the main task for Unesco is to make maximum use of this pause to consolidate, to recuperate, to regain some of its former energies and skills.

REFERENCES

MacBride, S. (1980). *Many voices, One world. Report by the International Commission for the Study of Communication Problems.* London: Kogan Page; New York: Unipub; Paris: Unesco.

Nordenstreng, K., & Varis, T. (1974). Television traffic—a one-way street? *Reports and papers on mass communication, 70.* Paris: Unesco.

Schramm, W. (1964). *Mass media and national development: The role of information in the developing countries.* Paris: Unesco.

Unesco (1970). *Mass media in society. The need of research.* Reports and Papers on Mass Communication. No. 59. Paris: Unesco.

CHAPTER

Media Policy Research: Conditions for Progress

DENIS MCQUAIL

COMMUNICATION AS POLICY MINEFIELD AND NO-GO AREA FOR RESEARCH

While media research in general has steadily developed in range and capacity, research with a direct bearing on media policy has always been faced with exceptional and deeply rooted difficulties. On the one hand, there are claims to professional autonomy on the part of communicators, which lead to a rejection both of research and of policy. On the other hand, the precepts of liberal communication philosophy offer little support for media policy of any kind and can be cited to devalue critical research and delegitimate policy. As a result, the very idea of policy for communication has often been controversial, and research has often been conducted in a minefield staked out by the varied, often conflicting, interests and points of view of governments and regulators, the media (either in their commercial or professional capacity), and the public, who are the supposed ultimate beneficiaries of media policy.

Policy is often perceived as a control in a domain that should not be controlled, and research in the interests of policy and planning has suffered as a result. Only in Third World countries is there much recognition of the need to plan and to have policies for communication, where resources are scarce and needs great. In more developed economies, major technological change has provided some boost for research; this has been outweighed by reassertion of liberal traditions. Communication policy remains a contested territory, and researchers have still to tread very warily.

These remarks are a necessary preamble to any consideration of the state of media policy research, partly because they help to account for a slower and more uneven pace of development, after an initial phase in the history in which policy of one sort or another was quite in vogue and provided a stimulus to innovation of theory and method. The seeming conservatism of much policy-related research has much to do with the nature of policy research commissions and with the need to address findings and interpretations to lay audiences of politicians, mass communicators, and the general public. This circumstance has often led to a lower status for policy research within the community of scholars, without much compensation by recognition in the world where politics is practice.

Policy-related research has also comprised a very fragmented, even miscellaneous category. The expression applies to several quite different issues and research tasks, but principally the following:

- critical diagnosis of communication problems and needs;
- planning to solve problems that are either structural (provision-related) or communicative (for example, information campaigns);
- evaluation of results of communication policies and interventions.

FROM COMFORMITY TO DISSENT

Policy-related research flowered first and most evidently in the decade or so after the Second World War, when needs seemed clear and optimism high, and policy and planning both were viewed in a positive light. Moreover, research tools, fashioned partly for purposes of war, seemed to be readily at hand. These tools were often those that later came to be identified under the (usually derogatory) label of *dominant paradigm.* They were, indeed, largely the instruments fashioned to pursue empirical, positivistic inquiry into the means of mass persuasion and control, and of planned social developmental change. Ideologically, the chosen methods and strategies of research often reflected an attachment to individualism, behaviorism, "modernism," hierarchy, manipulation, and progressivism of one kind or another.

The social and cultural world could, it was believed, be remade according to a plan conceived by the new masters of the universe, who, for once, however temporarily, were supposed to be acting for the good of mankind. It was also widely believed that some of the perceived ills of society—especially those manifesting themselves in the form of disorder, immorality, crime, and violence—were caused by mass media (and others might be cured by mass media—especially ignorance, underdevelopment, and related ills). In this moment of optimism about social engineering it was assumed that research could help to make charges of ill-doing stick and thus guide and legitimate prohibitions and cures. For the positive goals of social improvement, research was expected to uncover guidelines and often cures.

It proved much less easy than expected to reshape the world, to improve it, or even to diagnose its ills. Many of the efforts to secure development by way of communication appear to fail or were shown to have been fundamentally misconceived. The relatively very large research effort into the effects of crime and violence came to largely inclusive, inconsistent, or even unwelcome conclusions. The "powers that were" were not very pleased (although the media themselves were happy enough). The good intentions of authorities were also coming to be called into question by other media researchers.

Looking back, it seems as if the methods of research, although delivering quite useful knowledge, often became fatally implicated in the misconceived plans and the ideological motives of some of the planners and would-be social controllers. Any independent research interest was politically very weak, satisfied with small benefits, often glad simply of the opportunity to practice the research task. This frame of mind is not the most conducive to significant advance.

During the 1960s and 1970s, communication research came to bear a dual curse and some other burdens, not entirely merited, but not altogether the result of bad luck. As to the curse: research, in its applied, administrative, policy-related variety, became identified with the would-be manipulators of a capitalist or bureaucratic order, in a new counterparadigm of critical research (which was by then also the most creative and productive branch of the communication research enterprise). At the same time, this more creative, critical, and ideologically pure version of research came itself to be viewed with profound suspicion by a wide spectrum of media practitioners, politicians, and policy makers because of its critical stance in relation to the established media (and the media establishment).

A good deal of media research was perceived as being on the side of the protest movements of these decades and, in a global context, supporting the efforts to establish a more equitable "international information order." Research appealed, in effect, to few powerful friends, having become internally polarized as well as somewhat isolated from mainstream media institutions. This situation inevitably held back the acceptance of communication research as a reliable policy tool, even where researchers were willing to break critical ranks and engage in applied research.

The contribution media research made to its own difficulties was partly the result of its own success in relativizing the power of the media, demonstrating the limits to what can be achieved by communication, and also charting the complex interrelation between communication and other social and cultural processes. Research findings tended, to the naive at least, to undermine any claim to significance that the field might have by downplaying the significance of communication as an agent of change, influence, or effect. If communication is itself such a minor factor, it can reasonably be asked, why pay much attention to research? This is a caricature of a long period in which communication, research, and policy were each being manifested in quite diverse ways. Even so, it contains a core of truth and offers some lessons for the present.

BETTER TIMES

The prospects for communication policy and for research in relation to it have now, arguably, improved. One key to this improvement is that research has, with time, earned for itself a higher standing and won a degree of independence. It is not simply regarded as ancillary to policy, but has more claim to be able to offer policy guidelines of its own. To a large extent, this is due to the slow but steady growth of the research field over time. Fifty years ago, it was a little more than a set of tools borrowed mainly from social psychology and statistics, simple-minded ideas about media effects, and some very fragmentary factual information about media systems and audiences. There was really no instutitionalized field of communication inquiry and theory that could not set research priorities or define problems with any measure of autonomy.

The present degree of status and autonomy is limited but not negligible, and it is likely to grow as the subject of "communication science" or its equivalent is more widely studied in higher education. If we speak about tools for policy research now, we do not refer only to borrowed instruments used in the service of others, but to a set of instruments, including concepts, over which researchers have more intellectual control.

A second aspect of the improvement has already been noted—the growth, interconnection, and increasing centrality to society of communication institutions and activities. They are no longer seen just peripheral, superstructural phenomena or as instruments that can be used to achieve this or stop that. However liberal the climate of the times may be, communications media can no longer escape either from some form of regulation, planning, or monitoring, or be left entirely to their own devices. This paradoxical situation brings no joy to the media, which tend to respond by some form of self-regulation, but it is a stimulus to research.

Growth and change in communication arrangements have started to accelerate after a long period of postwar stability. The globalization of communication and the decline of national sovereignty over communication arrangements have tended to substitute international agreement for local freedoms and regulations, increasing the need for the kind of comparative information that communication research is able to supply, either generated from the concerns of communication science or collected on a commissioning basis. No small part of the growth and the increasing demands for knowledge comes from the private sector, where information is seen to play a key role in the promotion of new schemes, in planning investment, in marketing, and in monitoring progress of new ventures.

LESSONS LEARNED

Before surveying the current instrumentarium for policy research, it is relevant to recall some features of the communication process that were gradually and sometimes painfully uncovered in the rather drawn-out process of postwar development of research that has been referred to. On essential point that might have been obvious but had to be learned the hard way is that communication always takes place in an open and complex system of other changes. Communication is reflexive and interacts with an independently changing environment. Nothing stands still, and little can, in any direct or literal sense, be controlled, except, at best, through knowledge of what is going on.

Another essential fact, which it has taken time to learn and digest, is that communication—the purposes, effects, and messages—cannot be neutral or value free. Communication inevitably takes sides, and even if tries not to, it is perceived as doing so—which amounts to the same thing. The process of communication is governed at every stage by diverse, often conflicting, norms and ideologies. No research effort can succeed if it is not sensitive to such matters or has not the tools to handle them. This often means taking simultaneous account of perspectives on communication needs, purposes, and effects that may, logically, be quite irreconcilable. This is extremely taxing, to say the least, for a research practice that still has its roots in empirical and behavioral models.

The sometimes bitter lesson of experience is that a research practice adequate to emerging policy tasks has to be flexible and reflexive, able to cope with alternative values and cultural variations. Nevertheless, it cannot entirely escape from the requirement to dependable knowledge about a confusing and always changing reality. There is a strong expectation that any research knowledge that is usable in policy debate and development (which are always likely to be politically contested areas) has to have a hard core and a high degree of communicability in the public domain.

In practice, this means being able to deploy a form of discourse that has a wider circulation than that of the community of researchers. It means, at the very least, that general ideas and concepts have to be unambiguously defined and also firmly grounded in evidence. In practice, it also means that the empricial-behaviorist model has to be retained for purposes of policy research, despite the fact that, on its own, it will not serve to explain the complexity of what is going on.

THE POLICY TERRAIN: ISSUES AND TASKS FOR RESEARCH

From the early days of communication research, it was customary to divide the territory of research according to a basic model of communication that envisaged a process of *transmission* of (usually) purposeful *messages* from *senders* to *receivers*. Such a process could, in principle, be described in terms of its objectives and evaluated according to its success of failure in achieving these objectives. The same model has often provided the logic for classifying the main methods and types of communication research: organizational analysis, to deal with communication senders and their goals; content analysis, to deal with messages; surveys, to measure audiences and effects. Like the rest of the older dominant paradigm of research, this model does not suit the potential needs of modern policy research all that well, although it cannot simply be abandoned.

Policy research is now much more likely to be concerned with the underlying conditions of public communication arrangements, with the interactions between elements in larger systems of communication provisions, with the assessment of communication needs, with the long-term monitoring of performance for evidence of potential problems that have been identified at the level of the media structure and the larger society. Not all the problems identified are new, but priorities may be different, and new elements have entered the scheme of things. The key issues of current communication policy can be summarized as follows.

- The question of cultural autonomy and integrity, the protection of the national language and culture. Centrally at issue is the need to preserve opportunities for cultural expression by way of national mass media in the face of increasing, and inevitable, transnational flow. The problem has now become one for developed national societies, not just for the dependent Third World.

- The question of concentration of ownership and loss of diversity and independence of media. Concentration may be on the increase because of multinational financial activity, deregulation, and free trade, and as a result of pressures to rationalize production and distribution. The main underlying problems are those of loss of diversity and increased inequality in the balance of power within the "public space" of society.

- The effects of convergence of distribution systems, especially the loss of clear distinction between different communication technologies and systems (and policy regimes) of broadcasting, cable, telephone, satellites, etc. (Pool, 1984).

- The question of adequacy (in terms of quality) and the effectiveness (in range of access and universality of distribution) of the public information flows that maintain standards of information in increasingly complex modern societies. At issue is the quality of citizenship in the "information society" (Golding, 1990).

- The question of future roles and financing of the public broadcasting sector, which widely retains legitimacy but which can no longer claim continued monopoly status or unlimited access to its former sources of funding (McQuail, 1990).

- The old question of global imbalance between the information-rich and information-poor nations, which has been exacerbated by technological development and widening economic gaps between North and South. The failure to find any acceptable international political solution has left the problem ignored or festering, and it calls for new kinds of research (Mowlana, 1985) as well as for policy attention.

These are five widely encountered issues of policy that are prominent in public debate and on the political agenda of many countries. They are also issues that cannot very easily be handled by the traditional behaviorist research model referred to above. It is not even very obvious how the basic media research methods for studying organization, content, and audience would be of much help. In an obvious sense the task for research has become more difficult, but it has also been elevated to a higher level, above that of mere data-gathering technique. The task has to include much more complex forms of analysis on a wide front and also more creative, conceptual work that connects communication with the larger body of social and political theory.

TOOLS FOR RESEARCH

With these points in mind, we can review the main tools that might now be most relevant to the redefined tasks of policy-relevant research. In general, the lie of argument advanced implies that the notion of *tool* is itself somewhat inappropriate. Rather, what is now called for is an extended instrumentarium of theory, concepts, and methods. The entries that follow are intended to identify the main components of such an instrumentarium.

Political and legal analysis.   Questions of the kind raised above cannot be handled without attention to the context of conflict and competition in which decisions about media are forged. It is impossible to understand the background of these issues without weighing up wider costs and benefits, and without assessing the relative strength of the parties involved. On the matter of commercial inroads into public broadcasting, for instance, the principal actors include not only the new operators, the old broadcasters and the consumers, but also organizations of media workers, industrial interests, other media, political parties, advertising agencies, maybe transnational agencies, and so forth. The direction of events has often to be described and assessed by examining these matters. There is nothing new in the methods called for, but they have been relatively little used in the past, where system contexts were often relatively unchanging and also taken largely for granted.

Economic analysis. Communications research developed originally without any systematic connection with economics—giving rise to few economic analyses, benefiting little from economic thinking. Issues were largely defined in political or social-cultural terms, and the economic foundations and dynamics of media were generally regarded by the noneconomist media scholars as a basic *given*, which might either be safely left out of account or taken as an unexamined cause of problems that would be analyzed only in terms of their structural effects—for instance, the problems of monopoly, or commercialism, or the influence of advertising, or the global imbalances resulting from the economics of international communication. In other words, the tools of economic analysis were not regarded as important for communication research proper.

The general tenor of much public policy communication research has often seemed almost to imply that economic factors were, at best, regrettable necessities in the scheme of things. This attitude has largely disappeared, overtaken, to a large extent, by real-world events as media industries grew and diversified. There has been more coming to terms with economic factors, more recognition of their key role and the need to understand them, whatever one's attitude to commercialism. During the 1980s, this adaptation has been accelerated by the development and deployment of new communication technologies. These have a wider significance in the growing global information and hardware markets. Experience has shown that the implementation of policies for new technology depends very much on market conditions and forces. It is the economics of media technology that are currently more determinant than political-cultural considerations. The development of conceptual tools and research methods for economically literate communication policy research is still retarded, but at least the need has been recognized.

Communication and campaign planning tools.   There remains a wide terrain where communication is still regarded as a potential instrument for achieving other policy goals—for instance, as a means of stimulating social and technical change, or for promoting health, education, safety, and public information. There is no need to review all the methodological possibilities for this kind of communication task. The capacity to devise and to evaluate broad communication strategies has been at the core of the field from the beginning, and knowledge and skills have gradually accumulated, notwithstanding the many setbacks and reservations that the theoretical literature underlines. The central skills are those of constructing suitable messages, choosing the right channels, and measuring audiences reached and effects achieved.

The main qualitative gains over time have been the lessons already mentioned. Planned communication, if it is to have any chance of success, has to take account of the multiplicity of meanings in content, the variable experience and perceptions of intended recipients, and the operation of other, even competing, communication sources and networks. It also has to take account of great inefficiency, even counterproductivity, of mechanical models of information transfer and has had to build in considerations of audience negotiations and reflexivity. In practical research terms, this has meant that it is no longer enough to count and measure.

There is no easy shortcut to understanding what is going on in any significant sphere of communication and meaning—any of which touches peoples' lives deeply. Time-consuming analysis of the structure of texts and ethnographic knowledge of the audience and reception process have to be allowed for—as they are, increasingly, in trying to understand the normal process of mass communication (Ang, 1991).

While this has called for a development of *qualitative* theory and method, the demands for quantitative knowledge have also increased. In part this stems from the application of better research technology (the result of computerization for the most part). In part it stems from the increased complexity of media, of channel possibilities and audience behavior. Choosing appropriate vehicles and formats is more difficult, and keeping track of the audience, where the distributed message ends up, is also more difficult. This has not so much led to new tools than to adaptation of, and heavier demands on, the old ones—especially the use of multimedia, multinational surveys, and panels.

Content research.   A brief reference has just been made to developments in message analysis in applied communication research. Some of the earliest arguments for the policy relevance of research into media content have not been invalidated. Research played an important role in a wide range of policy research issues, including the effects of media concentration; the influence of media in relation to crime, violence, and disorder generally; the questions of political bias and/or diversity; general matters of the quality of mass media performance; international communication and the third world; the treatment of racial and other minorities in the media; and the role of the media in peace and war and international conflict (McQuail, 1991).

Essentially what content analysis did was to offer firm evidence of problems that might need media policy attention, and also to provide the basis for understanding the causes of problems. Over decades of much activity, methods were developed to incorporate much more sensitive ways of coping with the task of assessing evaluative direction, with uncovering structures and layers of meaning. There is little reason to be dissatisfied with the range of content research methods now available, although powerful challenges from the perspective of reception analysis have still to be answered.

CONCLUSION

The contribution that research can make to policy making or policy implementation will always be limited, especially because of the political and ideological sensitivity of much media work; the underlying tension between professional communicators, on the one hand, and media scientists and critical researchers on the other; the lack of unanimity within the research community; the gap between the privacy and self-containment of the research world and the uninsulated and often rough world of politics and business in which media operate; the fundamental inconsistency between freedom and planning; and the low capacity of research to explain or predict.

Nevertheless, the capacity of research has improved in other respects and the relationships among researchers, media communicators, and those concerned with policy are now less abrasive. Divisions of labor are recognized and mutual needs acknowledged, in an age, paradoxically, of more regulation. As the media institution itself matures, it is easier for research tasks in relation to policy to be more acceptably defined (Ferguson, 1990).

There still lingers an ambivalence on the part of some researchers in respect of policy research. Policy remains unfavorably associated with routine, managerial, and even manipulative practice, or with visions of technocratic utopia in the information society (Carey, 1989). Media practitioners, in turn, are still often suspicious of public policy and not always well disposed to researchers who align themselves with policy goals. The main improvements lie in the steady development of a policy-research discourse that is more widely shared among the various parties. Within this discourse, there is a place for recognizing some of the inevitable infringement on communication freedom, whether these result from the pressures of the market place or the political demands of the wider society. The discourse provides a means of coming to terms with the inevitable.

Policy may come to be perceived as less exclusively to do with "policing," but also with allocating, adjudicating, and even facilitating or promoting. It does not have to be seen only as a potential instrument of control. It can also operate as a monitor of trends and changes and a source of useful information in conditions of uncertainty. The widening range of activity of media communication also allows a wider and more varied role for research.

It is not out of place to end by noting the recommendations about research made by the MacBride Commission (MacBride, 1980, p. 225). The Commission asks that "current and future research should broaden its focus to deal with the truly fundamental problems of our time. It should not be content to serve to implement a given communication policy, or just to 'support' the media establishment, in order to make the existing system or various parts thereof more effective, regardless of its validity of the possible need to rethink certain dominant values or to suggest various alternative means or ends. Research, instead of dealing with value-free micro-questions, must therefore endeavor to apply independent critical criteria and to explore the potential of new forms and structures." They recommend, especially, the need to look at media institution in the light of a wider institutional context, and the need to devise "reliable indicators—such as exist in other fields—for communication policies and planning." In the end, the most critical condition for flourishing of policy research will be the survival or revival of a broad concept of a "public interest" in all matters to do with communication (Melody, 1990; McQuail, 1991).

REFERENCES

Ang, I. (1991). *Desperately Seeking the Audience*. London: Routledge.
Carey, J. (1989). *Communication as culture*. Boston: Unwin Hymen.

Ferguson, M. (Ed.). (1990). *Public communication: The new imperatives.* London: Sage.

Golding, P. (1990). Political information and citizenship. In M. Ferguson (Ed.), *Public Communication: The new imperatives* (pp. 84-100). London: Sage.

MacBride, S. (1980). *Many voices, one world.* Paris: Unesco.

McQuail, D. (1990). Caging the beast: Constructing a framework for the analysis of media change in Western Europe. *European Journal of Communication, 5* (2-3), 313-332.

McQuail, D. (1991) *Media performance.* London: Sage.

Melody, W. (1990). Communication policy in the global information economy. In M. Ferguson (Ed.), *Public communication: The new imperatives* (pp. 16-39). London: Sage.

Mowlana, H. (1985). *International flow of mass communication.* Paris: Unesco.

Pool, I. de Sola. (1984). *Technologies of freedom.* Cambridge, MA: Belknap Press.

CHAPTER

On Media Studies as a Breath of Air Across the Field of Sociology

TODD GITLIN

Sociology, properly understood, is less a science or a discipline than a field, which is all to the good. A field is more easily cultivated than a science and lays claim to fewer pretensions. A field, in the sense of high-energy physics, is a territory through which high charges work. It is diffuse. It radiates around a set of charged questions but lacks clearly defined boundaries. It is not a coherent, tidy body of knowledge. And if things work well, it illuminates.

In the past three decades, the scientific claims of sociology to be a "social science" have taken a well-deserved battering. The publication of Thomas Kuhn's work and its sequels helped spread skepticism about whether science could be an autonomous, ever-advancing concourse of knowledge. Radical student and feminist movements pointed the finger at science and found there unholy interests.

The critical spirit of those movements moved into a variety of professional circles and set out to demystify claims to objectivity and value-neutrality. Nevertheless, and paradoxically, in the United States at least, the widespread challenge of sociology's claim to be a positive science has not succeeded in exploding the hegemony of positivist models of research. Part of the reason is quite vulgarly material: the great bulk of empirical research, even under the Reagan cuts, is funded by federal agencies (and their private clones)—mainly small scale experimental and survey studies. Of course positivist research prevails partly by default, since the challenge to positivism has not generated a convincing alternative model for research. Still, for all the backsliding, the positivist style has lost some of the jauntiness and claim to universality it once embodied. At the same time, at the level of theory, the functionalist paradigm has suffered so many assaults—from paleo-, neo- and post-Marxisms, from symbolic interactionism and a range of other approaches—it can no longer so lightheartedly claim to be the master scheme that will eventually enfold and make sense of the "contributions" of this, that, and the other shred of "abstracted empiricism."[1] In short, English-speaking sociology has become an essentially contested terrain. In approach, method, and paradigm, sociology as a whole seems inalterably pluralist—though whether this recognition comes begrudgingly or enthusiastically depends on your location and point of view.

So much for a breathtaking general introduction. When I was originally asked to comment on the relation between sociology and media studies, I hazarded the glib, off-the-cuff guess that the recent revival of media studies, however admirable in itself, had left sociology as a whole rather unfazed. But further reflection suggests that this may not be the case. In fact, unexpectedly, recent work in media studies may have blown some fresh air throughout a good bit of sociology, or at least promised to open up sociology to critical thinking about the nature of modernity in general. By themselves, media studies make up a thriving enclave within sociology, but they may also be tonic for sociology as a whole, and for some unexpected reasons.

Curiously enough, one influence of media studies has been methodological. The recent waves of media scholarship have paid much attention to the workings of media *institutions* and to the *histories* of those institutions and the cultural forms they have sheltered and excluded. In the first realm, the fundamental question had been: How does this institution (newspaper, wire service, television news, or entertainment apparatus) make decisions? By what standards and codes does it make certain matters legitimate and render others unthinkable? Since the mid '70s there has been a range of new work in the United States along these lines, particularly on the production routines and ideologies of news (Epstein, 1973; Sigal, 1973; Tuchman, 1978; Gitlin, 1980; Hallin, 1986; Dorman & Fashaug, 1987). Here, the inspiration of British models—especially the pioneering study by James D. Halloran, Philip

---

[1] This is C. Wright Mills' (1959) ever-apt phrase in *The Sociological Imagination.*

Elliott, and Graham Murdock (1970), *Demonstrations and Communication*[2]—has been evident. Even in the '50s, the heyday of positivist media research in the United States, Paul F. Lazarsfeld had included on his agenda (or wish list) for the field the need for anatomies of decision making in media institutions. But the money, ideas, and effort flowed far more easily to fund effects studies, conducted in the spirit of marketing research if not as a footnote to it (Gitlin, 1978). So microscopic and misleading effects-of-media studies dominated the field for a long time. It took the political upsurges of the '60s, and the precedent of the careful and broad-gauged British research, to make the tracing of power and the formation of ideology central to a critical mass of scholars in the United States.

Suddenly sociology returned to media research, from which it should never have been expelled in the first place (Katz, 1983). The "targets" of mass media messages were rediscovered to be embedded in social worlds. Wonder of wonders, the media institutions themselves were discovered to have histories. Their conventions turned out to be problematic, changeable, contingent.[3] But most of all, the new wave of research centered on the working of media institutions. And this research found new use for un- and anti-positivist methods. Ethnomethodology, symbolic interactionism, and the varieties of ideology-reading practiced by the "cultural sciences"—all these ways of mapping the structures of human cognition and evaluation were ready-made for dissecting and criticizing the routines of choice in the command centers of the culture industries, of news in particular.

The application of these methods to a concrete body of material gave the methods a new raison d'être. No longer were they simply arid, abstract possibilities, of concern simply to connoisseurs of methodology. In the hands of such researchers as Harvey Molotch and Marilyn Lester (1974) and Gaye Tuchman (1978), they were working tools. The result was a rapidly growing number of media studies within sociology, sometimes grouped as the so-called "production of culture perspective" in the United States.[4] Influenced by

---

[2] When I began my own research on the mutual pressures of news and the New Left, *Demonstrations and Communication* was the only model I could find. It was, by the way, almost wholly unknown in the United States.

[3] The most striking sociological contribution to media history in the United States is Schudson (1978).

[4] Peterson (1979). On the limits to this perspective, see Mukesji and Schudson (forthcoming).

the spirit of Raymond Williams (especially Williams, 1977), if not the actual work, this viewpoint sees cultural work as social activity, not as a given array of free-hanging artifacts. The point is then to investigate the institutional conditions, for particular products. Such studies often borrow from the legitimacy of cultural anthropology within the social sciences as a whole (Geertz, 1973). They often employ the methods of ethnographic fieldwork (Gitlin, 1983). Starting from a base of close to zero, such studies added up to one of sociology's major growth industries in the past decade.

On the theoretical plane, the most ambitious media studies proved hospitable to a range of approaches to the analysis of images and discourse. This isn't the place for a close assessment of the uses and abuses of critical theory, structuralism, various post-structuralisms, and Foucaultian discourse analysis in the study of media content. Suffice it to say that media studies turned out to be a fertile ground for a hundred theoretical flowers. Media studies also turned out to be a site on which various methods of originally literature criticism could collect, cross-pollinate, and prove not only provincially titillating, but also germane to large projects. Eventually, by insisting on the constructedness of images, the fact that they are not accidental or arbitrary, media studies have helped restore the centrality of ideology to social studies as a whole—with effects on historical studies as well as the avant garde of literary criticism.

One more feature of the most advanced media studies—they were and are interested in the whole of a social process. This should not be remarkable in the social sciences, but sociology is still fairly new at this sort of thing in the United States. Starting with the cultural-studies work of Cohen (1978, 1983) and the Birmingham Centre for Contemporary Cultural Studies (Hall, 1973, 1977), it became not only mandatory but possible to look, at one and the same time, at the skews of discourse and image and also at the sources and consequences these skews. All the elements of media studies were seen to be rooted in society—although from today's vantage it is hard to imagine where else they could have been all along. There are complex tangles and loops, through which particular social activities and groups generate images and discourse that are selectively blocked and channeled through media, then go out into the world, in turn, to affect the styles in which deviant groups, movements, and finally everyone else understands themselves and each other (Gitlin, 1980). Instead of studying the news business, say, as an appropriator and broadcaster of meaning, a font of ideology that operates in a vacuum, various scholars began to lay out the news process on a larger canvas—as one important loop that is embedded in larger social processes and transformations at particular moments. Media studies started to think big. The totality of society caught at a particular historical moment—this essential crucible that tended to disappear when the close-up searchlights were turned on normal sociological microstudies—reemerged as the ground and condition of particular social processes. In other words, media studies at their most ambitious have turned out to be a sphere that has reminded sociology—or at least many sociologists—that the truth, or untruth, is the whole.

Conceivably, media studies and related forms of literary/cultural criticism will also push sociology toward addressing some of the bigger neglected questions of our present historical moment. I'm thinking of the question of how, in the most simple sense, "world-historically," we shall understand a society that routinely, profusely traffics in images; of the part played by technology in transforming human consciousness (and unconsciousness); of the shifts in cognitive infrastructure, which correspond to distinct historical periods; of the meaning and limits of the globalization of culture. Timid sociology, having wearied of its overly schematic childhood (Tönnies, Marx, Durkheim, even Weber) has signed many of the big questions over to the more daring or reckless cultural historians, or to certain rebels in its own ranks. On the image-centered society, there is notably the solid as well as self-parodying work of Jean Baudrillard (1981); on technology in general, Alvin W. Gouldner (1976); on the history of cognition and "deep structure" in consciousness, the cultural historians Carl Schorske (1979), Paul Fussell (1976) and Stephen Kern (1983). When both media studies and sociology think about big theory again, they will find ample reason to rack each other's brains.

REFERENCES

Baudrillard, J. (1981). *For a critique of the political economy of the sign* (Levin, Trans.). St. Louis: Telos.

Cohen, S. (1973). Mods and rockers: The inventory as manufactured news. In S. Cohen and J. Young (Eds.), *The manufacture of news: A reader.* London: Constable.

Cohen, S. (1983). *Folk devils and moral panics.* London: MacGibbon and Kee.

Dorman, W. & Fashang, M. (1987). *The U.S. press and Iran: Foreign policy and the journalism of deference.* Berkeley: University of California.

Epstein, E.J. (1973). *News from nowhere: Television and the news.* New York: Random House.

Fussell, P. (1976). *The great war and popular memory.* New York: Oxford.

Geertz, C. (1973). *The interpretation of cultures.* New York: Basic.

Gitlin, T. (1978). Media sociology: The dominant paradigm. *Theory and Society, 6.*

Gitlin, T. (1980). *The whole world is watching: Mass media in the making and unmaking of the new left.* Berkeley: University of California.

Gitlin, T. (1983). *Inside prime time.* New York: Pantheon.

Gouldner, A.W. (1976). *The Dialectic of ideology and technology.* New York: Seabury.

Hall, S. (1973). *Encoding and decoding in the television discourse.* Stencilled paper, Centre for Contemporary Cultural Studies, University of Birmingham.

Hall, S. (1977). Culture, the media and the "ideological effect." In J. Curran, M. Gurevitch, & J. Woollacott (Eds.), *Mass communication and society.* London: Edward Arnold.

Hallin, D. (1986). *The "uncensored war": The media and Vietnam.* New York: Oxford.

Halloran, J.D., Elliott, P., & Murdock, G. (1970). *Demonstrations and communication.* Harmondsworth: Penguin.

Katz, E. (1983). The return of the humanities and sociology. In Ferment in the Field [special issue] *Journal of Communication, 3.*

Kern, S. (1983). *The culture of time and space, 1880–1918.* Cambridge, MA: Harvard.

Kuhn, T. (1962). *The structure of scientific revolutions.* Chicago: University of Chicago.

Molotch, H., & Lester, M. (1974). News as purposive behavior: On the strategic use of routine events, accidents and scandals. *American Sociological Review, 39.*

Mukesji, C., & Schudson, M. (in press). *Introduction to rethinking popular culture: Contemporary perspectives in cultural studies.* Berkeley: University of California.

Peterson, R. (1979). Revitalizing the culture concept. *Annual Review of Sociology, 5,* 152–158.

Schudson, M. (1978). *Discovering the news.* New York: Basic.

Sigal, L. (1973). *Reporters and officials: The organization and politics of newsmaking.* Lexington, MA: Heath.

Schorske, C.E. (1979). *Fin-de-siecle Vienna.* New York: Knopf.

Tuchman, G. (1978). *Making news: A study in the construction of reality.* New York: Free Press.

Williams, R. (1977). *Marxism and literature.* New York: Oxford.

Wright Mills, C. (1959). *The sociological imagination.* New York: Oxford.

Mass Communications and Political Science

COLIN SEYMOUR-URE

To attempt a comprehensive comparison between the place of mass communications in political science now and 25 years ago would be foolhardy. It would read like a bibliographical guide. It would fail, anyway, in its aim of completeness: It would say more about the author (especially his or her limitations) than about the subject. The great growth of research and teaching has of course made political communications an established field within political science (or at least a largish meadow, lush with green grasses and an industrious hum). But now, as before, it is a peripheral field. It has grown with the discipline as a whole, yet in essence, if not in its details and emphases, its relation to the parent discipline has not changed. This essay concentrates more upon why I believe this to be so, and on the roots of the present relationship in the 1960s and 1970s, than upon the position today. Readers have their own vantage points upon the latter and will no doubt prefer to make their own comparisons. This is simply one person's view of the kinds of questions that may in general be asked about the relation of communication to politics, of the factors that determined what particular questions were studied in these decades, and of some of the developments since then.

At first sight it is puzzling to find political communication a peripheral field. Reduced to its essentials, the subject involves three kinds of questions, and each seems of central importance to the study of politics. The most ambitious involves the attempt to describe the workings of a political system entirely in terms of communication concepts—in short, the construction of a "communication model" of politics. The rationale for this starts from the preposition that communication is a basic social (and hence political) process. There can be no society without communication among its members; through communication, the organic nature of a society—its continuous recreation—is made possible. While the means and patterns of communication may be socially controlled, in the last resort social institutions are secondary and media of communication primary. In the words of Richard Fagan, "Communication as a process pervades politics as an activity." We should therefore expect to be able to offer at least a mechanistic explanation of political behavior by examining the flows of political communication. Such a model, of which the pioneering effort by Karl Deutsch (1963) remains the most prominent, goes far beyond just mass communication. But the rationale provides a strong basis nonetheless for the claim that mass communication should be an important subject in the study of politics.

The second kind of question involves normative theories of politics. The relevance of communication to these theories may be shown through its connection with the key political concept of power. Questions of how power is exercised, by whom, in what circumstances, and why, lead naturally into questions about how it ought to be exercised, that is to say, into the traditional normative problems about forms of government, or about freedom, justice, authority, and the like. But the exercise of power is critically affected by patterns of communication. At its simplest, we cannot obey someone unless we understand his or her command. Even then, whether we obey may depend also on other information: Will there be a reward or a punishment? Is the command legitimate? Is it unwise, because it is ill-informed or ignorant? Again, we may obey a command that was not intended as such, like Henry II's exasperated "Who will rid me of this turbulent priest?", which led to the overeager killing of Becket. In the context of a discussion of forms of government, it is clear that the patterns of communication necessary to democracy, for example, are more elaborate and involve much more communication upwards than those of a despotism. Indeed, one of the tests of a totalitarian society is the range of expression and openness of its communications.

The third kind of question is the least easy to encapsulate. It derives from the propositions underlying the first kind. For if communication pervades politics, we may suppose that most forms of political phenomena will be illuminated by taking that fact into account in our attempts to explain them. Not all may have a connection with mass communication, but mass media are so intrusive in people's lives that it would be perverse to start from the assumption that they are socially and politically insignificant. At this point, however, the argument falters. The very universality of communication as a factor in political behavior excludes a concise statement about its importance; for the number of questions about communications and politics is as great, arguably, as the number of questions about politics. Party identification, class relations, legislative behavior, problems of legitimation, even the control of civil servants or local government expenditure—you name it, and it must be affected to some extent by the flows of communication between those concerned. The point may be overstated, but it resolves the puzzle about why the study of communication is at once so central and yet so peripheral to political science. It is central in the sense that it has something to say about everything in politics, yet it is peripheral because what it has to say is of central importance to by no means all the questions people have thought worth asking. By analogy with road communications, the people who know about cars have a contribution to make in explaining how you get from A to B—indeed, whether you will actually succeed in doing so—and how you may feel at the end. But most journeys have a higher purpose, far transcending the journey itself.

That inadequate summary introduces only part of the problem. If it is true that all questions about communication and politics can be squeezed under one or another of those headings, the choice of particular questions is in practice determined by, to use a rough shorthand, the opportunities and attitudes of political scientists. The next point to consider, therefore, is the state of British political science, as it concerned communication—and especially mass communication—at the beginning of the 1960s. About this, too, it would be foolish to pontificate, and my comments aim simply to convey an impression of how the field seemed to me then, as someone embarking on research and planning to offer an undergraduate course in it.[1]

The political science community in Britain was still small in the early 1960s. (There must have been more scholars studying British politics in the United States than in Britain.) Its roots were chiefly in the disciplines of history, philosophy, law, and economics. The

---

[1] I mean a *course* in the sense of a unit in a degree program. In the system as it then was at the University of Kent, a course comprised one-sixth of an undergraduate's total workload in the last five terms of the degree.

dramatic expansion of higher education after the Robins report in 1962, exemplified in the foundation of seven new universities and the granting of university status to a number of existing institutions of further education, gave political science a new status. Many universities had hitherto tucked the subject into another department, such as Economics, or an omnibus Social Sciences Department. Now they gave it a department of its own. In the new universities in particular, the social sciences as a whole enjoyed a prominence not previously experienced elsewhere except at the London School of Economics and, in the case of economics, Oxford, Cambridge, the Scottish universities, and a few of the great civic universities such as Manchester. So rapid was the expansion of chairs in sociology—from about four to 40 in a few years—that some of them were left vacant or converted for lack of candidates.

So there were lots of new students to teach and lots of new staff to teach them political science. The new status of the subject might, I suppose, have led to a new concern for disciplinary coherence. But if anything its eclecticism was increased by two other factors. One, the less important, was that new staff did not always have a background in political science. (This was even more true in sociology.) The diversity of disciplinary roots was thus reinforced, the most glaring illustration to this day (and one that weakens the discipline as a whole) being the rift between *political theory* (meaning, broadly, the history of ideas) and *political institutions* or *behavior.* The other factor was a fashion for *interdisciplinarity.* In their search for a distinctive pedagogy to match their new foundation (and to make them attractive to good students), the new universities nearly all sought to break down barriers of departmentalism and strict disciplines. Sussex constructed an interlocking system of schools and disciplines, and Kent eschewed the word Department altogether and still organizes itself into Boards of Studies under large faculty umbrellas. What exactly interdisciplinary meant was not always clear, nor in particular how it differed from multidisciplinary, but whatever it meant there was no doubt that mass communication was a subject with great interdisciplinary potential.

For a variety of reasons, then, the early 1960s was a good time to develop an interest in mass communications—in politics, as in a number of other disciplines. Political science was a heterogeneous subject, tyrannized by no orthodoxy though conscious of the contribution that might be made to it by behavioral techniques and by sociology. The times encouraged experimentation. In the new universities, courses were starting from scratch, and there was no problem for staff of having either to teach courses that already existed or to weave a way through long-established personal and academic networks in order to innovate. The traditional cultural bias towards countries that "mattered"—Britain, the United States, France, the U.S.S.R., the Commonwealth nations—began to be corrected. Students were looking for new subjects; publishers scented profitable markets.

For research on political communication, as distinct from teaching, the circumstances were in practice more difficult. The S.S.R.C.[2] had not yet got going. The typical researcher was still the isolated scholar, funded by the U.G.C. and fitting in his (rarely her) research between teaching responsibilities, which took first place. If he was lucky, he would get a sabbatical every so often. There was a strong professional incentive, unless he was completely oblivious of promotion, not to become too specialized or esoteric, nor to splash and tumble in the shallows of a backwater.

In this respect, mass communications, though welcomed as legitimate for the reasons I have suggested, was still rather marginal. It would certainly have been professionally unwise—possibly suicidal, at least in career terms—to bill yourself in a British university in the early 1960s as a Lecturer in Communications with an interest in politics, rather than as a Lecturer in Politics whose field happened to be communications. The easiest research to organize, and the dominant form in British political studies, was library-based or desk research, in a tradition of simple empiricism. Survey work was mysterious and expensive (Butler & Stokes, 1969, were just cranking up the first major voting study in 1964), and fieldwork of all kinds ate dreadfully into the time available for reading and writing. It was undoubtedly true that your time was most productively used if your teaching and research interconnected (Seymour-Ure, 1968). This too discouraged the choice of very narrow research topics.

Acceptance of political communication as a legitimate and potentially worthwhile field, of course, did not imply that one's colleagues would personally acquaint themselves with it. Helping to plan our Part II courses at Kent in 1965, I paced along the university road with a senior colleague. When we started on political communication, picking our way past the chunks of left-over concrete and

---

[2] *Social Science Research Council,* now the *Economic and Social Research Council.* The *Science* was dropped in 1984, following appraisal of the S.S.C.R.'s position and status. It says more than it marks about the political climate surrounding social research, sociology in particular.

broken curbstones that dotted university campuses in the goldrush years, there was a certain clearing of the throat, and then my colleagues said, "Yes, but what will the students actually read?" The short answer was a hotchpotch ranging from ephemera such as *The Listener,* through heavyweight scholarly work (much of it American), to primary sources such as readership surveys produced by market research agencies.

Giving an indication of what there was to read 20 years ago will show at the same time, I hope, just how limited was the existing output of research. My course set out to explore the political role of mass media, mainly in Britain, with a focus on the determinants of the behavior of news organizations and their impact upon political groups and institutions and upon individuals. The limitations of the literature caused obvious biases. It was much easier to study the press than broadcasting (but not the regional and local press). There was more material on Parliament than on parties, interest groups, and the executive. The nearest approaches to a history of the press in the 20th century were the uneven and amateur volumes by Harold Herd (1952) and Francis Williams (1957). Volume One of Asa Briggs's (1961) history of broadcasting had just appeared, but it took the story only up to 1927. Undergraduates could not be expected to plough through the history of *The Times,* which in the interwar volume was anyway unbalanced by its guilt about the paper's attitude to appeasement. There was virtually nothing scholarly about the internal workings of news organizations or the interaction between journalists and politicians (of all kinds). Jeremy Tunstall was about to embark on the research that produced *The Westminster Lobby Correspondents* (1970) and *Journalists at Work* (1971). There was, admittedly, a lot of American material—about news values, for instance—that could be tentatively applied to the British context. But perhaps the two fields in which it was easiest to find material were the relevant bits of law and "effects." The former, so far as I was concerned, involved such topics as official secrecy and the political implications of libel, contempt of court, and what might be termed the *Sunday Times* problems: that is, legal constraints of all kinds against publication of matters in the public interest. There was a good new book by David Williams (1965) on the Official Secrets Acts, and for the rest it was a case of chasing up the normal legal sources. But this was for the political scientist a marginal area, even though it linked up to the historical arguments about press freedom.

Effects, on the one hand, were central. Questions about every kind of political influence of mass media eventually boil down to questions about their influence over individuals; and it was hardly surprising, if rather irritating, that effects had come to be synonymous with this kind of influence rather than, say, influence upon the role of the relationship of institutions. For an undergraduate course, however, there was no doubt that J.T. Klapper's (1960) survey of the research up to about 1959 was most useful. Moreover much of the American primary research (Katz, Lazarsfeld, the Langs, and so on) was easily available, even if very little related to Britain. But Trenaman and McQuail had appeared in 1961; Blumler and McQuail (1968) would soon be in the pipeline; and Himmelweit, Oppenheim, and Vince (1958) had tackled a subject—violence— about which discussion slid naturally into political channels.

Among nonscholarly literature (by which I mean work not written for a scholarly audience, nor according to the usual canons of scholarship; which is not to say, of course, that it is not often more stimulating, perceptive, and better informed than scholarly work), it was a matter of beachcombing. There is a long tradition in Britain of the self-aware journalist reflecting upon his or her craft—R.D. Blumenfeld (1933), Kennedy Jones (n.d.), Philip Gibbs (1923), J.A. Spender (1925), to name but four at random from the interwar period. Heirs to it postwar included Francis Williams (1946), Paul Einzig (1960, revealing on the Lobby in the 1940s and 1950s), and a generation whose experience increasingly included broadcasting (John Whale, 1967). Such books are always readable (and much shorter than most of their American counterparts) and are part of the scholar's raw material as well as revealing commentaries in their own right.

The same could be said about official publications. For a country whose dominant political culture excludes the idea of mass media as a general public policy area, Britain in fact generates a regular flow of inquiries and reports. Pilkington on broadcasting was out by 1962; so was Shawcross on the press, even though it did not contain much research. The B.B.C. and I.T.A. Handbooks included useful detail; so did Press Council Annual Reports and occasional parliamentary publications, such as the report of the House of Commons Committee on broadcasting Parliamentary proceedings (1966–1967).

But I am beginning to collapse into bibliography. Two other sources should not be omitted, however, for they helped the neophyte student and researcher in political communication substantially in the mid-1960s. One was market research. Some firms, such as Gallup, British Market Research Bureau, and Mark Abrams at the London Press Exchange, would readily make their findings available. If I had cast my net wider I could no doubt have found others. News organizations themselves varied. *The Guardian* was helpful, but *The Times,* still in its Astor ownership, was thoroughly obscurantist, or so it seemed to me. That suspicion of the social sciences that must have been encountered by so many researchers in the 1960s (even before the period covered by Malcolm Bradbury in *The History Man*) was well represented in Printing House Square. This was one aspect of the general difficulty for the media researcher in getting access. It is a perverse and ironic paradox that news organizations, which live by publishing information about other people's affairs, are no keener than the rest of us on people scrutinizing theirs. The first research proposal I ever put up to the S.S.R.C., in about 1966, would have involved, among other things, the selection of recordings from the B.B.C. sound archives. Naive and inadequate though the proposal no doubt was in many respects, it was turned down flat with the comment that I would be most unlikely to get access (no suggestion, alas, that the S.S.R.C. might use its good officers to overcome the problem). In 1962, similarly, I had breezed into the Sergeant-at-Arms's office at Westminster to pick up a copy of the Lobby Correspondents' list—and slunk out a few minutes later feeling lucky not to have been accused of a breach of privileges. In Ottawa, whence I had just returned to do a thesis about political journalism, the corresponding list was printed and publicly available. Many lobby correspondents were still writing anonymously then; but even so, it seemed a nonsense. Interviewing journalists on an individual and informal basis was a different matter, once I could get to them, and many, of course, were willing to come and talk to student audiences as well.

The other indispensable source, then as now, which means that however bad a course on mass media may be, it should never be boring, was newspapers and broadcast programs themselves. Every student could be his or her own researcher. This, I assume, is partly why mass media is such a good field for courses in continuing education and at the Open University. (It is interesting to note that both Richard Hoggart and Raymond Williams started their careers in adult education.) In political science, though, the value of content analysis is strictly limited. It tells you nothing about how audiences understand or react to what they see or read, and little about the intentions of those who produce the papers and programs. Even the extent to which it indicates the boundaries of what is available to be understood is limited and unclear, as the notion of "reading between the lines" (that is, inserting content that is not explicitly there) makes clear. By comparison, audience research and studies of news organizations tend to be much more fruitful.

There was no difficulty, then, in finding material for students in the 1960s, and possibly there was virtue in the need for them to extemporize and to use so many sources that, though strictly secondary, were primary in their relevance to a course about politics and mass communications. The most uncomfortable thing was the absence of undergraduate literature offering either communication models of politics or a theoretical framework for the course as a whole. Too much data referred to other disciplines' theories.

I have already said that this situation seems to me essentially unchanged—but comparatively, not absolutely. In absolute terms the picture was transformed by, say, the late 1970s. No textbook about British politics could be taken seriously unless it had a substantial chapter about communications. Students of specialized fields such as elections and voting behavior became acutely conscious of the importance of mass media in shaping the patterns of behavior described as "the campaign" and the reactions of electors to it (Seymour-Ure, 1974). The communication processes involving political institutions in general and the political potential of institutions that are explicitly "for" communication—the mass media—are widely recognized. Media institutions no longer appeared as monoliths, symbolized by domineering proprietors or editors. Problems of access became progressively fewer. Blumler, Gurevitch, and Ives (1978) talked to 200 broadcasters and politicians and analyzed 150 hours of videotaped election programs in a study of election broadcasting in 1974. Philip Schlesinger (1978) interviewed 120 staffers and spent 1,260 hours observing them at work over a 4-year period for his book on B.B.C. News. Michael Tracey's (1977, 1983) studies involved both research in depth about key individuals such as Hugh Greene and particular programs such as *Panorama*. Oliver Boyd-Barrett, Phillip Elliott, David Morrison, Jeremy Tunstall, and many others carried out comprehensive interview schedules unheard of 20 years earlier. The change is epitomized in the experience of Tom Burns (1977), who was permitted to interview 200 B.B.C. staffers in 1963—but not to publish his findings. By the mid-1970s the climate had changed: he interviewed a further 60 people, and publication of *The B.B.C.: Public Institution and Private World* was no problem.

The textbooks adapted; the media organizations, by and large, opened up. Case studies abounded—of individuals, of interest groups, of events, of topics. Even officialdom was partly converted, if the Ministry of Defense's cooperation in research about mass media and the Falklands War is anything to go by. The memoirs and more-or-less reflective volumes by journalists flourished—

James Margach (1978), Joe Haines (1977), Charles Wintour (1972)—as well as less autobiographical studies, including those of Hugh Cudlipp (1980) and Simon Jenkins (1979). Fads and fashions came and went (official secrecy, parliamentary broadcasting).

In all that, and in what came later, political scientists did not make the running. Some of the work, certainly, such as that of Blumler and his colleagues at Leeds, or some of the researchers at the Leicester Centre and at the City University, was rooted fairly firmly in political science. But other work, whether by the Glasgow Media Group (1976, 1980) on industrial relations, Hartmann and Husband (1974) on race, Stephen Koss (1981) on the rise and fall of the political press, or the forays against secrecy by Crispin Aubrey (1981), was highly relevant to the concerns of political scientists without being rooted in the discipline.

Precisely why the sociologists made the running is for them to say. But one reason, I dare say, is connected with the failure of political science to develop an adequate theoretical base to the study of communication. This is not surprising, given the nature of the substantive concerns of politics. Yet the universality of communication in society seems to demand an overarching theory, and the scope of sociology makes this a more natural discipline to provide one. Equally, it is easy to see why mass society theories, and, latterly, Marxism, can accommodate the analysis of mass communication so comfortably, although in undergraduate hands they can quickly degenerate into crude determinism and circular argument, with the voice of Dave Spart[3] raised high. More recently still, the application of semilogical theory seems especially exciting, although, unlike Marxism, it is inaccessible to the conventionally trained political scientist.

The most important substantive change affecting mass communication and political science, therefore, has been the growth of sociological research in the field. (It may well be true for other fields in political science too, such as parties, voting behavior, and bureaucracies. Indeed the growth of sociology in Britain has broadened the horizons of political science no end.) But it is naturally an oblique change, shifting the focus of questions about political communication towards processes and away, to some extent, from formal structures and legalities.

The most important institutional change has been the growth of research units. Isolated scholars still beaver away, but the typical

---

[3] An infantile Marxist, created by the satirical magazine *Private Eye* to characterize the "mad left."

researcher must now, surely, be located in Leicester, Birmingham, Glasgow, Leeds, and the rest. Moreover, the numbers proliferate, with such newcomers as the Broadcasting Research Unit, the European Institute for the Media at Manchester, and the concentration of research, alongside teaching, at the Polytechnic of Central London and Goldsmith's College.

To someone working outside such units, one of the striking things about them has naturally been the degree to which their choice of research topics must depend upon success in fund raising. It used to puzzle me why the university-based units did not become involved in undergraduate teaching and strengthen their U.G.C. bases earlier, though there would have been costs as well as benefits and perhaps it was not practical. Nor has the E.S.R.C. been generous. In any expanding field it is difficult by definition to fund enough good people to do all that the field might justify. But between 1970 and 1979 the S.S.R.C. made only 30 project grants for media studies. This was one percent of the total number; and the money involved, £292,929, amounted to much the same percentage of the total sum dispensed (£24.7 million). According to the Annan Committee on Broadcasting (Annan, 1977, p. 45–52), the B.B.C. and I.B.A. spent more than £800,000 on their audience research in 1974 to 1975 alone.

The units thus have not always done the research they might have liked, no doubt. But they have constituted an important community of scholars, able, not least, to stand up to the media organizations, especially the publicly accountable broadcasters. Also—and not to be underestimated—they have provided a body of people who will read media research as well as undertake it.

The growth of mass communication teaching, ironically, has accentuated the disjunction of teaching and research, since the teaching has happened mainly in the polytechnics. Despite the handwringing of the C.N.N.A. Communication Studies Board about the lack of a central core of communication theory, it is easy to see why the polys seized on communication studies degrees. It was clear in the 1970s that the universities were not ready to do so, yet the subject had all the advantages of student appeal, inderdisciplinarity, and flexibility in staffing and course combinations. But in theory there was supposed to be less time for research in the polys—a theory on the whole resoundingly disproved.

The community of scholars was widened further, so far as political scientists were concerned, by the success of the annual workshops of the European Consortium for Political Research, founded in 1970. This increased the contact English political scientists had, particularly with Scandinavian, French, and German scholars. The International Political Science Association and other professional bodies have increasingly had the same beneficial effects.

Political scientists interested in mass communications will always, in my view, be to a considerable extent the customers of researchers based in other disciplines. We adapt their findings to those questions about politics that seem important for the moment. Mass communication is bound to be a factor in explanations of many political phenomena (indirectly, perhaps, in all). But with the exception of the search for specifically cybernetic models of politics—and no one yet, to my knowledge, has tried to apply Deutsch's (1963) *The Nerves of Government* to a particular country—it is a peripheral field. No more peripheral than many others, I hasten to emphasize; for the experience of the last 20 years has been to establish it firmly as a legitimate area of the discipline. But if mass communication is peripheral also to other disciplines, researchers will always struggle for research funds, as experience with the S.S.R.C. suggests, since energies are diffused. This, in the last resort, is the justification for a strong group of research units. Long may they thrive.

REFERENCES

Annan, Lord. (1977). *Report of the Committee on the Future of Broadcasting.* Cmnd. 6753. H.M.S.O.

Aubrey, C. (1981). *Who's watching you?* Harmondsworth, UK: Penguin.

Blumenfeld, R.D. (1933). *The press in my time.* London: Rich and Cowan.

Blumler, J., Gurevitch, M., & Ives, J. (1978). *The challenge of election broadcasting.* Leeds, UK: Leeds University Press.

Blumler, J., & McQuail, D. (1968). *Television in politics.* London: Faber and Faber.

Briggs, A. (1961). *The birth of broadcasting.* New York: Oxford University Press.

Burns, T. (1977). *The B.B.C.: Public institution and private world.* London: Macmillan.

Butler, D., & Stokes, D. (1969). *Political change in Britain.* London: Macmillan.

Cudlipp, H. (1980). *The prerogative of the harlot.* London: Bodley Head.

Deutsch, K. (1963). *The nerves of government.* New York: Free Press.

Einzig, P. (1960). *In the centre of things.* London: Hutchinson.

Gibbs, P. (1923). *Adventures in journalism.* London: Heineman.

Glasgow Media Group. (1976). *Bad news.* London: Routledge and Kegan Paul.

Haines, J. (1977). *The politics of power.* Jonathan Cape.

Hartmann, P., & Husband, C. (1974). *Racism and the mass media.* Davis-Poynter.

Herd, H. (1952). *The march of journalism.* London: Allen and Unwin.

Himmelweit, H.T., Oppenheim, A.N., & Vince, P. (1958). *Television and the child.* New York: Oxford University Press.

House of Commons. (1966–1967). *Report from the Select Committee on Broadcasting etc. of proceedings in the House of Commons.* H.C., 146.

Jenkins, S. (1979). *Newspapers: The power and the money.* London: Faber and Unwin.

Jones, K. (n.d.). *Fleet Street and Downing Street.* London: Hutchinson.

Klapper, J. (1960). The effects of mass communication. New York.

Koss, S. (1981). *The rise and fall of the political press in Britain* (Vol. 1). London: Hamish Hamilton.

Margach, J. (1978). *The abuse of power.* London: W.H. Allen.

Pilkington, Sir H. (1962). *Report of the Committee on Broadcasting, 1960.* Cmnd. 1753. H.M.S.O.

Schlesinger, P. (1978). *Putting 'reality' together: B.B.C. News.* London: Constable.

Seymour-Ure, C. (1974). *The political impact of mass media.* London: Constable.

Seymour-Ure, C. (1968). *The press, politics and the public.* London: Methuen.

Shawcross, Lord. (1962). *Royal Commission on the Press, 1961–1962.* Cmnd. 1811, H.M.S.O.

Spender, J.A. (1925). *The public life.* (2 vols.) Cassell.

The Times. (1935–1952) *History of the Times.* (4 vols. in 5). London: The Times Publishing Co.

Tracey, M. (1977). *The production of political television.* London: Routledge and Kegan Paul.

Tracey, M. (1983). *A variety of lives: A biography of Sir Hugh Greene.* London: Bodley Head.

Trenaman, J., & McQuail, D. (1961). *Television and the political image.* London: Methuen.

Tunstall, J. (1970). *The Westminster Lobby correspondents.* London: Routledge and Kegan Paul.

Tunstall, J. (1971). *Journalists at work.* London: Constable.

Whale, J. (1967). *The half-shut eye.* London: Macmillan.

Williams, D. (1965). *Not in the public interest.* London: Hutchinson.

Williams, F. (1946). *Press parliament and people.* London: Heineman.

Williams, F. (1957). *Dangerous estate.* New York: Longman.

Wintour, C. (1972). *Pressure on the press.* London: Deutsch.

CHAPTER

Games Media People Play* (Changes in the Mass Communication System of Hungary)

TAMAS SZECSKÖ

> If traffic lights are green for every direction, this does not yet mean to have democracy.
>
> *(J.Z. Elky, Murphy's Hungarian Laws, Budapest, 1989)*

Sweeping events in a society bring the social scientist into an odd situation. He or she tries to be on the beat of history, but, at the same time, his or her professional self feels a kind of uncertainty. Being confronted with an almost impenetrable mass of social novelties, meeting unprecedented events, the scholar finds it extremely difficult to employ the usual tools of investigation: The material to be dealt with is more than volatile. It is just as if a chemist were starting the analysis of an unknown substance, but each time he or she pours reagents into the test-tube, a large hand from the outside changes it, adding a new dose of liquid.

The fundamental changes of the last few years in the East European societies have piled up a huge stock of raw material for further scientific inquiry. But the pace of these changes has been so accelerated, and the transformational process of some basic structures compressed into such a brief time-span, that the social scientist rubs his or her eyes and, in a dizzy excitement, begins wondering about feasible methodologies for the study of these events and processes. Very soon, however, he or she might realize that it is not possible to be more than an open-eyed observer and humble chronicler of the changes, meticulously recording the

---

* Manuscript completed in January 1990.

events, trying to distinguish between organic and incidental preeminent political ones. And, last but not least, formulating hypotheses to be verified later, when phenomena are not *in statu nascendi* any longer.

In the light of these considerations I will present here some characteristics of the Hungarian mass communication system in transition. Following the traditions of classical dramaturgy, I first offer a glimpse of the scene where the play has been unfolding. In the second part I introduce the main actors. The third part describes, rather concretely, the games the actors played in 1988 through 1989. After this overview I will make some summary statements, acknowledging that my position is similar to that of a drama critic who leaves his or her seat before the play has ended. Because the curtain has not yet come down—the play is going on, and there are more games to follow.

I. CHARACTERISTICS OF A SYSTEM IN TRANSITION

In September 1989 the newly elected president of the National Association of Hungarian Journalists said at his inauguration: "The Hungarian press and broadcasting of today is already a power, because there has not been any other institution, organ, or organization in the country which has contributed to the demolition of the old, bad power—that is, to the democratic development of the society—as effectively as the press, the mass media (*Magyar Sajtó*, 1989, p. 22).

This, I think, is not a journalistic overstatement. The legitimate and official mass media played a much greater role in the "peaceful revolution" of Hungary than those of the other East European countries in their respective revolutions. (This fact, probably, also contributed to the peaceful, gradual character of the [nevertheless fundamental] changes in the political structures.) This can be explained by several factors.

Probably the most important among them is that, during the 32 years of the Kádár era, Hungarian society has developed, as a leading Hungarian political scientist rather persuasively puts it (Hankiss, 1989), into a "double-decked" or split society, with a very peculiar relationship between the first and the second societies. Its most spectacular expression was the coexistence of the first and second economy (not only coexisting but taking each other for granted!). This split pervaded other social spheres as well, including the information system of society (Szecskö, 1984).

Considering that there was an overlap, a grey zone between the two societies where, as Hankiss (1989, pp. 134–135) shows, beside clientelism, nepotism, oligarchic mechanisms, and corruption, one could also find a broad field for informal bargaining processes between the actors of both (official and nonofficial, legitimate and illegal) societies, communicators also found ways and means of expressing ideas that were sometimes very different from the ritual or official standpoints. (Even in the most heavily controlled media, including Hungarian Radio and Hungarian Television, broadcasters could develop programs—mostly during off-peak hours—where they aired critical, sometimes openly oppositional, views.) There were, certainly, repercussions for the most blatant cases (mostly temporary bans, which prevented publication or transmission), but nothing really serious. The Kádár regime, rather shrewdly, did not want to create public martyrs, so the journalists, for their part, just shrugged and said: "Well, this everyday fight goes with the job!"

Another factor in explaining why mass communications could act as a battering ram stems from another Hungarian peculiarity, the fact that communication policies and cultural policies have never been organically linked to each other. The highest level decision makers in the cultural field usually behaved in a much more liberal (albeit paternalistic) way than their counterparts in the domain of mass communications. At a lower level, the Department of Science, Culture, and Education of the Communist Party and the Department of Agitation and Propaganda rarely acted in a coordinated way. This resulted, on the one hand, in a cultural system that was far more liberal than that of the other East European societies (with the possible exception of Poland). On the other hand, it also offered room in which the communicators could maneuver. While part of the mass communication system was supervised by Agit-Prop Department and the Government's Information Office, and the other part by the Cultural Department and the Ministry of Culture, the journalists evoked the old Latin proverb *Inter duos litigantes*...and realized that—if they were careful—they could be the third party in the game...the one who has the last laugh.

A third factor that explains the crucial role of the communication system in promoting changes in Hungarian society is rooted in the fact that since the mid '80s, most of the shrewd politicians were preparing themselves for the post-Kádár era, for a change of the guard. They did belong to the generation that already appreciated (sometimes even overvalued) the power of the media, in contrast to

Kádár and most of his associates in the old Politbüro.[1] Consequently, they began to build up informal contacts with some of the most prominent media personalities, giving them background information in the hope that their own political careers could be promoted by pampering the media.[2] Here again a field opened for journalists: If one politician attacked them, they could look for another to defend them.

There could be yet another historical factor to the explanation. If we accept Hugo Grotius's distinction between negative and positive stratagems—further elaborated by Hans Speier (1989, p. 191) in his essay on concealing the truth—we could say that, while the Rakosi regime in the early '50s was following a positive stratagem, a simulation strategy of lying in the media, the Kádár era brought along a negative stratagem: dissimulation; that is, withholding some important information from the population.[3] It is rather easy to understand that for a journalist, it is easier to smuggle in additional information than to expose views diametrically opposed to lies already printed or broadcast. So the whole period of the '60s and '70s could serve as an introduction to the revolutionary '80s.

Last but not least, a subjective component has also to be considered: the person of the journalist, who dares to face the challenges or who tries to avoid them. In 1988, roughly 70 percent of the Hungarian journalists were 30 to 50 years old (*Magyar Sajtó*, 1989, p. 2). This was a generation that had already been socialized, both politically and professionally, into the Kádár era, and learned the moves and tricks of the power game and the whereabouts of the escape-doors that led out of tight situations. Moreover, in the second half of the '80s some members of that generation by then had responsible editorial posts. These people thought of themselves as the "Children of 1968," the year of the student revolts in the

---

[1] Kádár's attitude to television is well reflected in an interview that one of the earlier presidents of the Hungarian Television gave to the press: "He [János Kádár] spoke to me about the TV for one hour. I asked him if he watches the programmes. He said: No!" (Népszabadság, 21 Nov. 1989).

[2] This personal race for media-power sometimes resulted in quite extraordinary cases. One day in 1989, for example, Károly Grósz, chairman of the Communist Party at that time, gave an interview to the Hungarian Radio, saying that he had agreed with the Prime Minister that emergency economic measures should be introduced. The Prime Minister, Miklós Németh, upon hearing this broadcast, immediately phoned the studio, stressing that no agreement of this kind had been reached. And this denial was on the air a few minutes later.

[3] There was even a "positive" ideology for the dissimulation in existence, suggesting that the population should be safeguarded from a critical and/or dramatic public information.

West, the Prague Spring, and large-scale economic reform in Hungary. I guess that a deeper cohort analysis could show the determinant role of this generation in the transformation of the Hungarian mass communication system.

All these factors, taken together, could help us to understand how it was possible that a basically Party-controlled media system contributed to such a large extent to dismantling those same political power structures among which it had developed. This also shows that this was a result of a several-year-long battle between the press and the holders of political power, between reform-minded and conservative forces both inside and outside the profession (and, one should add, inside the Communist Party itself). This was a kind of guerilla warfare, with small victories and step-by-step tactical moves; a slow process built upon minor quantitative changes.

The first signals showing qualitative changes came right after the party conference in May 1988, which brought an overwhelming victory for the reformists. Not much later the party resigned of its controlling role over the media system as a whole and proclaimed that it was only the party papers over which it wished to keep control. Both the Agit-Prop Department of the Central Committee and the powerful Agit-Prop Committee, which had had an absolute say in communication policy matters, were dismantled. As a consequence, the Information Office of the government—an administrative arm of the party—also came to the end of its existence.

So the backbone of the political control and regulation of the media system was broken at once. The issues relating to legal regulation posed more intricate problems. The Press Law of 1986 was already in place, but it served more to preserve the old structures than facilitate the buildup of new ones. According to the law, starting the operation of a communication medium—be it a paper, or a radio or a TV station—was reserved only for "legal persons" (some forms of collectives) and not for individual citizens. Moreover, under the stipulations of the law, ownership of communication infrastructure was not allowed for most of these "legal persons" either, in order to keep this under State ownership. In addition, all the media were supposed to undergo a prior licensing arrangement (with the so-far-nonexistent Information Office) before they were allowed to start their operations.[4]

---

[4] For the debates around the Press Law of 1986 see: Szecskö, T.: "The New Hungarian Press Law," in: "The Vigilant Press" *Reports and Papers on Mass Communication*, Unesco, Paris, 1989.

In the political atmosphere of 1988–1989, however, it became clear for both the (still one-party) government and the opposition parties and groups that, according to the new laws under consideration by the parliament, a modern law on communications was also required. This new law would not only resolve the contradictions and limitations of the Act II of 1986 but it would also be fully compatible with those international covenants related to freedom of expression, communication, and information to which Hungary was a signatory. In the meantime, however, until the new law could be enacted, the Hungarian Government hastily abolished by decree the mandatory licensing of media operations, and extended the right to start them to private individuals.

With all these modifications, however, the Hungarian media system has come to an *ex lex* state, a transitory stage for the beginning of the new decade. Old mechanisms do not work any more, and new ones have not yet been elaborated. But this is characteristic of the whole society. The public does not seem to be worried about the necessary lapses, deficiencies, and contradictions of a mass communications system in transformation. Just the contrary: they highly appreciate its contribution to the build-up of a new society. In 1989 several polls—including a Gallup poll— showed that, among the different social institutions, it is the media that people consider to be best serving their interests.[5] So the audience is satisfied. But what about the actors?

II. THE ACTORS

In 1989 I wrote a short essay for the West German professional paper Rundfunk und Fernsehen (Szecskö, 1989) where I tried to sketch out the profile of those pressure groups and lobbies that act on the communication scene in Hungary. Here I have to do it again, because some concrete issues that have emerged in the field of communications since that time (issues that I will enumerate in the next part of this chapter) have slightly restructured the scene. This is not a fundamental change but involves smaller shifts of the actors from one position to another and—in some cases—a better definition of their policy lines (if such lines exist at all). So the cast to be presented here already bears the imprint of the events of the second half of 1989.

---

[5] On a 5-point scale the media got a score of 4, followed by the churches and the environmental movements (both at 3.6). The political parties (old and new ones as well) reached only scores of 2.9–3.0 (HangSúly, No. 6–7, 1989, p. 13).

1. Political actors
    a. *The Government.* Until the general elections held in
        March 1990, it was still a one-party government, com-
        posed of members of the Hungarian Socialist Party and
        others without party affiliation. Enjoying only relative
        legitimacy and confronted with an economic crisis, it
        was usually very lenient on communication matters,
        rather deregulating than regulating anything.
    b. *The Hungarian Socialist Party.*[6] Although weakened in
        political power, its economic power in the domain of
        communications is considerable due to its large assets
        (including newspapers and publishing companies). At
        the same time it has some experts in communication
        policies in its ranks, well practiced and sharing mostly
        socialist or social democratic values regarding
        communications.
    c. *Other parties and political groupings.* Several dozen
        exist, of which some 18 defined themselves as political
        parties up to November 1989. A poll conducted at that
        time showed that six or eight of them could surpass the
        four percent threshold of the votes necessary for par-
        ticipation in the elections (Hungarian Institute for
        Public Opinion Research, 1989). On the one hand they
        are fighting for access to the media but, on the other
        hand not more than three or four of them showed any
        sign of having a communication vision.
    d. *Club of Openness.*[7] A small group of professionals—
        mostly journalists—with a watchdog role over the com-
        munication and information freedoms. In 1987, when
        it was first established, the club proved to be a counter-
        weight to the official association of journalists. Since
        the refurbishing of the association in 1989, however,

---

[6] Although its predecessor's official name was the Hungarian Socialist Workers'
Party (HSWP), to avoid confusion I called it the *Communist Party*—at least for the
period before October 1989. This Communist Party (officially HSWP), during its
congress at that time, was transformed into a reformist party, under the name of
the *Hungarian Socialist Party.* The conservative faction, however, made a
comeback, under the name *HSWP.* So, when mention is made in this chapter of
the Communist Party, we are referring to the old, united HSWP, while the HSWP is
used to mean this new-old political formation.

[7] "Openness" in this context is equivalent to the concept of the Frankfurt
School, "Offentlichkeit," for which there is no precise word in English. (In some
scholarly papers it is translated as the "public sphere.")

the club's basic function began fading away. If it acts, it usually does so simultaneously with the association.

2. Professional actors

   a. *National Association of Hungarian Journalists.* Traditionally it played a rather servile role vis-à-vis the political powers, serving mostly to transmit the central political will. Since its renewal during two general assemblies in 1989, it raises its voice each time professional interests are at stake.

   b. *Publishers.* A loose group with diverging interests. Their main worry is how to sail through the turbulent waters of market competition from the hitherto calm bays of government subsidies. In some instances, however, they act congenially under the aegis of the Union of Publishers (earlier also a "transmission" organ).

   c. *National media.* The dominant political forces complied with the principle of preserving the public service character of Hungarian Television, Hungarian Radio, and the Hungarian News Agency; hence the expression *national media.* Usually they act together with the respective professional and/or political organizations, but in some clashes of interest they have to go it alone.

   d. *Hungarian Post.* Due to a deregulatory process, its administrative monopoly is shrinking. However, efforts have been made to replace it with a kind of market monopoly.

   e. *The Ministry of Justice.* In the process of preparing new fundamental laws (among them laws on communications, social information, and postal services) the legal experts of the ministry gained a certain kind of procedural power, which comes into play in the public debates on communication issues as well.

   f. *Independent media.* The ad hoc grouping of the proliferating commercially oriented media that are not (overtly) affiliated to any political or social organization. Generally they are in competition with each other, but in some cases (for example, in trying to find alternative sources of information besides the Hungarian News Agency) they act in unison.

3. Financial actors
    a. *Banks.* While earlier they played a negligible (and mostly administrative) role in the operation and development of the media system, with the strengthening of market forces and the partial privatization of the economy their importance is soaring (for example, they have extended credits to new media ventures and bought in to already existing ones).
    b. *Foreign capital.* Some of the large multinational media conglomerates are already present on the Hungarian market. Because of the fast-changing scene—and due to the ex-lex state of the media system—not even intelligent guesses can be made regarding their present market shares.
    c. *Small private capital.* Up to now, its role has not been important, but there are indications that on certain levels of the media system (for example, in local media) it is being tempted into making small-scale investments.

This relatively neat listing and typology of the actors is, of course, far from being conclusive, since the whole system is on the move. The distinction between the different actors is also more blurred in reality than in the picture presented above. Ad hoc or more durable coalitions are produced from one day to the next. And there are some important, sometimes undetectable, personal liaisons between the different actors, too. But this is also an organic component of the picture.

III. THE GAMES

In the following I try to present the "games" that these actors have played in 1989. (Some of them had already started in the preceding year, but they gained real impetus in 1989, when the already legitimized political fight between the different parties and organizations warmed up.) Almost all of them would deserve a separate analytical case study, but here we cannot offer anything but a brief descriptive listing. Even given this superficial treatment, however, this overall picture may help the reader to realize the peculiar ambiguity of these games. If one looks at them from the traditional

viewpoint of the Party-State—that is, the perspective of the past—
they are nothing other than elements of a huge two-player zero-sum
game where the Party is fighting the opposition. Nevertheless, from
another perspective—the perspective of a future democracy—it is a
series of multifarious games, mostly involving several players,
having both zero-sum and cooperative outcomes possible. And
because in Hungary nowadays the present does not exist, but only
the past and the future, these two perspectives happen to be
interwoven in the minds of most of the actors. Consequently, it is
not possible even to describe these games with mathematical
precision.

Game I

Perhaps the most important game is about the national media—
national radio, television, and the national news agency—although
it is television where most conflicts really occur. Very soon after the
Communist Party resigned its control over the whole media field in
1988, the government declared Hungarian television, Hungarian
radio, and the Hungarian News Agency to be government-controlled
"national media." Perceiving that this cryptic definition was not too
satisfactory, a minister of state—then responsible for the media on
behalf of the government—gave the following explanation: "Radio
and Television, albeit operating under the direct supervision and
orientation of the government, should serve and express the entire
public sphere of the society, of the nation. This means that the
government does not consider these media exclusively as its own
political instrument: in the programs the most varied social views
and efforts could be expressed. The government must take care to
keep this expression of views within constitutional limits, in
accordance with the Press Law's stipulations" (Pozsgay, 1989).

The opposition, however, were not much happier with this
explanation, primarily because they did not see any remarkable
changes in the programming policies of the national broadcasting
institutions. Under the resulting pressure, the government and the
Communist Party retreated further and during the trilateral coordinating talks in the summer of 1989.[8] The talks produced an
agreement that said that for the interim period leading up to the

---

[8] Political talks between the Communist Party, the opposition parties and the
nonparty organizations in the preparation of the most crucial laws to be voted
upon in parliament.

parliamentary elections, the supervisory responsibilities for the national media should be taken over by an ad hoc committee composed of the representatives of the more important political forces. So in November 1989 the Supervisory Committee for Hungarian Television and Hungarian Radio was set up, and, at the same time, the Hungarian News Agency, the Magyar Hirlap (a semiofficial daily of the government) and the Hungarian Institute for Public Opinion Research—all up until then the responsibility of the Minister of State—came under the supervisory authority of the Minister of Culture.

But this move, instead of calming things down, added further fuel to the debates. The broadcasting organizations protested because no communication expertise was reflected in the composition of the committee. The National Association of Hungarian Journalists also raised its voice, partly because it was not consulted beforehand and partly, too, because of the lack of expertise in the committee. Some of the opposition parties also attacked the decision (they did not even send their representatives to the committee) saying that the whole concept was a misinterpretation of the agreement reached during the summer: A politically neutral, high-prestige body was needed. The government retreated again, at least partially: The Prime Minister promised that the supervisory committee would be assisted by a group of experts.

As we have seen before, the heat of the debate was concentrated on television, "which is in the age and in the conditions of Christ: not only because it will be 32 years old, but also its crucifixion of today and its resurrection to be hoped for the day after tomorrow puts it among similar conditions."[9] Others use less Biblical language. One of the two program directors who resigned right after their first meeting with the supervisory committee said in an interview: "The government let us down. It increased the license fees but—in spite of firm personal promises—Hungarian Television received only a small fraction of that money...in today's top-level power-struggle the institution was thrown in as a prey." (Esti Hirlap, November 24, 1989). He adds, however, that primarily it is not the political pressure from the outside that is difficult to cope with, but the friction inside the organization: Personal ambition and individual professional fads and foibles are coated with political rhetoric, making television ungovernable.

---

[9] The expression of the vice-president of the Hungarian Television in a roundtable debate on the future of broadcasting, Film-Szinhaz Muzsika, No. 17, 1989.

Game II

This game revolves around the allocation of frequencies. At first sight the game seems to be on a smaller scale, but broadcasters know that its outcome will have a long-term influence on the future of broadcasting in Hungary.

With the legal liberalization of media operations, the number of applicants seeking access to broadcasting frequencies suddenly multiplied. In the first half of 1989, 61 such applications were tabled (29 for radio, and 32 for TV broadcasting). In the preceding three years, due to the legal constraints, there had been no such requests, and even for urban cable-systems not more than three dozen licenses had been given (Heti Világgazdaság, September 2, 1989). Without having any concept of communication policies, the government showed an understanding attitude: through its competent authorities it began distributing frequencies. After an outburst of professional protests (including those of national broadcasters and the association of journalists), however, it made a new assessment of the situation and proclaimed a moratorium on frequency allocations until the new laws on communications and postal services had come into operation.

Nevertheless, some licenses had already been handed out at that time. This is the explanation, for example, of a unique case: from August 1989 until the end of the year a private commercial channel, Sun-TV, broadcast on the frequencies of Hungarian TV's Channel 1 early in the morning. This was because they had been given a license before the moratorium, and the PTT did not have any prior consultation with Hungarian Television regarding this decision.[10]

The main actors in this game are the government (via the Ministry for Transport, Communications, and Construction, the national broadcasting organizations, and the *Hungarian Post*) and, certainly, those commercial companies and social organizations that are seeking frequencies. Their interaction is perhaps even more complex than those in Game I. The *Hungarian Post* was earlier an integral part of the Ministry's predecessor, so they have similar interest even now. At the same time the *Hungarian Post* is being split into three parts, two commercial and one a public service company, while keeping some elements of its administrative authority. As for the contenders for frequencies, behind some of

---

[10] What makes the case even more bizarre was that anchors of Sun-TV were also leading reporters on the staff of Hungarian Radio who, on other days, worked on the morning radio news program.

them one can find foreign capital—and even lobbying ambassadors (Heti Vilaggazdasag, September 2, 1989).

So, it seems, in this third game several others are hidden.

Game III

"It can happen that the Parliament curtails press freedom well before it deals with it" (Jakab, 1989). This Sybillean statement in one of the articles dealing with the new laws about the postal services is trying to say that debating and enacting the three laws related to communication and information should follow a strict, logical sequence: Giving priority to the law on the postal services might endanger some of the essential elements of the law on communications. (The law's working title is *Law on the Freedom of Expression and on the Freedom of the Press.*) On the other hand, some parties and the Club of Openness are stressing that the law on social information is also of primary importance, because it is designed to curtail the traditional secretiveness of the political and administrative power, and, moreover, because it should guarantee the privacy of the citizens.

Basically all these suggestions are right; notwithstanding, it seems that there is considerable delay in the preparation of all three laws. (The law on communications, for example, was scheduled to go before Parliament in autumn 1989.) Legal experts in the Ministry of Justice have never been as overburdened with preparing new laws as they are nowadays, and the most eagerly awaited of them are the drafts of the so-called "Crucial Laws."[11] At the same time, due to the critical state of the telecommunications infrastructure in Hungary, which is seriously hindering economic development, it is rather probably that, among the three laws related to mass communications, it will be the law on the postal services that will be considered first in Parliament. In crisis situations it is not always rational or long-range thinking that dominates.

Game IV

This one is a softer game, which revolves around the ethical questions of journalism. As a rather professional game, it brings

---

[11] The laws on political parties, on electoral procedures, on amendments to the Constitution, etc.: all the basic laws that create the necessary legal framework for the transition to democracy.

into motion (and emotions) almost exclusively the journalists, broadcasters, and the National Association of Hungarian Journalists, because the public so far—as we showed earlier—is enjoying the Saturnalia of their newly liberated media...with all the factual mistakes, bad reporting, and even slander. After all, if we can trust Marx, a free press is never well groomed.

In professional circles, however, there is growing concern because of the rapid deterioration of professional/ethical standards. This phenomenon could be explained by several factors. One—and perhaps the most important—is that journalists had been socialized into a profession where they were usually told what was important and what was not. And now, suddenly, they are supposed to turn from outer-oriented persons into inner-oriented ones... which is not an easy task. (In a different version, this is true even for those autonomous journalists whom we mentioned earlier and who were in the front line of the battle with political power: earlier, they saw, at least, where the wall to batter was. But when there are no walls?)

The second reason comes from the fact that the so-called "socialist journalism" was decidedly antisensationalist. Postmen biting dogs have never been news items, and absolutely never if they had any political undertones. So journalists now try to quench the natural thirst of the public for sensations. Some use those sensations that history has produced lately, and some use sensations that involve intrusions into privacy.

We must add that the existing press and penal laws do not curtail but rather facilitate this tendency. Civil and penal codes allow for very little material compensation for "nonmaterial damages" caused by slander. So the proliferating new tabloids, if sued for slander, can leave the courtroom with a fine equivalent to but not exceeding one month's salary for a journalist. These parts of the codes are under revision now.

The commercialism overcoming the media also contributes to the deterioration of ethical standards, as well as to that subjective factor that causes communicators who earlier were very well integrated into the political system, writing servile editorials or serving as "microphone-stands,"[12] to think that they now must resculpture themselves.

The National Association of Hungarian Journalists plays a positive—it is to be hoped, even a decisive—role in this game. At its

---

[12] In journalistic professional slang those broadcasters who were insiders enough to interview the top-level political bosses, and also servile enough not to ask any disturbing questions during the interview.

General Assembly in September 1989, the association adopted a new code of professional ethics, which, in contrast to the earlier one, is not a compendium of ideological statements but a kind of practical guideline for value-laden behavior in the profession. Nevertheless, one cannot feed illusions: It is easier to come out of an ex-lex state than the moral vacuum that had been imposed earlier on the whole society.

Game V

This is clearly a game of less importance. Nevertheless, it is rather symptomatic, because it shows how former monopolies try to use their power to sustain their dominant position in the market. It is about the distribution of newspapers. It is about the *Hungarian Post* (again).

Up until now the *Hungarian Post* [HP] was exclusively authorized to distribute the press nationwide. For this operation it charged the papers 30 percent to 35 percent of their sales price. The distribution nevertheless was rather sloppy: the *Post* did not have enough workers, so the morning papers usually arrived at subscribers' homes late in the morning, after most of them had already left for work. Usually readers got the morning news in the afternoon—in the age of instantaneous electronic mass communications.

Despite the shortcomings of the distribution system it was still in the red. With reference to this economic fact, and saying that in the future—as we also mentioned earlier—most of the operations of the *Hungarian Post* should be of a profit-seeking character, in November 1989 the *Hungarian Post* leaked the information that, from 1990, they wanted to increase the distribution tariffs by an average of 40 percent. (This means that of the 4.60 Ft price of a daily, some 2.50 would go to the *Hungarian Post*) (Népszbadság, October 31, 1989).

Needless to say, this leaked information led to an uproar in the printed press. The *Hungarian Post* irritated the journalists even more when it proclaimed that if the press did not accept these conditions, the distributors would go on strike; and that if some of the papers did not comply with the new conditions, from 1990 they would not be distributed.

The editorial boards of some 15 national papers sent an open letter about this case to the Prime Minister. In it, alongside the strong protestations, there is a very meaningful paragraph: "The *Hungarian Post* is abusing its market power. Although, in words, it does not insist any more on holding on to its distribution monopoly, the exclusivity of several decades cannot be wiped out by a mere change in a provision of the law. The *Post* is acting at times as an actor in a provision of the law. The *Post* is acting at times as an actòr in the market and other times as a national authority— depending on which is more favorable for it (Népszbadság, November 18, 1989).

The final outcome of this game is almost negligible from our point of view. It is the tactics of the monopolies that are revealing.

Game VI

Another game shows how difficult it is to give up monopolistic positions. This time the actors are the editorial boards of the regional dailies, the Communist Party (later the Hungarian Socialist Party) and the association of journalists.

The regional dailies (one or two in every county), with their total circulation of 1.2 million, have been a rather powerful means of molding opinions in the countryside. They used to be supervised by the Party Committee of the county and published by the small-scale county publishing houses, which were also owned by the Party. During the last few decades they had become even more important, while the circulation of the national dailies stagnated or decreased, but their circulation grew from year to year.

In 1989, however, journalists working on these newspapers revolted. County by county, they began to declare that they did not want to be "party papers" anymore. Their proposals for changing their status were varied. Some of them declared that the county's municipal council should be their master. Others thought that they should be independent papers, allowing all the parties and political organizations to express their views in their columns. There were also some who suggested that regional dailies should become a kind of national media, like Hungarian Television and Hungarian Radio.

The Party's opposition to these proposals has been very obstinate. (On this issue the Hungarian Socialist Party took the same position as its predecessor, the Communist Party.) Seemingly it did not want to give up this stronghold. First, in the wake of the general elections they insisted on keeping these media for their campaign purposes. In addition, it meant quite a lot of money for the party budget. Half of the after-tax profit of these dailies goes to the Party, and the other half remains with the papers (Népszabadság, November 10, 1989).

The National Association of Hungarian Journalists also raised its voice to lend support to the proposal that these dailies should become part of the national media (Magyar Nemzet, November 15, 1989), but the Hungarian Socialist Party did not go any further in its publicized stand against this other than to declare that it "supports the far-reaching creative independence of the journalists and, on its behalf, ensures it. It offers an alliance for all those who accept those left-wing values which—in accordance with the progressive forces of our country—the Hungarian Socialist Party endorses" (Népsabadság, November 18, 1989).

Game VII

The greatest game, the economic one, is so complex and confused that here we cannot do anything other than to indicate—in a thesislike way—some of those whimsical elements that are so characteristic of this transitory period.

- In 1986 Hungarian Radio established a commercial competitor for its own programs, Radio Danubius. Later, in 1989, it leased part of Radio Danubius's daily program time to another commercial service, Antenne Austria. In the same year another commercial venture, Radio Calypso, began its broadcasts on the wavelengths of Hungarian Radio.
- We have already spoken about the commercial Sun-TV, which worked on the frequencies of the Hungarian Television's first channel allotted to it by the *Hungarian Post*. The second channel itself became partly commercial from 1989, and there are plans that Hungarian Television will broadcast on a third, fully commercial channel.
- It has been reported in the press (Kapu, November 1989) that the managing director of Axel Springer Budapest Ltd. (earlier the economic director of Hungarian Television) served as a personal advisor to both the (now resigned) president and the (now arrested) economic director of HTV. The same reports hint that—due to these veiled connections—Springer has been using some of the production facilities of HTV at a rather moderate price.[13]
- HTV's news channel introduced commercials into its broadcasts. The money so earned (yearly some 43 million forints)

---

[13] The Springer group already applied for frequencies for two TV channels (cf. heti Világgazdaság, 2 Sept. 1989).

(Heti Vilaggazdasag, November 23, 1989) is separated from HTV's overall budget and can be used only by the TV News.

- Mirror Group Newspapers (Robert Maxwell), with a 40 percent participation, entered into a newly established company that will punish the Magyar Hirlap (the semiofficial duty of the government).[14] There are also plans to set up an alternative system of newspaper distribution (Magyar Hírlap, November 1, 1989).

- There are also talks about establishing a new company for the publication of the daily Magyar Nemzet (until now the organ of the National Patriotic Front). Three foreign groups showed an interest in participating: those of Andrew Sarlos (Canada), George Soros (USA),[15] and the Frankfurter Allgemeine Zeitung. The council of the National Patriotic Front decided on the second variation, where the NPF, the Pallas Publishing House, the Postbank (belonging to the Hungarian Post), the Soros Foundation, and the journalists of the paper would be the shareholders (Magyar Nemzet, November 27, 1989). The talks dragged on, because the Front insisted on having a right of veto in appointing the editor-in-chief and the Soros representatives could not accept that (Magyar Numzet, December 11, 1989).

As we said earlier, these are but small moves in the vast financial game, with the media organizations, Hungarian banks, and foreign capital cast as the main actors. For the right interpretation of these mosaics, however, one must know that the mass communication system of Hungary has been built on heavy State subsidies, as everywhere else in Eastern Europe. And although elements of the marketplace have begun to appear gradually since the end of the '60s, with the beginning of economic reform, the determinant factors of financing media operations were based upon the "benevolence" of the Party-State. This State money has to be taken up by free capital now, at a time when the whole Hungarian economy is in need of capital.

---

[14] Seemingly the Maxwell group was not bothered by this fact. Probably, it was more important that the Magyar Hírlap was the only national daily that did not lose readers. Instead, it increased its circulation during the last few years.

[15] Both are well-known businessmen of Hungarian origin. G. Soros has established and operated a foundation—run jointly with the Hungarian Academy of Sciences—to promote the intellectual opening of the Hungarian society for the last few years.

IV. SUMMARY

What kind of summary statements can be made after this overview of the Hungarian communication scene? (We do not dare to call them conclusions, because the processes have not yet ended. The play is still going on.)

Perhaps the most important point to make is that the Hungarian media system is undergoing fundamental structural and functional transformation, which, in their historical scope, can only be compared to those that have occurred three times before in Hungarian history. The first of these transformations took place in the early decades of the 19th century, when the independent Hungarian language press was established. The second took place around the turn of the century, when the media system became fully Europeanized, both quantitatively and qualitatively. The third transformation happened shortly after the Second World War, when the Stalinist concept of mass communication was imposed on the system. One cannot yet see clearly which model will be the final result of this fourth transformation, an overwhelmingly commercial one, a mixed one where market forces and State intervention are in an ever-moving balance, or a third conceivable model in which there are three constitutive actors—the market, the State, and the political forces of self-organized, grass-root democratic movements of citizenry.[16]

There is a lack of farsighted concepts of communication policies among the actors on the scene.[17] On the one hand, this bars a clearer vision of the possible outcomes of the games described earlier, and consequently prevents a prognosis about where the system is going. The lack of strategic thinking also has some side effects. One is that media, which—by definition—do not have long-term goals but aim rather at quick, instantaneous profits (the tabloid-like press, for example) can flourish. As we have shown, the

---

[16] In her latest book, the Hungarian sociologist Zsuzsa Ferge (1989) recommends a strategy for social policies that should be based on the interplay of these three actors. Without pushing the analogy between social and communication policies, I feel that there is a strong homology between the two sectors: sound, democratic communication policies also could be built on that triangle.

[17] Only one concept of this kind has been elaborated in recent years by the Mass Communication Research Center (1988, pp. 53–65), on the commission of the National Planning Office. But although it sketched out several scenarios, even the most daring proved later, in the light of the developments of 1988–1989, to be too timid.

deterioration of professional/ethical standards of journalism[18] could also be attributed at least in part to this fact. At the same time, those actors who have their own well-conceived strategies (the large multinational communication conglomerates) are finding it easier to penetrate the Hungarian market.

It is remarkable how Parliament is absent from today's communication games. This could be explained partly by its traditional structure and by its lack of expertise in communication matters.[19] More important is that, among the peculiar power relations of this transitory phase, it is primarily the old monopolies (albeit in disintegration) and the new market forces (as yet unregulated) that are bargaining with each other, usually behind closed doors, so both Parliament and the public confront important communication issues in an ex post facto state.

Nevertheless, the social scientist could feel a certain kind of optimism. Recalling Tacitus, who wrote "Rara temporum felicitas, ubi quae velis sentire et quae sentias dicere licet," one can hope that in this "rare lucky period where both emotions and the communication media expressing them have been liberated" after decades of political and ideological constraints, an essential element of democracy, rational argument, will also come into play.

REFERENCES

Ferge, Z. (1989). *Van-e negyedik út? A társadalompolitika esélyei.* [Is there any fourth road? The chances of social policies]. Budapest.

Hankiss, E. (1989). *Kelet-europai alternativak* [East European alternatives]. Budapest.

Hungarian Institute for Public Opinion Research (1989). *Osztódik a baloldal* [Left goes divided]. Budapest.

Jakab, Z. (1989). Frekventált téma [A frequent subject]. In *Heti Világgazdasag.* October 7.

---

[18] One of the well-known Western observers of the Hungarian media system, Paul Lendvai of Austria, is reported to have remarked that Hungarian mass communications is not only free, but libertarian (Magyar Hírlap, November 23, 1989).

[19] In the Hungarian parliament today, for example, there is no committee to deal with issues of communication or information. It is only the Cultural Committee that, from time to time, oversees some matters of communication—primarily those of broadcasting. It is also rather symptomatic of the present situation that the newly created radio and television supervisory body's relation to parliament was not defined.

Magyar Sajtó (1989). No. 19–20.

Pozsgay, I. (1989). An interview with Hungarian Radio. January.

Speier, H. (1989). *The truth in hell and other essays, 1935–1987.* New York.

Szecskö, T. (1984). *Notes on the value of information.* Paper presented at the XIVth scientific conference of the IAMCR, Prague.

Szecskö, T. (1989a). Kommunikationspolitische Veränderungen in Ungarn-Momenaufnahme. In *Rundfunk und Fernsehen, 2–3,* 276–282.

Szecskö, T. (1989b). The New Hungarian Press Law. In Unesco, *The vigilant press: Reports and papers on mass communication.* Paris: Unesco.

PART

II

On Mass Media Effects

Are We Asking the Right Questions? Developing Measurement from Theory: The Influence of the Spiral of Silence on Media Effects Research

ELISABETH NOELLE-NEUMANN

INTRODUCTION

My inaugural lecture at the University of Mainz in the fall of 1965 was devoted to the subject of "Public Opinion and Social Control." My point of departure was the confusion about the term *public opinion*. In 1904 Hermann Oncken had written: "Fluctuations and flow are not understood by locking them up in a formula...After all, anyone who is asked knows exactly what public opinion is" (Oncken 1904, p. 236; see pp. 224 ff). In 1962 Jurgen Habermas complained that "it is not only colloquial speech...which retains the term public opinion; scholarly fields such as jurisprudence, political science and sociology are also evidently not in a position to substitute more precise definitions for traditional categories such as...'public opinion'" (Habermas 1962, p. 13). Harwood L. Childs, professor of political science at Princeton, included 50 definitions of *public opinion* in one of the introductory chapters of his book *Public Opinion* (Childs, 1965).

I was convinced that we could not leave it at that: "How can we study the effect the mass media have on the way public opinion is formed, and conversely, how public opinion is expressed in the media when there is no agreed upon definition of public opinion?" (Noelle-Neumann, 1966, p. 4 ff).

I was moved to develop the "spiral of silence" theory (Noelle-Neumann, 1973a, 1974a, b, 1984, 1989a, 1991) by questions arising out of research into the effect of the mass media. Today tools to study the effect of the mass media are being derived from this theory. This suggests that it was correct to assume that an understanding of the process of public opinion is a prerequisite for progress in understanding the effect of the mass media.

There is no need at this point to go into the many reasons why research on the effect of the mass media is especially difficult (For a detailed discussion of the special problems connected with effects research, see Noelle-Neumann, 1977b, 1982, 1986a, 1986.) A brief sketch of the theory of the spiral of silence, however, will serve as an introduction to the tools themselves.

From the perspective of the spiral of silence theory, public opinion is seen as a social psychological process lending cohesion to human communities—from small tribes of primitive peoples to the major industrial nations—a process in which agreement about the values of the community and the acts derived therefrom is continuously reestablished.

The power of public opinion over the ruling class resides in the fact that any government depends upon the support of the governed. The English philosopher David Hume summarizes this idea when he wrote in 1741: "It is, therefore, on opinion only that government is founded; and this maxim extends to the most despotic and most military governments, as well as to the most free and most popular" (Hume, 1963, p. 29). The power of public opinion over the individual member of the community is based on fear of isolation, which is innate and drives people to seek to be well liked and so avoid being rejected and ostracized. Thus the process of public opinion ensures that both the rulers and the individual members of society make a constant effort to agree with what they believe to be the general consensus.

Insofar as they are hidden in the private sphere. thinking, speaking, and behavior are not important to the cohesion of the community; it is only when they are visible, audible, and out in the open, when they occur in public, that they are important to cohesion. This is what is meant by the "public" component in the concept of "public opinion." The individual should not violate the values of the community in his or her speech and behavior in public. Otherwise he or she will be threatened with isolation, with rejection and ostracism. The opinion component does not simply refer to opinions in the narrow sense but also the publicly visible expression of opinions in behavior and symbols (badges, clothing, hair styles).

In operational terms, for purposes of empirical study, public opinion is defined as opinions and behavior in morally loaded areas that can be publicly expressed and shown with the expectation of meeting with approval, or, conversely, without running the risk of isolation.

There is not much danger of isolation on issues of fact. The process of public opinion always involves a debate on values, however; most imortantly moral values but also aesthetic values, insofar as they are publicly visible, for example, in clothing and hair styles. Politics is imbued with a moral dimension in order to win over public opinion and impose the threat of isolation on opinions that deviate.

Speaking out and keeping silent are of great significance in the process of public opinion. This is most obvious with regard to the formation of new public opinion, for example in the process of value change or in connection with current events. In a tense situation like this, individuals constantly observe which opinions and behavior are on the increase and which are on the decrease. When someone finds that his or her opinion is on the increase, this serves to confirm his or her views, which he or she then expresses more forcefully and without fear of isolation. When someone finds that his or her opinion is losing ground, he or she feels insecure and falls silent. The former group thus seems stronger than it really is, since its opinions are expressed loudly and confidently and continue to attract supporters; the other group seems weaker than it really is, since supporters of these views fall silent. This, in turn, influences others to fall silent or to change their views, until one view dominates entirely in public and the opposing view largely disappears. This is the process I have called *the spiral of silence.*

Literature and the media—television, radio, newspapers, and magazines—play an important role in the process of public opinion. They are themselves the public. Thus it is possible to identify in public with the point of view represented by a majority of the media in the area of political morality without danger of isolation. They also influence the individual to observe the environment continuously, so as to determine how most people think. In addition, they perform an important articulation function: They provide words and arguments to speak up for one's views in public as well as in private situations.

HYPOTHESES ABOUT INDICATORS
FOR MEDIA EFFECTS

Several hypotheses about media effects can be derived from this theory and empirically tested. This chapter presents the tools of media effects research.

1. People continuously try to find out by observing their
    environment which issues (modes of behavior) are contro-
    versial and how the relative positions of the opposing
    camps are developing.

    The most important source of their observations and
    determinant of their view of the climate of opinion is the
    media. If there is a definite gap between the population's
    opinion on a controversial issue and its assessment of how
    most people think on that issue ("pluralistic ignorance"),
    the suspicion is that a media effect is involved—that is,
    impressions about frequency distributions that are con-
    veyed by the media.

    Attitudes towards nuclear energy may provide an example.
    Sabine Mathes (1989), in a master's thesis based on
    Allensbach surveys and presented at the University of
    Mainz, finds that "from the beginning the population
    completely misjudged the relative strength of supporters
    and opponents of nuclear energy."

2. Both pluralistic ignorance relating to prevalent opinion
    and pluralistic ignorance relating to the population's atti-
    tudes, experience, and situation in life strongly suggest
    that media effects are involved (Table 7.1).

TABLE 7.1
Federal Republic of West Berlin Population 16 and over

Climate of Opinion and Personal Experience of Reality

QUESTIONS: "Do you have the impression that most people here in the
Federal Republic are satisfied with their life on balance, or are
they not really satisfied?"

"Are you actually satisfied with your life on balance, or are you
not really satisfied?"

	Own feeling	Most people
	%	%
Satisfied	79	47
Not really satisfied	21	40
Other response, undecided	x	13
	100	100
	n = 988	1009

x = less than 0.5 per cent
Source: Allensbach Archives, IfD Survey 4012, August 1982

3. The same applies when opinion of persons, groups of persons, institutions, places and countries differ significantly, depending on whether they are arrived at based on one's own knowledge ("insider's view") or not ("outsider's view") (Table 7.2).

4. If there is a significant difference in assessments of the climate of opinion (how most people think) depending on exposure to the media ("dual climate of opinion" [Noelle-Neumann, 1977c], media effects are to be expected. The same applies if there is a significant difference in the assessment of the general situation or of controversial persons, depending upon media use (Tables 7.3a-b).

   The phenomenon of the dual climate of opinion was first observed in a panel analysis prior to the West German Federal election of 1976. It was only maintained briefly in the two-step flow of communication (Noelle-Neumann, 1977c, 1980). The dual climate of opinion was also evident from surveys conducted immediately after a famous German domestic affair involving the minister of defense (Noelle-Neumann, 1985).

5. If there is evidence of significant differences in attitude on a subject that is by its nature not included in a political party platform, depending upon the population's position on the right–left spectrum, it may be surmised that media effects—the different positions taken by media that are relatively farther to the right or to the left—are involved.

6. If there is a significant difference in the willingness of the two camps to speak out on a controversial issue, media effects are possibly involved. We must differentiate between four kinds of media effects:

   a) One camp appears stronger in the climate of opinion than it is according to its numerical strength, thus encouraging supporters to speak out (Table 7.4).

   b) While one camp knows that it is in the minority, it receives support from the trend-setting media and thus does not fear isolation and is willing to speak out (Tables 7.5a-c).

   c) One camp knows that is is in the majority but nonetheless fears isolation and thus falls silent because the trend-setting media are on the other side ("the silent majority"—Table 7.6).

   d) Independently of its majority or minority status, the camp that is receiving support from the trend-setting

TABLE 7.2
Federal Republic of West Berlin Population 16 and over

Striking difference between views based on own experience and stereotypes of how things are in general are interpreted as the effect of the media

An example: Insider's and outsider's view of the hospital

QUESTION: on the insider's views: "Several things which are said about hospitals are listed on these cards. With the hospital that you are most familiar with in mind: Which of these things might apply to this hospital, according to what you know or have heard?" (Presentation of a set of cards)

QUESTION: on the outsider's views: "...In your opinion, which of these things applies to our modern-day hospitals?" (Presentation of a set of cards)

	View based on own experience	Generalized view
—Excerpt from the replies—	%	%
Positive views:		
Helpful nurses	67	64
Good food	55	39
Completely up-to-date medical and technical facilities	49	68
Pleasant, well furnished rooms	41	31
Spacious rooms	40	25
Everything is quiet; you don't hear many sounds	38	25
Negative views:		
The doctors don't have enough time for the patients	36	69
The senior physicians don't have enough time for the patients	35	63
Cold and unimaginative furnishings	32	43
Not enough nurses	28	54
An impersonal operation, you're just a number	22	44
Not enough doctors and specialists	15	39
People are sometimes treated improperly	13	38
Strict rules on visiting hours	19	17
	n = 1016	1033

Source: Allensbach Archives, IfD Survey 4012, August 1982

media is more willing to speak out because it has an abundance of words, expressions, and arguments at its disposal—articulated for it by the media.

7. If one camp is significantly more willing to speak out than the other in a debate, it is likely that the camp that is willing to speak out will increase. Insofar as there is an obvious connection between the willingness to speak out and the tenor of the media, the success of the camp supported by the trend-setting media is to be classified as an effect of the media (Tables 7.5a-b).

TABLE 7.3A
Federal Republic of West Berlin Population 16 and over

Dual climate of opinion: Depending upon use of the media, people have different ideas about how most people think about nuclear energy

In her master's thesis, Sabine Mathes finds a long-term climate of opinion on nuclear energy: People who do not watch much television had a different attitude toward nuclear energy for many years than people who watch an average of more than one hour of television daily.

QUESTION: "Aside from your own opinion for the moment, do you think most people in the Federal republic are in favor of or opposed to the construction of new nuclear energy plants?"

	Total*	Light viewers*)	Heavy viewers**)
	%	%	%
Supporters of nuclear energy			
Most are in favor	34	45	30
Most are opposed	21	14	23
About fifty-fifty, impossible to say ...	45	41	47
	100	100	100
	n = 426		

* significant at the level of 5%
*) Light viewers are persons who watch less than 1 hour of television daily
**) Heavy viewers are persons who watch more than 1 hour of television daily

Source: "Sabine Mathes: Sozial-optische Täuschung durch Massenmedien? Die Einschätzung des Meinungsklimas im Konflikt um die Kernenergie durch Personen mit viel und wenig Fernsehen," Master's thesis, Mainz 1989, Tables 2.7, 2.8 and 2.9 The survey data are from the Allensbach Archieves, IfD Survey 3070, May/June 1979
Additional examples of the dual climate of opinion:
Elisabeth Noelle-Neumann (1980), Table 23, p. 231 and Elisabeth Noelle-Neumann (1985), Tables 1 and 2, p. 53

TABLE 7.3B
Federal Republic and West Berlin Population 16 and over

Troubled summer 1989

An indication of television's effect: Concern about influx of foreigners in the Federal Republic grown with increased television viewing

That the Federal Republic will become a nation of guest workers and foreigners

	Total population	Average daily TV viewing time;		Respondents interested in politics		Respondents not (esp.) interested in politics	
		less than 1 hour %	1 hour and more %	less than 1 hour %	1 hour and more %	less than 1 hour %	1 hour and more %
I am presently very concerned about this	24)	16)	28)	14)	30)	20)	26)
I am often concerned about this	}45 21)	}33 17)	}51 23)	}29 15)	}50 20)	}39 19)	}51 25)
I am sometimes somewhat concerned about this	29	34	27	35	27	32	28
I am not at all concerned about this	23	30	19	35	21	25	18
Undecided, no response	3	3	3	1	2	4	3
	100	100	100	100	100	100	100
n = 1111	1111	379	731	198	331	181	401

Source: Allensbach Archives, IfD Survey 5021, June 1989

TABLE 7.4
Federal Republic of West Berlin Population 16 and over

Willingness to Speak Up

Great differences in the willingness to speak out as illustrated by the issue of the peace movement

QUESTION: "In the Federal Republic there is a peace movement which advocates complete disarmament in the East and in the West. All things considered, are you in favor of the peace movement or opposed to it?"

	Total population %
In favor	52
Opposed	20
Undecided	28
	100
	n = 2206

QUESTION: "Assuming you are on a five-hour train ride and someone in your compartment starts talking and says that he is absolutely *in favor* (in one out of two interviews: *opposed to*) the peace movement. Would you like to talk to this person or would you prefer not to?"

	Supporters of the peace movement (majority) %	Opponents of the peace movement (minority) %
Would like to talk to him (willing to speak out in public)	60	37
Prefer not to (silent in public)	30	54
No opinion	10	9
	100	100
	n = 1199	417

Source: Allensbach Archives, IfD Survey 4049, Oct. 1984

TABLE 7.5A
Federal Republic of West Berlin Population 16 and over

Willingness to speak up

A second example based on the question of whether the East can be trusted shows the greater willingness of the minority to voice an opinion which, however, is in agreement with the majority of journalists

QUESTION: "In your opinion, can we actually trust the East or not?"

	Total population %
Can trust the East	12
Cannot trust the East	58
Undecided, impossible to say	30
	100
	n = 1967

TABLE 7.5B
Federal Republic of West Berlin Population 16 and over
—Subgroups—

QUESTION: "Assuming you are on a five-hour train ride and someone in your compartment starts talking very *favorably* about…(in every other interview: very *unfavorably* about) trusting the East. Would you like to talk to this person, to get to know his or her point of view, or would you prefer not to?"

	Persons with the opinion that the East—	
	can be trusted (Minority) %	cannot be trusted (Majority) %
Would like to talk to him (willing to speak out in public)	65	30
Would prefer not to (silent in public)	28	60
No opinion	7	10
	100	100
	n = 124	532

Source: Allensbach Archives, IfD Survey 4008, May 1982

TABLE 7.5C
Federal Republic and West Berlin Population 18 and over and journalists

Contrasting attitudes between journalists and the public

QUESTION: "A variety of political demands are listed here. Which of them do you personally consider especially important? Could you please set aside the cards." (Presentation of a set of cards)

	SUMMER 1976	
	Population %	**Journalist %**
—Excerpt from the responses—		
Think it is especially important:		
Not to give in too easily to the East, no concession without a *quid pro quo*	55	20
Prevent the influence of communism from penetrating Europe	51	26
No cooperation with communist groups in the Federal Republic	46	14
Strengthen NATO and the West German federal armed forces to prevent the Russians from gaining an ever greater military lead over the West	40	15
	n = 1265	100

Source: Allensbach Archives, IfD Surveys 2185, 2187

TABLE 7.6
Federal Republic of West Berlin Population 16 and over
—Subgroup—

Silent majority

Although the majority is perfectly aware of being in the majority, it remains silent without the support of the media. The minority, although aware of being in the minority, is very outspoken when it senses support from public opinion.

QUESTION: "Assuming you are on a five-hour train ride and someone in your compartment starts talking very *favorably* about...(in every other interview: very *unfavorably* about) appointing members of the communist Party as judges. Would you like to talk to this person, to get to know his or her point of view, or would you prefer not to?"

	The majority: People who are against appointing Communist Party members as judges, and who know that they are in the majority (56% = 100%) %	The minority: People who are in favor of appointing Communist Party members as judges, and who think that they are in the minority (13% = 100%) %
Would like to talk to him (willing to speak out in public)	26	57
Would prefer not to (silent in public)	66	36
No opinion	8	7
	100	100
	n = 526	117

Source: Allensbach Archives, IfD Survey 3028, April 1976

TOOLS: TYPES OF QUESTIONS AND MODELS OF ANALYSIS

Since 1971 questions to test the hypotheses derived from the spiral of silence have been included in many surveys by the Institut fur Demoskopie Allensbach. In the following, variety of types of questions and models of analysis—connected with the study of media effects—will be presented.

PLURALISTIC IGNORANCE

The research model consists of two basic questions: a question about the respondent's own opinion, and a question about how most people think about this subject. There are analogous questions about how he or she behaves and how most people behave, as well as about his or her situation and the situation of most people.

Since available findings indicate that the expectation as to which camp will be successful in the future ("Success," Mutz, 1989) influences the process of public opinion and the willingness to speak out more strongly than which camp is currently stronger, it is also important to ask about expectations for the future: "How do you think things will develop in the future—will more people be for _____ in a year or will fewer people be for _____?" A variation on questions about expectations for the future, which has been the focus of scholarly literature since the Erie County study of 1940 (Lazarsfeld, Berelson, & Gaudet, 1944), is: "Who do you think will win the election?"

When analyzing the data, it is not only the comparison of the respondents' answers about their own opinion, experience, and situation and their answers about what most people think, most people's experience, and the general situation that is of interest but also the self-confidence of the opposing camps in the controversy. The so-called "looking-glass perception"—that is, an overestimate of one's own opinion when assessing "how most people think"—will always be found. The stronger this distortion in favor of one's own opinion is, the more secure this camp will be thought to be and the more it will be thought to receive support from the media. Conversely, a high proportion of undecided responses (including "yes and no" and "fifty–fifty") indicates the weakness of one camp and a lack of support from the media. Based on the difference between how the climate of opinion is assessed for the two camps, the "degree of polarization" can be calculated. The measure of discrepancy introduced by Osgood, Suci, and Tannenbaum (1957), $D = d^2$, can be used for this purpose (Noelle-Neumann, 1978, pp. 29ff.). The stronger the deviation between the climate of opinion for the two camps, the more tense the debate is. The degree of pluralistic ignorance is often not symmetrical; the stronger camp tends to err more in its own favor in assessing the climate of opinion than the weaker.

DUAL CLIMATE OF OPINION

This requires additional questions about exposure to the media—exposure in general and exposure by degree of intensity. Since population groups with different exposure to the media also differ in many other characteristics—for example, in their interests in politics or in their position on the political spectrum—additional questions on such characteristics are needed to avoid spurious correlations.

Panel designs are especially effective for checking spurious correlations. If the same persons are interviewed repeatedly, and changes in attitude only appear for certain media user groups, the panel design serves to keep most of the characteristics on which spurious correlations could be based constant, and the probability that changes should be interpreted as the effect of the media thus increases (Noelle-Neumann 1977c, pp. 423 ff.).

Since impressions derived from the trend-setting media spread quickly due to the "two-step flow of communications" (Lazarsfeld, et al., 1944)—in part being adopted in other media, in part being incorporated into conversations—it is best to select new topics and new developments as far as possible in studying the dual climate of opinion, and to begin the study at the earliest possible date, before the differences between the groups with different media exposure have become blurred (Noelle-Neumann, 1982, pp. 121ff.; 1977c, p. 437).

In studies of this sort, it is useful to establish trends to observe how long such a dual climate of opinion is maintained. This tests the hypothesis that it is only maintained briefly on topics that are much discussed but is quite long-lasting on other topics (Mathes, 1989).

WILLINGNESS TO SPEAK OUT

The question form that was first developed to test the willingness to speak out and that is mot used today is the train test (Noelle-Neumann, 1984, pp. 16 ff.): "Assuming you are on a five-hour train ride, and someone in your compartment starts talking very favorably about _____ (a parallel interview reads: very unfavorably about

_____). Would you like to talk to this person, to get to know his or her point of view, or would you prefer not to?"

The question was adapted as follows for countries where train trips are not customary: "Assuming you are on a five-hour bus trip, and the bus stops for a long rest stop and everyone gets out for a long break. In a group of passengers, someone starts talking about whether _____. Would you like to talk to this person, to get to know his or her point of view, or would you prefere not to?" (Allensbach Archives, 1987, 4093/II).

The train (or bus) test has the advantage that the situations can be varied systemically in the interview: The speaker described is presented as someone who favors A or B or the situation if described in neutral terms. The willingness to speak out may vary considerably, depending upon how the speaker in the train compartment is presented.

Another question tests the willingness to speak out in front of a relatively large public: "Assuming that a television reporter with a microphone is asking people on the street about their opinion of _____. If the television reporter holds the microphone out to you, would you be willing to state your opinion or would you prefer not to?" (Donsbach & Stevenson, 1984; Tokinoya, 1989). The disadvantage of this question is that a systematic variation of the point of view dominating the conversation is not as easy to arrange in the television interview format as in the train or bus format.

Situations that are essentially private are not suited for this sort of inquiry—for example, the willingness to speak out in the family or with friends—for it is the willingness to speak out in public (*coram publico*) that is important to the process of public opinion.

Situations should, however, be chosen in which the "public" ("Everyone has access") is kept as small as possible: according to Michael Hallemann's findings (1989, section 3.2.3.2.), fear of isolation increases in proportion to the size of the public. The larger the public, the more personal characteristics—security, self-confidence, practice in speaking, education, role—will influence responses, independently of the climate of opinion. Thus the reaction to the climate of opinion is increasingly concealed by "personal characteristics" as a factor influencing the willingness to speak out. In addition to the choice of a situation involving a "small public," characteristics that influence the willingness to speak out must be established in order to keep these characteristics constant.

While another test of willingness to speak out is not so graphic, it is less prone to be influenced by the particular conditions in a given country. In the interview, three topics are introduced briefly, one of which is controversial and two of which are neutral. The subsequent question in the interview reads: "You can't ask questions about every last subject in an interview. So I have three subjects here—which of them would you prefer to answer questions on?" When the data are analyzed, the percentage of persons on both sides of a controversial subject who are willing to answer additional questions on this topic are compared (Allensbach Archives, 1983, 4021/B).

Another test of the willingness to speak out is geared to the person addressed rather than to the speaker. The question reads: "Has someone recently talked to you about topic XY?" If the answer is "yes," "What was his opinion, was he more in favor of or more against?" (Noelle-Neumann 1986b, p. 81). This is another way to determine which camp is more active and more willing to speak out on a controversial issue.

By systematically varying the phrasing of a controversial topic, the willingness to speak out can also be recognized from the tenor of the discussion. Other variations can be established by introducing questions suggesting a climate of opinion that is favorable or unfavorable to the respondent, for example by a sentence completion test with an aggressive tenor ("Threat test," Noelle-Neumann 1984, pp. 42 ff.). The willingness to speak out can also be investigated through tests that focus on wearing badges and displaying bumper stickers: To what extent are the two camps willing to take a stand like this in public?

With a specific view to the study of media effects, both camps' willingness to speak out is to be studied according to media use, similarly to the test of the dual climate of opinion.

The analysis of findings on the willingness to speak out has in part been done in terms of an oversimplified version of the theory of the spiral of silence. According to this version, only two variables are considered:

1. Does the respondent belong to the majority or minority camp?
2. Does he or she feel in agreement with the climate of opinion, "the way most people think," or in conflict with the climate of opinion?

According to this simplified version of the spiral of silence theory, it is assumed that respondents from the majority camp, and respondents who feel they are in agreement with the climate of opinion, will be the ones who are willing to speak out.

This approach has resulted in analyses of the willingness to speak out that proceeds independently of which of the two camps in a controversial issue someone belongs to—an abstraction that blurs the asymmetrical modes of behavior in the process of public opinion rather than clarifying them. Such an abstraction is based on the assumption that media effects do not favor one side or the other. The study of media effects using tools derived from the social psychological theory of public opinion demands that analyses always be conducted separately for the two sides in a controversy.

SALIENCE

Studies on media effects using the tools of public opinion theory turn out to be disappointing if the topics chosen are not limited to those currently being debated. The current debate is preceded by an early stage, in which leaders act as an avant garde in the process of public opinion (Noelle-Neumann, 1974a, p. 319); a later stage closes the debate, with a hard core barricading itself, as it were—a rather tragic development. *Don Quixote* may be interpreted from this point of view (Chuliá-Rodrigo, 1989) but media effects research has not yet dealt with these extreme situations.

In everyday media effects research, questions determining salience are required. One question, which is used in election research, reads: "Many different issues are discussed during an election campaign. But there are usually a few issues that really receive a lot of attention. Could you please read through this list and tell me all the issues that people are talking about especially these days?" (Noelle-Neumann, 1987). The higher an issue ranks as being much discussed, the more suitable it is to study media effects. This makes apparent the connection between another approach to media effects research, the agenda-setting function (McCombs & Shaw, 1972; Funkhouser, 1973), and the theory of the spiral of silence: Agenda setting creates the issues on which the public opinion process will work.

THE MORAL COMPONENT

Media effects research using the tools derived from the spiral of silence will also disappoint, if the topics chosen are such that you cannot isolate yourself with your opinion—that is, if the topics are not morally loaded. This would represent an aberration, such as happened with studies on selective perception when they were conducted on subjects impossible to identify with emotionally (Jecker, 1964; Mills & Ross, 1964).

The question most frequently used on morally loaded issues reads: "There are certain subjects about which friends can have different opinions; this can sometimes even lead to heated arguments and the end of a friendship. These cards list different subjects—please read them through. Which subjects do you think that even good friends could get into heated arguments about?" (Noelle-Neumann, 1983a, p. 561a).

THREAT OF ISOLATION, FEAR OF ISOLATION

Since the concepts of threat of isolation and fear of isolation play a key role in the theory of the spiral of silence but almost no research has been devoted to them—they do not appear in the established encyclopedias of social research—a special effort has been made, in developing the empirical tools, to find methods of studying the threat of isolation and fear of isolation or of simulating them in interviews, and to link up the findings with media content analysis.

An example is provided by the following question, drawn from Allensbach election research, in which an illustration of a car with slashed tires is shown: "Here is a picture of a car that has had its tire slashed. On the right rear window there is a sticker for a political party, but you can't read which party the sticker was for. What is your guess: With which party's stickers do people run the greatest risk of having a tire slashed?"

A question was also developed to test the threat of isolation: "I want to tell you, now, about another case and ask you what you think. Someone drives into a strange city and can't find a parking space. He finally gets out of the car and asks a pedestrian: 'Can you tell me, please, where I can find a place to park?' The pedestrian replies, 'Ask somebody else, buddy!' and walks away. I should mention that the driver is wearing a political badge on his jacket. What do you think: Which party did this badge support? What is your guess?"

Another variant: "In the election campaign, posters again were ripped up and defaced. According to what you saw, which party's posters were most often damaged?" This question fits into this context, because it is assumed that ripping up and defacing posters is perceived as a symbolic threat of isolation.

In order to test the danger of isolation outside of specific election campaign situations, the following question was developed: "I would like to tell you about an incident which recently took place at a large public meeting on nuclear energy. There were two main speakers; one spoke in favor of nuclear energy and the other opposed it. One of the speakers was booed by the audience. Which one do you think was booed, the speaker supporting nuclear energy or the speaker opposing it?" (Table 7.7). Another question of this type is: "I would like to tell you about an incident which recently took place at a large public meeting. The main speakers were a left-wing extremist and a right-wing extremist. One of the two was jeered a the meeting. Which one do you think was jeered? The left-wing extremist or the right-wing extremist?" (Allensbach Archives, 1989, 5019).

This kind of question represents the application of findings arrived at by systematic studies on the threat of isolation (Holicki, 1984) and on the role of laughing and smiling in the threat of isolation (Albrecht, 1983).

TABLE 7.7
Federal Republic of West Berlin Population 16 and over

Testing the threat of isolation for any given issue

Which opinions voiced in public lead to isolation?

QUESTION: "I would like to tell you about an incident which recently took place at a large public discussion on nuclear energy. There were two main speakers. One spoke in favor of nuclear energy and of the breeder reactor in Kalkar being put into operation and the other opposed this. One of the speakers was booed by the audience. Which one do you think was booed: The speaker supporting nuclear energy and the breeder reactor or the speaker opposing this?"

	Total population %
Supporter of nuclear energy	72
Opponent of nuclear energy	11
Undecided	17
	100
	n = 2213

Source: Allensbach Archives, IfD Survey 3029, April 1976

In connection with the threat of isolation and the fear of isolation, the pillory effect of the media needs to be studied.

TENOR OF THE MEDIA

The study of the effect of the media on the process of public opinion cannot be conducted without media content analysis. The work this entails serves as a deterrent. But even small-scale media content analysis is more useful than the attempt to ask questions about the tenor of the media in survey interviews. Perceiving the tenor of the media requires a degree of detachment that is obviously not in tune with the unconscious view of the media, as described by MacLuhan, as an extension of one's own sensory organs, one's own eyes and ears. This what makes it so difficult to perceive the tenor of the media. Selective use of the media, and selective perception, are additional influences that result in distorted perceptions of the tenor of the media Noelle-Neumann, 1977a, pp. 67 ff.; Kepplinger, 1988a).

SPECTRUM ANALYSIS AS AN APPROACH IN MEDIA EFFECTS RESEARCH

According to the fifth hypothesis mentioned initially, one may expect that the polarization on issues that are irrelevant to the programs of political parties is due to media effects. It is assumed that the media that tend to take a right-wing position, and those that tend to take a left-wing position represent different values on these issues. To test this assumption, a variation of media content analysis, *spectrum analysis*, has been developed.[1] The yardstick for an assessment as being on the right or the left is derived from the rating of print media by experts (Schönbach, 1976; Stolz, 1987) according to their position from right to left on the spectrum. The yardstick thus derived can be applied to radio and television programs according to a method developed by Hans Mathias Kepplinger (Kepplinger, 1985).

---

[1] The concept first appeared in the title of a communications seminar given by the author at the University of Mainz during the summer term of 1973: "A Contribution to the Theory of Consonance: Spectrum Analysis."

CONCLUSION

This contribution set out to show how hypotheses and tools used to study media effects are derived from a theory about the role of the media in the process of public opinion. The achievement of these tools is not that they *prove* media effect; rather, they focus attention on indications of possible media effect, and as the observations accumulate, the probability increases that media effect is involved (Kepplinger, 1982, p. 109). The findings arrived at using tools derived from the theory are difficult to explain if media effect is not assumed. On the other hand, a theory should prove itself, in communication research as elsewhere, by the fact that tools may be derived from it that enable us to conduct research on such important questions as media effects.

SUMMARY

This chapter is based on the premise that the media's most important effect is its influence on public opinion and on the climate of opinion. Thus, the first step was to clarify the concept and process of public opinion. Using the spiral of silence theory of public opinion, which was developed between 1965 and 1980, the chapter focuses on hypotheses which can explain how the effect of the media—as described by this theory—can be demonstrated and on tools which have been developed to investigate the effect of the media on public opinion.

REFERENCES

Allensbach Archives, JFD (Survey 3028) (1976, April).
Allensbach Archives, JFD (Survey 4008) (1982, May).
Allensbach Archives, JFD (Survey 4012) (1982, August).
Allensbach Archives, JFD (Survey 4021b) (1983, January).
Allensbach Archives, JFD (Survey 4049) (1984, October).
Allensbach Archives, JFD (Surveys 2185 & 2187).
Allensbach Archives, JFD (Survey 4093b) (1987, September).
Allensbach Archives, JFD (Survey 5019) (1989, April).
Allensbach Archives, JFD (Survey 5021) (1989, June).
Albrecht, A. (1983). *Lacheln und lacheln—Isolation oder integration?* FRG: University of Mainz.
Childs, H.L. (1965). *Public opinion: Nature, formation and role.* Princeton, NJ: Princeton University Press.

Chulia-Rodrigo, M.E. (1989). *Die öffentliche Meinung in Cervantes Roman Don Quijote von der Mancha*. FRG: University of Mainz.

Donsbach, W., & Stevenson, R.L. (1984, May) *Challenges, problems and empirical evidences of the theory of the spiral of silence*. Paper presented at the Conference of the International Communication Association, San Francisco.

Funkhouser, G.R. (1973). The issues of the sixties: An exploratory study in the dynamics of public opinion. *Public Opinion Quarterly, 37,* 62–75.

Habermas, J. (1962) *Strukturwandel der Öffentlichkeit. Untersuchen zu einer Kategorie der burgerlichen Gesellschaft.* Neuwind: Hermann Luchterhand.

Hallemann, M. (1986). Peinlichkeit und Öffentliche Meinung. *Publizistik, 31,* 240–261.

Hallemann, M. (1989). Peinlichkeit. Ein Ansatz zur Operationalisierung von Isolotionsfurcht im sozialpsychologischen Konzept Öffentlicher Meinung. Dissertation. Mainz.

Holicki, S. (1984). *Isolationsdrohung: Sozialpsychologische Aspekte eines Publizistikwissenschaftichen Konzepts.* FRG: University of Mainz.

Hume, D. (1963). *Essays moral political and literary.* London. (Original work published 1741/1742)

Jecker, J.D. (1964). Selective exposure to new information. In L. Festinger (Ed.), *Conflict, decisions and dissonance* (pp. 65–81). Stanford.

Kepplinger, H.M. (1982) Die Grenzen des Wirkungsbegriffs. *Publizistik, 27,* 98–113.

Kepplinger, H.M. (1985). *Die akteulle Berichterstattung des Horfunks: Eine Inhaltanalyse der Abendnachrichten und politischen Magazine.* FRG: Freiburg.

Kepplinger, H.M. (1988a) *Die Kernenergie in den Massemedien ode die Rhetorik der Angst.* Paper presented at the Conference on Nuclear Energy, Bonn.

Kepplinger, H.M. (1988). *Künstliche Horizonte. Die Darstellung von Technik in der Presse und ihr Einflub auf die Ansichten der Bevölkervng 1965–1986.* Mains: Institut für Publizistik.

Lazarsfeld, P., Berelson, B., & Gaudet, H. (1944). *The people's choice: How the voter makes up his mindin a presidential campaign.* New York: Columbia.

McCombs, M., & Shaw, D. (1972). The Agenda-setting function of mass media. *Public Opinion Quarterly, 36,* 176–187.

Mathes, S. (1989). *Sozial-optische tauschung durch massenmdien? Die einschatzung des Meinungsklimas im konflikt mit der kernenenergi durch personen mit viel und wenig fernsehnutzung.* FRG: University of Mainz.

Mills J, & Ross, A. (1964) Effects of commitment and certainty upon interest in supporting information. *Journal of Abnormal and Social Psychology, 68,* 552–555.

Mutz, D. (1989). The influence of perception of media influence: Third person effects and the public expression of opinions. *International Journal of Public Opinion Research, 1.*

Noelle, E. (1966). *Öffentliche Meinung und soziale Kontrolle*. Tubingen, FRG:

Noelle-Neumann, E. (1973a). Return to the concept of powerful mass media. *Studies of Broadcasting, 9*, 67–112.

Noelle-Neumann, E. (1974b). Die Schweigespirale: Über die Entstehung der offentlichen Meinung. In E. Forsthoff & R. Hörstel (Eds.), *Standorte im Zeitstrom* (pp. 299–330). Frankfurt, FRG.

Noelle-Neumann, E. (1974c). The spiral of silence. *Journal of Communication, 24*, 43–51.

Noelle-Neumann, E. (1976). *Mass media and the climate of opinion*. Paper presented at the International Association for Mass Communication Research, University of Leicester, England.

Noelle-Neumann, E. (1977a). Auflagenkonzentration and freie Meinungsbildung: Das Springer-Problem. In J. Wilke (Ed.), *Öffentlichkeit als Bedrohung: Beitrage zur empirischen Kommunikationforschung* (pp. 62–68). Munich, FRG:

Noelle-Neumann, E. (1977b). Turbulences in the climate of opinion: Methodological applications of the spiral of silence theory. *Public Opinion Quarterly, 41*, 143–158.

Noelle-Neumann, E. (1978b). The dual climate of opinion: The influence of television in the 1976 West German federal election. In M. Kaase & von Beyme, K. (Eds.), *Elections and Parties: Socio-political change and participation in the West German federal election of 1976. In German Political studies, Vol. 3* (pp. 137–169). London: Sage.

Noelle-Neumann, E. (1982). Der Konflikt zwischen Wirkungsforschung und Journalisten: Ein wissenschaftsgeschichtliches Kapitel. *Publizistik, 27*, 114–128.

Noelle-Neumann, E. (1983a). The effects of media on media effects research. *Journal of Communication, 33*, 157–165.

Noelle-Neumann, E. (1983b). Öffentliche Meinung in der Bundestagwahl 1980. In M. Kaase & H.D. Klingeman (Eds.), *Wahlen und Politische system: Analysen aus Anlass der Budestagwahl 1980s.* (pp. 540–599). Opladen.

Noelle-Neumann, E. (1984). *The spiral of silence: Public opinion—our social skin*. Chicago, London.

Noelle-Neumann, E. (1985). Theorie and methode. In W. Mahle (Ed.), *Fortschritte der Medienwirkungsforschung? Neue theoretische und methodische Ansätze und Fortschritte der Medienwirkungsforschung* (pp. 51–61). Berlin, FRG: Volker Spiess.

Noelle-Neumann, E. (1986a). Zur Forschungsstrategie der medienwirkungsforschung. In W. Schultz (Ed.), *Medienwirkungsforschung in der bundesrepublik Deutschland* (pp. 129–141). Weinheim

Noelle-Neumann, E. (1986b). Election research and the climate of opinion. In *Seminar on Opinion Polls*, Strasbourg, November 26–28, 1986. Amsterdam.

Noelle-Neumann, E. (1987). Arger Uber die Steuern schadet der CDU/CSU. *Die Welt, 19*, 6.

Noelle-Neumann, E. (1989a). Die Theorie der Schweigespirale als Instrument der Medienwirkungsforschung. *Kolner Zeitschrift fur Soziologie und Sozialpsychologie, 30,* 359–399.

Noelle-Neumann, E. (1989b). Wirkumg der Massenmedien. In E. Noelle-Neumann, W. Schultz, & J. Wilke (Eds.), *Fischer Lexicon Publizistik—Massenkommunikation* (pp. 359–399). Frankfurt, FRG.

Noelle-Neumann, E. (in press), The theory of public opinion: The concept of the spiral of silence. In J.A. Andersson (Ed.), *Communication Yearbook, 14.*

Oncken, H. (1914). *Historirisch-politische aufsatze und reden von Hermann Oncken, Vol. 1.* Munich, Berlin, FRG.

Osgood, C., Suci, G., & Tannenbaum, P. (1957). *The measurment of meaning.* Urbana, Illinois.

Schönbach, K. (1976). *Trennung von nachricht und meinung: Empirische untersuchung eines journalistischen qualitatskriteriums.* Freiburg, Munich, FRG:

Stolz, H.G. (1987). *Die redaktionellen linien ausgewahlter publikumsorgane.* FRG: University of Mainz.

Tokinoya, H. (1989). Testing the spiral of silence theory in East Asia. *Keio Communication Review, 10.*

Whose Effects Are They, Anyway? Or How Can You Locate Effects in All This Fog?

BRENDA DERVIN

At the outset, it is important to say that this commentary is concerned with something called *effects* but is not limited to mass media effects.[1] Rather, it cuts across the genres of communication studies: intrapersonal, interpersonal, organizational, media, and societal; psychological, sociological, anthropological, and semiotic; political, informational, educational, and otherwise.

Each of these genres represents a strength in communication studies. Taken together, they conveniently anchor our work in time and place and line up our allegiances and networks within and between. In any one of these genres, it is clearly an exciting time to be in communication studies. One sees better discourse and more sophisticated commentaries of all kinds. Without any disrespect to any of these genres, however, this chapter sets out not to be bound within them but to cut across them. There is no adequate description of the slice that this chapter attempts to take. It is neither vertical nor horizontal, for either of these directions would accept the genres as given. Rather, it is diagonal, but more properly described as chaotically diagonal. The goal is to play a version of let's pretend. Let's pretend that our research genres as we currently

---

[1] Although many of the examples will be derived from mass media research, particularly the active vs. passive audience debate. The author found the following useful in understanding that debate: Biocca (1988), Fejes (1984), Gunter (1988), Jensen (1987), Lindlof (1988), Price (1989), Swanson (1987).

know them, as they currently define our field, are a fog.[2] Let's pretend that we can be free of them and then think about this term *effects.*

If one were to take a stereotyped portrait of our field right now, in the main we seem divided into those who admit the word "effects" (and its synonyms, such as "impacts") into our vocabulary, and those who don't. In mass media studies, this plays itself out in extreme versions through debates over the active versus passive audience. But we see the same debate in different forms throughout our field. Is the individual a passive inhabitant of the structures/cultures/organizations within which he or she lives? Is the individual a passive recipient of the messages/norms/lessons/to make what he or she will of the structures and messages that abound around?

Admittedly the statement of the debate in this polarized form leaves behind most of the subtlety and rich complexity of the current discourse. But the simplicity will serve our purposes. It is fair to say that most of those who inhabit our field have made a choice one way or the other on this matter—either they acknowledge and search for effects, impacts, and if—then patterns or they don't. In one extreme version of this debate, we find, for example, proponents of the most polarized arguments about methodologies—those who argue, for example, that given the enormous creativity of individual behavior, methods must be responsive to that creativity and, thus, systematically unsystematic. At the other extreme we find proponents of more traditionally presented scientific positions.

All of the arguments nested in the paragraphs above have strength, particularly when they are understood in the context of the vantage point from which they are cast. But there is something going on here that deserves attention. Indeed, in recent years we see attempts to reach across this structure vs. theory of audience reception, for example, and effects researchers who formerly focused on psychological states are reaching out to introduce structural considerations.

But amidst all the debate and new connecting, there are actually

---

[2] The author has relied heavily in developing this commentary on the work of Richard Carter (Carter, 1989, 1980, 1973). Others whose writing have been useful include: Dewey (1915), Geertz (1973), Giddens (1984, 1989), Habermas (1984, 1987), and Hall (1989). For further development of these ideas in different contexts, see Dervin (1990a) (applied to comparative theory); (1990b) (applied to research on users of communication systems); (1989) (applied to audience research).

few who focus on the communicative nature of the relationship between individual or society, not the individual-in-society or the society-implemented-by-individuals. And the conceptual frame continues to proceed as if searching for invariant generalizations: proof, for example, that active audience arguments are weak; or, alternatively, proof of the opposite.

There are signs of this virtually anywhere one looks in our field. We continue to look for ways to describe the impacts of messages/institutions/cultures, and so on, on people as if these were taken as whole units. And we continue to look for ways to describe individual humans as if they were one way or another—he is a local news viewer, she is a gullible recipient of editorials, and so on.

In essence, despite our protests to the contrary, in good part we continue to look at communication as monolithic transmission. Even the term *a theory of reception* is confined to this definitional frame. Even within this frame, when we search for variations in reception, we look in essence at meanings made, not meaning making.

This brings me to my central point. Whether we want to or not we continue to be victims of our inherited conceptualizations of communication. We do not conceptualize communication as process, as activity, as behavior...but rather as state, as input and output, as result. This does not mean that I am suggesting that a focus on states is entirely wrong and without value. Rather what I am suggesting is that there are consequences of using *only* a state orientation. The main consequence, I propose, is that we end up conceptualizing individual behavior as either too chaotic or too individualistic and cannot find the meeting ground between.

When we apply a state orientation to the study of communication, we in essence search for descriptors of state conditions that will be explanatory or predictive or useful to us in some way. We focus on human entities—individuals and collectivities—in terms of their demographics, personality, skill, resources, and other state characteristics. Given our heritage, this makes sense. It leads us to divide our field into all our current genres. Levels of analysis concern how many humans are involved and whether the state condition is internal or external: intrapersonal, interpersonal, organizational, and so on. Contexts such as political communication, health communication, and so on delineate areas of activity in which these human entities specialize—experience is captured as if it were a state condition.

I propose that our emphasis, actual and implied, apparent and hidden, on state conditions demarks our current field's contests and debates more than any other characteristic. On the one hand we have those who continue to search for if–then propositions of understanding about the relationship of one set of state conditions to another. Sometimes this is done at the structural level: if media ownership patterns are x, then information flows are y. Sometimes this is done at the individual level: if the audience member is a regular x, then the audience member focuses on y. Sometimes this is done in situational terms: when people find themselves in x situation, they then do y; or, if a person shows these characteristics, then other people show these characteristics.

On the other hand, we have those who completely opt out of the search, preferring instead to describe individual and case uniquenesses. This work, for a variety of reasons, is often peppered with illuminating discussions of the ethics of researcher involvement. Given the uniquenesses of the meanings made by people, these discussions ask whether the researcher has the right to find patterns in those meanings or to link those meanings to larger structural conditions of which lay people may not have the same privileged knowledge.

Again, it is important to reiterate that I am polarizing the arguments for purposes here and do not intend to denigrate any of the research genres to include myself in it. The one thing that is very clear about our work right now is that we have many writers reaching across barriers and pushing limits. I take this as symptomatic of a simultaneous awareness that something is not as it should be.

Whether we search for patterns in state conditions or retreat from the search, we have defined communication not as process but as state condition and have therefore not developed theories of communication as behavior. As a result, we know very little about either human rigidities or human flexibilities. The former is obvious in our continued concern for our lack of ability to predict human communication behavior (for example, exposure) resulting in the often cited "low variances account for." It is also obvious in our legion of revaluations, in which we move in cycles from emphasis on individuals to emphasis on structure and back again.

The fact that we know little about human flexibilities is obvious in our field's acceptance of individual uniqueness as capricious and recalcitrant. In essence, we have defined flexibility as chaos and see it as without pattern and therefore not admissible to any framing that would also include the word "effects."

Our polarizations between individual vs. structure, individual vs. message, individual vs. organization, are manifestations of our implied and actual emphasis on state conditions rather than process conditions. The way to explain this is to pursue, again, a let's pretend argument. Let's start with the assumption that without behavior there is no structure, no message, no institution. Individual humans do things, both internal things (such as thinking, categorizing, defining, illustrating) and external things (such as shouting, writing, illustrating, agreeing, disagreeing).

Let's also assume, as most researchers in our field do, that there is no direct observation of reality. A behavioral act always stands between reality and person, person and reality. Let's assume that these behavioral acts—these communications—are the strategies and tactics by which human entities (individual and collective) define situations and act to face them. Since instruction from reality is not given, humans make it. In some situation-definings, humans focus on creating individual sense; in others, they focus on moving together; in others, they try to cope with impositions from other people; in others, they merely repeat what they have learned in the past.

The important point in this set of let's pretend assumptions is not that individual behavior is either free or constrained, but rather that it is sometimes free and sometimes constrained; sometimes rigid and sometimes flexible; sometimes oriented to being part of, assisting, or maintaining a collectivity, sometimes at odds with that collectivity; sometimes an unconscious energizer of collective rigidity.

To say that is not to assume that humans are totally conscious of and able to explain all their acts. Rather, it is to suggest that by focusing on state conditions we may have found both too little rigidity as well as too little flexibility. It is as if we have been looking for something through the fog but the thing we have been looking for wasn't even there...or wasn't as important as we thought.

There are a number of myths and illusions which come at least in part from these blinders we wear. One set of these myths relates to how we conceptualize individuals. The other relates to how we conceptualize structures, including message structures. Many of these myths are contradictory. The individual, for example, is presented all at once as chaotic, capricious, rigid, untrustworthy, unconscious, and unsophisticated, as well as creative, unique, active, and responsive. The structure or message is presented as hegemonic and forceful as well as irrelevant and subject to interpretation. Each one of these contradictory myths may arise in part because of our emphasis on state conditions.

If what is patterned about humans is not the entity characteristics that we ascribe to them (for example, demography or personality) but rather the entity defining and behaving at specific moments in time-space, then we would miss these patterns by searching for entity characteristics. Assume, for example, that it is not social class that explains negotiated decoding but rather defining social class as relevant to self at a particular moment in time and space. Then, searching for differences in decoding based on social class would have limited observational productivity.

The individual's behavior would, thus, look chaotic, but the chaos would result from our searching for constancy in the wrong place. We have not looked at how situation defining has consequences for situation facing, at how communication strategy and tactic interrelate, at how one's tactical behavior impacts one's definitions, and how one's definitions impact on one's tactical behavior. We have sought to find similarities in meanings between people who look the same to us, either because they carry entity characteristics that are the same (such as personality, demography) or they are structurally positioned in the same way (perhaps culturally) or exposed to the same message. We have not sought to find similarities in meaning making between people who define themselves as similarly situated, or tactically approach their communicating in similar ways.

Within such a framing, the individual would fall out of favor as a locus of attention for those searching for constancy, and fall into favor for those captured by unique case material. But, likewise, our assumptions about individual rigidities may also be myths arising from our emphasis on state conditions. If anything, it can be said that the social sciences have a far more developed understanding of human rigidities than human flexibilities, because, in essence, our theories have drive us to observe them. Given the line of reasoning presented above, it is understandable that we are better able to explain and predict channel access patterns (media exposure) than we are to interpret messages. The former are far more constrained and habitualized by socioeconomic conditions. It is also understandable that we are better able to explain rigid human responses in organizational settings—angry reactions to authority, for example—than we are able to explain why someone who behaved one way yesterday behaves another today.

The examples are legion of how badly the social sciences have done in predicting and explaining many major human events—public response to the Vietnam war, for example, or recent events in Eastern Europe. Again, the important point here is not that people are always flexible or always rigid but that we have not pursued understandings of the behavior they go through to define and face situations—understandings which would get us closer to understanding both rigidity and flexibility.

The entire polarization of individual vs. structure is another aspect of this problem. The structure has been conceptualized as having a monolithic impact on the individual. When that impact hasn't been found one response has been to reject the emphasis on individuals as too individualistic. Clearly, the blame-the-individual ideological position prevalent in much U.S. communication research in the 1950s and 1960s has been shown to have been both limiting and biased. But the individual has not fallen into disfavor only for ideological reasons. We have, in essence, been unable to keep the individual in our theorizing at the same time that we have focused on structures. We have been unable to develop understandings of how individuals communicatively create, maintain, reify, and change the structures they live in. We have relegated research on the human struggle with structures to a "critical" position without comprehending that each human is daily mandated, no matter how conformist the culture or structure within which he or she lives, to make sense of his or her relationship to that structure within which he or she lives, to make sense of his or her relationship to that structure. This struggle is the rich context that folklore, oral and media, draws on. Yet, ironically, we have not been able to draw it in systematically to all corners of our field.

There are other myths about the individual that may be seen as derivative of our emphasis on state conditions. Some of these result from how our emphases impact our methods. Our ways of interacting with lay people generally either opt out into individual uniqueness (the case study, the highly individualistic ethnographic account) or into the imposition of our world views via such research techniques as the close-ended survey. Our involvement with our respondents is not a strategic or tactical involvement. Because of this, we can conclude too easily that lay persons are untrustworthy (they lie, they bend to our opinions), or unsophisticated (they are unaware of all manner of realms of human existence to which our privileged knowledge gives us access), or unconscious (they are unaware of the true causes of their own behavior, their own rigidities).

In this context, our conceptions of communication impact the communicating that is involved strategically and tactically in interacting with our data collection approaches. The idea that a dialogue can ensue with the respondent in which we mutually define the situation does not often occur to us—we attempt to give the individual total control or none at all. We do not consider, for example, developing tactics for dialoguing with lay persons that guard against unduly impacting each other's perceptions, or assist in consciousness raising, or provide mutual education about each other's realities and then capitalize on the communicative results of this sharing. In fact, we take great pains, for different reasons—both in our qualitative research genres and our quantitative—not to interact unduly with the respondent.

The discussion above has a number of implications for the study of effects. One is that the fact that effects may seem so elusive may be due in part to our looking for effects in the wrong place—across time rather than in specific moments in time; in state conditions rather than process conditions. The second is that we have confined our meaning of the word "effects" to a search for patterns in rigidities and have not allowed for the possibility that effects may be found as well in patterns of flexibilities. The third is that even while protesting otherwise, we have excluded constructing human beings from our enterprise. We have not allowed for the possibility that the humans whom we study themselves have stories to tell about effects, and that these stories may be entry points for systematic and qualitative understandings.

REFERENCES

Biocca, F.A. (1988). Opposing conceptions of the audience: The active and passive hemispheres of mass communication theory. In J. Anderson (Ed.), *Communication yearbook 11* (pp. 51–80). Newbury Park, CA: Sage.

Carter, R.F. (1973, August). *Communication as behavior.* Paper presented at annual convention of Association for Education in Journalism, Fort Collins.

Carter, R.F. (1980, November). *Discontinuity and communication.* Paper presented at the East-West Center Conference on Communication Theory East and West, Honolulu, Hawaii.

Carter, R.F. (1989a, May). *Comparative analysis and theory in communication.* Paper presented at the annual meeting of International Communication Association, San Francisco.

Carter, R.F. (1989b, May). *What does a gap imply?* Paper presented at the annual meeting of International Communication Association, San Francisco.

Dervin, B. (1989). Audience as listener and learner, teacher and confidante: the sense-making approach. In R.E. Rice & C. Atkin (Eds.), *Public communication campaigns* (2nd ed., pp. 67–86).

Dervin, B. (1990a). Comparative theory reconceptualized: From entities and states to processes and dynamics. *Communication Theory, 1*(1).

Dervin, B. (1990b, January). Users as research inventions: How research categories perpetuate inequities. *Journal of Communication,* special issue on "The information gap," pp. 216–232.

Dewey, J. (1915). *Democracy and education.* New York: MacMillan.

Fejes, F. (1984). Critical mass communications research and media effects: The problem of the disappearing audience. *Media, Culture, and Society, 6,* 219–232.

Geertz, C. (1973). *The interpretation of culture.* New York: Basic Books.

Giddens, A. (1984). *The constitution of society: Outline of the theory of structuration.* Cambridge: Polity Press.

Giddens, A. (1989). The orthodox consensus and emerging synthesis. In B. Dervin (Ed.), *Rethinking communication 1: Paradigm issues* (pp. 53–65). Newbury Park, CA: Sage.

Gunter, B. (1988). Finding the limits of audience activity. In J. Anderson (Ed.), *Communication yearbook 11* (pp. 108–126), Newbury Park, CA: Sage.

Habermas, J. (1984). *Theory of communicative action I: Reason and the rationalization of society* (T. McCarthy, Trans.). Boston: Beacon Press.

Habermas, J. (1987). *Theory of communicative action II: Lifeworld and system* (T. McCarthy, trans.). Boston: Beacon Press.

Hall, S. (1989). Ideology and communication theory. In B. Dervin (Ed.), *Rethinking communication 1: Paradigm issues* (p. 53, Communication 65), Newbury Park, CA: Sage.

Jensen, K.B. (1987). Qualitative audience research: Toward an integrative approach to reception. *Critical Studies in Mass Communication, 4,* 21–36.

Lindlof, T.R. (1988). Media audiences as interpretive communities. In J. Anderson (Ed.), *Communication yearbook II* (pp. 81–107). Newbury Park, CA: Sage.

Price, V. (1989, May). *Public opinion and communication: Theoretical and empirical dependencies among levels.* Paper presented at International Communication Association, San Francisco.

Swanson, D.L. (1987). Gratification seeking, media exposure, and audience interpretations: Some directions for research. *Journal of Broadcasting and Electronic Media, 31*(3), 237–254.

PART

III

On Violence

The Politics of Media Violence: Some Reflections

9

GEORGE GERBNER

Humankind has had more bloodthirsty eras but none as filled with images of violence as the present. We are awash in a tide of violent representations unlike any the world has ever seen. There is no escape from the massive invasion of the colorful mayhem into the homes and cultural life of ever larger areas of the world.

Of course, there was blood in fairy tales, gore in mythology, murder in Shakespeare. It *is* a violent world. Cruelty was, if anything, more rampant in the past. Massacres and genocides are becoming difficult to hide. Such facts are often invoked to argue that violent storytelling is not new and that it did not make us into monsters (which may be a dubious claim). But what if it did something else, something perhaps even more intimidating and serviceable? And what if its apparent audiovisual realism, stable formulas, steady flow, and critical mass represents a change in the symbolic lifeblood of human development that is without precedent?

Audience appeal and just plain broadcaster greed are also said to play a part in the prevalence of violence on television. But neither these nor historical rationalizations can fully explain, let alone justify, drenching every home with graphic scenes of expertly choreographed brutality.

The pervasive symbolic overkill is not without social and institutional costs. Its persistence, despite the risks it entails, the price it extracts, and the marginal profits, if any, it nets, requires more than the conventional explanations. Doing justice to its global challenge requires more than the usual public rituals.

Charges of speech corrupting the young and innocent have been heard in the Western World at least since the time of Socrates. The rise of print, the spread of media to the "lower" classes, and every new extension to those presumed to be more vulnerable than their elders and betters sent the charge echoing through ruling circles and the academy.

Cheap literature in the late 19th century was blamed for making workers lazy and indolent. In his *Ladies Guide*, published in 1882, J. H. Kellogg railed against the "pernicious habit of reading fiction which, once thoroughly fixed, becomes as inveterate as the use of liquor or opium" and "is one of the greatest causes of uterine disease" and other painful maladies. Immorality and violence in comics and movies generated new fears, codes, regulations, and the first large-scale media research project, the Payne Fund Studies.

The rise of television in the United States coincided with post-World War II social ferment and concern about juvenile delinquency, crime, and general unrest. A series of Congressional hearings heard the traditional charges and denials of media violence focusing on television for the first time. Subsequent hearings, commissions, and reports energized citizens' movements for greater public participation in broadcasting, and provoked a fierce backlash. The ensuing debacle paved the way for the great retreat of the 1980s.

The received arguments of the popular culture debate failed to illuminate the new problems of the television age. A global sea-change in the symbolic environment has overtaken the old parochial formulation of the issues. The collapse of the reform movement exposed the bankruptcy of the traditional terms and tactics of the debate.

Violence is a legitimate and necessary feature of cultural expression, balancing deadly conflict and compulsion against tragic costs. Even catering to morbid and other pathological fascinations may have its poetic or commercial license. The historically limited, individually crafted, and selectively used symbolic misanthropy of the past is not the issue today. All that has been swamped by violence with happy endings produced on the dramatic assembly-line, saturating the mainstream of our common culture.

Our children are born into a symbolic environment of six to eight violent acts per prime-time hour alone, four times as many in presumably humorous children's programs, and two entertaining murders a night. Contrary to the hype that promoted them, most actual uses of cable, video, cassettes, and other new technologies make the dominant patterns penetrate even more deeply (but not more cheaply) into everyday life.

The incremental profits on manufacturing, inserting, and exporting such a troubling commodity (as distinct from other dramatic qualities of programs) is hardly worth its human and institutional risks and costs. Most highly rated programs are nonviolent. Though economies of scale in cheaply produced violence formulas may have some small financial advantages to program producers, there is no general correlation between violence and the ratings of comparable programs aired at the same time.

Why would mainstream media, the cultural arms of established society, undermine their own security for dubious and paltry benefits? Why would they persist in inviting charges of lawlessness? Why would they suffer public and legislative criticism and face international condemnation—unless the essential balance of institutional costs and benefits did tip, however precariously, to the positive side?

James D. Halloran suggested an answer when he wrote in 1977 that the conventional approach to media violence, focusing on imitation and incitation as major causes of criminal violence, misses the point. His own research on protest demonstrations showed that in focusing on even trivial or irrelevant violence, the media achieve certain positive values; positive, that is, from their own standpoint, although not necessarily from the standpoint of those seeking reform.

The only positive value equal to that of profits for commercial institutions is, of course, power. Politics is the art of getting, holding, wielding, or catering to it. Violence is its cheapest and clearest symbolic expression.

Violence in its most reliably observable form is a physical show of force. It is making one do or submit to something against one's will on pain of being hurt or killed. It demonstrates who has the power to impose what on whom under what circumstances. It illuminates the ability to lash out, provoke, intimidate, and annihilate. It designates winners and losers, victimizers and victims, champions and wimps.

In life that demonstration is costly, risky, and disruptive. In story-telling, it is usually clear, compelling, and instructive. Depictions of violence thus have important social functions. They symbolize threats to human integrity and to the established order. They demonstrate how these threats are combated, how order is restored (often violently), and how its violators (though rarely its violent enforcers) are punished. They display society's pecking order and show how the social order deals with attempts to subvert it. The ability to define violence and project its lessons is arguably the single most essential requirement for social control.

Media violence is a political scenario on several levels. As a symbolic exercise, it is a demonstration of the distribution of power. As a subject of media research, it has been a source of funding, supplying ammunition for various positions in a debate purportedly about violence but really about media control. The media themselves shape and manipulate the terms of the debate. And legislators milk it as long as there is political juice in it.

The assassinations of President John Kennedy, Senator Robert Kennedy, and the Reverend Dr. Martin Luther King, Jr., led to the establishment in 1968 of the National Commission on the Causes and Prevention of Violence. Its Mass Media Task Force commissioned me to provide a reliable analysis of violence on television. That was the beginning of what has become the longest-running ongoing media research project. Called Cultural Indicators, the project relates the analysis of television content to a variety of viewer conceptions.

The Task Force by Baker and Ball (1969) presented our content analysis. It established a standard format for tracking violence in network drama and revealed the high level of its frequency, a level that has not changed much over the years. Equally important was its systematic description of television violence not as a simple act, but as a complex social scenario of power and victimization. The risks of life in prime time are not evenly distributed. When involved in violent encounters, women and minorities are more likely to become their victims.

Only the frequency findings, accompanied by charges and denials of violent imitation and incitation, were reported in mainstream media. The Task Force called for remedial action by government and the media, calls that, like many others that followed, went unheeded. But it moved Senator John Pastore to ask President Nixon for a larger investigation to safeguard public law and order.

A Scientific Advisory Committee to the United States Surgeon General found indications of a causal relation between violence on television and "aggressive behavior" among some viewers (Comstock, Rubinstein, & Murray, 1972). In 1980, another Surgeon

General's Advisory Committee was formed to review and summarize progress since the 1972 Report (Pearl, Bouthilet, & Lazar, 1982). The report noted that television cultivates exaggerated beliefs about the prevalence of violence and heightens feelings of insecurity and mistrust among most groups of heavy viewers, and especially among women and minorities.

The Cultural Indicators research, which was the source of these conclusions (see Gerbner, Gross, Morgan, & Signorielli, 1986a,b), also found that these consequences are not necessarily identical for all groups. They tend to erode traditional differences over time so that the perspectives of heavy viewers of otherwise divergent groups are closer to each other than are the perspectives of light viewers.

Subsequent research confirmed, refined, and extended these findings into other areas of television "cultivation" (see Morgan & Signorielli, 1990). These studies and their implications represent a new approach to media violence effects research.

Research on the consequences of exposure to mass-mediated violence has a long and involved history. Most of it focused on limited aspects of the complex scenario. It has been motivated (and dominated) by charges of individual imitation, incitation, brutalization, or subversion. Research has concentrated on observable and measurable psychological traits and states—such as aggressiveness—that were presumed to lead to violence and could be attributed to media exposure.

Research on aggression has been the most prominent "media violence story." Although ostensibly critical of media, it may have been the preferred story because it is the easiest to neutralize and the least damaging to basic instructional interests and policies.

Aggressiveness is an ambivalent concept with positive as well as negative connotations. It is a traditional part of male role socialization. Its link to most real violence and crime, which is organized and systemic, is tenuous, to say the least. It can even be argued that too many people submit too meekly to exploitation, injustice, indignity, and intimidation.

Approaches that focus only on aggression and lawlessness view violence from the law enforcement point of view. Their critical edge represents media (and other) institutional interests. They distract attention from wholesale "official" violence and state terrorism, from the disproportionate victimization of women and minorities, and from demographic and social conditions that are much more closely related to actual violence and crime. And they fail to take into account the crucial difference between television and all other media.

Universal exposure to televised images of violence goes on from cradle to grave. Conventional research concentrations on imitation alone, selective exposure, before-and-after exposure attitude change, viewer preferences, and the recurrent notion of "powerful" audiences miss the essential problem of television culture and its cultivation of conceptions about social relationships in deadly conflict.

Seldom asked and rarely publicized are broader research questions of media policy. They focus on the implicit message of open season on the different and the deviant. They deal with victimization and the consequences of control, as well as with aggression. The key question in the new approach is not what causes most violence and crime, as that goes far beyond media. It is what contribution does constant exposure to particular scenarios of violence and terror make to different groups' conceptions of their own risks and vulnerabilities.

These questions do not fit the typical media effects research mold or media violence story. On the contrary, they expose their assumptions and challenge their social and political functions.

Television viewing is a time-bound and relatively nonselective activity. Prime time, when most people watch television, and children's programs have been found to have the highest frequencies of violent representations.

Of course, there are many other elements in televised storytelling. And one must give credit to the creative artists and other professionals who seize opportunities—few and far between though they may be—to challenge and even counter the massive flow of formula programming. But most people watch television by the clock, not by the individual program. The overarching dramatic messages and images found in many programs tend to cultivate common conceptions most relevant to public policy, which is my focus. Violence is probably the most vivid and prominent of these hard-to-avoid presentations. Signorielli's (1986) analysis shows that the program mix is such that the average viewer has little opportunity to avoid frequently recurring patterns such as violence. Large audiences watch violent programs scheduled in time periods when large audiences watch television.

The world of prime time is cast for its favorite dramatic plays—power plays. Men outnumber women at least three to one. Young people, old people, and minorities have many times less than their share of representation. Compared to White American middle-class heterosexual males in the "prime of life," all others have a more restricted and stereotyped range of roles, activities, and opportunities, and less than their share of success and power. But they have more than their share of vulnerability and victimization.

The cultivation of conceptions of self and society implicit in these portrayals begins in infancy. For the first time in human history, major responsibility for the formative socializing process of storytelling has passed from parents and churches and schools to a small group of transnational conglomerates who have something to sell, as well as to tell, and can tell it all the time.

The moderate viewer of prime time sees every week an average of 21 criminals (domestic and foreign) arrayed against an army of 41 public and private law enforcers. There are 14 doctors, six nurses, six lawyers, and two judges to handle them. An average of 150 acts of violence and about 15 murders entertain us and our children every week, and that does not count cartoons and the news. Those who watch over three hours a day (more than half the people) absorb much more.

The violence and terror we see on television bears little or no relationship to their actual occurrence. Neither their frequency nor their nature resembles trends in crime statistics. Rather, they follow marketing formulas that call for injecting relatively cheap dramatic ingredients into otherwise often dull "action programs." But the action goes far beyond markets.

Our analysis has found that exposure to violence-laden television cultivates an exaggerated sense of insecurity and mistrust, and anxiety about the mean world seen on television. Furthermore, the sense of vulnerability and dependence imposes its heaviest burdens on women and minorities.

These are highly exploitable sentiments. They contribute to the irresistibility of punitive and vindictive political slogans ranging from "lenient judges" to capital punishment presumably to enhance security. They lend themselves to the political appeal of "wars" on crime, terrorism, and drugs that heighten repression but fail to address root causes.

Typical publicity deals with threats media violence might pose to the social order. Legislative attempts are similarly oriented. Focusing on potential threats obscures the symbolic functions and utility of media violence to the existing structure of power.

Rowland (1983) ascribes political motives to the choice of media violence research in the first place. The changes brought about by television after World War II reenergized the debate about the impact of modern communications, he wrote. As the television industry had no concrete obligation to fulfill any responsibility but the commercial, it had everything to gain from reducing its accountability for other effects. The political establishment needed leverage to use in dealing with the rising political power of television.

The most promising approaches were those that confronted typical charges and appealed to popular fears but formulated problems in limited and easily controlled ways; that set up straw men to be knocked down; and that, while anxiety provoking and emotionally arousing, and thus politically attractive, would not be likely to lead to any provocative legislative action. If, in addition, they could cater to public insecurities and mobilize support for defense of "law and order," so much the better. The ideal candidate fulfilling these criteria was television violence research.

Riding the wave of citizen activism and reformist sentiment, Senator John Pastore espoused television violence as his issue and held a series of legislative committee hearings on it. In a climactic session in 1974, I reported our findings of both the incidence of violence and an indication of what some consequences of exposure might be. But the cultivation of insecurity and dependence seemed too complex and academic for Pastore. He kept pressing for an answer to the usual law-and-order question: "Does it lead to violent behavior?"

The hearings were, of course, pure theater. Research testimony was used to extract public promises from network executives in exchange for less visible deals in more concrete areas of broadcaster interest, such as licensing. Having served its political purpose, the actual meaning and implications of the research, or the actual performance of the networks, was of little importance.

One notable exception occurred in the late 1970s at the height of the citizens' reform movement. A decade of commissions, research reports, and committee hearings had produced nothing. A short-lived "family hour" (which only its originator, CBS, ever observed) resulted in an antitrust legal challenge and quick retreat even from existing network codes of broadcast standards. Not even a committee report and recommendation, let alone legislation, attempted to address the policies imposing the violence formula.

Upon Pastore's retirement, a House subcommittee headed by Lionel Van Deerlin took up the television violence cudgels. This group, newly elected, more independent-minded, and more militant than previous committees, armed with critical research, decided to cut through the ritual.

Dragging their reluctant chairman along, these Young Turks produced a well-documented draft report. It was the first time that a committee even attempted to write a report. Furthermore, the draft called for an investigation of the structure of the television industry as the only way to get to the roots of the "violence problem."

When the draft mentioning industry structure was leaked to the networks, all hell broke loose. The National Association of Broadcasters, one of the most powerful Washington lobbies, declared war on the committee. Local broadcasters contacted campaign contributors in home districts. The NAB threatened reprisals on other bills dear to Van Deerlin's heart, including a rewrite of the Communications Act of 1934, the basic law of American broadcasting. Members of the subcommittee told me that they had never before been subjected to such relentless lobbying and pressure.

The report was delayed for months. Van Deerlin caved in and tried to downplay the recommendation. The staffer who wrote the final draft was summarily fired.

The day before the decisive vote, a new version drafted by a broadcast lobbyist was substituted. It ignored the evidence of the hearings and gutted the report, shifting the source of the problem from network structure to the parents of America.

When the network-dictated draft came to a vote, members of the full committee (including those who had never attended hearings) were mobilized. The watered-down version passed by one vote. The press featured it as the "anti-violence" report. The blistering minority report of the Young Turks received no attention.

The surrender was in vain. The rewrite bill was still scuttled. Van Deerlin was defeated in the next election. The broadcast reform movement collapsed. Foundation support for citizen action dried up. Advocates for the public interest were paralyzed when deregulation dismantled most protections built up through the years.

The battle over the first and only Congressional violence report had nothing really to do with violence. It was a test case fought on the industry's favorite battleground. It was a watershed marking the demise of the public trustee concept in broadcasting, the ascendancy of the plutocracy of market forces, and the full transfer of culture power to the newly merging and consolidating conglomerates. It demonstrated politically, as media violence does symbolically, who can do what to whom in a conflict.

The Young Turks of 1977, smarting from their defeat and dismayed at the collapse of their public constituency, made another attempt in 1981. Under the leadership of then Congressman Timothy Wirth a series of hearings attempted to revive the media violence issue. As it turned out, the hearings only exposed its political liabilities.

Many of the actors of 1977 were trotted out on the same stage. Our Cultural Indicators Violence Profile was introduced. It showed record levels and continued cultivation of insecurity, mistrust, and acceptance of repression.

Only one reference was made to our most telling basic findings. Representative Cardiss Collins, a member of the subcommittee, noted that our "research shows that when women and minority types encounter violence on television they are more likely to end up as victims than the majority types." Then she said: "You stated, 'The real questions that must be asked is not just how much violence there is, but also how fair, how just, how necessary, how effective, and at what price.'" And she wondered aloud: "Are you saying that the price to the well-being of our society is much too high?" (Hearing, 1982, pp. 230–231.) There was no answer or follow-up to her question.

The trade paper *Broadcasting* (October 26, 1981, p. 40), but no general media, noted my attempt to rekindle the spirit of the 1977 report:

> The way to reduce violence is to "extend the economic support for a broader view of the social and cultural mission of television," said Gerbner. "Further hearings are needed to examine the ways in which democratic countries manage their TV systems," and the subcommittee "should recommend a mechanism that will finance a freer commercial system, one that can afford to present a fairer, more peaceful, and more democratic world of TV."

Mindful of the debacle of 1977, I also observed that, "without economically and politically viable alternatives, and despite all good intentions, going through the same motions every few years remains in my opinion an exercise in futility" (Hearing, 1982, p. 149).

In the course of the final hearing a network executive found it "ironic... that while Gerbner attacks television for its fear-inducing elements, he is quite doubtful of the extent to which it generates serious violence.... To his mind, television's danger is not that it undermines the social order but that it 'cultivates acquiescence' to the powers that be" (Hearing, 1982, p. 55). I think the real irony was

lost on those focused on the problem of media violence, conventionally defined.

The last substantive remark of the hearing was made by Representative Al Swift, who, recalling the fiasco of 1977, concluded that
"we ought to be careful in our frustration of what television is doing
to us that we do not take an axe to the tail of the tiger and think we
have accomplished something. We may have accomplished a little
bit, but it is the other end of the tiger that is ultimately going to get
us" (Hearing, 1982, p. 235).

The tiger is riding high. Its power to thwart discussion or shunt
it into convenient channels was displayed on the night of February
24, 1983, when I appeared on Ted Koppel's "Viewpoint" program on
ABC dealing with television violence. (A transcript of Show #469 is
available from ABC NEWS, Box 234, Ansonia Station, New York,
N.Y. 10023.)

Of the seven men and one woman on the program, four were
broadcasters or their representatives and one a U.S. Associate
Attorney General. The prior agreement was that each participant
would have one minute to introduce his or her position on television violence. Koppel called on me first. "Is there," he asked, "a
direct causal relationship to violence in our society?" That of course
was just the question that begs the larger issue, so I said "Well,
Ted...first we have to ask what is media violence?" when Koppel cut
me off far short of the one minute to insist: "Humor me, over-
simplify the answer for a moment. Do you think there's a direct
causal relationship?"

Koppel has his finger on the button that switches cameras.
"Humoring" him, or at least appearing to do so, is a good idea. So I
continued to complete my one-minute answer: "Media violence is a
demonstration of power. There is a direct causal relationship, our
15 years of research has shown, between exposure to violence and
one's feeling of where one belongs in the power structure—one's
feeling of vulnerability, one's feeling of insecurity, one's demand for
protection, and one's welcoming even repression if it comes in the
form of security. That is the direct relationship."

"All right," said Koppel, seemingly satisfied, and turned to the
ABC Research Director who hastened to point out that "Well, I think
the answer Dr. Gerbner suggests was, no, there is no causal
relationship between television and crime, violence, the things that
we're all concerned about."

Lest things go off the narrow track assigned to them, ("the things
that we're all concerned about") and roles get confused, Koppel now

cut *him* off insisting that I *did* say "there was a direct causal relationship" and tried for the rest of the evening to fit my comments into the conventional law-enforcement script. The star of the show was the federal prosecutor and later Republican mayor of New York City, who used it for vigorous crime-fighting on the air.

Persistent exposure to the media violence scenario has several social consequences. These include the cultivation of aggressive tendencies as well as of relative insecurity and anxiety; the sporadic triggering of violent acts; and a relatively high sense of potential victimization especially by the more dependent groups in a stereotypic social hierarchy.

Differential vulnerability, rigidity, and resistance to change seem to be the most telling consequences of exposure. Bombarding viewers with violent images of a mean and dangerous world remains, in the last analysis, an instrument of intimidation and terror.

A never-to-be-declared state of symbolic emergency is pitting white male heterosexual "prime-of-life" middle-class power against the majorities of humankind living in the ghettos of America and the Third World. Probably the least affected by this particular offensive were the countries that until recently had been insulated from the influx of television violence "Made in the U.S.A."

This is a time of flux in the international communication and information order. The floodgates are opening for unrestrained penetration by a handful of transnational conglomerates in the name of democracy. If the Cold War turns into a new Holy Alliance, as those who declare themselves its winners seem to hope, the superpowers can concentrate on securing their ever more precarious hold on the remaining privileges and shrinking resources of a world liberated from some bankrupt forms of domination but increasingly free and open to symbolic invasion.

The mass production of images and messages of violence plays a perhaps small but critical part in the new imperial network. The questions we must ask are those of Congresswoman Collins: How just and how necessary, not just how much? And how long can the benefits outweigh the costs and the risks? Isn't the price much too high already?

We need to build a broad constituency to halt the public offensive. It should not be focused on violence alone. Only new global environmental movement can arrest the degradation of the cultural mainstream we share in common. That is the habitat in which those who survive the deterioration of the physical environment will live and learn to act human.

REFERENCES

Baker, R.K., & Ball, S.J. (1969). *Mass media and violence* (A report of the Task Force on Mass Media and Violence to the National Commission on the Causes and Prevention of Violence). Washington, DC: U.S. Government Printing Office.

Comstock, G.A., Rubinstein, E.A., & Murray, J.P. (Eds.). (1972). *Television and social behavior* (Report to the Scientific Advisory Committee) (5 vols.) Washington, DC: U.S. Government Printing Office.

Gerbner, G., Gross, G., Morgan, M., & Signorielli, N. (1986b). Living with television: The dynamics of the cultivation process. In J. Bryant & D. Zillman (Eds.), *Perspectives on media effects*. Hillsdale, NJ: Erlbaum.

Hearing Before the Subcommittee on Telecommunications, Consumer Protection, and Finance of the Committee on Energy and Commerce, House of Representatives, Ninety-Seventh Congress First Session, October 1981. (1982). Washington, DC: U.S. Government Printing Office, 1982.

Halloran, J.D. (1977). *Violence and its causes*. Unpublished paper. Leicester, UK: Centre for Mass Communication Research.

Kellogg, J.H. (1982). *Ladies' guide*. Des Moines, IA: W.D. Conduit Co.

Morgan, M., & Signorielli, N. (1990). *Cultivation analysis*. Beverly Hills, CA: Sage Publications.

Pearl, D., Bouthilet, L., & Lazar, J. (Eds.). (1982). *Television and behavior: Ten years of scientific progress and implications for the eighties*. Rockville, MD: National Institute of Mental Health.

Rowland, W.D. (1983). *The politics of TV violence: Policy uses of communication research*. Beverly Hills, CA: Sage.

Signorielli, N. (1986). Selective viewing: Limited possibilities. *Journal of Communication,*

CHAPTER

10

Media Violence—Research Perspectives in the 1980s

CECILIA VON FEILITZEN

Within the field of mass communication research, particularly in the United States, a great deal of resources have been invested in studies of the effects of entertainment violence on the individual. The researchers, like policy makers and other participants in the public debate, have concentrated on the physical (and sometimes on the verbal) violence shown on television and in film. Studies of violence in other media are less common. Above all, researchers have focused on the causal effects of violence, particularly among children and adolescents.

Even if this traditional violence research has given certain well-founded results (see below), it has been criticized as too limited by many researchers who also have wished to redefine the research problem to get more relevant answers. In this chapter international and Nordic examples of such redefinitions will be presented. The aim of the chapter is to show that, in the course of time, the redefinitions have become frequent—in the 1980s it was no longer reasonable to talk about *one* perspective within media violence research. The research was not, however, always empirical but consisted to a great extent of ontological, epistemological, theoretical, and methodological outlooks and critical questions.

Here, four main perspectives will be put forward, according to the researcher's starting point on what, slightly taken to the extreme, is most determining for the importance of media violence: *the media violence itself, the culture, the audience,* and *the power relations in society.*

PERSPECTIVE I: EFFECTS OF MEDIA VIOLENCE— THE TRADITIONAL MODEL AND ITS FURTHER DEVELOPMENT

The traditional research on media violence and aggression is based on theories that aggression originally arises via cultural learning and/or frustration (but hardly on theories on human aggression as biologically innate or as a psychic internal instinct). It further assumes that the media violence is the cultural learning factor. The traditional aggression studies up to and including the 1970s may be said to have arrived at the following results:

- Violent actions in the media can lead to *imitation* among younger children. (In a similar vein but to a much lesser extent, young people and adults can copy "tips" on how to perform violence.) But even if the media contents often activate children in particular to say, do, or play something of what they have seen, these impulses are most often short-term. And while imitation can be modeling, this does not mean as such that one has incorporated conceptions, norms, and values that lead to an intentional action.

- The media contents seldom have a direct or sole influence on our actions. We get instead mental impressions that are mixed with conceptions, norms, values, feelings, and experience from our own practice, and from family, school, peer groups, and so on—impressions of much greater importance—that, taken together, increase and diminish the disposition to act. In this indirect and most often reinforcing way, in interplay with the more important factors, entertainment violence contributes in some measure to increased *aggression* in the short term for certain individuals under certain circumstances.

- Mass communication research has not been able to discern any corresponding causal relation between entertainment violence and *violent crimes*. The criminologists, too, find completely different factors from media essential (Hurwitz & Christiansen, 1983). In Sweden, for example, the cause of youth violence (which is not the most widespread; persons in their 30s and 40s commit most violent crimes) is in part societal changes. Young people nowadays are consumers instead of producers, and because of that control over them has lessened, and opportunities for crimes have increased through, among other things, the spread of cars, supermarkets, and the superfluity of goods. In addition, the risk of violent crimes is heightened by bad family conditions and by being in certain milieux and groups where narcotics or alcohol are present (Svensson, 1985; Sarnecki, 1988).

During the 1980s great resources were still invested to analyze the influence of TV violence according to this traditional approach, but the perspective also widened: Even though short term effects were studied, too, a characteristic trait of recent investigations is that they are made up of longitudinal field studies (often initiated in the 1970s); in which the same individuals have been followed in order to analyze causal relations in the long term. Furthermore, several new theoretical assumptions have been developed about the mental processes that lie behind or facilitate aggression. Neither is TV studied in isolation or in a vacuum as often as it used to be, but the role of family, school, and peers is more and more observed.

What the long term studies indicate, in sum (e.g., Milavsky, Kessler, Stipp, & Rubeuns, 1982; Huesmann & Eron, 1986; Viemerö, 1986; Sonesson, 1989) is that viewing of entertainment violence seems to explain *at the most* five to 10 percent of children's and young people's aggression over time (1–10 years), while at least 90%–95% of the aggression is dependent on other factors:the child's and adolescent's personality, capacities, and earlier aggression; conditions in family, school, and peer groups (for example, aggression at home, a school that does not encourage one's capacity, lack of popularity among peers); sociocultural background and societal conditions (although the last-mentioned conditions have not been empirically studied). Thus, the entertainment violence plays in the long (as in the short) run only a contributing role and comes in as a faint reinforcement in a syndrome of other far more important circumstances.

Moreover, certain longitudinal studies point to a reciprocal causal relation, a circular or spiral effect: the case is both that more aggressive children and adolescents seek entertainment violence, and that the entertainment violence reinforces the aggression. But, accordingly, in this interaction the latter causality appears to be somewhat stronger.

Besides the development towards longitudinal studies and more sophisticated and widened theories on the aggression and socialization processes, other effects, as well, have more and more been studied within the traditional approach, and many researchers underline that these are more relevant to examine than aggression. It is clear, for example, that media violence can be the source of *fear* among children and young people (e.g., von Feilitzen, 1981). Some studies also indicate that influences of a cognitive nature—for example, those who watch violence a lot are reinforced in their *norms and values*, and aggressive behavior is an adequate means of solving conflicts (e.g., Dominick & Greenberg, 1972). Another question is whether entertainment violence leads to erroneous *conceptions* of violence in real life (e.g., Johansson & Larsson, 1976; Cernerud, 1987). One may wonder, for instance, if children and adolescents, by watching entertaining violence, get insufficient understanding of how serious the consequences of blows and kicks can be. Still another type of influence is *emotional and cognitive desensitization or habituation* (decreased excitement, decreased fear, lowered inhibitions against violence), something that may make us indifferent and increasingly tolerate violence as an adequate solution of conflicts. Desensitization and habituation in the form of decreased excitement and fear after violence-as-entertainment has been verified in the short term (e.g., Thomas & Drabman, 1975, 1978; Roe, 1983). But nobody has yet been able to certify that desensitization and habituation after media violence also lead to an indifferent attitude towards violence in real life.

The traditional violence research has, during the 1980s, also given attention to new media, such as horror videos, violent music videos, and computer games based on aggression and the player's active participation. However, this research is similar to the earlier short-term TV and film research and is yet in its infancy.

Critical Question: What is Aggression?

Aggression means an attack. Attacking societal evils, defending oneself against oppression, and applying aggression to meaningful activity are examples of constructive aggressive acts; submission and inhibited aggression would in such cases be something negative. In public debate and in research, however, aggression has become a negatively loaded concept. What is referred to is, in fact, destructive aggression—injuring without a conscious end or assaulting and oppressing in order to maintain or strengthen a superior position. Similarly, there are problems with the concept of *violence*. Some violence, albeit not very much, can have positive consequences (as when smashing crockery relieves a person of her or his aggression).

The traditional studies on media violence would, then, become more fruitful if they were to leave the composite notion of aggression (which in many studies has been measured as general nuisance on the whole among children and young people) and in exchange were to differentiate between: (a) constructive aggression, violence with positive consequences, and aggression that is a defense or a struggle against oppression; and (b) destructive aggression, the negative consequences of violence and that aggression that is a real oppression.

Besides, several studies are very diffuse on whether they concern aggression in the form of feelings or actions. Likewise, research has emphasized physical aggression, something that often results in more aggression among boys than girls, among working class children/adolescents than middle class ones, or among adolescent gangs compared with adults. But such aggression may partly depend on gender differences, and on class and generation conflicts in society; partly it may be a way of expression that is more useful in boys'/working class/young people's intercourse and culture. At the same time this aggression may be only apparently higher—girls, members of the middle class, and adults, respectively, have more ways to express their aggression verbally. Middle-class individuals and adults can also more easily give aggression the shape of individual competition, achievement, and self-assertion at the expense of others, since these kinds of aggression are more appreciated and functional in their subcultures. Research ought to compensate for the biased view of aggression also in this sense.

Critical Question: Can Other Media Contents Contribute to Aggression?

The traditional research can be criticized not only for its biased definition of aggression, but also because only in exceptional cases has it dealt with influences on entities other than the individual, for instance on groups, politics, industry, culture in a wide sense, societies, animals, and nature. Furthermore it has focused on manifest physical (sometimes verbal) entertainment violence. Thus, even if there are exceptions, the effect research is meager regarding the realistic, the psychic, the structural, and the latent violence. Moreover, energy has been directed towards popular culture and not towards high culture in media output.

For a long time some researchers have asked themselves, too, if violence is really required in the program or film for viewers to become more aggressive. The theory of emotional arousal, or the instigation theory, which is empirically supported by studies with adults, points to the possibility that any media content, in fact, that is found exciting or inspires strong feelings, reinforces the viewer's mood already prior to viewing (aggression, depression, or erotic disposition, among other things). This leads in the short run to more intensive behavior corresponding to that very mood (Tannenbaum, 1980).

Another assumption with empirical support is that sustained viewing of programs where the tempo is very fast contributes to aggressive and uneasy behavior, so-called *hyperactivity*, among young children (Singer & Singer, 1983).

A third hypothesis is that a great deal of the entertainment media output as a whole contributes to increased expectations in the viewer about a more glamorous life-style, expectations that cannot be fulfilled for all groups due to their relative deprivation in society. The result may be frustration, which in its turn can be a cause of aggression (e.g., Halloran, Brown, & Chaney, 1970a). Such a possible influence of the media is reinforced by a societal development that is also built on steadily increasing expectations—societies that emphasize increased production, increased consumption, achievement, and individual competition, in spite of the fact that different groups have different economic, social, and cultural possibilities of realizing such goals (von Feilitzen, 1975).

It is conceivable that media advertising, as well, might lead to too-high expectations and frustration (and therefore aggression) within the viewer. Content analyses show that advertising is characterized by images where leisure and well-being dominate, by an existence free of conflicts and full of glamour, and by the hedonistic message that it is a pleasure and associated with happiness to own and consume. Furthermore, the values in advertising have an indirect impact via programming, as many TV programs are financed by enterprises that have the object of reaching as large an audience as possible, and therefore most often avoid contents that may appear objectionable to the audience (von Feilitzen, 1987).

The assumption that general entertainment output and advertising might lead to frustration and aggression is, in fact, in the light of criminal statistics, more plausible than the assumption that media violence does so. By way of example, since the 1960s Sweden has had only a slight increase in the number of violent crimes. On the other hand, we have had a substantial increase in theft and other economic criminality (Svensson, 1985; Sarnecki, 1988).

More direct and short-term evidence of "aggression effects" of advertising comes from the United States. Children want sweets and toys, for instance, which they have seen in the TV ads, and they become dissatisfied and angry when their parents try to offer resistance. Moreover, advertising sometimes contributes to an unpleasant and irritated atmosphere during viewing, when the ads make breaks in a funny or exciting program, or when the fast tempo and the high sound level instill uneasiness and aggressivity (Atkin, 1980).

PERSPECTIVE II: THE POWER OF CULTURE

During the 1960s and 1970s, many researchers in the field of mass communication came to view the media and media output as being part of the total cultural or symbolic environment, and so reflecting the values and/or myths of its society. This cultural environment—which, according to Williams's (1974) definition, is sometimes thought of as a flow—in turn has power over the culture as whole, nourishing it and exerting a long-term influence over it. The cultural environment is a life-long reflection of (and influence on) individuals' common world views, ideals, norms, and values. This view is rooted in the critical theory of the Frankfurt school, Gramsci's theory of media hegemony, structuralism, semiotics, linguistics, and anthropology, among other things. It opposes the concentration of traditional research on the specific effects of specific media and on the effects of specific media contents on specific individuals.

The media contents may, thus, be regarded as a ritual, cultural narrative according to linguistic conventions and form traditions (genres). The myths being told symbolize the collective discomforts and pleasures of human, subcultural, and national character (people's problems, conflicts, anguish, uneasiness, fear, fantasies, wishes, hopes, dreams, needs of identification). For instance, Girard (1972) has presumed the media staging of crime and punishment to be a conjuring rite of sacrifice with the function of reassuring an anxious audience, diverting insight into the real state of things, and maintaining social order. The idea is that media violence is escalating when the social system of law and control is weakening and the crimes in society are increasing. The increasing criminality is, in reality, desirable for societal economy, as it keeps the market of products and services going. But for the audience the media give an illusion that crime will not do and that crimes are cleared up, and therefore the social machinery is relieved of blame.

More empirically based research is represented by Gerbner and his colleagues (e.g., Gerbner, Gross, Morgan, & Signorielli, 1986; Signorielli & Morgan, 1990), who, through their cultural indicators approach and cultivation analyses, have performed continuous content analyses of the violence on TV and correlated them with studies on children and adults in the population. The results indicate that the audience, due to TV viewing, can get exaggerated ideas of the amount and kind of violence in society. Such erroneous conceptions can, in their turn, give rise to fear in the viewer of meeting with violence himself or herself—perhaps when walking alone in a park—as well as to a pessimistic outlook that it is impossible to trust people and that the state of things in the world is just getting worse. This wrongly founded fear and pessimism might, further, lead to more clamoring for law and order and increased dependence on authorities.

In spite of the fact that the cultivation analyses, in particular, have been criticized methodologically, "Gerbner-inspired" research has been performed in many countries. Perhaps as a result of national differences, these studies have yielded divergent results (e.g., Wobner & Gunter, 1988). In Sweden, for example, the amount of TV or video viewing generally has not been found to have such relationships, but identification and parasocial interaction during TV viewing seem to reinforce exaggerated conceptions of violence in real life in young people (Hedinsson, 1981; Wall, 1987).

Cannot news violence also influence conceptions of violence in real life? In Sweden many adolescents overrate the number of real murders and manslaughters, and believe, too, that violence among the young has become more brutal, probably as a result of how the violence is presented in the news (Wall, 1987). Press and TV news often greatly exaggerate how violent the violence is (e.g., Halloran, Elliot, & Murdock, 1970b). A well-known study in the British cultural studies tradition on how a row between adolescent gangs was overdramatized by the press shows what the further consequences can be (Cohen, 1972). Even though all causal relations in the link are not clearly confirmed, there is nevertheless support for the claim that this vilifying of adolescent groups led to a groundless moral panic among the newspaper readers, which legitimized more police actions and contributed to a more antagonistic attitude between the gangs than existed originally—something that in its turn, led to more news about the violence and further escalated the moral panic. Hall, Chritcher, Jefferson, Clarke, and Roberts (1978) has used other empirical data to further develop the theory on this deviancy amplification spiral and connected it to racial conflicts, economic crises in society, political disagreement, and readiness for governmental control, which were at hand even before the fictitious news in the media. Fictional as well as nonfictional portrayal of terrorism and political violence, which is often described by the media as threat beyond human control, can have similar functions (Schlesinger, Murdock, & Elliott, 1983).

According to this perspective, then, culture defines for the people both the violent events that are important and how the events should be interpreted. Fictional and nonfictional violence appear to contribute to a public opinion that reinforces the interests of the dominating strata of society and legitimizes that strata's means of control.

But, latently imbedded in the violence-as-entertainment, there is another kind of victimization, too (Gerbner, 1980). In U.S. TV programming there is a pecking order that includes those who commit the violence and those who are subjected to it. At the top, among the assailants, there are white male adults; at the bottom, among the victims, are women, elderly people, black people, members of the working class, children, adolescents, and poor people. Thus, the dramatized commission of violence seems, as a matter of fact, to reflect the societal hierarchy of power. This, too, indicates that TV is the cultural control of society that has the function to maintain social order.

Moreover, the categories of people who are victims in this myth of aggression correspond to those groups in the media culture generally that, according to much empirical research, are more or less symbolically annihilated—women, children, old people, the working class, people with occupations of low prestige, and linguistic, ethnic and other minority and immigrant groups. The underrepresented groups are depicted in less diversified and more uninteresting roles as well, or in a ridiculous, comical, and villainous way. Even certain peoples as a whole are often negatively depicted in the media output of other nations.

Underrepresentation and a negative portrayal of a group or a people may have several undesirable consequences (e.g., von Feilitzen, 1984). Prejudices that the majority of the audience brings to the screen might be reinforced, in some cases prejudices might be created, and the idea about the marginality of the subordinated groups may be heightened. For the subordinated groups in the audience, the symbolic annihilation may be conceived of as contributing to a weakened identity and self-esteem, less solidarity with equals, and continued internalized oppression by means of transferring low self-esteem to the next generation. Besides, it is possible that these groups may accept their subordinated situation, as well as other people's hegemony in society—they may accept the right of the *superior* groups to continue dominating and committing destructive aggression. At the same time there is a tendency for a person who is oppressed himself or herself to oppress those who are still more subordinated. Thus, it is a question about a cultural violence that might have far worse influences than the manifest violent content.

Critical Question: Are the Effects of Media Violence and the Power of Culture Always Something Negative?

The dramatized and the true-to-life media violence, or the valuating reflection of power in the culture, ought to give the audience insight into the causes and consequences of violence/power, and, in this way, *realistic conceptions* reinforce *democratic norms and values* and contribute to *constructive actions.* In all likelihood such cultural contents with positive influences exist, although the traditional media violence research, as well as the research on the power of culture, have focused on negative consequences—something for which these perspectives have been criticized.

Another positive influence is *excitement.* Violence, hatred, and death—and power, fame, and money—are, like love, important phenomena for the individual and therefore exciting. They have a dramatic value in themselves, which agrees with the audience's preferences, needs, and identification. They are particularly exciting if they are portrayed dramatically—as conflicts or struggles with threats and obstacles—and if they mean testing where the limits are, for example defying something forbidden or showing what the characters are ultimately able to do, dare, and endure.

It is, however, wrong to believe that entertainment violence as such always inspires feelings of excitement. The human being's need for excitement is not the same as an alleged genuine need for entertainment violence. TV programs other than those with entertainment violence—sports, other fiction, erotic programs, quizzes, and news—are sometimes felt to be more exciting. (Berg & von Feilitzen, 1979; Pearl, Bouthilet, & Lazar, 1982).

Excitement and *fear* are emotions along the same dimension, at least if one believes in Spinoza's (1678/1959) analysis of the contents and mutual connection of different feelings. He would have called positive excitement hope with a little strain of fear. Negative excitement (fear), on the other hand, consists, according to Spinoza, of fear with a little strain of hope. It is also shown empirically that those kinds of media contents that children and adolescents like because they are exciting often are the same as those that are frightening. Children and young people *want* to be a little frightened (von Feilitzen, 1989a).

The ability to become afraid is a biological gift, a condition of survival. Accordingly, more genuine fear can have positive consequences, for instance when it makes us guard ourselves against real external dangers like accidents, assaults, and outrages of power and fight them.

It is also conceivable that media fear is positive in another way— if the symbolic vicarious experience of fear relieves the individual of real inner agony, if it lifts up unconscious and tabooed conflicts and problems to a more conscious level. Such hypotheses about catharsis (purification), which are quite common in the next perspective dealt with here, come from Aristotle's ideas on the Greek tragedy (3rd century B.C.), Bettelheim's (1975) view of folktales, and psychoanalysis. Catharsis on a societal level may be imagined, too, if the media reproduction of myths of violence and power relations releases human fantasy, treats collectively experienced problems, and functions as rituals in an anthropological sense.

But there are no empirical data that support the hypothesis of catharsis being the decisive influence. Also, *arguments* can be found against the assumption that precisely what the entertainment violence would be releasing. According to Aristotle not all tragedies purify fear—only a good tragedy can do so. Moreover, he put up a number of demands that a tragedy should meet to be good. Much of the entertainment violence of today, which is based on exterior effects and does not situate the violence in a well-motivated context, does not fulfill these demands (von Feilitzen, 1978). Similarly, Bettelheim asserts that only the genuine fairy tale can further the child's experience. Among other things, the fairy tale has to agree with the child's emotional experience and needs, and the unraveling has to give self-confidence and hope about future. The fact that violence-as-entertainment attracts young people certainly means that it partly agrees with their needs and conflicts. But does it give self-confidence and hope about the future? A treatment and relief of the fictional media violence seems mainly to occur for especially imaginative children (Biblow, 1973).

Neither has the mass communication theory that posits cathartic effects for the individual—that the vicarious experience of viewing entertainment violence relieves the viewer from prior *aggression* so that he or she becomes *less* aggressive after viewing (Feshbach, 1955, 1961; Feshbach & Singer, 1971)—received much empirical support. However, perhaps such *smaller* cathartic effects can occur, even though they do not neutralize other influences or are not the most common aggressive influence.

Quite another thing is the idea, mentioned above, that aggression in certain cases can be something positive.

Also, *imitation* of violent acts can sometimes be desirable, especially for small children. Imitation and play are fundamental factors in the socialization process, and both function as a working upon, and freeing oneself from, impressions, and as a learning of things. Thus, even if imitation sometimes means learning by modelling (negative impact), it is, from the view of treating impressions, now and then necessary (positive impact) for children after watching entertainment violence (Feilitzen, 1989a).

Critical Question: Are Different Kinds of Influences Valid for Different Individuals?

We have seen how excitement and fear can sometimes be connected, and that decreased excitement and fear can imply desensitization. Moreover, erroneous conceptions of violence seem to result in fear and uneasiness (and reinforce prevalent societal interests). Nor is it, in principle, impossible that smaller effects of catharsis can occur during viewing, even though viewing of violence contributes somewhat more to increased aggression. The complex relations between different kinds of influences of media violence are far from clear, however. Let us take a closer look at the relation between aggression and fear.

Certain empirical results from the traditional media violence research point to either fear or aggression (if anything at all) after entertainment violence (Björkqvist, 1985). As more viewing of violence can lead to desensitization in the form of decreased fear reactions, is it, then, this process that paves the way for increased aggression?

Some researchers are of that opinion. It is contradictory to other results, indicating that fear and aggression act together in a spiral in the same children. In some children agony and aggression can bring about increased viewing of exciting violent programming that in its turn both causes more fear and reinforces the aggression (Viemerö, 1986; Sonesson, 1989).

At the same time anxious children are often the nonaggressive ones (Viemerö, 1986). And some children find fictional violence frightening and therefore dissociate themselves from it, while others, who are more aggressive themselves, find entertainment violence less violent, appreciate it more, and identify more with it (van der Voort, 1986).

However, a frightening film can also be worked upon quite differently. While certain children frankly show their anxiety, others become anxious and activate various defensive strategies, and still others become anxious and aggressive. (Moore & Wallqvist, 1979). For certain children this last-mentioned aggression may be a constructive treatment of fear. For others it may be that wrongly treated fear becomes problematic and grows into more permanent uneasiness, anxiety, or destructive aggression (von Feilitzen, 1981).

In sum, different persons experience excitement, violence, horror, and power—as well as other media and cultural contents—very differently, need it differently, and attach different meanings to it. In order to understand these processes, research has to consider the fact that the causes for influences of media violence and culture are not only the manifest and latent depictions of violence and power as such, but also the individual's situation and intentions in the use of media.

PERSPECTIVE III: THE ACTIVE AUDIENCE

The traditional media violence research and the perspective of the powerful culture have been criticized for looking upon the media output as too homogeneous, media and cultural influences as too negative, and the individual as too passive. A contributing cause, it is said, is that the studies seldom have been profound and qualitative with smaller groups for whom the media are of more or less importance. The media may have an agenda-setting function (McCombs & Shaw, 1972), defining for the audience what to think and talk about it—but not *how* to think about it. Much empirical research shows that individuals, both adults and children, are active in the process. Each person will select media content according to his or her own specific aims, pay attention to it, and comprehend and remember what is useful and has meaning to him or her. Each individual will interpret the media content in his or her own special way. The individual is creative and partly construes his or her own media content based on his or her own gender, sociocultural background, experience, interests, expectations, and needs, and through more or less imagination, identification, and emotional engagement. Family, peer groups, preschool, school, work, and various interested parties are often more essential than the media, and also often the cause for which media contents are used, what import is put into them, and which underlying meanings are perceived. "The texts" (media contents) are "read" on the basis of socially formed conventions and codes, but readers (viewers) of different subcultures may, thus, decode other meanings, oppositional or negotiating, from what was encoded (Hall, 1980).

Some empirical examples about media violence: Eight to 12-year-olds have the capacity to understand the underlying myth in a cartoon on a werewolf—to decode the media violence as a signifier of conflict. Construction of meaning also differed according to personality, gender, and class (Hodge & Tripp, 1986). Media violence, which in content analyses has been coded as equally violent, is seen as more or less violent by the audience, whether adults or children (van der Voort, 1986). Violence is perceived differently by different individuals, depending on which groups they belong to, normative expectations, and national cultural values. For example, British audiences interpret American and British media violence differently in several respects (Gunter & Wobner, 1988).

According to this theory, as a result of different personal interpretations and cultural competencies the media culture cannot become very homogeneous, and so cannot be so much a strong negative factor as a powerful exerciser of cultural control.

Some people, therefore, have described the worry about media violence in public debate as *moral panics*. And in line with Bourdieu's (1984) thought that tastes and preferences are part of cultural hierarchies, it is also claimed that the researchers—who belong to the dominating carriers of taste (the educated middle class with its verbal culture)—through their way of formulating the research problems, are cherishing the high culture, condemning the taste for popular culture as "bad," and by that also ascribing to the *people* with the bad taste (the working class who use the visual media more) a lower value. Adults' tastes and preferences, compared to children's, may be looked upon in a similar hierarchy.

Not least within the humanities, which earlier mostly paid attention to high culture or analyzed the ideology of popular culture critically, popular culture during the 1980s has been studied from the perspective of the active audience and their positive usage of it. The starting points include literary theory, reception theory, film theory, aesthetics, cultural history, anthropology, structuralism, linguistics, semiotics, and psychoanalysis. A certain amount of this media violence research implies drawing conclusions from textual analysis about the readers' use of the text and the needs it fulfills. Other research includes empirical qualitative (ethnographic, ethnomethodological) studies of readers' reception. But quantitative and/or social scientific studies are also at hand.

Among other things, researchers have tried to understand the fascination of media violence. One hypothesis (among many) is that in our postmodern, rational society we are allowed to give expression to our sadistic impulses less often than we would have been in earlier periods, and so we have become increasingly attached to media viewing (Hartwig, 1988). Another common conclusion is that a youth's viewing of film and video horror is a ritual of initiation, which on a deeper level means treatment of bodily and erotic crises of puberty, the feeling of isolation, psychic identity seeking, powerlessness against parents and school, and feelings of hatred and revenge for the oppression exercised by adults and bullying peers (Sjögren, 1985). Computer games, too, have been regarded as a way for the player to give vent to his or her feelings, since the intensive emotional fluctuations of puberty involve aggressions that must get an outlet (Breitenstein, 1989).

There is empirical support for the finding that TV viewers, children as well as adults, all within the frame of normality, often select programs to regulate their emotional state. One reason for choosing action, sensations, and strong feelings is boredom. For instance, adults with monotonous and tedious work (more often working class) choose action on television to decrease their weariness, whereas those who return home overstimulated and stressed (more often middle class) select more restful programs to reduce the stress (Zillman, 1980; Zillman & Bryant, 1986).

The context of reception also plays a role in the meaning of media violence. It has been shown that watching horror film fits into the socialization of gender-specific roles. Young men have a chance to show off their fearlessness—something expected of men—and young women to display fear response, obtain protection from men, and admire men for their heroics—something expected of women (Zillman, Weaver, Mundorf, & Aust, 1986). And the competent readers of action videos among teen-age boys, those who are acquainted with the filmic conventions and narrative structures, maintain, by means of their comments during viewing, their leading position in the group and their ability to control their less experienced companions (Rasmussen, 1989).

A subcultural stream of the research on the active audience starts from the total life situation of children and young people. Media and media contents, popular culture and popular music especially, are included as important ingredients, symbols and signs of children's and adolescents' own practices—their play and identity work, cultural forms of expression, development of life styles, and social acting. Also, the usage of media is related to sociocultural conditions, and the individual's cultural practices can sometimes signify protest and resistance that emancipatorily counteract dominant ideologies of media, family, school, and so on. This view is rooted in, among other things, West German socialization theory, British cultural studies, the uses-and-gratifications model, and a structural-cultural approach that combines traditional socioeconomic differences with new hierarchic differences caused by the explosion of education and by cultural capital.

Interviews with 15 and 16-year-olds has made it clear that viewing of violent and horror videos is a way of measuring toughness, a test of manliness in the circle of male peers, and also a countercultural manifestation of protest, as a consequence of negative attitudes to and low marks in school. The latter result is valid, as well, of special youth groups' adoption of less socially accepted forms of music, like punk and hard rock (Roe, 1983, 1984; Holmberg, 1988).

It ought to be underlined that since this media violence research has directed its energy on sub- and countercultures that are seen, heard, and noticed, mainly male and not female cultures have been observed. Watching films with extreme violence on TV, video, and in the cinema, and playing computer games are chiefly male occupations. The culture of violence is to a great extent built on male values.

Critical Question: What Happened to the Overall View?

Research on the active audience has constructively criticized perspectives that are too one-sided. At the same time, however, it has a tendency—*even if* the causes of aggression and violence are mainly to be found outside the media and culture—to ignore the fact that media output and culture nevertheless *have* influences in the short and long term. Often, those influences are negative. in all likelihood, the individual is *both* active, selective, working and creative, *and* positively and negatively influenced by the media and the environment. Moreover, even though the research perspective underlines the fact that the sociocultural situation plays a role for the usage of media, it disregards the fact that the communicators, the institutions, and the economy behind the popular products impinge upon the spreading and use of popular culture. Furthermore, it does not deal with the question of whether other political and economic forces in society exert an influence on media violence and culture.

Thus, the perspective of the active audience has a tendency to be too one-sided, as well; it places itself on a microlevel and over-emphasizes individualism and freedom of human acting. In addition, in its most simplified form it starts solely from the viewer's subjective opinions and needs. According to Rönnberg (1989), for example, that culture is good if the user likes it and finds good use for it; entertainment violence becomes automatically releasing, or children do not perceive the violence and then it is not violence. This populism too easily complies with the argument of the enter-tainment industry: "We give people what they want."

Carey (1978) says that different theories and results may be valid for different periods and societal circumstances. The fact that many now lay stress on the individual's activity might, accordingly, be a consequence of the individual's greater independence in the changing and flexible society of today. It could also be, however, that the *view* in itself of the individual as active and creative is functional for societal development. The high-technological, chang-ing society urgently needs independent, mobile individuals who cope with choosing among the contradictory pluralistic value systems. A theoretical view does not always tell what the whole is like. In other words, it *might* be that the researchers, due to the character of society, more or less unconsciously overemphasize the individual's activity.

PERSPECTIVE IV: ECONOMY AND POWER RELATIONS IN SOCIETY

Some researchers underline that the political, economic, tech-nological, and other material conditions in society, as well as the conditions of media production, direct culture, and media con-tents, owning, and power are, in their view, more fundamental factors of cultural control than thought structures. Even if media and cultural contents are admitted to exert a certain influence, this perspective is, consequently, more materialistic than, for example, the perspective of the power of culture.

During the 1980s, it was less common for researchers of media violence to emphasize societal economy and power relations as primary agents than it was for them to focus on the three perspec-tives already discussed in this chapter. Since the 1960s and 70s, more traditional Marxism has been kept at the periphery of many other social sciences as well.

Therefore, many fewer media and communications researchers have asked themselves how the media could survive while offering their audience sensational fictional violence, which is so often condemned. Few have come up with the same answer as De Fleur (1966), who concluded that the function of popular entertainment is to maintain the financial balance in the mass communication system, which is tightly integrated into the economy of the whole society. Not many researchers have followed up Schiller's (e.g., 1976) analyses of the economic structure and technological development of the media industry, its relationship to the military, space, computer, and telecommunication industries, transnational enterprises, and other world traders—a development, according to that theory, that means that companies such as American Motors and General Foods have an interest in disseminating entertainment violence in the industrialized and Third World countries.

But research on media violence becomes distorted if it does not also ask questions about the policy-making process of the media and the political and economic institutions and control agencies that feed and sustain the media (Murdock, 1982). A 1980s analysis of the reasons why research has not been able to make the media industry in the United States reduce the violence also indicates that the violence is partly a question of cultural values rooted in the whole of American society, and in part the economic factors that steer the industry are too strong (Rowland, 1983).

As entertainment violence and certain other media violence is economically functional for society, it legitimizes the activity of the media. Several studies that we have mentioned earlier seem to show that media violence is functional for society in other respects as well. Depictions of violence reflect the power of hierarchy and in so doing appear to legitimize and reinforce it, stabilize economic structures, and be convenient to the intentions of established groups and institutions.

Analyses of violence and power in the media and culture can, then, be a starting point, not only for further studies about its influence on the audience, but also for studies about societal conditions, particularly if comparisons of media outputs and cultures are made between nations and in an historical perspective. What does it mean, for instance, that in Japanese television entertainment, compared to that of the United States, the hero is more often subject to violence, and the suffering is shown more clearly and for a longer time? What does it mean that U.S. TV entertainment, the subject of violence is more often the villain, and the consequences of violence are shown to a much lesser extent or not at all (Iwao, de Sola Pool, & Hagiwara, 1981)? What does it mean that the violence in American detective stories on TV is committed between two or a few individuals, and the motives for murder are almost exclusively to get hold of money or things (Nordlund, 1977)? And while American entertainment violence is individual and connected to personal success, achievement, and private property, the violence in Soviet drama programs, is, or at least during the 70s was, more often committed collectively and in order to support or counteract a society (Pietilä, 1976). (Since then, perhaps democratization, glasnost, and perestroika have had some importance for entertainment programming in the former Soviet Union.)

Next, what does it mean that the entertainment programming exported over the globe emanates chiefly from the United States (Nordenstreng & Varis, 1974; Varis, 1985; UNESCO, 1989)?

One explanation may be that the violence is produced, imported, and presented in different cultural contexts, and that the function is to reinforce the norms and values of the society in question. However, cultural or symbolic violence does not only have different meanings in different nations and epochs, and different ways of glorifying and condemning violence are not only due to different cultural intentions—but also to other social conditions (Golding & Middleton, 1982).

A political, economic, and cultural elite dominates the media institutions as well as the media output—both through its presence and its ideology—*because* it has a stronger economic function in society, a greater political power, and a more extensive cultural influence. With another economy and other power relations, culture would, consequently, be different. In the interplay between media violence, culture, the individual and the economy, and power relations in the society, the last-mentioned are, after all, the motor of the changes—those decisive of, among other things, the manifestations, functions, and influences of the media violence and media power (Feilitzen, 1989b).

CONCLUDING REMARKS

Media violence research has been criticized for not asking the right questions. However, the policy questions it asks are important, and they will continue to be asked as long as recent research on media violence and power, with its redefinitions of the research problem, can be of some practical importance. Can the research change the media output and culture for the better, or will any changes that it produces be irrelevant and merely surface-level, as the changes made by more traditional media violence research have been? The examples of research perspectives in the 1980s seem to indicate that if the research of the 1990s is to properly comprehend the import of the media violence and get any practical results, it must be diachronous, focus on processes, and be directed by an overall view; that is, it must embrace the media violence as well as the power of culture, the active audience and the economy, power relations, and media technology in society. Quite likely, it must also combine teleological understanding and causal explanations, quantitative and qualitative methodology. In particular, comparative studies between different countries and periods ought to be carried out, and the results would be clearer if the analyses are performed in parts of the world where great changes are occurring.

REFERENCES

Atkin, C.K. (1980). Effects of television advertising on children. In E.L. Palmer & A. Dorr (Eds.), *Children and the faces of television. Teaching, violence, selling.* New York: Academic Press.

Berg, U., & Feilitzen, C. von (1979). *Metodstudie om spännande program.* Publik- och programforskningsavdelningen, nr 19. Stockholm: Sveriges Rado.

Bettelheim, B. (1975). *The uses of enchantment: The meaning and importance of fairy tales.* London: Thames and Hudson.

Biblow, E. (1973). Imaginative play and the control of aggressive behavior. In J.L. Singer (Ed.), *The child's world of make believe.* London: George Allen & Unwin.

Björkqvist, K. (1985). *Violent films, anxiety and aggression: Experimental studies of the effect of violent films on the level of anxiety and aggression in children.* Helsinki: Commentationes Scientiarm Socialium.

Bourdieu, P. (1984). *Distinction: A social critique of the judgment of taste.* London: Routledge & Kegan Paul.

Breitenstein, O. (1989). *Spela basket i vardagsrummet. Om datorspel. Uppväxtvillkor,* nr 1, 59–64.

Carey, J. (1978). The ambiguity of policy research. *Journal of Communication, 28*(2), 114–119.

Cernerud, L. (1987). *Skolhälsovardens verksamhet.* Stockholms skolor.

Cohen, S. (1972). *Folk devils and moral panics: The creation of the Mods and Rockers.* London: MacGibbon & Kee.

DeFleur, M. (1966). *Theories of mass communication.* New York: David McKay.

Dominick, J.R., & Greenberg, B.S. (1972). *Attitudes toward violence: The interaction of television exposure, family attitudes, and social class.* In G.A. Comstock, & E.A. Rubinstein (Eds.), *Television and social behavior, Vol III: Television and adolescent aggressiveness* (pp. 314–335). Washington, DC: U.S. Department of Health, Education, and Welfare.

Feilitzen, C. von. (1975). *Children and television in the socialization process.* Stockholm: Swedish Broadcasting Corporation, Audience and Programme Research Department.

Feilitzen, C. von. (1978). Aristotles, katharsis och underhallningsvald. *Författaren,* 1/2, 22–26.

Feilitzen, C. von. (1981). Barns rädsla och tv. *Barn och Kultur,* 27(6), 123–130.

Feilitzen, C. von. (1984). On the cultural oppression of children. In G. Melischek, K.E. Rosengren, & J.G. Stappers (Eds.), *Cultural indicators: An international symposium* (pp. 71–84). Wien: Verlag der Österreichischen Akademie der Wissenschaften.

Feilitzen, C. von. (1987). *Barnet i ett samhälle med masskommunikation och konsumtion. n ForbrukerlAEre i utdanningen av fOrskolelAErare* (pp. 40–58). Nordiska Ministerradet, NEK rapport nr 7.

Feilitzen, C. von. (1989a). Spänning, rädsla, aggression och vald. In C. von Feilitzen, L. Filipson, I. Rydin, & I. Schyller (Eds.), *Barn och unga i mediealdern. Fakta i ord och siffror* (pp. 188–208). Stockholm: Rabén & Sjögren.

Feilitzen, C. von. (1989b). Ungdomar som problem ideal och identitetssöokare. Synen pa ungdomar i mediekulturen. In H. Wulff (Ed.), *Ungdom och medier. Klass, kommersialism och kreativitet.* Stockholm: Stockholms universitet, Centrum för masskommunikationsforskning, MASS 17.

Feshbach, S. (1955). The drive-reducing function of fantasy behavior. *Journal of Abnormal and Social Psychology,* 50(1), 3–11.

Feshbach, S. (1961). The stimulating versus cathartic effects of a vicarious aggressive activity. *Journal of Abnormal and Social Psychology,* 63(2), 381–385.

Feshbach, S., & Singer, R.D. (1971). *Television and aggression: An experimental field study.* San Francisco: Jossey Bass.

Gerbner, G. (1980). Children and power on television: The other side of the picture. In G. Gerbner, C.J. Ross, & E. Zigler (Eds.), *Child abuse: An analysis and agenda for action.* New York: Oxford University Press.

Gerbner, G., Gross, L., Morgan, M., & Signorielli, N. (1986). Living with television. The dynamics of the cultivation process. In J. Bryant & D. Zillman (Eds.), *Perspectives on media effects* (pp. 17–40). Hillsdale, NJ: Erlbaum.

Girard, R. (1972). *La violence et le sacré.* Paris: Bernard Grasset.

Golding, P., & Middleton, S. (1982). *Images of welfare: Press and public attitudes.* Oxford: Martin Robertson & Co.

Gunter, B., & Wober, M. (1988). *Violence on television. What the viewers think*. London: John Libbey & IBA.

Hall, S. (1980). Encoding/decoding. In S. Hall, D. Hobson, A. Lowe, & P. Willis (Eds.), *Culture, media, language* (pp. 128–138). London: Hutchinson.

Hall, S., Chritcher, C., Jefferson, T., Clarke, J., & Roberts, B. (1978). *Policing the crisis. Mugging, the state, and law and order*. London: MacMillan.

Halloran, J.D., Brown, R.L., & Chaney, D.C. (1970a). *Television and delinquency* (Television Research Committee, Working Paper No. 3). Leicester, UK: Leicester University Press.

Halloran, J.D., Elliott, P., & Murdock, G. (1970b). *Demonstrations and communication: A case study*. Harmondswort, UK: Penguin Books.

Hartwig, H. (1988). *Grymhetens bilder, bildernas grymhet. Skräck och fascination i gamla och nya media*. Göteborg: Daidalos.

Hedinsson, E. (1981). *TV, family and society. The social origins and effects of adolescents' TV use*. Stockholm: Almqvist & Wiksell International.

Hodge, B., & Tripp, D. (1986). *Children and television: A semiotic approach*. Cambridge, UK: Polity Press.

Holmberg, O. (1988). *Videovald och undervisning*. Stockholm/Lund: Symposion.

Huesmann, L.R., & Eron, L.D. (Eds.). (1986). *Television and the aggressive child: A cross-national comparison*. Hillsdale, NJ: Erlbaum.

Hurwitz, S., & Christiansen, K.O. (1983). *Criminology*. London: Allen Unwin.

Iwao, S., de Sola Pool, I., & Hagiwara, S. (1981). Japanese and U.S. media: Some cross-cultural insights into TV violence. *Journal of Communication, 31*(2), 28–36.

Johansson, B., & Larsson, G-B. (1976). *Barns tankar om döden*. Stockholm: Natur och Kultur.

McCombs, M.E., & Shaw, D. (1972). The agenda-setting function of the press. *Public Opinion Quarterly, 36*, 176–87.

Milavsky, J.R., Kessler, R.C., Stipp, H.H., & Rubens, W.S. (1982). *Television and aggression: A panel study*. New York: Academic Press.

Moore, R., & Wallqvist, I. (1979). *Försvarsstrategier och beteenden hos femoch sex-aringar vid oroskapande film*. Lund: Lunds universitet, Institutionen för tillämpad psykologi.

Murdock, G. (1982). Mass communication and social violence: A critical review of recent research trends. In P. Marsh & A. Campbell (Eds.), *Aggression and violence* (pp. 62–90). Oxford: Basil Blackwell.

Nordenstreng, K., & Varis, T. (1974). *Television traffic—A one-way street? A survey and analysis of the international flow of television programme material*. Paris: Unesco.

Nordlund, R. (1977). *PM angaende underhallningsvald*. Stockholm: Radionämnden.

Pearl, D., Bouthilet, L., & Lazar, J. (Eds.). (1982). *Television and behavior. Ten years of scientific progress and implications for the eighties.* Washington, DC: U.S. Department of Health and Human Services.

Pietilä, V. (1976). Notes on violence in the mass media. *Instant Research on Peace and Violence, VI*(4), 195–197.

Rasmussen, H.A. (1989). Actionfilm og drengekultur. In L. Hojbjerg (Ed.), *Reception af levende billeder* (pp. 221–234). Kobenhavn: Akademisk Forlag.

Roe, K. (1983). *The influence of video technology in adolescence.* Lund: Lundsuniversitet, Sociologiska institutionen, Mediapanel nr 27.

Roe, K. (1984). *Youth and music in Sweden. Results from a longitudinal study of teenagers' media use.* Lund: Lunds universitet, Sociologiska institutionen, Mediapanel nr 32.

Rönnberg, M. (1989). *Skitkul! Om s k skräpkultur.* Uppsala: Filmförlaget.

Rowland, W.D., Jr. (1983). *The politics of TV violence: Policy uses of communication research.* Beverly Hills, CA: Sage.

Sarnecki, J. (1988). *Föredrag om valdet i samhället.* Stockholm: Folkpartiets Kvinnoförbund, Studieförbundet Vuxenskolan, 12 mars.

Schiller, H. (1976). *Communication and cultural domination.* New York: International Arts and Sciences Press.

Schlesinger, P., Murdock, G., & Elliot, P. (1983). *Televising terrorism. Political violence in popular culture.* London: Comedia Publishing Group.

Signorielli, N., & Morgan, M. (1990). *Cultivation analysis. New directions in media effects research.* Newbury Park, CA: Sage.

Singer, J.L., & Singer, D.G. (1983). Implications of childhood television viewing for cognition, imagination and emotion. In J. Bryant, & D.R. Anderson (Eds.), *Children's understanding of television.* London: Academic Press.

Sjögren, O. (1985). Den förbannade tröskeln. Skräckfilm som modern övergangsrit. In T.M. Forselius & S. Luoma-Keturi (Eds.), *Valdet mot ögat. Filmforskareom film-och videoskräck* (pp. 13–58). Stockholm: Författarförlaget.

Sonesson, I. (1989). *Vem fostrar vara barn—videon eller vi? TV, video och emotionell och social anpassning.* Stockholm: Esselte studium.

Spinoza, B. (1959) (original work published 1678). *Ethics.* London: J.M. Dent & Sons.

Svensson, B. (1985). Välfärd och kriminalitet i Sverige. *BRA Apropa, 11*(1), 25–32.

Tannenbaum, P.H. (1980). Entertainment as vicarious emotional experience. In P.H. Tannenbaum (Ed.), *The entertainment functions of television* (pp. 107–131). Hillsdale, NJ: Erlbaum.

Thomas, M.H., & Drabman, R.S. (1975). Toleration of real life aggression as a function of exposure to televised violence and age of subject. *Merrill-Palmer Quarterly, 21*(3), 227–232.

Thomas, M.H., & Drabman, R.S. (1978). Effects of television violence on expectations of others' aggression. *Personality and Social Psychology Bulletin, 4*(1), 73–76.

Unesco. (1989). *World communication report.* Paris: Unesco.

Varis, T. (1985). *International flow of television programs* (Reports and papers on mass communication, No. 100) Paris: Unesco.

Viemerö, V. (1986). *Relationships between filmed violence and aggression.* Abo: Abo Akademi, Department of Psychology.

Voort, T.H.A. van der (1986). *Television violence: A child's-eye view.* Amsterdam: North-Holland.

Wall, J. (1987). Enkätundersökning - rapport. Hur använder ungdomar video?. In Eklundh, C. *Videovald. En rapport fran valdsskildringsutredningen* (pp. 89–114). Stockholm: Utbildningsdepartementet, DsU.

Williams, R. (1974). *Television. Technology and cultural form.* Glasgow: Collins/Fontana.

Wober, M. & Gunter, B. (1988). *Television and social control.* Avebury, UK: Gower.

Zillman, D. (1980). Anatomy of suspense. In P.H. Tannenbaum (Ed.), *The entertainment functions of television* (pp. 133–163). Hillsdale, NJ: Erlbaum.

Zillman, D., & Bryant, J. (1986). Exploring the entertainment experience. In J. Bryant & D. Zillman (Eds.), *Perspectives on media effects* (pp. 303–324). Hillsdale, NJ: Erlbaum.

Zillman, D., Weaver, J.B., Mundorf, N., & Aust, C.F. (1986). Effects of an opposite-gender companion's affect to horror on distress, delight, and attraction. *Journal of Personality and Social Psychology, 51,* 586–594.

CHAPTER

Visualizing Violence: Television and the Discourse of Disorder

GRAHAM MURDOCK

Over the last two decades or so, a damaging division has developed within the study of television. On the one side stand the political economists, sociologists, and political scientists, whose major interest is in the organization of broadcasting systems and their links to wider social, economic, and political formations. On the other side stand the practitioners of cultural studies, who approach television as a key site for the articulation of public discourse and are mainly concerned with the way meaning is organized in programs and negotiated by audiences.

This bifurcation is unsustainable theoretically and profoundly unhelpful to the development of a more comprehensive account of the way television works in modern societies (Murdock, 1989). What is needed now is a renewed commitment to exploring the interplay between the two dimensions of television's relation to contemporary life. The presentation of violence provides an interesting departure point for this enterprise, since how we define and explain violence within our major public medium is central to sustaining our conceptions of power, legitimacy, and social order.

This perception forms the basis of the work on cultural indicators developed by George Gerbner and his colleagues at the Annenberg School. As he puts it, "TV violence is a dramatic demonstration of power which shows who gets away with what, when, why, how and against whom" (Gerbner & Gross 1976a, p. 178). Because his elaboration of this basic insight offers the most comprehensive counter to the discourse of effects research that we have, it has become something of an alternative orthodoxy. Most of the criticisms leveled against it have centered on his investigations of audience cultivation effects. His analysis of representations has attracted rather less attention. Yet, as I shall argue, they are based on assumptions that need to be surpassed if we are to move the debate forward and open up new lines of research inquiry.

MESSAGES AND DISCOURSE

Gerbner concentrates on the major forms of televised fiction— series, comedies, and movies—broadcast in prime time. He sees these programs as constituting a "message system" with a relatively stable structure. His aim is to identify the "repetitive pattern of television's mass-produced messages and images" through an analysis of the "gross, unambiguous and commonly understood facts of portrayal" (Gerbner, Gross, Jackson-Beeck, Jeffries-Fox, & Signorielli, 1978 p. 178). Accordingly, his research team is under instructions to count "only clear, unambiguous, overt physical violence" that involves actual hurt or the credible threat of harm (p. 179). This definition immediately rules out any analysis of talk about violence. Yet the meaning of any violent act is seldom clear and unambiguous. It has to be negotiated within the text through discussion and argument among the principle characters. Talk about violence—in the form of interviews, studio discussions, and presenters' commentaries—is even more central to news and current affairs output. By excluding these program categories from his analysis, Gerbner underestimates both the importance of discourse within the television system and the mediating role of cultural forms.

It is instructive to compare his approach to the analysis of U.S. prime-time TV that Raymond Williams (1974) offers in *Television: Technology and Cultural Form*, which he wrote while visiting the Department of Communications at Stanford. Like Gerbner he accepts that people watch television rather than particular programs so that their "characteristic experience is one of sequence or flow" (p. 86) linked by a series of metathemes or master values. At the same time he continues to insist that form is crucial in organizing discourse, producing variations in the meaning of ostensibly similar acts.

Gerbner acknowledges that "not all violence is alike" and that "a blow by the oppressed against unbearable odds or by the exploited against the exploiter may be a message of liberation rather than of established power. (Gerbner & Gross, 1980, p. 153). But he argues that such exceptions are rare and do not effect the remarkable consistency in the general patterns of televised drama. In his view, "different time and programme segments complement and reinforce each other as they present aspects of the same symbolic world" (Gerbner & Gross, 1980, p. 159). This assumption of a unitary symbolic system misses the fundamental point that the raw material out of which TV programs are made is not individual depictions of overt aggression but the discourses that define and explain them by placing them within wider meaning systems. Violence is not so much a quantity that can be counted as it is a form of action whose meaning—in any particular instance—has to be established through discourse and may be open to dispute.

Although Gerbner's work runs counter to the core assumptions of effects research in some respects, it shares the same basic *transportation* model of meaning, which regards cultural forms as vehicles for moving overt content from one place to another. To get beyond this, we need to develop a *translation* model, which sees television as an organizational system for converting social discourses into completed programs through the mediation of specific cultural forms.

Since the notion of *discourse* is central to my argument, I should make it clear that I am using the term in a particular sense. Recent years have seen an explosion of work in this general area and a corresponding proliferation of definitions. As a result it is now "perfectly possible to have two books on discourse analysis with no overlap in content at all" (Potter & Wetherell, 1987, p. 6). One of the main divisions is between researchers who focus on the organization of particular spoken or written texts, and those who are interested in exploring more general clusters of linguistic practice. If we are concerned with television as a signifying system, we need to combine both levels, the micro and macro. We clearly have to pay attention to the way discourse is organized within particular programs. But equally, we need to investigate the wider discursive systems that particular programs draw upon and rework. To avoid confusion, I will use the term *discursive formations* to describe these macrostructures.

Discursive formations are systematically organized ways of describing and explaining the social world or segments of it. They are historical phenomena that emerge at particular points in time and have traceable careers. They are made up of four main elements:

1. systems of classification and framing that situate particular phenomena within a grid of affinities and antagonisms;
2. preferred linguistic tags and images, which concretize these relations and provide detailed descriptions of who and what belongs inside and outside the relevant boundaries;
3. forms of argumentation and reasoning that legitimate these boundaries and explain the basis of the differences separating "us" from "them";
4. evaluative principles that convert differences into moral distinctions.

These formations provide a basic pool of discursive resources that can be drawn upon to produce particular instances of discourse, and it is in this restricted sense that I shall use the term here. *Thatcherism*, for example, is most usefully seen as a discursive formation constructed out of the myriad pronouncements of Mrs. Thatcher and her intellectual and political supporters, whereas a particular televised speech or interview given by Mrs. Thatcher is an example of discourse. These two levels are dynamically related. To continue in existence, discursive formations have to be reproduced and reconstituted through concrete discursive acts, in the course of which they are amplified, added to, and altered. This process, in turn, is part of a more general struggle to maintain the centrality and legitimacy of Thatcherism against the claims of counter discourses. To this end, "the Thatcherites have problematised and de-structured the political discourses of their opponents, and attempted to impose their own restructuring" (Fairclough, 1989, p. 178). More particularly, they have tried to combine the neoliberal discourse of the free market with the "organic conservative themes of tradition, family and nation, respectability, patriarchalism and order" (Hall, 1988, p. 2). Theoretically these emphases are clearly incompatible. As Marx grasped better than anyone, the dynamism of capitalist markets has no respect for traditional values and hierarchies or for national borders. But this does not matter since the crucial links are established through discursive practices that bypass theorists and appeal directly to the common sense of "ordinary people." Television plays a privileged role in these dynamics by virtue of its position as the central site for the public presentation of discourse.

DISCOURSE AND VIOLENCE

As Gerbner points out, messages about violence are also always messages about power and authority—about who has the right to use coercion and against whom, and in what circumstances it is legitimate to resist. Unfortunately, he does not follow the full logic of this argument through. Because his analytical procedures are only concerned with acts of interpersonal aggression, he fails to consider the crucial role of discursive formations in making them meaningful.

The need to do this becomes abundantly clear if we look at the case of *terrorism*. At first sight, it seems obvious what terrorism is. Certainly, Jeane Kirkpatrick, President Reagan's former representative at the United Nations, had no difficulty recognizing terrorism wherever she saw it. For her, "The first step in understanding politics is to see things as they are, without confusion or mystification—simply to observe who does what to whom. What the terrorist does is kill, maim, kidnap, torture. His victims may be schoolchildren, travelers...industrialists returning home from work, political leaders or diplomats" (Lost in the Terrorist Theatre, 1984, p. 44). This definition is operationalized in the statistics for terrorist incidents collected by the CIA and other official agencies in the major Western nations. They are frequently cited as authoritative indicators of levels of international terrorism. However, as Edward Epstein has argued, these acts of definition cannot be taken at face value. They have to be seen as part of a strategy of persuasion aimed at presenting the problem of terrorism in a way that advances the goals of American foreign policy. As he points out, "One of the commonest means of creating approval for particular aspects of policy is the use of political labelling...using emotionally positive terms to describe supposed friends of the United States and emotionally negative terms to malign enemies...terrorism is an excellent example of this process" (Epstein, 1977, p. 67).

To label an act as terroristic is to condemn it as unjustified and to accept the legitimacy of the state against which it is aimed. Political leaders of all persuasions understand this very well, which is why Mrs. Thatcher objected to some British journalists describing the opposition forces in Afghanistan as rebels (since this suggested an endorsement of the Soviet-backed government in Kabul) and argued forcefully for them to be called resistance fighters. Conversely, to accept the prevailing definition of international terrorism as directed primarily against friendly regimes is to ignore the ways in which states endorsed by the United States and her major Western allies use systematic terror against civilians as an instrument of rule. Nor are these arguments purely semantic. They have real and often fatal consequences. As the "dirty war" in Argentina demonstrates, by labelling their opponents as terrorists, the junta was able to justify the wholesale use of terror by the security forces. Their conception of who counted as a terrorist was elastic enough to embrace almost anyone who protested conditions in the country. As the then head of government, General Jorge Videla, put it, "a terrorist is not just someone with a gun or a bomb, but also someone who spreads ideas that are contrary to western and Christian civilization" (quoted in Latin American Bureau, 1982, p. 67). This definition extended to students protesting against high transport charges. Most of those arrested joined the more than 6,000 documented cases of people who had been made to disappear in the two years after the military first assumed power from Isabel Peron.

The meaning of these events is therefore open to two diametrically opposed interpretations, depending on whether one works with the definitions of retail terrorism promoted by the dominant discursive formation and extended by the junta, or with the alternative definition, which locates the problem with the wholesale terror practiced by secret states (see Chomsky & Herman, 1979, pp. 6–7, 85–95).

Another instructive example of the way in which the meaning of events depends on the mobilization of discursive formations is provided by the media coverage of the inner city riots in Britain in 1981. These were major incidents of public disorder involving running battles between police and young people, particularly black youths, and sporadic acts of arson and looting. In interpreting these events, the news media drew on three major discursive formations: the Thatcherite discourse of *authoritarian populism*, which located the causes in the "natural" disorder of black communities and in the decline of traditional values and authority; the Laborist discourse, which saw the riots as a logical response to the mass unemployment and youthful alienation produced by government policies; and a radical discourse, which focused on the long-standing antagonism between the police and inner-city communities (Hansen & Murdock, 1985). Hence, although the television coverage of the violent incidents that occurred during the riots could have been coded using a schema similar to Gerbner's, their meaning and significance was far from clear and varied considerably depending on which discursive formation was being drawn upon.

Research on the riots also highlighted the key role of program forms in organizing the presentation of discourse. In particular, it suggested that certain forms of television documentary are likely to be more open to alternative and oppositional discourses than the relatively closed forms of news (Murdock, 1982).

FORMS AND FORMULAS

The way cultural forms organize meaning has been a central theme in the analysis of popular culture derived from literary studies. From this perspective, acts of violence are only rendered meaningful within "the moral and dramatic context provided by individual stories and by the generic conventions which underlie these stories" (Cawelti, 1975, p. 523). This argument was taken up in one of the earliest pieces of research undertaken by the Birmingham Centre for Contemporary Cultural Studies.

The study was a part of a program of work sponsored by the Television Research Committee, which the British Home Secretary had appointed in the summer of 1963 to investigate the influence of television on the values and behavior of young people. James Halloran, the Committee's secretary, was instrumental in placing the work with Birmingham, where Richard Hoggart, whom he had known personally for some time, had just established the Centre within the English Department. The study set out to examine the presentation of violence on television as a complement to research on the role of television in the lives of adolescent boys, directed by James Halloran himself (see Halloran, Brown, & Chaney, 1970). In common with the Annenberg team, the Birmingham work concentrated on prime time television fiction, but unlike Gerbner they undertook detailed readings of particular texts, on the assumption that "individual violent incidents must be referred to their context in programmes" (Shuttleworth, 1975, p. 19). In developing their analysis they paid special attention to the "necessary moment when the representation of an action obeys or submits itself to the structuring effect of the dramatic form in which it is cast" (p. 19). They particularly emphasized the way that generic conventions work to produce a familiar range of characters, settings, and plot structures. Genres were seen as historically based "codes" that frame and organize representations. This idea was developed in a paper written by one of the researchers on the study, Marina Carmargo Heck, in which she emphasized their role in structuring "not only what is said but also the way it is said, and what is not said but could be said" (Heck, 1980, p. 214). Although this formulation points us to the relations between discourse and cultural forms, the lead was not pursued at the time.

Gerbner's lack of interest in the mediating role of program forms follows logically from his analysis of the American network system as a machine for converting forms into formulas. In terms strongly reminiscent of Adorno and Horkheimer's celebrated critique of the standardization of American popular cultural production, he argues that "The economics of the assembly line and the requirements of wide acceptability assure general adherence to...clear-cut characterisations, tested plot lines, and proven formulas for resolving all issues" (Gerbner & Gross, 1976a, p. 182). "Unlike the real world, where personalities are complex, motives unclear, and outcomes ambiguous, television presents a world of clarity and simplicity" (Gerbner & Gross 1976b, p. 44).

Although he never conducted the detailed studies of television's institutional processes that his original research program called for (Gerbner, 1973, pp. 559–562), Gerbner's pessimistic analysis is broadly confirmed by other people's work on network production. These suggest that, even when "the system that cranks out mind candy occasionally proves hospitable to something else" (Gitlin, 1983, p. 273), that something is sooner or later pulled back into the mainstream. Take the case of *Hill Street Blues*. A rare combination of being in the right place at the right time with an idea that found executive favor allowed the show's creators to develop a new kind of police show, one that combined elements of the precinct-based series (like *Kojak*) with some of the characteristics of soap operas like *Dallas*: the overlapping story lines, the large cast of core characters, and the carry-over of plot lines from one episode to another. However, as the show's subsequent career demonstrates, it is next to impossible to sustain an innovatory thrust for long within the network system. For "all its singularity, Hill Street in the end was also commercial television banging up against its limitations, revealing at the moment of its triumph just how powerful are the pressures and formulas that keep prime time close to dead center" (Gitlin, 1983, p. 274). Or, as one of the show's original creators, Michael Kozoll, put it rather more bluntly; "No matter how well intentioned you are when you go out to do a cop show it's almost impossible not to end up with a bag of shit afterward" (Kerr, 1984, p. 153).

The pull of the safe and the mainstream is also strong within the British broadcasting system, but unlike the U.S. networks, its advance has been partially checked by an ideology of authorship that gives a limited number of designated auteurs a license to go against the grain of prevailing tastes and opinion. Where a fully commercial system celebrates the audience's sovereign right to pleasure and confirmation, the ethos of public service privileges the producer's right to personal expression and creative innovation, including the right to provoke and shock (Murdock, 1980). As a consequence, there is arguably a greater diversity in the available forms of prime time television in Britain—both dramatic and documentary—than in America. This has important implications for the way the television system organizes the field of discourse around violence, since the system's openness to varying positions will depend in part on the range of available program forms.

At the most general level, we can distinguish two basic dimensions to the relation between social discourses and program forms. The first concerns the *range of discourses* that a particular form allows into play. How far is it organized around the discourses of central power centers—whether corporate, governmental, or party political—and how far does it provide space for the articulation of counterdiscourses? The second has to do with *the way discourses are handled* within the program. Are they arranged in a clearly signalled hierarchy of credibility that directs the audience to prefer one over the others, or are they treated in a more even-handed and indeterminate way that leaves viewers with an open choice?

Gerbner is not interested in exploring these dimensions, since according to him, the imaginary space of prime time fiction "presents a world of clarity and simplicity" from which ambiguity and openness are banished (Gerbner & Gross, 1976b, p. 44). This may or may not be true of American television (though a number of critics would wish to take issue with him), but it certainly cannot serve as an adequate description of the British situation, for the present at least.

Exceptions may not be frequent, but they continue to occur. Even in an area such as terrorism, where official discourses are continually reproduced within a range of mainstream program forms, prime time drama provides spaces for counterdiscourses (Schlesinger, Murdock, & Elliott, 1983). And if we take the field of social violence more generally, we find a number of instances where the standard forms are deconstructed to provide an extended discursive space. One of the most interesting recent examples is Dennis Potter's drama series *The Singing Detective*, which draws on a variety of forms and genres, from the Hollywood musical to the hospital series and film noir, to present a multilayered and open-ended meditation on crime, betrayal, illness, and authorship.

Openness and ambiguity can also be found in mainstream actuality programs, though in recent years the available spaces have come under increasing pressure. The bitter row between the BBC and the Government over the documentary *At the Edge of the Union* is particularly instructive, since it illustrates the way in which questions of program form are central to struggles over television's relation to the field of discourse.

DISCOURSE AND FORM

The BBC's coverage of Northern Ireland had long been a bone of contention among senior Conservative politicians. As early as 1977 (two years before Mrs. Thatcher's election as Prime Minister), they complained that the Corporation's notions of impartiality and their commitment to providing a full range of relevant opinion, including the views of the IRA, was undermining the Government's propaganda offensive and giving the "impression that they are not really on the side of the civil power in Northern Ireland" (quoted in Bolton, 1990, p. 26). Their suspicions of disloyalty were confirmed (to their satisfaction) by a series of later incidents. In the summer of 1985, Mrs. Thatcher returned to the issue in a speech to an American Bar Association meeting in London, arguing that it was time "to find ways to starve the terrorist and the hijacker of the oxygen to publicity on which they depend" (Hughes, 1985a, p. 7). Though she was quick to add "In our societies we do not believe in constraining the media, still less in censorship."

A few weeks later she was in the United States. A journalist working for Rupert Murdoch's *Sunday Times*, operating under instructions from the paper's London office, asked her what her reaction would be if she learned that a British broadcasting organization was about to transmit a program containing an interview with the IRA's alleged Chief of Staff. She replied that she would "condemn them utterly." At that time she didn't know about the BBC's plans and was speaking hypothetically, but it was sufficient to allow the *Sunday Times* to run a story headed "Thatcher Slams IRA Film."

The film is constructed around profiles of two prominent figures on opposite wings of the Northern Ireland political spectrum: Martin McGuiness, the alleged IRA Chief of Staff; and Gregory Campbell, a vocal spokesman for the hard-line Union position, which sees no possibility of a negotiated settlement with the IRA and advocates a shoot-to-kill policy. The presentation is relatively open, in the sense that it gives extended space to discursive positions that are seldom voiced directly on British television. It is also organized in a way that refused to privilege any one position. The filmed portraits of the two men are carefully matched, sequence by sequence. We see them established in their communities as respected figures; we see them in graveyards, meditating on the meaning of the conflict in Northern Ireland; and we see them at home, surrounded by their families. They speak for themselves, addressing the viewer directly. There is no voice-over offering a seemingly disinterested interpretation, and no definite conclusion, resolving the conflict of positions in favor of a middle way. Viewers are simply left to ponder the irreconcilable differences.

This unusually nondirective form was particularly problematic in relation to McGuiness. The scenes of him playing affectionately with his children ran directly counter to the standard stereotype of the ruthless, dehumanized IRA activist. Moreover, the fact that he had been elected as a Sinn Fein representative in the last local elections gave him an ambiguous status within the dominant discourse. On the one hand he was widely thought to have been involved in planning bombings, while on the other hand he was a spokesman for a legal political party who had been interviewed a number of times previously. However, this was before Mrs. Thatcher's uncompromising remarks on the need to starve terrorists of the oxygen of publicity.

Taking this cue from her, the then Home Secretary, Leon Britten (who under the British system is responsible for both broadcasting and counterterrorism), wrote to the Chairman of the BBC's Board of Governors, asking in the strongest terms for the broadcast to be cancelled. "What is at issue," he argued, "is not the overall balance of the programme or whether its impact on reasonable people is to make such people more hostile to terrorism than they are already. Even if the programme and any surrounding material were, as a whole, to present terrorist organisations in a wholly unfavorable light, I would still ask you not to permit it to be broadcast." The Governors responded by convening an emergency meeting, during which they took the highly unusual step of opting to view the film. Several prominent members were outraged by what they saw as the overly sympathetic presentation of the two protagonists. The chairman, Stuart Young, complained that "it made them out to be nice guys, bouncing babies on their knees" while another member dismissed it as "a Hitler loved dogs programme" (Milne, 1988, pp. 199–190). Having debated the issues, they decided to cancel the scheduled screening. This very public repudiation of the editorial judgment of the Corporation's senior managers (who had seen and approved the film) was unprecedented, and was met by an equally unprecedented one-day protest strike by BBC and ITV journalists.

The program was eventually shown, with only minor changes, and in an effort to head off a crisis of confidence among their staff, senior BBC personnel were at some pains to restate their commitment to open debate on Northern Ireland. As the then-assistant director general, Alan Protheroe, put it

> It is necessary for the maintenance of democracy that unpopular, even dangerous, views are heard and thoroughly understood. The argument about "the national interest" demanding the censorship (for that is precisely what it amounts to) of such voices is glib, and intrinsically dangerous. Who determines the "national interest"? How far does the "national interest" extend? (Protheroe, 1986, p. 17)

This last question was answered on October 19, 1988, when the Home Secretary, Douglas Hurd, issued notices under Clauses 13(4) of the BBC Licence and Agreement and section 29(3) of the Broadcasting Act 1981 (which regulates the ITV system), restricting live interviews with representatives of 11 named Irish organizations, including Sinn Fein.

Sinn Fein remains a legal political party, with elected councillors in Northern Ireland and one elected Westminster MP, but its spokespeople cannot speak directly to British television viewers, though they may be quoted indirectly or have their words read out by a journalist or actor or printed as subtitles. They can be seen but not heard. The logistic problems these strictures impose have reduced both the number of screened interviews with Sinn Fein representatives and their length (Henderson, Miller, & Reilly, 1990, p. 25), marking a significant move towards closure in the discursive field relating to violence in Northern Ireland.

The ban on direct interviews with Sinn Fein is one among a number of recent measures imposing new restrictions on broadcasting. They include the revisions to the official secrets legislation and the new impartiality requirements in the 1990 Broadcasting Act. These initiatives are part of a pincer movement designed to squeeze the space available to counterdiscourses and reinforce the centrality of official discourse. The other significant source of pressure is coming from the accelerated commercialization of the media system produced by a decade of privatization and deregulation. This has reinforced the control that the major multimedia groups can exercise over the moving image industries and has opened up new spaces for corporate publicity and for commercial speech more generally (Murdock, 1990).

These extensions of market dynamics and state regulation are absolutely central to a full understanding of the forces currently reshaping television program production. But they are not the whole story.

We also need to bear in mind that reportage, in all its forms, involves "the processing of text and talk" (Van Dijk, 1988, p. 179), and that every program is a selective reconstruction from the available field of discourse. Hence, a full analysis of the production process must examine both the social relations of production and the way cultural forms mediate the translation of social discourse into finished programs. Unfortunately, research has tended to separate these two levels, with sociologists of communication focusing on the first and writers in the cultural studies tradition concentrating on the second. Stuart Hall's seminal paper on encoding/decoding is a case in point. Having argued, rightly, that the analysis of discourse must "be integrated into the social relations of the communication process as a whole, of which it forms only a part," he opts to focus on the moment when the raw materials of the program-making are translated into the "aural-visual forms of the television discourse" (Hall, 1980, p. 129). The problems of not examining the social relation of production in any detail emerge very clearly in one of the key Birmingham studies, *Policing the Crisis*, which explores the moral panic over violent street attacks in Britain in the early 1970s, and their characterization as muggings. The link between the general field of discourse and the media coverage is accomplished through the notion of *primary definition*, which sees official sources as having privileged access to the media by virtue of their structural position (Hall, Chritcher, Jefferson, Clarke, & Roberts, 1978). This position ignores both the conflictual processes within central social institutions that lie behind the moment of definition, and the strategies sources adopt in their pursuit of visibility and legitimacy within the media system (Schlesinger, Tumber, & Murdock, 1991). Primary definition is the outcome of this competition. It cannot be read off directly from structural location.

This emphasis on discursive struggle both inside and outside program systems runs directly counter to all variants of the dominant ideology thesis, including Gerbner's formulation.

DISCURSIVE STRUGGLES

Gerbner works with a straightforward instrumental model of power in which network television operates as an agency or cultural arm

Hall, S. (1988). *The hard road to renewal: Thatcherism and the crisis of the left.* London: Verso.

Hall, S. (1989). Ideology and communication theory. In B. Dervin (Eds.), *Rethinking communication Vol. 1: Paradigm issues.* London: Sage Publications.

Hall, S., Chritcher, C., Jefferson, T., Clarke, Y., & Roberts, B. (1978). *Policing the crisis: Mugging, the state and law and order.* London: Macmillan Education.

Halloran, J.D., Brown, R.L., & Chaney, D.C. (1970). *Television and delinquency.* Leicester, UK: Leicester University Press.

Hansen, A., & Murdock, G. (1985). Constructing the crowd: Populist discourse and press presentation. In V. Mosco & J. Wasko (Eds.), *The critical communications review, Vol. III: Popular culture and media events.* Norwood, NJ: Ablex.

Heck, M.C. (1980). The ideological dimensions of media messages. In S. Hall, D. Hobson, A. Lowe, & P. Willis, (Eds.), *Culture, media, language.* London: Hutchinson.

Henderson, L., Miller, D., & Reilly, J. (1990, October 15). The sound of Irish silence. *The Guardian,* p. 25.

Hughes, R. (1985, July 16). PM plea on terrorism publicity. *Financial Times,* p. 7.

Kerr, P. (1984). Drama at MTV. *Lou Grant* and *Hill Street Blues.* In J. Fuer (Eds.), *MTV 'quality television'.* London: British Film Institute.

Latin America Bureau. (1982). *Falklands/Malvinas: Whose crisis?* London: LAB.

Lost in the Terrorist Theater. (1984, October). *Harper's,* p. 44.

Milne, A. (1988). *DG: The memoirs of a British Broadcaster.* London: Coronet Books.

Murdock, G. (1980). Authorship and organisation. *Screen Education, 35.*

Murdock, G. (1982). Disorderly images: Television's presentation of crime and policing. In C. Sumner (Ed.), *Crime, justice and the mass media.* Cambridge, UK: Cambridge University, Institute of Criminology.

Murdock, G. (1989). Cultural studies: Missing links. *Critical Studies in Mass Communication, 6.*

Murdock, G. (1990). Redrawing the map of the communication industries: Concentration and ownership in the era of privatization. In M. Ferguson (Ed.), *Public communication: The new imperatives.* London: Sage Publications.

Potter, J., & Wetherell, M. (1987). *Discourse and social psychology: Beyond attitude and behaviour.* London: Sage Publications.

Protheroe, A. (1986). The broadcaster's greatest hazard is fear. *Index on Censorship, 1.*

Schlesinger, P., Murdock, G., & Elliott, P. (1983). *Televising 'terrorism': Political violence in popular culture.* London: Comedia.

Schlesinger, P., Tumber, H., & Murdock, G. (1991). The media politics of crime and criminal justice, *British Journal of Sociology, 42,* 397–420.

Schudson, M. (1989). The sociology of news production. *Media, Culture and Society, 11*(3).

Shuttleworth, A. (1975). *Television violence, crime-drama and the analysis of content.* Unpublished report, University of Birmingham, Centre for Contemporary Cultural Studies.

Van Dijk, T.A. (1988). *News as discourse.* London: Lawrence Erlbaum Associates.

Williams, R. (1974). *Television: Technology and cultural form.* London: Fontana.

PART

IV

On Journalism and Society

CHAPTER

The Study of Women and Journalism: From Positivist to Feminist Approaches

GERTRUDE J. ROBINSON

The complex relationship between communication and feminist studies is difficult to unravel. In spite of this a number of scholars have begun to lay the groundwork for an assessment of the theoretical influences of the two disciplines on each other. Among these are Lana Rakow (1986b) and Paula Treichler and Ellen Wartella (1986), as well as Brenda Dervin (1987) in the United States and Helen Baehr (1986) and myself (Robinson, 1986), in Great Britain and Canada, respectively. I have noted elsewhere that part of the reason for this difficulty lies in the fact that communications studies are what Littlejohn calls an *interdiscipline*, in which scholars from a variety of disciplines come together to investigate communications related themes (Littlejohn, 1982, pp. 243–245). This interdiscipline presently lacks a proper intellectual history that identifies and locates different strands of scholarship in relation to each other and to a particularly historical time and place (Robinson, 1988a, p. 99). Such a historiography would show that communication—and feminist research approaches and methodologies themselves—have undergone change over time, starting with different assumptions and methods of work for studying sex and gender than are accepted today.

Much of this research, furthermore, fell into the period of the seventies, when functionalist social methodology came under critical fire and new theoretical initiatives were launched in both interdisciplines (Giddens, 1983). Yet another obstacle to the development of a historiographical account arises from the lack of agreed-upon criteria for classifying research on women. Should the historical period into which the research falls or the theoretical assumptions on which the research is based be made the defining characteristic? The first would label as feminist all investigations carried out since the North American women's movement began in the late sixties. The second would designate as feminist only that research that distinguishes between sex and gender, the biological and the social aspects of women's existence. Drawing the distinction on theoretical grounds permits the communications historiographer to illuminate the impact of different methodological styles of work within and across disciplinary boundaries. Up to now most writers in both interdisciplines fail to use the feminist research label systematically.

SEX DIFFERENCE STUDIES IN COMMUNICATIONS (1966–1976)

According to Jagger and Rothenberg (1983) four different types of scholarship initially dominated the study of women in the sixties. All of these focused on women's inferior status in society and assumed that gender was a biologically based variable that was able to explain social status and behavior differences between women and men. Liberal feminists such as Betty Friedan (1963) documented how the ideology of "difference" was translated into social practices that excluded women from the public sphere. Radical feminists argued that these exclusionary practices were complexly interlinked into a system called *patriarchy*, which constructs and legitimates a hierarchal system of power in which women possess fewer economic and social privileges than men. Traditional Marxists clarified the intricate relationships between sex and class inequality in capitalist societies and noted that they exploit the female both as a paid worker and as a form of property in the family (Eichler, 1978). Socialist Marxists in turn began to investigate the reinforcements that capitalist and patriarchal practices offered each other in oppressing women in different societies and historical epochs.

In communication studies these positivistic theories led to two major research foci, according to Lana Rakow: sex difference and gender studies (Rakow, 1986b, pp. 11–14). Sex difference inquiries, like my journalist study, focused on women's different social and work force participation, as well as on differences in social status between professional media women and their male colleagues

(Robinson, 1975/1980). Gender research, in contrast, probed media images and effects and demonstrated that media content legitimated the prevailing social ideology of female inferiority. This strand of research is more correctly described as *images and representation* research, because it too assumed that sex was an unproblematic biological variable. Little did we know at the time that all of these critical research approaches, which took gender as given, were themselves molded by a set of inadequate 19th-century assumptions. These, according to Rosalind Rosenberg, include the belief in a *gendered* individual whose sexual division of labor was a result of biological imperatives; the notion that the sexes were antagonistic interest groups; and the idea that the nuclear family was a natural rather than a culturally produced human phenomenon (Rosenberg, 1982, p. 33). The sex difference studies of women's media role ignored the sociopolitical context in which women live, and thus led the superficial hypotheses and misdirected research strategies (Janus, 1977, p. 20). Even the various strands of neo-Marxist scholarship, which experienced a rebirth after the student revolutions in North America and Europe, did not escape these theoretical inadequacies. Their theorization of the family in terms of production relationships alone failed to account for this institution's crucial role in language and consequently identity acquisition (Saunders, 1983).

FEMINIST CRITIQUES OF POSITIVISTIC MEDIA RESEARCH APPROACHES

Feminist scholars offered two types of criticisms of the early positivistic studies of women and media. The first questioned the adequacy of translating "sex" into "role," on the grounds that such a translation tends to flatten and homogenize women's experiences and depoliticizes them (Elshtain, 1981). The second points out that the variable of sex is unable to account for the workings of patriarchal social ideology. We now know that women media personnel in North America as well as Europe are "minorities" in their professions, that they tend to cluster in the lowest ranks and receive unequal pay (Crean, 1987; Gallagher, 1986). Social profiles of female journalists furthermore discovered that women journalists and broadcast personnel tend to be single (66%), while their male colleagues are overwhelmingly married (71%) (Robinson, 1974/1981). The reasons for these discrepancies lie in the patriarchal family structure, which expects women to play a dual role that is often incompatible with the long hours of media work. What is demonstrated here, feminist theorists Helena Lopata and Barrie Thorne (1978) explain, is that gender is *not* role specific. It is instead a pervasive identity and set of self-feelings that affect *all* social roles. As such, gender is part of a complex set of interrelationships that structure *every* social interaction.

Positivistic sex-based research was additionally criticized for ignoring the working of patriarchal social ideology and the ways in which it structures social practice. Though sex role research discovered organizational barriers to women's media careers, such as difficulties in access, promotion, and pay equality, it was unable to pinpoint the *ideological* roots of these barriers, which are grounded in organizational power differentials. A 1975 Canadian Broadcasting Corporation (CBC) study discovered that one powerful deterrence to women's promotion lay in male managers' stereotypical notions or working women (1975, pp. 50–52). Interviews with male supervisors revealed that they failed to advance female broadcast journalists because they believed that women were unwilling to change their domicile in case of job transfer, that they should not work night shifts, and that they were emotionally unstable and therefore unfit for management positions (Robinson, 1977b, p. 125).

These examples illustrate how the symbolic realm of sense making directly affects all working conditions and systematically discriminates against women and minority journalists. Yet until the late seventies, neither feminism nor communication studies offered a convincing theory of the media as ideological apparatuses. The positivistic theoretical edifice of *sex differences* overlooked sexism in its social and ideological context, including the media's modes of production and structures of political organization (Janus, 1977, p. 20). Women and their concerns were either identified with mainstream notions of the guardian role in the "private" sphere or essentialized as man's "other" (Schwichtenberg, 1989, p. 205). Both of these research approaches fail to illuminate what gender means on both the personal and the social levels.

1980S FEMINIST AND CULTURAL STUDIES CONTRIBUTIONS TO THE STUDY OF WOMEN AND JOURNALISM

Since the 1980s a number or researchers with varied theoretical approaches have investigated what gender means. Among these are British cultural studies researchers at Birmingham, U.S. feminist theorists, including Suzanne Kessler and Wendy McKenna, symbolic interactionists such as Ervin Goffman (1979), and a number of such phenomenologists as Gaye Tuchman (Tuchman, Daniels, & Benet, 1978) (see Robinson & Straw, 1982). All of these have enlarged the theoretical variety and methodological approaches for studying the media and gender. They share the common assumption that human beings are not only finished products of biological evolution, but symbolizing, conceptualizing, meaning-seeking creatures. The culture thus created consists of a system of practices, values, and ideas about the world that meaningfully organize an entire way of life (Geertz, 1973, p. 100). *Culture*, Clifford Geertz demonstrates, cannot be studied like an experimental science. It must contain an interpretive hermeneutic element in order to explain meaning. Consequently, as Anthony Giddens notes, semiotic, rhetorical, and phenomenological approaches gained theoretical ascendancy in 1980s social and communications theorizing. They enriched scholarship in both feminist and communication studies.

Saussurian linguistics was at the core of this theoretical revolution that reconceptualized a number of key concepts. Among these are the distinction between language and speech, the arbitrary nature of the sign, the tripartite signification process, and the fact that language codes are based on "absent knowledge." This absent knowledge provides common-sense understandings of life situations that support and make social behavior both intelligible and possible (Giddens, 1983, p. 253). Both cultural communication and feminist scholarship have shown that sex is not a transparent variable that can be separately studied, but a culturally constructed and unstable category of social organization. In Lana Rakow's (1986b, pp. 20–21) elegant phrase, "gender is both something we do and something we think with." Through it, information about which gender should be assigned to a person is conveyed to others in the communicative situation.

At the level of meaning, Marilyn Frye (1983, pp. 21–22) and others note, gender operates in three different ways: as a classificatory system, as a structuring structure, and as an ideology. As a classificatory system gender arrangements presently order women into a dominant/subordinate caste system that is maintained by requiring women continuously to announce and act this subordination. This marking of distinction is ubiquitous and creates the impression that it is crucial and fundamental to all human life. The dual nature of gender as something we do and something we think with is revealed in the four different kinds of classificatory activities that help maintain the dominant/subordinate class system.

Among these are *gender assignment*, which classifies an individual into a gender at birth; *gender attribution*, which assigns an individual to a gender classification in a social interaction; gender role *practices*, which refer to *behaving* like a female, and gender *identity*, which identifies the *feelings* one has as female or as male (Kessler & McKenna, 1978, p. 168). These classificatory categories provide a means for studying the elusive gender-related aspects of professional behavior that have up to now escaped attention. Subordinate gender attribution does lead to differences in role practices and professional behavior for female and male journalists.

As a structuring device, the categories of female and male have been used to describe, define, and categorize much of the daily world, both animate and inanimate. This structuring of the structure of thinking is primarily achieved through metaphor (justice = female) and metonomy (men = humans). Metaphors are particularly effective, because they present facts belonging to one category in the idioms appropriate to another. Levi Strauss demonstrated how the culturally produced structure of gender relationships serves as a model for other structures in the symbolic order. He shows how the relationships between women and men in our own and other cultures become templates for juxtapositions such as nature/culture, sun/moon, or virtue/vice. Recently a number of communications and feminist scholars have begun to investigate the influence of gender templates on popular culture images of women. They demonstrate how the so-called woman's genres and characterizations and the pleasures women derive from media programming are denigrated (Rakow, 1986a). Not only are women less highly regarded in television situation comedies and in radio programming (Baehr & Ryan, 1984), but their enjoyment of such entertainments as rock video and film (Kaplan, 1987), romance novels (Radway, 1984), and certain types of popular music (McRobbie, 1982) are classified as "less worthy" than men's enjoyment of sports and crime shows.

Even less well understood is the use of gender as a model for structuring thought processes themselves. Here Susan Hekman (1987, p. 67), like other phenomenologists, has begun to investigate the dichotomies on which Enlightenment epistemology itself rests. Among these are the dichotomies of subject/object, rational/irrational, and reason/emotion, which she considers fundamentally mistaken. Antifoundationalists question the rational model's idea that knowledge must have an absolute foundation and that it is achieved through a process of abstraction from the social world. Phyllis Rooney (1989, pp. 22–29) carries this critique a step further into what she calls the problem of "gendered reason" on which Enlightenment epistemology is based. In this schema "reason" is associated with male characteristics and "unreason" with female ones. She argues that the problem is not whether women can reason, but whether the parameters of rational method diminishes the full force of women's voices. According to Rooney, "the question that I want to raise here is whether under the influence of dominant metaphors we try to force our analyses into simplistic structures which...set up oppositions and 'paradoxes' that reside primarily in the *frame* through which we view the problem...(not in the problems themselves)" (1989, pp. 22–23).

This line of analysis is close to that of phenomenological and symbolic interactionist scholars within the communication studies tradition who have probed the beliefs on which the meaning structures of everyday life are based. Women's ways of knowing, psychologists Belensky, Clinchy, Goldberg, and Tarule (1986, p. 15) found, are not only modeled by different socialization patterns for women and men, but also by different structures of consciousness that are developed through being a women rather than a man living in 1980s North America. According to Keohane, Rosaldo, and Gelp (1982, pp. IX–XI), this differential consciousness arises from three unique sources of knowledge. These she calls *feminine consciousness*, which involves the consciousness of oneself as the object of attention of another person; *female consciousness*, which refers to the age-old conservative experience of women in giving and preserving life, in nurturing and sustaining; and *feminist consciousness*, which is developed and refined as women reflect on the asymmetries in power, opportunities, and situations that have marked their lives.

Communications and cultural scholars will have to explore the relationships between these consciousnesses and popular culture selections and uses. Like Carol Gilligan, they will also have to investigate whether these styles of consciousness lead to different underlying value systems for women and men. Her discovery of a female definition of *equality* based on differences in need, and a male ethic stressing *fairness* criteria legalistically defined, provides tantalizing food for thought (Gilligan, 1982). Together these findings suggest that female value systems may be rooted in an epistemological outlook that is differently oriented and that thus challenges the male prerogative to structure the very structure of human thought (Hawksworth, 1987, p. 123).

British cultural studies made the relationship between ideology and sex inequality and women's special relationship to the media two of their major research agendas in the eighties (Baehr, 1986,

p. 141). The former investigated what kind of a voice women have in a patriarchal media system where preferred meanings reside in a male discourse. The Birmingham Women's Study Group, like many other researchers, discovered that the cult of femininity marginalizes women's voices in both media production and in the ways women's contributions in the public realm are described (Robinson, 1980/1983). My own research of television news programming, tracing women's issues, showed that female broadcasters cover disproportionately more (60%) women-related topics, and that the latter appear in the bottom third of the news line-up. This positioning, and the shorter amount of time assigned to their coverage, together indicate that these topics are less important (Robinson, 1978). Feminist insistence on women's special relationship to the media has furthermore led to the reworking of the whole notion of media professionalism in terms of the clockwork of male career patterns and the mainstream interpretations of professional practice. Else Fabricus Jensen (1982) found evidence that Danish women television producers go about their work differently, treating interviewees as equal to themselves in the news program. They also select different news angles for story construction while maintaining the same code of professionalism as their colleagues (Jensen, 1982, p. 15; van Zoonen, 1986).

REASSESSING THE INFLUENCE OF FEMINISM ON COMMUNICATION STUDIES

Because communication studies straddle the grey area between the social and the humanistic sciences, they are theoretically more open to the hermeneutic agenda than, for instance, economics and psychology (Press, 1989, p. 196). Our evidence shows that within the interdiscipline there are today more communication scholars who have learned from feminism and its critical questioning of received truths. These scholars hail primarily from post-Marxist, interactionist, and phenomenological critical traditions. There is also increasing evidence that communication scholarship using a feminist perspective has been more readily and widely published since the 1980s. Lana Rakow (1989, p. 209) opines that "feminist scholarship" seems to be a "go" word. In spite of these developments, however, the question remains where this scholarship is going? Institutionally it is going nowhere. Though its value is hinted at in mainstream publications, feminist writing on communications issues appears mostly in special journals where it is stigmatized as a special interest concern, as something of interest to women *only*. Feminism's agenda is also erased from the wider disciplinary debate about the theoretical ferment in the field. Among the five paradigm essays in the recently published *Rethinking Communications* (1989), the feminist voice is absent. It appears only in the *Commentary* section, where Caren J. Deming (1989, pp. 162–163) answers yes to her title question "Must Gender Paradigms Shift for Themselves?"

Why has the feminist interest in examining and challenging the power of gender construction in all human endeavors not been taken up more widely? Different researchers have offered a variety of reasons for this oversight. The most obvious reason is probably lack of numbers, especially in the older generation of female communication researchers. This state of affairs prompted Lana Rakow (1989, p. 210) to suggest that the visibility of feminist scholarship can best be improved by a coalition between older "liberal feminists" and the younger generation of researchers who have studied feminist work. Others have argued that feminism's absence is simply one more example of the ways in which status inequality plays itself out in the academy, where newer strands of scholarship are excommunicated through silencing. Yet others see it as an outcome of the very interdisciplinarity of communication studies themselves, which are theoretically "soft" at the core. Still others ascribe it to the profound influence that gender has had on all modes of thought for the last three centuries. These practices make it easy to erase gender from the theoretical agenda (Deming, 1989, p. 164).

While all of these explanations are probably true, we should ask ourselves what our interdiscipline is missing by ignoring feminist insights. The analysis presented here demonstrates that positivistic sex role and sex difference approaches, which grew out of functionalist media agenda, are theoretically flawed. They treat gender as a mere variable, rather than as a structuring feature of all human life. In addition, it has become clear that feminist scholarship is essential for the restructuring of the discipline itself. The argument for the crucial role of feminist scholarship has been made on three persuasive grounds. Brenda Dervin (1987, p. 113) has argued that it supplied a missing perspective that addresses the experience of one half of the human race not presently accounted for. Lana Rakow (1986b, p. 24) adds that feminist scholarship is essential because it will help transcend the traditional theoretical boundaries between different domains of communication research such as sociolinguistics, speech communication, and interpersonal, organizational, and mass communications, which are currently informed by incompatible theories and methods. Andrea Press and Caren Deming note that feminist critique goes further than other critical approaches in that it calls for a rethinking of the very assumptions, methods, and underlying bases of knowledge on which communication studies are based (Press, 1989, p. 198; Deming, 1989, p. 126).

The historiographical evidence amassed here lends credence to these claims. It shows that there has been a movement away from positivistic sex-based to culturally situated gender-based inquiries of women and media over the past 40 years. It also shows that the rethinking of communication studies will not amount to more than an empty promise, unless scholars are willing to rethink their own praxis as social actors, dramatic language users, and gendered individuals.

REFERENCES

Baehr, H., & Ryan, M. (1984). *Shut up and listen: Women and local radio.*London: Comedia.

Baehr, H. (1986). The impact of feminism on media studies: Just another commercial break? *Medie/Kultur* (Copenhagen), *4*, 132–154.

Belenky, M.F., Clinchy, B.M., Goldberg, N.R., & Tarule, J.M. (1986). *Women's ways of knowing: The development of self, voice and mind.* New York: Basic Books.

Brown, P., & Jordanova, L. (1982). Oppression dichotomies: The nature/culture debate. In E. Whitelegg, M. Arnot, E. Bartels, V. Beechey, L. Birke, S. Himmelwhite, D. Leonard, S. Ruehl, & M.A. Speakman (Eds.), *The changing experience of women* (pp. 389–399). Oxford: Basil Blackwell with Open University.

Canadian Broadcasting Corporation. (1975). *Women in the CBC.* Montreal: CBC Publishing.

Crean, S. (1987). Piecing the picture together: Women and the media in Canada. *Canadian Women's Studies Association. 8*(1), 15–29.

Deming, C. (1989). Must gender paradigms shift for themselves? In B. Dervin, L. Grossberg, B. O'Keefe, & E. Wartella (Eds.), *Rethinking communication* (pp. 162–165). Newbury Park, CA: Sage.

Dervin, B. (1987). The potential contribution of feminist scholarship to the field of communication. *Journal of Communication, 37*(4), 107–120.

Eichler, M. (1978). *Ten theses on sex in the economy.* Toronto: McLelland & Stewart.

Edelsky, C. (1981). Who's got the floor? *Language in Society, 10,* 383–421.

Elshtain, J.B. (1981). *Public man, Private women.* Princeton, NJ: Princeton University Press.

Friedan, B. (1963). *The feminine mystique.* New York: Dell.

Frye, M. (1983). *The politics of reality: Essays in feminist theory.* Trumansurg, NY: Grossing Press.

Gallagher, M. (1986). Myth and reality in women's broadcasting: Ten years of equal opportunity. *Medie/Kultur* (Denmark), 4, 197–219.

Geertz, C. (1973). *The interpretation of cultures.* New York: Basic Books.

Giddens, A. (1983). *Central problems in social theory* (2nd ed.). Berkeley, CA: University of California Press.

Gilligan, C. (1982). *In a different voice.* Cambridge, MA: Harvard University Press.

Goffman, E. (1979). *Gender advertisements.* Cambridge, MA: Harvard University Press.

Hawksworth, M.E. (1987). Feminist epistemology: A survey of the field. In M.J. Falco (Ed.), *Feminism and epistemology* (pp. 115–127). New York: Hayworth Press.

Hekman, S. (1987). Feminization of epistemology: Gender and the social sciences. In M.J. Falco (Ed.), *Feminism and epistemology: Approaches to research in women and politics* (pp. 65–83). New York: Hayworth Press.

Jagger, A., & Rothenberg, P.S. (1983). *Feminist frameworks: Alternative theoretical accounts of the relations between women and men.* New York: McGraw Hill.

Janus, N.Z. (1977). Research on sex-roles in the mass media: Toward a critical approach. *The users of literacy.* London: Penguin.

Jensen, E.F. (1982). *Television newscasts in a women's perspective.* Stockholm: Nord-Publication.

Kaplan, A. (1987). *Rocking around the clock.* London: Methuen.

Keohane, N., Rosaldo, M., & Gelp, B. (1982). *Feminist theory and critique of ideology.* Chicago: University of Chicago Press.

Kessler, S., & McKenna, W. (1978). *Gender: An ethnomethodological approach.* New York: John Wiley.

Littlejohn, S.W. (1982). An overview of contribution to human communication theory from other disciplines. In F.E.X. Dance (Ed.), *Human communication theory* (pp. 243–286). New York: Holt Rinehart and Winston.

Lopata, H., & Thorne, B. (1978). On the term 'sex-roles'. *Signs, 3*(3), 717–721.

McRobbie, A. (1982). Settling accounts with subcultures: A feminist critique. *Screen Education, 34,* 37–49.

Press, A. (1989). The ongoing feminist revolution. *Critical Studies in Mass Communication, 6,* 196–202.

Putnam, L. (1982). In search of gender: A critique of communication and sex role research. *Women's Studies in Communication, 5,* 1–9.

Radway, J. (1984). Identifying ideological seams: Mass culture analytical method, and political practice. *Communications, 9*(1), 93–123.

Rakow, L. (1986a). Feminist approaches to popular culture: Giving patriarchy its due. *Communication, 9*(1), 19–42.

Rakow, L. (1986b). Rethinking gender research. *Communication, 36* (4), 11–26.

Rakow, L. (1989). Feminist studies: The next stage. *Critical Studies in Mass Communications, 6,* 209–215.

Robinson, G.J. (1977a). The future of women in Canadian media. *McGill Journal of Education, 12*(1), 124–132.

Robinson, G.J. (1977b). The future of women in the Canadian media. *McGill Journal of Education, 12*(1), 124–132.

Robinson, G.J. (1978). Women, media access and social control. In L.K. Epstein (Ed.), *Women and the News.* New York.

Robinson, G.J. (1980/1983). The media and social change: Thirty years of magazine coverage of women and work (1950-1977). *Atlantis, 8*(2), 87–113.

Robinson, G.J. (1986). The feminist paradigm in historical perspective. *Medie/Kultur* (Denmark), *4,* 113–131.

Robinson, G.J. (1988a). Here be dragon: Problems in charting the U.S. history of communication studies. *Communication, 10*(1), 97–119.

Robinson, G.J. (1988b). Feminism and communication studies. In H. Dagenais & D. Piche (Eds.), *Women and development.* Montreal: McGill Queens Press.

Robinson, G.J., & Straw, W. (1982). Semiotics and communications studies: Points of conflict. In M. Voigt (Ed.), *Progress in communication science* (Vol. 4, pp. 91–144). Norwood, NJ: Ablex Publishing Corp.

Rooney, P. (1989). *Gendered reason: Sex metaphor and conceptions of reason.* Unpublished paper, University of Iowa, Department of Philosophy.

Rosenberg, R. (1982). *Beyond separate sphere: Intellectual roots of modern feminism.* New Haven, CT: Yale University Press.

Saunders, E. (1983). Women in Canadian society. In D. Forces & S. Richter (Ed.), *Social issues: Sociological views of Canada.* Toronto: Prentice-Hall.

Schwichtenberg, C. (1989). Feminist cultural studies. *Critical Studies in Mass Communication, 6,* 202–208.

Treichler, P., & Wartella, B. (1986). Interventions: Feminist theory and communication studies. *Communications, 9*(1), 1–18.

Tuchman, G., Benet, S., & Daniels, A. (Eds.). (1978). *Hearth and home: Images of women in the mass media.* New York: Oxford University Press.

van Zoonen, L. (1986, August). *Rethinking women and the news.* Paper presented at the IAMCR Conference, Delhi, India.

CHAPTER

Some Thoughts On The Press–Polling Connection

GLADYS ENGEL LANG
KURT LANG

Do the news media pay too much attention to the results of public opinion measurement? Especially after the long drawn-out nominating process that culminated in the election of George Bush, the amount of coverage itself became a political issue. Poll-driven campaign reporting was held responsible for changing a race between donkeys and elephants into a mere horse race and, in turn, contributing not only to an issue-less campaign but to low electoral participation. Wedded to each other, both pollsters and the press shared the blame. Nor has adverse comment on polling and its publicists been purely an election year phenomenon: At least one United States senator is reported to have jested that "we will never have real tax reform unless we line up all the pollsters and shoot them!" And, of course, long before 1988 the early broadcasting of election returns had become a special target of political critics and legislators, with exit polling singled out as a special villain.

To ask about the overreporting of polls may be, however, to ask the wrong question. Should we not be inquiring whether the news media pay sufficient attention to the kind of polling information that their consumers need if political polling and public opinion research are best to fulfill democratic needs? The news media may pay too much attention to certain kinds of polls—such as trial heats, presidential popularity ratings, and immediate reactions to televised debates—that invite the public to follow politics as a spectator sport (who's ahead?) while underplaying the more de-layed, thoughtful analysis of statistics garnered over time that help put opinion change into more meaningful perspective. Even an informed and attentive public needs guidance through the maze of seemingly contradictory findings.

Any fair judgment of media performance requires that its role in both *generating* and *disseminating* news about public opinion be evaluated. The purpose of the media-sponsored opinion poll is to generate news while other polls, whether or not intended as news products, become news only when they are reported in the media.

Generating news about public opinion.   Media-generated polling encompasses both the work of the in-house pollsters, some of them bonafide members of the journalistic profession familiar with scientific survey methodology, and that of polling firms or consultants commissioned by individual print or broadcast organizations to conduct their surveys. With media demand having proliferated, some firms poll almost exclusively for the news media.

The connection between scientific polling and journalism goes back a long way. In the 1930s scores of newspapers subscribed to the column written by George Gallup, himself a journalist, and Elmo Roper's poll was published in *Fortune* magazine. Self-generated media polls also have a long tradition, the most famous being that of the *Literary Digest*, which fell into disrepute only after it confidently predicted Alf Landon's victory in the 1936 election.

While most opinion inquiries initiated by newspapers and magazines were once apt to be "straw polls"—in which respondents were either self-selected into the sample or nonrandomly chosen—these have been mostly, though not entirely, replaced by more scientific surveys. In the United States ersatz polls survive mainly in the broadcast industry, where the solicitation of responses from listeners and viewers is one way of stirring audience interest. In fact, with advances in communication technology making it possible to get an "instant reply" and a "quick tally" from an entire nation, such "dirty polls" are conducted almost daily to measure response to breaking news. These counts, the brainchildren mainly of local broadcasters but not infrequently of national networks, confound honest efforts by media and public opinion professionals to teach the public to discriminate between polls that are scientifically sound and those that are not. And worse—such quickie polls can be readily manipulated by true believers with a vested interest in the resolution of a particular issue to promote a false picture of opinion that serves their cause. More charitably, one can reasonably argue that such nonscientific polling can serve a democratic purpose, however serendipitously: many people who don't trust polls because "Gallup has never called them" will willingly pay the price of a phone call given the opportunity, as they see it, to make their opinion count. Also, such call-in polls might have a latent function in countries such as the former Soviet Union, which are newly emerging from opinion repression by encouraging people not used to formulating opinions on public issues to do so. Given the down side of such nonscientific polls, however, it is fortunate that the leading public opinion analysts in the former USSR have yet to emulate us along these lines.

Long-standing as it is, the tie between the media and polling worlds is now closer than ever. Major news media have their own in-house expertise, with print and electronic media cooperating and sharing expenses. CBS does some of its polling in conjunction with the *New York Times*, NBC with the *Wall Street Journal*, ABC with the *Washington Post*. These and other news organizations in high repute produce high-quality polls. With in-house or contract arrangements in place, many news organizations have the capability to go into operation almost instantaneously whenever anything happens.

USA Today, which collaborates with CNN, turns out more polls than any of the three major networks. Certainly it is more often the first out with a poll on a breaking story, concentrating on "overnights." Thus, the Supreme Court's ruling on June 21, 1989, that state laws could not prohibit the burning of American flags as a form of political protest protected by the First Amendment was front page news the next day (June 22). By June 23 *USA Today* could inform its readers that an overwhelming majority (69%) of the people wanted the flag protected by amending the Constitution. Was this the public expressing an opinion on an issue, or was it an expression of patriotic indignation that dissidents might burn the flag with impunity? It is unlikely that most poll respondents had yet read about the decision or heard arguments pro and con a constitutional amendment to undo the Court decision. Yet this early and hardly surprising measure of response to the ruling surely encouraged President Bush in his call for an amendment to protect the flag. In the months that followed public opinion ultimately settled for a law against flag desecration as passed by Congress. Newspaper editorials throughout the nation had deplored tinkering with the Bill of Rights, and members of Congress had implored their colleagues not to allow "the blindness of passion to cloud their judgment." Still, the initial polling to serve news needs was not without effect on the debate that ensued.

What have been the implications for the political process of media-generated polling? Any acceptable assessment would have to address the effects on (a) the media organizations themselves; (b) the public's understanding and responses to various kinds of issues; (c) the decision-making activities of political actors; and (d) the quality and influence of public opinion research. It is these consequences that we are presently investigating in a series of case studies involving political decision making (at the Congressional level). At least three of these controversies, all of which surfaced in 1989, have come to some kind of a resolution. We have examined the published polls and their use in the media; we have examined the television and news reporting of these controversies, paying special attention to references to public opinion; we have consulted with any number of political consultants and pollsters to test our hypotheses; we have collected a number of Congressional polls and talked to staff members who keep track of constituent response; and, of course, we have read the records of the relevant Congressional debates. Right now we are involved in a pilot survey with plans to look more directly at the self-images of public opinion analysts and their conceptions of their responsibility to the democratic process.

A final report on our research is, as of this publication deadline, not yet ready, but let us record here some of the frequent claims and charges (pro and con) about the effects of media polling that are at the heart of our inquiry. Each one contains at least a kernel of truth:

1. Polls conducted by the news media produce the events that they cover and thus, under certain conditions, change the course of political events. This contradicts the self-concept of the journalist as an observer of the political process, not as a participant;

2. The attention given to polling results has led the press to neglect other manifestations of public opinion that affect policy;

3. Inasmuch as opinion surveys can be used to arrive at and bolster editorial positions, a reliance on the majority view (as measured by polls) can drown out the independent editorial voice;

4. The potential value of scientific polling as a tool of democracy is not fully exploited as media-generated polling becomes part of the attempt to make news programs interesting;

5. Too many newspapers and broadcasters have gone into the polling business without adequate resources, trained

personnel, or attention to sampling procedures. Where surveys are contracted out, journalists may not be able to assess adequately the validity of the data on which reports are based;

6. Because media sponsored polls are mostly geared to a hard news format (timeliness, big stories, etc.) and rarely used for guidance or investigative reporting, policymakers cannot usually get much guidance regarding public desires and preferences from them;

7. The way polls are presented makes it easy for everybody— including the journalists—to impute to them more accuracy than is factually warranted.

8. The findings from polls (both media generated and media reported) influence the amount and kind of press coverage given to political figures.

9. Media-generated polls serve as a check on the power of those who use proprietary polls to manipulate public opinion.

10. The ubiquitous spread of media polling leads to a misdirected battle for prestige among competitors, which favors corner-cutting and less rigorous research. (The assumption is that polls conducted with methodological rigor do not necessarily enjoy more credibility than others, so why bother?)

11. When polls contradict each other's findings, editors are apt to favor their own and ignore, perhaps even squelch, those of the competition in order to make the most of their investment. This is at the expense of the public's need to know.

12. The press—polling connection is a constant invitation to plebiscitary excess, with constant intrusions into policy debate threatening "the proper balance between the direct and representative dimensions of democracy in a complex society."

Disseminating news about public opinion.   If the media did not disseminate news about polling results, we could hardly speak of public polls. American public opinion analysts can hardly fathom the task that has faced their counterparts in countries where the content of the press is strictly controlled by the ruling government. Glasnost has meant, for our Soviet colleagues in public opinion research, encouragement, not only of their efforts to undertake scientific surveys, but to circulate their findings by way of the media. Both the electronic and print media now carry news of poll findings. The National Center for Public Opinion Studies (NCPOS), whose function is to collect information on opinion countrywide, has in the two years of its existence amassed extensive information about present-day opinion in all the republics and all the country's major regions and published the main results of their investigations in a series of bulletins entitled "Public Opinion: Facts and Figures." When they began issuing their bulletins they expected a rush of orders but, as they frankly pointed out at a colloquium in Moscow last December (1989), "it did not work out quite like that." There seemed to be "no urgent need to know what people think and feel" in Soviet society—at least as of the end of 1989. Yet, on the brighter side, most requests for the bulletins came from people in the mass media and from the people's deputies. Such publicity helps to counteract the power of organizations that make socially significant decisions to suppress the dissemination of findings that displease them. When officials do try to ban such news, this tends to backfire, as both the polling results and the interference with publication becomes "big news" in the foreign press, especially on television.

To invoke the situation with regard to public opinion in the former USSR is to put into perspective some of the criticisms of American media reporting of public opinion research. We take as given the proposition that the American press has not only the right but the responsibility to report fully and fairly within the limits of its resources the significant findings of scientifically produced polls on politics and public affairs. At the same time it is the responsibility of experts in and out of journalism to monitor the media performance.

Most debate about media performance in reporting on polls has centered on the disclosure of standards. This has involved disputations among pollsters themselves as well as between the pollsters and the media organizations that make use of the polls. It concerns mainly disclosure requirements: What must the reader or listener or viewer be told about the methodology employed in order to judge the soundness of the conclusions? For long years, the American Association for Public Opinion (AAPOR) Code has called for minimal disclosure: the identification of the sponsor, question wording, dates and method of interviewing, and details about the sample design and its precision. Yet today most news stories about polls—especially radio and television stories—do not meet even this level of disclosure. One leading media researcher has recently argued that disclosure must go further to make known to consumers all flaws in the research design that can affect conclusions drawn from the study. As is, most journalists who report on polls have learned some magic words—such as "margin of error" and "confidence level" and "randomly drawn"—that assure the public that it may accept the headlined statistic at face value, giving the statistic an authority it may not deserve. What has not been reported about methodology may, however, be just as important for such evaluation as what is now commonly reported.

Less frequently debate about the use of polls in the press has concerned which polls get reported and which do not. Most such criticism is reasonably charitable, the assumption being that omissions, in particular, are mainly the product of space or time constraints and the hard choices that news managers have to make. Thus it is quite obvious that the broadcasting networks favor news based on findings from their own polls over those of their competitors. It is also apparent that, despite the proliferation of polls, the results of most are mainly unpublished. For one thing, statistics from the myriad of proprietary political polls find their way into public print only when it is in the client's interest to leak them; for another, only those polls on public affairs that are judged to be newsworthy get picked up by news services and are widely publicized.

More chilling are charges of the selective employment of poll findings to advance the editorial goals of a particular newspaper or broadcast organization. While such manipulation can involve policy making in the domestic field, it appears to us that it is more prevalent in matters involving foreign policy matters. But this is a matter we have not yet explored in depth.

In general the news media treat polls as they treat stock market reports, sports rankings, and best seller lists. They annually report "the most admired woman or man," and any poll that rates the popularity of presidents, dead or alive, is sure to be printed. It may be that this is what people have come to enjoy and expect from opinion polling. Our question is, of course, whether there is not more news value to polling than serving as a kind of hit parade or as a barometer that a politician can use to intimidate the opposition.

When polling results are misleading—for whatever reason—how much responsibility do the media have for alerting the public? When polled responses to some news development are contradicted by the results of another poll, are the media responsible for printing both polls—even though the second may no longer be "news"? It seems to us that we may need ombudsmen for both media-generated and media-reported polls, just as we have ombudsmen who seek out mistakes in other types of news. Given the number of references to opinion trends that find their way into journalistic and social science accounts of politics, how else will history ever be purged of what turn out to be false impressions?

Information, Knowledge, and Journalistic Procedure: Reporting the War in the Falklands

DAVID E. MORRISON
HOWARD TUMBER

It wasn't a news war, it's as simple as that. It was in the wrong place.
(Martin Clever, Press Association Photographer)

Too often, studies of news concentrate either on the formal editorial control of content or on the informal control whereby the journalist is socialized into the news values and procedures of his or her organization. What is missing is any notion of the journalist as person. That is, he or she is first and foremost regarded as a performer of a specific role with certain attributes rather than as an individual with his or her own biography of sensibilities. For example, following the fall of Port Stanley, Ian Bruce of the *Glasgow Herald* was talking by phone to his editor, who complained that Bruce's stories sounded very bitter, to which Bruce replied "That's because I am fucking bitter."[1]

A soldier Bruce had known well and with whom he had shared a drink on many occasions failed to make it to Port Stanley, having

---

[1] The quotations given in this paper are taken from interviews that the authors conducted with the journalists who accompanied the task force. The study involved interviewing every journalist who sailed with the British fleet, editors, and personnel at the ministry of defence and Downing Street, plus performing a content analysis of the main evening television news bulletins shown throughout the conflict and analyzing a national representative survey of 1,000 individuals, that asked questions about their attitude to the war and attitudes to media coverage of the war. The full account the study can be found in David E. Morrison and Howard Tumber's *Journalists at War: The Dynamics of News Reporting during the Falklands Conflict* (Sage Publications, 1988).

been badly wounded, possibly crippled, at the very close of the war. Bruce was upset, it affected him, so it molded his copy.

Of course it would be sociological madness to deny the vital importance of structural factors influencing the manner in which journalists report; the journalist does not, after all, write for himself or herself, but for an organization. Nevertheless, insufficient attention has been paid to how the journalist as an individual exercises his or her role, and more than that, the critical politicizing of research in the area of mass communications has meant that the journalist as news gatherer has been pushed out of sight. He or she no longer fits, or rather researchers cannot find a place for him or her, in the grand indictment of the news as the reproduction of dominant ideology.

This is not to deny the value and contribution to mass communication research of the "critical tradition," but there is a need alongside this for a more humanistically inclined individual perspective. One needs to know how those at the cutting surface of news collection operate before making statements drawn from general understanding of social processes. Content analysis can help, but, even then, its major benefit is in determining values; it cannot go beyond its own methodology to explain how the picture was arrived at. The values say something in that they do not appear by chance; indeed, they represent the workings of social relationships that go beyond even the news industry itself and into social formation. Yet to understand the creation of news, as distinct from social relationships as demonstrated by the news, it is essential to come to grips with people as operatives within a system rather than operators of a system. The latter too easily leads to notions of conspiracy on the one hand, and on the other, gives social structures a life of their own.

Although the individual as such is not the object of sociological study, this does not mean that there is no room in sociological explanation for biographical placement, especially when the subject under investigation (the news) is constructed in the first instance by individual investment of meaning. The observer must be observed. The events in the Falklands offered a unique facility for observing journalists going about being journalists.

DEPARTURE AND UNPREPAREDNESS

When the British task force moved down the Solent and out into the open sea on Monday, April 5, 1982, very few of the journalists on board the ships thought that the fleet would see action. Very few supported the government's decision to send the task force. And most journalists who were gathered on the guardrails of the various craft had never covered a war, or even a troublespot for that matter. Events in the South Atlantic had caught everyone unawares, and the journalists who were sent tended to be those who had been on duty at the time that the Ministry of Defence decided that journalists could go with the troops. Most editors considered that the real story would be in London and hence held their senior correspondents in reserve. The story was going to be political, not military.

To say the journalists turned up for embarkation unprepared is an understatement. David Norris of the *Daily Mail* informed us that he was

> completely clueless. Until the invasion I didn't know the capital was Port Stanley. I knew the basic details: that it was mainly sheep farming and that the Argentinians had this sort of claim to them, but that's about all really. Usually in other countries there is an embassy you can go to and get the background.

Badly briefed, the journalists were no better prepared physically for the assignment. John Witherow of the *Times* was contacted by the Ministry of Defence late on the Sunday evening before the sailing and told to go immediately to the embarkation point in Portsmouth and to "make sure you bring a dark suit." Witherow sailed on the aircraft carrier *Invincible* with four other journalists from the national press. Stuck without any proper equipment or clothing to withstand the freezing cold of the Falklands, they went ashore literally with a suitcase, oddments of naval attire, and a packet of cheese and pickle sandwiches that Tony Snow of the *Sun* had the presence of mind to bring along. They were thrown off the island by the military on the supposed grounds that they could not survive without proper equipment and thus failed to cover the landings.

Those journalists who came later on the P&O liner *Canberra* with the main body of the troops took advantage of the delay in sailing. Kim Sebido of Independent Radio News (IRN), for example, bought a "whole lot of little Antarctic equipment from the Alpine sport shop" before boarding, while, according to Charles Lawrence of the *Sunday Telegraph*, others were fitted out as thoroughly as the intrepid William Boot, the hero of Evelyn Waugh's *Scoop:* "It was the cleft stick routine. Alastair McQueen from the *Mirror* was by far the best equipped. He turned up with the whole lot, including his own water bottle, mug and camping stove."

INDIVIDUALITY AND CONSPIRACY AS KNOWLEDGE

The Navy is a very closed world, and some of the senior officers were aghast at the motley crew of individuals who descended on their ships. Life for all was not going to be easy. More than anything, however, what separated the journalists from both the Navy and the Army was cohesion: The military were disciplined and worked as a team; the journalists were unruly and in competition with each other. As John Shirley of the *Sunday Times* observed:

> The whole military were about co-operation and obeying orders and if the colonel said do something it was done. Whereas they suddenly came up against this group of probably the most anarchistic, competitive group of individuals you could meet. We found it difficult to cooperate.

The journalists' very individuality, both professionally and by dint of personality, was to tell against them and affect their performance. The psychiatrist attached to the task force, Surgeon-Commander Morgan O'Connell, forecast that the journalists would suffer exceptional strain, their competitiveness and lack of cohesion making it difficult for them to support the harsh conditions of the expedition. David Norris of the *Daily Mail* agreed: "I think he's quite right that journalists tend to operate in cutting each other's throat." As time went on, however, some of the journalists did modify their behavior. Ian Bruce from the *Glasgow Herald* told us: "Initially there was great rivalry but it tailed off. When we got ashore co-operation increased. There was no point in cutting someone's throat for a story; he'd get his throat cut very easily by staying where he was, probably."

It is true that the necessity of circumstances—the danger and sheer physical difficulties of the reporting situation—at times drew the journalists together into supportive units. Bruce himself, however, attacked Max Hasting, then of the *London Evening Standard* and now editor of the *Telegraph,* with a bayonet, seriously intending to kill him, in the bar of the Upland Goose in Port Stanley after the war was over for what he falsely believed were overcompetitive practices—he believed that Max Hastings had deliberately mislaid his fellow journalist's copy of the fall of Port Stanley, which had been entrusted to him to file.

When interviewed, Bruce was unrepentant about the attack but did say, "I must confess I tried to bayonet him. Soberly and quite rationally. Now it seems crazy but in the circumstances...there is no rational explanation for it." Bruce was not alone in wishing to kill Hastings, and by this stage in the proceedings, since the journalists had armed themselves with discarded weapons, such an act would not have been difficult, but the point to stress is that Bruce's act was not beyond "rational explanation." His act had much to do with the conspiratorial view that journalists have of the world, a *Weltanschauung* that was given extreme expression in the difficult circumstances of the Falklands.

Individuals who believe that a conspiracy is at work are difficult to pacify by evidence that rests outside the logic of the conspiracy, but, by their nature, conspiracies are not easily open to evidential examination. In fact, as a source of understanding or making sense of proceedings, that is their strength: Something is going on, the detail of which is not quite understood, but everything occurring seemingly fits, in terms of its consequences, into some kind of deliberate design.

Thus Bruce and his colleagues, who were only too painfully aware in talking with their editors by phone that their stories of the fall of Port Stanley had not reached London, knew that something had gone wrong, and in good conspiratorial fashion looked no further than Hastings as the carrier of their copy for the explanation of why their reports had failed to appear.

That something had gone wrong was not seen as an accident or product of circumstances, or as a fateful calamity, but as evidence of purposeful intent to restrict their efforts. Hastings was not at fault and that ought to have been fairly obvious to those present in the Upland Goose—some copy other than his own with which Hastings had been entrusted did get through.

What journalists do, and it is not that their estimations of the way the world is organized are entirely wrong, is to emphasize the conspiratorial side of it. Emphasis is given to the engineered and engineering aspects of human conduct and unfolding of events, to the detriment of processes over which individuals do not have the imagined precise control or influences they are credited with.

Most individuals probably view the world this way, but journalists operate with it as part of their professional practices. What shows as understanding becomes a performance of suspicion, making all unfavorable explanations that do not conform to the practices of a conspiracy difficult to accept. It not only fits their knowledge of the world, it also fits their own self-image of the journalist as "fixer." Because the gathering of news requires the development of persuasive skills—the setting up of difficult interviews, the establishment of trust with sources, the pressuring for facilities not readily forthcoming, the detection of more information than that revealed—the occupational value developed is the good journalist as someone who skillfully and tenaciously gets his or her own way.

This professional value, the ability to manipulate the environment so that hindrances to performance are removed or lessened, based as it is on a very individually developed talent, accounts in part for the development of the conspiratorial mind itself.

It is not argued that conspiracies do not exist; they indeed do, or there would be no basis in reality for the conspiratorial mind that journalists demonstrate. What is suggested is that the high level of suspicion that journalists harbor means that, when conspiracies do occur, they act to overdetermine the view of a conspiratorial world, so that when events possess even the weakest clue of a conspiracy, a conspiracy is registered. The attack on Hastings is a perfect example of this. Therefore Bruce's action in the bar of the *Upland Goose* was not, as he presented it, beyond "rational explanation," but was the product of a collectively suspicious mind operating on an incident that possessed certain features sufficient for those involved readily to invest it with planned interference. Given that Bruce and others believed Hastings to be the agent of the interference, he was fortunate, given the atmosphere and the recent experiences of the journalists, to escape with his life.

Within that framework of thinking and understanding of their colleagues' propensity to scheme and their conspiratorial view of social processes, it would have been surprising had they arrived at a different type of conclusion. It does, however, make for a type of personality that is not easily satisfied with explanations that run counter to their interests, which instead sees explanations as part of a conspiratorial attempt at limitation. Although functional for journalism, such refusal is awkward for those who wish to control journalists. Descriptions of journalists as unruly, or as incapable of doing what they are told—frequent complaints by the military—while accurate from one perspective, from another describe no more than journalists going about their business in a manner that their personality traits well equip them for.

ENVIRONMENTAL DOMINANCE

Yet this general element of the journalists' makeup has a second part to it. That is, they have difficulty in recognizing the needs of any system other than that for which they work. For example, the fact that some of the journalists, somewhat amazingly, did not realize that the Marisat (satellite communication system) was an insecure system of communication was not some cerebral weakness but a product of viewing the world from one obsessive perspective. Access to communication facilities meant that the journalist's basic logistical problem of his or her trade had been solved. The Marisat was the magical link to the journalist's office and audience. The perception, therefore, was one of narrow professional sight, disallowing the intake of other information that was of concern to the military. Graham Hammond, one of the Ministry of Defence public relations officers, or minders as they were commonly known, gave us an example of this at work:

> On the *Hermes*, even when you arranged for helicopters and you said, "Right, helicopters will be ready at 6 o'clock," and the helicopters would be on the deck at 6 o'clock, burning and turning, ready to go, and the guy would turn up and you'd say, "You're not dressed. Where's your survival suit?" "Oh Christ, I've left it in my room." So he'd be ten minutes late getting onto the helicopter. Meanwhile, the pilot was sitting there waiting for the bloody journalist to turn up. And it was little things like that which showed, not disregard, but an insensitivity to the needs of the rest of the ship.

The minders gave us innumerable examples of incidents of this kind. It was not a straightforward disregard, but rather the social working of a job encasing the journalists so tightly in its grip that everything is seen to be for their use. For example, Michael Nicholson, of *Independent Television News (ITN)*, gave a tape that he had produced to a helicopter pilot on the *Hermes*, with the instruction to take it to the *Resource*, which had facilities to transmit it. According to Hammond, the pilot "took off, it was foggy, the first thing he saw of *Response* was the mast as it went past his cockpit, and he said, 'Bugger this,' and came back." The pilot could land on *Hermes* but not *Resource*, because it had superior navigational equipment, but as Hammond said, "Getting back to Nicholson and explaining was very difficult, to put across to him that actually we had tried very hard to get his stuff across and we weren't being deliberately obstructive." Exasperated by Nicholson's refusal to accept the situation, Hammond said, "Look out of the window, Michael, you can't see the end of the deck. There isn't a helicopter flying." Hammond informed us, "You began to despair about what explanations you had to give some of these guys before they'd accept it."

If the minders despaired about making the journalists understand the objective facts of meteorological states, the journalists despaired at the performance of the minders. But the minders, in many instances, were powerless to grant what the journalists wanted: Conditions in the South Atlantic defeated them also. Yet this professional value, the ability to manipulate the environment so that hindrances to performance are removed or lessened, based as it is on an individually developed talent, accounts in part for the unprintable nature of the vehemence of the journalists towards the minders. What was at work in the journalists' anger was the frustration of the professional value of being able to manipulate their environment—the ability to do so is a mark of their journalistic esteem. Yet whichever way they attempted to operationalize that skill, by bullying and threatening or by being pleasant and seemingly cooperative, it had no effect on the minders. They were defeated, and in that defeat, furious. The defeat irked because they failed to make the environment respond to their demand, and the less it responded, the more the journalists doubled their efforts at manipulation and the more they became suspicious of each other.

DESTRUCTIVE COMPETITION AND SUSPICION

Bob McGowen and Tom Smith, both of the *Daily Express*, were cross-decked from *Sir Lancelot* to join other journalists on *Canberra*. They were not displeased, as McGowen informed us:

> The MoD minders wanted us all together so they could keep an eye on us...always being suspicious characters we felt that while we're on this ship [*Sir Lancelot*] some bugger's getting away with murder on the other one. We were all happy to keep an eye on each other.

This suspicion led to strained relationships, as McGowen reported:

> A journalist is a very strange animal. If he thinks that somebody else is getting more copy out through Fleet Street than he is, he sweats, he smells a plot, which probably doesn't exist. Looking back on it now, I don't think there were any plots—it was just the circumstances of the way it was. But when you listen to the *World Service* and you know quite clearly that people are getting more stuff out than you, you get bloody angry. You think they are getting facilities that you're not getting.

The generally suspicious atmosphere meant that it was very difficult for the minders to convince the journalists that conspiracies were not being hatched, and that events were not the result of plots. Patrick Bishop of the *Observer* remembered the weariness of it all:

> All the professional things about nicking each other's stories. People getting on each other's nerves, you know, people always arguing that someone is screwing up arrangements with the military and they were all putting the military's backs up, just constant arguments.

Weary it may have been, but the suspicion that journalists have of each other is common to many reporting situations, as McGowen noted. Yet this distrust and the competitiveness that O'Connel, the military psychiatrist, had observed, and which he considered would lead to personal strain for the journalists, when added to other features of the reporting situation led to consequences that were not so predictable. The journalists began to identify with the troops whom they were supposed to report on and about.

ADMIRATION AND IDENTIFICATION

We have already seen that the journalists were physically ill-equipped to deal with the harshness of conditions in the Falklands; hence they had to be provided, where possible, with equipment borrowed from the military. They began to look like their subjects. Charles Lawrence of the *Sunday Telegraph* said: "It was only after a while I realized I looked like these guys...and because I was filthy dirty, wearing the same fatigues and sort of camouflaged, they thought I was one of them." However, he went on to describe his time on the top of Mount Kent:

> We were absolutely shattered and I had a blister. There was a ferocious storm coming in very quickly before we had time to get bivouacs up and I was absolutely soaked to the skin and it was about to get dark and I suddenly knew I wasn't going to survive that night, you know there was nowhere I could get shelter—we hadn't been issued with all the equipment. Fortunately a bloke, one of the battery commanders, knew that one of his sergeants had got an eight-man tent set up near some rocks and he took me up there. I had exposure. It's amazing how good these guys are to you...they've got problems, but they make sure you've got a dry sleeping bag and if not they'll borrow one from a squaddie and they'll spend hours making you tea and see you all right.

Lawrence did in fact collapse into a very poor state indeed, and undoubtedly the care that was taken of him that night saved his life.

Lawrence's dependence on the troops, although extreme in that instance, was a common experience for all the journalists. But this dependence on the troops for their safety and well-being was also matched by admiration for the troops.

Whatever the feelings of the journalists towards the decision to send the task force, one thing is for sure: the journalists were impressed by the troops they sailed with. John Shirley informed us that he had "more to do with the Marines than I did with the Paras," and then added, "They were enormously impressive. They were very serious blokes." And McGowen reported, "I think you'll find that most of the journalists made lifelong friends with some of the units. I certainly have." This friendship, however, was not based simply on admiration for the troops' professional ability but rather on sharing the social world of the troops. John Shirley explained:

> I was in the Lebanon last year with the PLO for three weeks. OK, they show you around, they take you down to the front. You talk to people, but you go back to Beirut at the end of the day to your hotel.

According to Shirley this inability to physically and mentally remove themselves from the troops, remaining instead within the closed world, affected the traditional role of the reporter: Instead of being observers, they became participants:

> [In Beirut] you've got the opportunity of withdrawing. You've also got the freedom to write what you want. You're an observer, and that's how you attempt to retain some objectivity—some distance from it. But on this thing (a) we were actually directly involved because we had been made captains; (b) we were absolutely dependent on the military—literally, for food, anything, company, survival—and there was nowhere else to go, you had no choice but to say with them. You could get back to your cabin on *Canberra*, but you were still surrounded by these guys, and when we were on the Islands you were marching with them, you were cooking with them and eating with them, you were part of the unit. You were just as likely to get killed as they were. And your actions could affect their safety.

And Shirley's conclusion: "I think the thing that really differentiates it [Falklands War] from anything else, is that we weren't observers, we were participants in the damn thing. This really affected what we wrote." It is not surprising.

Jeremy Hands, for example, admitted that he had become quite fond of the military, and then went on to say:

> I was constantly aware that I was reporting for a nation of civilians and living in a very, very close-knit service environment; and being welcomed by them, you tend, unless you're careful, to become slightly swamped by it. You start talking in initials, using their phraseology sometimes....You'd suddenly find yourself saying "I'm just going down to the bar for a razz and a bottle of Scotch." And you'd think: Hang on a second. Come back to life, son, you're a civilian.

Recognizing that a process is at work does not necessarily enable one to resist its influence. The journalists' adoption of military jargon, however strenuously they sought to excise it from their vocabulary, indicates how efficiently they were being assimilated. It showed in the journalists' copy. David Norris, for example, mentioned:

> I found I was referring to "us" collectively when we were on shore; not on the ships [when] I still felt a little divorced from the whole thing because it still wasn't certain whether there was going to be a landing and it was still in my mind—was the whole thing necessary? But I think once they were on shore and fighting, and we were with them, I couldn't help but think of myself as part of the operation. I suppose people might say that's a bad thing, you should still maintain some impartiality. It's very difficult.

Peter Archer of the *Press Association* mentioned that living with the troops gave him more insight into his subjects but that "the more insights you have, the more sympathetic you tend to be."

Aware that news agencies demand that their reporters be impartial, he added, "it's difficult when you are being shot at by the other side not to refer to them as 'the other side.'"

EMOTIONAL INVOLVEMENT: OBSERVER VERSUS PARTICIPANT

Indeed, the values that serve an occupation well in peacetime, or amid the pain of someone else's war, do not necessarily serve the individual journalist well in the midst of his or her war. The values of impartiality and objectivity, when compared to other people's efforts—the soldiers'—can look wrong or misplaced or even shabby. Away from the sounds of battle, it is easier for producers and editors, 8,000 miles away in England, to hold on to the central idea of objectivity even as their representatives in the field find the concept less easy to grasp. The journalists were deeply affected by what they saw.

John Martin, a soundman for *BBC Television*, said:

> We did an absolutely horrendous massacre in Uganda; we actually fell upon it just [after] it happened...children mutilated and everything. That's no problem at all—it's not pleasant, but you do it with no feeling. And Beirut is the same; it's not your problem. It becomes different when it's people you're involved with.

Some of the journalists were personally very affected by the sights that they witnessed. John Shirley certainly was:

> I'd just delivered some copy and I was getting a cup of tea or something, and a Sea King helicopter came. A general shout went up for people to go and help unload it. I went over because I had nothing else to do, and it was dead bodies of paratroopers who had been killed at Goose Green....It was like the Burghers of Calais....There's a copy of it outside the House of Commons. It's a very dramatic statue of five men who are in some state of agony. There are limbs sticking out all over the place and it's a very grotesque statue. And that's what they looked like. They weren't all neat and tidy and done up in body-bags. They were all wrapped in sacking and there was blood everywhere and bits sticking out all over the place. I helped unload the helicopter and take the guys over to the hospital. I am still affected by it. I went to have a look at the statue the other week and burst into tears....And those are guys I'd known. I'd seen them in the bar on *Canberra*. You get very emotionally involved in it. And yet it's not my job to get emotionally involved.

The enmeshing, the identification, the whole process of involvement, had nothing to do with each individual's private views, feelings about war, or the attitudes of his organization. The dynamics of the situation were so powerful that they overwhelmed all this. Not surprisingly, the degree to which each journalist sympathized with the military depended on his or her own personality and experience during the conflict, but overlaying any specific individual aspect of experience was the general social fact of reality maintenance: the journalists had to make social sense of, and give meaning to, a totally new world—organized death.

THE CONSTRUCTION OF MEANING
AND THE VIEWING OF ACTS

Hardly anyone with the task force had experienced the type of combat situation met with in the Falklands. It was a new experience for both the military and the journalists alike, and this newness meant that it had to be made sense of. Meaning structures, however, are not built from nothing, they are negotiated in interaction with the elements already there—language, culture, beliefs— and with others in the shared community. It is by and large not an individual enterprise at all, therefore, and it is consequently hardly surprising that the journalists, in common with the troops, when faced by new conditions, were presented with the necessity of constructing a new reality by which to make sense of their experiences, not just in terms of circumstances physically going on around them, but in order to give meaning to new emotions. In fact, the social construction of reality, the activity itself, is the process by which the emotions become known.

In discussing the behavior of the troops with the journalists, John Shirley informed us:

> I didn't see so much myself, but [one journalist] told me that he has seen occasions on which people had shot unarmed men, unarmed Argentinians who were in the process of surrendering. He didn't report it because he said that, although he disapproved of it, he felt he could understand it. In the tension of battle and given what was going on, it was an understandable action. That is not a very objective journalistic judgment. That is the judgment of a participant, and to that extent it's wrong. You see, I think that this is an absolutely central problem—this kind of crisis of identity. This problem of participant versus observer.

Yet it is not just a question of becoming a participant, of being with the troops; the question also becomes one of accommodating a world that shifts to include behavior no "decent" person would consider possible of himself or herself outside the sanctions of that particular situation. Even so, it is not a straightforward matter of sanctioned behavior; engagement also involves the psychological adjustment to, and accommodation of, gradations of acts. Without even considering questions of desensitization, then the meaning that acts have, whether sanctioned or not, must shift in the changed conditions of combat. They cannot possess the same meaning as in civilian life. The horrors of war cannot, in effect, be understood from within civilian values, they can only be judged by them. The point is that to hold to a set of values is to exist in a social world where the plausibility structure supporting those values remains sufficiently intact. Thus, to be witness to, or author of, macabre permutations of death is not to place other acts in perspective, as if ontologically there was a correct perspective, but, rather, to alter perspectives so that acts such as rape, looting, or summary execution are no longer capable of possessing their original values and meanings. It is a problem of credibility.

There is something incongruous in holding onto civilian notions of the sanctity of human life in a situation where the whole point of the exercise is to destroy as much life as possible in order to defeat the enemy. Death becomes a technical question, the conclusion of which is a framework of statements about the ability to kill, not a fine concern for individual life. Thus, it is not just the scale of killing that is a contributory factor in the journalists' glossing over of individual deaths, but the lack of a civilian reality by which to hinge the significance of death.

The fact that the journalist did not bother to report the killings because, according to Shirley, "he felt he could understand it" ought to be viewed, therefore, in terms of the dismantlement of the plausibility structures within which violent death draws its usual meaning and the construction of a new world of realities. Indeed, it would be surprising if what was deemed acceptable behavior, especially at the margins of the permissible, was not shared to some degree by the soldier and journalist alike. To disapprove, therefore, but yet not report because "one could understand it" takes on a somewhat different meaning when one understands the *context* within which the event occurred. Had, for example, the killings been of members of the IRA in Northern Ireland, then no matter what the sympathies of the journalists, such incidents if witnessed would no doubt have been reported because within the setting of Northern Ireland, the plausibility structures supporting civilian values and notions of appropriate behavior remain sufficiently intact for such killings to produce shock and thus register as news items. They are, in other words, out of place in reality as constructed in and about Northern Ireland.

It is not a question, however, of a reality, some ultimate base of being—or, at least, operationally it is not—but of a variety of realities containing a variety of assembled meanings that jostle together, producing tension and confusion. The soldiers' fond letters from home, for example, can disturb at the same time as they comfort. The letters bring voices from a reality where violent death is not present, where behavior and values prevail that are totally inappropriate to, and at odds with, the soldiers' setting, and it is from within that context that one must understand how, for example, the correspondent did not choose to report what Shirley clearly considered ought to have been reported if one was acting as an objective journalist. It is no good saying what journalistically ought to have occurred if that "ought" excludes lack of appreciation of what was likely or possible within the particular context.

Attitudes to death are revealing, for the world of the civilian tends to be built around an assumption of its absence. Yet for the soldier death, or at least its possibility, is part of the nature of things.

The journalists went to war without the benefit of military symbolic support to sustain them in the face of acts they were to witness and, in the case of some, friends they were to lose. How was reality to be constructed?

News does not exist independently of someone defining events, happenings, or processes as news; but news values, as collections of occupational understandings about what is of interest to specific publics, are basically the worked-through knowledge of civilian interpretation. For example, the firefighter visiting one of the world's troublespots retains within him the civilian's sensibilities and values and so is capable of moral outrage at acts outside the norm of civil experience. It is possible therefore to talk of thresholds of morality as well as cognition. In practice they are not unconnected. It may be, for example, that something that at first stands out visually because it is uncommon to the nature of the event examined, after repeated exposure becomes no longer noticeable as special and thus not reported; until, that is, within its own terms it becomes so extreme an example that it once again forces itself on the journalist.

Thus, for the correspondent who is operating alongside the action and living with the troops, it could be expected that he or she would adjust to the routines of war so that sights and experiences once beyond the imagination became not accepted—the correspondent did not become narcotized—but, rather, expected and taken for granted: They were accepted as part of the nature of things, and it is this acceptance that helps to explain the nonreporting of killings. It is not, as suggested by Shirley, a question, as with similar "oversights," of professional torpor or poor practice, but a matter of the new construction of reality that allowed the entry of values that downgrade insignificant acts that would normally have been reported, and it is from within that framework that the position of war correspondent ought to be understood, not from the accepted understandings of Fleet Street. It could not be expected that the larger social values, drawn from a different reality and upon which news values themselves are structured, would not, on entering a closed military world and military activity, change, and in doing so change or at least affect news values.

In fact, it makes sense to talk of military life in a way that does not make sense for most other occupations. The more enclosed a particular world, the greater the applicability of such notions of totality. Thus, in the case of war or of other postings, not only are people physically transferred, but all the established meanings of *their* world are also carried along. The journalists, however, in the sense of social anchorage, left their world behind but in doing so still managed to take with them competitive practices and thought processes—the conspiratorial mind—that overdetermined the likelihood of identification and the construction of a reality that was more military than it was civilian.

V

On Communication
and Development

CHAPTER

15

Communication Research and Development in Africa—An Overview

PAUL A.V. ANSAH

From a rather slow and late beginning, communication research has gained ground as a legitimate field of scholarly inquiry in Africa. Though research in mass communication has made some remarkable strides, in concrete terms the output is rather small and the quality uneven, leading an African scholar in the field to remark that "the amount of studies carried out in mass communication in West Africa is but a drop in the bucket, in relative terms, even though a significant progress has been made" (Edeani, 1987, p. 168). The unevenness in the quality of output can be explained partly in terms of the problems associated with doing any type of social research in Africa. Particular approaches, such as the survey method, carry their own problems, and these have been amply documented (see, for example, O'Barr, Spain, & Tessier, 1973). The situation is further aggravated by the lack of systematic and reliable baseline data on mass communication facilities in many countries.

In addition to the general problems encountered in doing social research in Africa, mass communication research poses other specific problems, mainly arising out of the fact that because mass communication is a new academic field in Africa, no research tradition has been established, and consequently, no authentic theories and methodologies appropriate for mass communication research have been formulated. This has many consequences for the quality, relevance, and validity of research findings—an issue that will be addressed in the latter part of this paper. This is what led the MacBride Commission to observe with general reference to the Third World that "the few researchers available for necessary national studies have usually been trained abroad and are often uncritical of research methodologies and priorities existing elsewhere" (MacBride, 1980).

African communication researchers have not been left untouched by the debate on the administrative versus critical research approaches, and while most of the research output is in the area of administrative or service research, there are some notable critical approaches. It has in fact been observed by one scholar that given the various areas in which research needs to be undertaken, a "hybrid" approach or what Halloran has called "pluralism or complementarity of approaches" may eventually emerge as the most appropriate method in the African context.

The need to develop and formulate appropriate mass communication theories and methodologies for Africa is clearly recognized. At the level of finding a philosophical basis for theory construction, Charles Okigbo has put forward some interesting ideas that will be discussed later. In the same vein, Isaac Obeng-Quaidoo has put forward some proposals, arguing strongly in favor of the focus group interview instead of the survey method, and basing himself on what he considers to be the "core value boundaries" of African culture.

But whatever theoretical frameworks or methodological approaches are going to be used, it is important first of all to identify the areas in which mass communication research is needed as a matter of priority in Africa. What are some of the areas in which mass communication research has been done, and what are the issues that need to be addressed in further research work? Broadly speaking, one can identify general areas such as media structures, including the history, development, and control of the mass media; studies of communication content and audience analysis; development type studies, the phenomenon of "cultural imperialism" through the media and other NWICO related topics; the social, political, and cultural impact of the new technologies; and aspects of traditional media. To what extent have these topics engaged the attention of African mass communication researchers? This is another of the questions that we shall be seeking to address in this chapter.

COMMUNICATION ENVIRONMENT

The main reason why it is essential to develop theories and methodologies that will be used in relevant communication research in Africa is that the environment in which a communication system operates determines the role that it can play or the effect that it will have. The communication environment in Africa is completely different from that which obtains in the western industrialized nations. Whereas access to and availability of mass communication facilities are fairly even and widespread in the west, one notices glaring disparities in Africa. On the one hand, there is a relative abundance of mass media facilities in the urban areas, where the elite minorities live and where the situation is close to what obtains in western societies; on the other hand, there is a media scarcity in the rural areas, where the vast majority of the people live. This means that in terms of penetration and possible effects, the situation is not comparable to that of the west, and in the African situation it may be more accurate to examine issues at two different levels.

In terms of structures, too, it is necessary to point out that the political, social, and economic environments in which the mass media operate in the west are different from what obtains in Africa. Whereas in the west there generally exists a privately owned, competitive, free, market-oriented system, what prevails in Africa is generally a publicly owned, highly centralized, monopolized, and controlled system that acts as an instrument for political legitimation and is at least theoretically geared towards public service objectives. Given these different environments, it should be obvious that media performance will be different in the two contexts, and that the approaches and philosophical underpinnings for assessing it will automatically be different.

But before addressing the central issues in this chapter as outlined above, it is perhaps necessary to explain the context in which the term *African* is used here. When scholars use the term "African," the assumption is that there is a uniformity or homogeneity of social systems and cultural outlooks. But is this in fact the case for the whole of the continent, or at least of that portion lying south of the Sahara? Can one really identify a common concept or ethos by which the various societies are regulated? Perhaps there is a set of characteristics or a common field of experience that distinguishes what one may call African society from others, but it is more debatable if one can go on from there to speak of a cultural or world view that is common to all African societies without seriously qualifying it. Even within individual national entities occupying specific geopolitical boundaries, one cannot always speak of a national culture. It is therefore within the context of a common field of cultural experience that distinguishes African society from others that the term "African" is used in this chapter.

DEVELOPMENT OF COMMUNICATION RESEARCH
IN AFRICA

In certain areas, Africa seems to have been overresearched. In some disciplines, most notably history and anthropology, the academic research tradition goes all the way back to the early colonial days. This trend became very noticeable during the period of the nationalist struggle and continued during the postindependence period, when a composite discipline called African Studies was pursued in a number of universities both in and outside of Africa.

However, the proliferation of general social science research on Africa was not seen in the field of communication. Certain studies about social systems and customs in Africa had made reference to communication behavior in some traditional societies, but one cannot speak of systematic studies of communication patterns. The situation was to change later, in the period following the Second World War, but studies and publications on communication were more descriptive than analytical.

If Africa has been underresearched in the field of communication, this is for a number of reasons. Research requires training in a particular discipline, and as far as communication is concerned, this type of training was late in coming to Africa. Journalism, communication, or media studies at the university level are of fairly recent origin; the first such institution, at the University of Nigeria at Nsukka, was opened in 1961. Around this period, a few institutions were set up to train print and broadcast journalists, but the emphasis was on practical training, and in most cases the teaching staff did not possess the necessary skills to undertake research into communication problems.

But even the university-based mass communication courses were at the subdegree diploma or undergraduate level and did not equip the students with many research skills. Such skills are imparted at the graduate level, and graduate level courses in communication studies in Africa south of the Sahara were started only in 1974 at the University of Ghana, Legon. The longer established programs in Nsukka and Lagos began to offer graduate level courses only at the beginning of the 1980s, and this trend has been followed by a number of departments in the region. The main reason that one can deduce for the late introduction of media studies in Africa is that the discipline was not part of the educational traditions established by or inherited from the colonial overlords in Britain, France, and Portugal.

But all this is not to say that Africans were not being trained in communication or that no research was being done in the field of communication studies. While a few foreign scholars were studying the media systems and communication behavior in Africa, Africans were pursuing communication studies up to the masters and doctoral levels abroad, especially in U.S. universities. It was these generations of students who were to become lecturers in African journalism schools, do research, and train students in research techniques at various levels.

Even though it still remains a relatively new discipline, within the last 20 years communication studies has become established in Africa and is producing a copy of indigenous practitioners and researchers. Still, the field has not yet had time to establish an academic tradition. Despite this development, and in addition to the reasons given earlier, there are other reasons to explain the paucity of communication research in Africa.

Among the reasons may be cited the fact that in most cases, the authorities responsible for the operations of the mass media do not appear to appreciate the value of research. Newspapers are published, radio and television programs are broadcast, without the originators of the messages trying to find out whether anybody is reading or listening, and if they do, how they react to what they read, hear, or see. Some broadcasting stations have audience research units, but quite often such units are starved of the human and material resources that will enable them to undertake research in a systematic and scientific manner. Because of this lack of appreciation of the need for research, the authorities don't find it necessary to commission feedback and effects studies from institutions that have the personnel and facilities to undertake such studies in a systematic way.

This lack of interest in or appreciation of the need for research in Africa does not provide encouragement or challenges to communication scholars. In many cases, the major motivation for doing any particular type of research is either to submit a dissertation for a higher degree or to publish an article for academic advancement. Depending on the inclination of the researcher, the topic of the research may or may not have any relevance to the communication problems facing the society in which he or she is operating. For this reason, most of the research findings by African scholars are stored away in university libraries at home or abroad, or published in academic journals. This lack of collaboration between researchers and policy or decision makers has an adverse effect on the establishment of a socially relevant, policy-oriented, and problem-solving research tradition. This has two direct results: firstly, research findings are hardly utilized; and secondly, because the authorities see no need for research, interested researchers cannot obtain the necessary funds and facilities to carry out research that may be relevant and useful to the society. Another consequence of this lack of appreciation of the need for research is that the authorities do not encourage the gathering of relevant baseline data on which to base any studies, and this is a very big handicap. Either people have to work with outdated and unreliable data, or precious time will have to be spent gathering basic facts that can be obtained for the asking in another environment (for a fuller discussion of this, see Edeani, 1987; also see Okigbo, 1987).

Happily, however, the situation is changing. In recent times, university communication departments and other relevant research institutions have been commissioned by government agencies to do feasibility or evaluation studies or even sometimes to execute communication projects, all of which involve research. In most cases, such studies have been supported financially by international agencies, including UNESCO, UNFPA, FAO, and UNICEF, on behalf of the various governments. This is a happy development, because such commissioned research projects are geared towards finding solutions to practical problems, and with time and the implementation of the findings of the research, policy makers may come to appreciate the value of communication research.

As mentioned earlier, within the last 20 years the study of mass communication or communication studies as an academic field or discipline has come into its own as a result of the increase in the number of scholars doing research in it with varying degrees of sophistication, and the research output, though naturally uneven in quality, is relatively impressive. One handicap used to be the lack of avenue for the publication of research findings—there is a very intense competition for space in the well-established and respected foreign journals. This problem appears to have been partially solved with the publication of the *Africa Media Review*, a quarterly published by the African Council on Communication Education (ACCE) since 1986 and providing great service in this area to African communication researchers.

But even with such positive developments, communication research still faces problems in Africa. Some of these problems have been mentioned already, others are too well known to engage much attention, but a few will be singled out here briefly only for the purpose of emphasis. First, there is the general problem of finding the appropriate methodology to use in the rural or urban context, with particular reference to sampling, the attitude of respondents, and the research tools. We shall revert to the methodological question later. Secondly, there is the difficulty in having access to data, especially from official sources, since sometimes even routine information is classified as restricted or confidential. Third is the uncooperative attitude of civil servants and other officials who don't appreciate the need for research and who consequently refuse to recommend or to release funds and other facilities for research.

EPISTEMOLOGICAL AND METHODOLOGICAL QUESTIONS

Even though a reasonably good amount of communication research has been undertaken by African scholars within the past 20 years, questions have been asked about the relevance of such studies to the African situation. More importantly, questions have also been raised about the validity of the findings, since one is not too sure of the theoretical basis on which certain assumptions and hypotheses were put forward. There is a vital link between communication research and communication theory, and communication theory is based on the manner in which the act and process of communication are perceived in a given society. But since communication does not take place in a vacuum, it is necessary to understand the nature of the society within which communication takes place. This is the point which Dissanayake (1988, p. 4) makes when he points out that "it is manifest that social research is largely guided by the social context in which it operates and is influenced by the cultural ethos which sustains it." What this means is that a prerequisite for meaningful and relevant communication research is the formulation of a communication theory that is applicable to the social environment in which communication research is to be conducted, or in any case the adaptation of established theories to suit the local situation.

Most African scholars (and in fact other Third World scholars) undertaking communication research have been trained in the west, particularly in the United States, and the models, conceptualizations, and paradigms that constitute the theoretical basis of their research are embedded in western culture. It has therefore been asked whether the findings from studies based on such theories have relevance or validity or applicability in a different cultural context. It is this concern that has necessitated a call for a reexamination of the various communication theories in the light of the cultural values of Third World countries.[1]

An examination of communication research output by African scholars shows a tendency to base their studies on models, theories, and paradigms developed in the western tradition without much effort to adapt them to the African context, as if such theories could be presumed to have universal validity and hence to be value free. This concern prompted the MacBride Commission to the assertion that "the historical circumstances in which research has developed in these countries have helped to create a dependency situation which is aggravated by the unsuitability of foreign research for their needs, with the theoretical and methodological models of developed countries continuing to serve as reference points for research and teaching" (MacBride, 1980, p. 225).

It is this same concern that leads Charles Okigbo (1987, p. 19) to lament the fact that "three decades of communication have not resulted in many research studies. More unfortunately, no theories have been developed to assist in scholarly explication of the African communication context." Okigbo argues that specific communication theories were developed by U.S. scholars on the basis of a certain concept of life in their society. He goes on to assert that the gate-keeping theory was derived from the social philosophy of liberalism, while the agenda-setting hypothesis was formulated on the basis of the social philosophy of rationalism. Similarly, he attributes the origins of the knowledge-gap hypothesis to the political philosophy of realism, while he sees the social philosophy of pragmatism as engendering the uses and gratification theory (pp. 22–26).

Whether one agrees with Okigbo's analysis or not, the question he seems to be asking is this: How applicable are theories based on liberalism, rationalism, realism, and pragmatism to social contexts and cultural environments that are not guided by such philosophies? In other words, should these communication theories and hypotheses and models not be tested and adapted to the African context before they can provide a valid basis for research? It is just possible that such theories may be universal and therefore applicable to Africa and other non-western areas, but they have to be tested first, and that point must be clearly established before the theories

---

[1] This is a point that keeps recurring in the literature dealing with communication research in Africa. The same concern has been expressed in Asia and Latin America. See for example, Dissanayake and Said (1983); Halloran (1981), and Beltran (1976).

can be used. It is the uncritical application of theories that leads Okigbo to describe African communication research efforts as "episodic, casual, serendipitous and non-systematic. Most tragically, these efforts are not informed by any identifiable philosophies, be they indigenous or foreign" (p. 27).

Okigbo's observations and strictures tend toward some exaggeration. Though there is a paucity of explicit communication theory formulation in communication research output in Africa, there are significant studies related to rural development and rural communication, the impact of the modern media, media use among the urban poor, and political communication that are informed by local usages and cultural values. Okigbo further observes that "the absence of theory-based research in African communication is attributed to the under-development of a philosophy of African communication." But is this really a fair observation? The weakness in communication research in Africa is not that it is not theory based. Most of the research is theory based, but the question is whether the theory can be said to be applicable to the African situation. Since, as has been earlier observed, communication theory is based on the cultural values and world view of the society that is being studied, is there any justification for using communication theories developed in a different social, political, and cultural environment as a framework for research in an African context? This is really the issue to address as far as communication research in Africa is concerned.

Looking at the issue of making communication research relevant and meaningful to the African context, Isaac Obeng-Quaidoo adverts to the questions of appropriate methodology that should be informed by the cultural values of Africa. Obeng-Quaidoo thus looks at the issue from both an epistemological and a methodological level. He recalls a conversation with Hamid Mowlana a few years ago in which the latter said that it takes the foreigner who has earned a Ph.D. in Mass Communication from a developed country about six years to divest himself or herself of the concepts and models he or she learned during his or her studies and which may not be applicable to his or her country. This is because in addition to learning the techniques of research he or she also imbibes a certain cultural outlook, and divesting himself or herself of this foreign culture takes a long time.

Obeng-Quaidoo makes a strong plea for undertaking the necessary methodological adaptations and innovations to make communication research relevant to the African situation in the light of the underlying cultural imperatives. He points out that each culture has a set of core values that are basic to it and cannot be altered without changing that culture. In order to establish the core values of African culture(s), one has to examine the anthropology, sociology, psychology, religion, history, and politics of African society, and it is suggested that the cumulative result of such a study will help in designing appropriate communication research methodologies.

Basing himself on the works of a few distinguished Africanists, Obeng-Quaidoo identifies four key areas that come close to or define the core value boundaries of African culture. These are (a) the role of the Supreme Being or lesser gods in the life of the African; (b) the African's concept of time and its influence on his or her behavior; (c) the African's concept of work and how this shapes his or her relationship with nature; and (d) the nonindividuality of the African and how this affects his or her world view and social relationships. One may or may not agree with what Oben-Quaidoo identifies as the "core value boundaries of African culture," and passing value judgment on the validity of his assertions is outside the scope of this chapter (Obeng-Quaidoo, 1986). However, the important point to retain is that unless we set ourselves to have a clear understanding of the society in which we operate as social science researchers, we cannot clearly identify the problems and select the appropriate tools to tackle them.

From the epistemological level, Obeng-Quaidoo moves to the issue of appropriate methodology. Basing himself on the nonindividuality of the African, he suggests that in the rural areas of Africa, survey methods involving interviewing don't seem to be appropriate because it appears more natural to interview people in groups. Field experience from many social scientists who have done research in Africa has shown them how difficult it is to draw individuals aside and interview them without others interfering. Obeng-Quaidoo proposes other research approaches based on the core values and concludes:

> A broad outline of an African theory in this area would facilitate the emergence of certain useful methodologies. For instance, it might likely be that in future, we shall not arm ourselves with prepared questionnaires for the villages. Rather, we shall live in the villages as participant observers, partake in the activities of the shrines...before we engage villagers in free open-ended discussions of their spiritual activities vis-a-vis the physical realities of their surroundings. Such an approach will help us find the intuitive communicative behavior of the African. (p. 97)

In the light of what he identifies as the core value boundaries of African culture, Obeng-Quaidoo calls for certain adaptations and innovations in methodologies and models that African communication researchers have borrowed from the academic tradition and environments in which they have been trained. He identifies three research traditions or approaches that can be explained in terms of the background of the researcher. There are, firstly, "those with American communication bias who consider the testing of hypotheses as the supreme effort in arriving at the truth"; secondly, "those who hate the very idea of 'chi-square' and consider the European critical approach as sine qua non of any truth seeking"; and thirdly, those "scholars trained in the Soviet Union or the eastern bloc who look through the ideological prism in finding truth" (1987, p. 53). This means there is no unified communication research tradition or approach in Africa—and this is as it should be; such a unified approach would be unnatural, and in fact does not exist in any part of the world. Obeng-Quaidoo himself agrees with Halloran that "we must develop a critical, eclectic methodology capable of doing justice to the complexity of our subject" (Halloran, 1986, p. 55).

Obeng-Quaidoo argues that it is inevitable that African scholars should adapt and replicate research formats learned elsewhere, but they should constantly have in mind the cultural context in which they operate. Blind imitation of methodologies and the application of theories not embedded in a given culture cannot produce reliable results. To illustrate the need for taking the cultural context into consideration, Obeng-Quaidoo argues convincingly why the focus group interview methodology is more suited than the traditional survey method to the African context. He concedes, of course, that this qualitative approach has its strengths and weaknesses and may be applicable to only a limited number of situations, but he gives a concrete example to show how the focus group method is more in tune with social behavior in the African context, whether rural or urban.

He argues that group norms of behavior still operate in Africa, especially in the rural and semiurban areas where the majority of the people live. Even in the urban areas, people from particular ethnic groups tend to congregate regularly in clan associations and attend birth or funeral rites as a way of reducing the isolation and anonymity created by the urban setting. This expression of group solidarity takes various forms and fulfills people's social, psychological, and other needs. It can be said that belonging to one group or another constitutes a natural cultural context for the African, which leads Obeng-Quaidoo (1987, p. 61) to "consider it very natural for communication researchers in Africa to shift some of their quantitative individualized methodologies to qualitative group ones."

ADMINISTRATIVE AND CRITICAL RESEARCH

Undertaking research is not an end in itself; its purpose is to assemble and analyze data with a view to explaining phenomena, finding solutions to problems, or providing a basis for policy formulation. Another purpose of research is to augment the store of knowledge in a particular field. In the African context, it would appear that there is justification for using research directly as a means for finding solutions to our communication problems and for formulating communication policies. It is this concern that prompts Nwosu to observe that "rural communication development research should focus more on applied, functional, utilitarian, field-operational, need-based and culturally-relevant studies"; but he hastens to add that "what is needed here is a shift of emphasis and not a complete neglect of the prototype and theory-building studies aimed at general development of scholarship and research in mass communication" (1987, pp. 77–78). What this means, in effect, is that though basic research that generates theories and hypotheses is important, functional rural development communication studies deserve greater attention.

In a related context, this line of reasoning brings up the issue of the position that the African communication researcher should take in the debate between advocates of administrative research and those of critical research. In administrative research, "the emphasis was on improving the effectiveness of the media or the communication system as well as improving methods to facilitate the achievement of specific goals rather than on refining concepts, developing theories or achieving social change" (Halloran, 1987, p. 137). Critical research, on the other hand, seeks to examine social issues and media institutions as they relate to other institutions in the society. It conceptualizes research in terms of structure, socialization, participation, and organization. Critical research takes a look at the social structures in which people live and the type of interest groups and their interrelationships, as well as the economic, political, and cultural arrangements that regulate conduct. The issue of power relationships, organization, and control are of concern in critical research, but not in administrative or service research.

Given Africa's needs in terms of communication facilities and development objectives, which of the two schools should African communication researchers follow? The simple answer is that there is a need for both types of research approaches. The modern mass media system is relatively new in Africa; it has been superimposed on a traditional system, and sometimes the two operate side by side. We need to know how the new system works. There is therefore the need to undertake administrative research that will generate data on such issues as audience behavior, readership analysis, media credibility, and audience perception of sources of information. This type of research will provide us with the well-organized baseline data that are required for communication policy formulation and planning. For example, it will be useful to find out who is reading foreign newspapers or listening to foreign broadcasts, and why they do so; such a study may provide useful insights into people's perception and evaluation of local media.

This administrative research will provide us with aggregate data, which should provide the basis for further research. With the data available, it will be necessary to move a step further to find out what kinds of social structures and arrangements determine how people relate to the mass media, and this brings us back to the area of critical research. To the African communication researcher, the two approaches are not mutually exclusive. In a sense they are even complementary in view of the role communication is expected to play in a developing country. As Ugboajah (1985, p. 281) observes: "If we consider critical research as having affinity with policy research, then it behooves the researcher to fully understand the environment and the system to enable the formulation of a policy for changing any particular media system."

Looking at the possible choices open to the African communication researcher, M'Baye and Nwako (1989, p. 8) speculate that, "as has been observed among Latin American communication researchers, neither the administrative nor the critical school tradition will dominate in Africa, and that what may eventually emerge will be a hybrid of the two research traditions, with a tendency towards more critical research." But the authors go further and throw a challenge to the African researcher when they say:

> Both the administrative and critical schools of thought should be seen merely as two different sides of the same coin, i.e., the Eurocentric philosophy and ideology. Drawing from the unique African cultural and historical experience, the African contribution should be geared toward generating either a hybrid approach that takes into

account the operations of both the modern and traditional modes of communication, or an altogether authentic African perspective of the study of communication problems. (p. 10)

In a similar vein, James D. Halloran who, perhaps more than anyone else, has written very copiously on the administrative versus critical research debate, and has not hidden his preference for the critical approach, which he considers to be "less likely than conventional research to be encumbered by historical and institutional relationships with journalism and broadcasting," finally settles for what he variously calls "a critical, eclectic approach," "complementary approaches," pluralism and complementarity of approaches," "critical, multi-perspective diagnosis" (Halloran & Jones, n.d., pp. 48–49).

It is even just possible that the debate may in the final analysis be of no more than mere academic interest to the African scholar, for such a debate may "have no meaning for Third World conditions where communication scholars are grappling with the daily and mundane issues of development and in so doing, are finding to their discomfort that Western models have neglected the structural and sociological factors present in countries such as India" (Reddi, 1986, p. 27).

RESEARCH ON TRADITIONAL COMMUNICATION

Most of the research that has been done in or about Africa has dealt with various aspects of the modern mass media that are mainly an urban phenomenon. However, it is well known that Africa is not for the most part urbanized, and that about two-thirds of the population live in the rural areas. This means that the impact of the modern mass media on the rural dwellers is limited, or in any case not as marked or decisive as is the case in the industrialized countries. One other sociological reality that should be kept constantly in mind is that there are several cultural layers even within a single nation. There are the majority of rural dwellers, who are generally untouched by foreign culture and who have remained faithful to their traditional culture. Then there are the social elite, who have come in touch with Western culture, are heavy consumers of Western media products, and are astride two cultures. These two groups attend to different media—the traditional and the modern—although sometimes they overlap.

A number of studies have shown that in the rural areas of Africa, traditional communication structures and modes still play a very important part in information distribution and sharing. But not much is known of the exact contexts in which traditional communication modes are used, and research in this area is urgently called for. What exactly are folk media, and how can they be integrated with modern mass media, or should they be in the first place? To what extent can the modern communication technology be used to extend the scope and reach of traditional communication formats, acting in this case as "magic multipliers"? How effectively can the traditional communication processes be applied in an urban or semiurban situation where the social context changes altogether?

Frank Ugboajah (1987) paid some attention to traditional communication processes and the social setting in which communication took place. He referred to this type of communication as *oramedia,* but its distinctive features were never clearly delineated or convincingly explicated. One point which Ugboajah clearly makes about oramedia—which he uses interchangeably with the terms folk media or traditional media—is that they reach fewer people than the mass media, but whereas the mass media have only an influence in the cognitive realm in increasing knowledge and awareness, oramedia, with their limited reach, "serve the motivational functions of communication (behavioral and attitude change, proximity, transaction, interpersonification, instrumentation, legitimacy and grassroots gratification)" (1985, p. 41).

In order to create a total communication environment and draw maximum advantage from the ancient and the modern, Ugboajah calls for "a fusion of oramedia and relevant modern mass media towards an equilibrium." He further adds:

> The communication effort should be to reconcile the total mass media environments of Africa so as to exploit mixedly those of the rural, the slum and the urban sectors in order to make communication audience-relevant. The aim would be to add speed to oramedial credibility in information diffusion in the villages—where the populace suffers from information underuse and ambiguity syndrome of the urban elite. (p. 47)

One further area of research, after the preliminary issues about traditional communication have been clarified or resolved, will be to find out how folk media can best be used: for mobilization, awareness creation, or persuasion and attitude change, or all of these.

Although there is recognition of the need to harness the resources offered by traditional communication processes to help in mobilization and other areas of development, because they are more

natural and more closely related to the customs, social organization, and value systems of the rural people, little research has been
done in this area. This dearth of research can probably be explained
by the fact that there has not been enough collaborative or interdisciplinary research in communication in Africa. In the particular
case under discussion, a combination of sociological, anthropological, psychological, and communication research skills should yield
useful and interesting insights. It is only such a systematic approach that will help us escape from a certain romantic hankering
after the past—the kind of sentiment that has led an African
scholar to suggest seriously that it might perhaps be worth our
while to reduce attention to the modern mass media and experiment to see whether the gongman cannot be equally useful as a
communicator even in the modern urban setting (Wilson, 1989). It
might well be that the idea is not all that romantic after all, but a
systematic study is needed before any conclusions can be drawn. It
is in this sense that, echoing the sentiments expressed by the
MacBride Commission, Frank Ugboajah writes:

> The main challenge to policymakers, communication practitioners
> and researchers is to find a formula that forges a relationship
> between traditional and modern forms of communication without
> damaging the traditional ways nor obstructing the necessary march
> towards modernity. (1987, p. 174)

THE IMPACT OF THE NEW COMMUNICATION
TECHNOLOGIES

The phenomenal growth and rapid development of new communication technologies should have a lot of implications for Africa and
provide interesting topics for research. The first issue is that of
access. What percentage of the population, or what sections, can
and do have access to the new technology? The available evidence
shows that it is a small minority, and that the new technology,
especially the video revolution, is rapidly widening the communication gap between the rural and urban populations. What are the
implications of this development in terms of national integration
and social cohesion (Ugboajah, 1987, p. 47)?

Another related issue that needs research is the production of
communication gadgetry. In terms of the manufacture of communication hardware in Africa, to what extent can the commercial

arrangements encourage self-reliance, or on the other hand increase the dependency situation, and with what consequences? Again, given the limited capacity of Africans to produce appropriate programs for their mass media, is the use of the new technology not likely to increase the incidence of cultural imperialism? And what will be the implications of direct broadcast by satellite, which has now become a virtual reality, on the cultural identity of various societies?

One further area that deserves the attention of African communication researchers is how the possibilities offered by the new technology will affect the issue of ownership and control, and what this means in terms of the balance of power and social forces. In Africa almost all electronic media are owned and controlled by the governments, and so is a large percentage of the print media. With the possibilities offered by video and satellite technology and cheap, fast, and efficient printing facilities, it is going to be increasingly difficult for governments to control the flow of information within individual countries. How will this affect the balance of forces within the society, and how is it likely to affect media legislation and regulation in Africa?

In brief, then, the potential and actual social and cultural impact of the new information technologies provides a very fertile field for communication research in Africa, and this is an area in which both the administrative or policy research approach and the critical research approach can make their appropriate contributions to the studies to be undertaken.

CONCLUSION

It is obvious from the volume of published research that communication research in Africa has seriously engaged the attention of communication scholars. While a few non-African scholars who have an academic interest in Africa continue to research and publish on communication issues related to the continent, the bulk of the research is being undertaken by Africans. The expansion of communication studies, the higher levels at which the discipline is taught, and the acquisition of appropriate skills account for the steady progress in communication research in Africa.

But recognizing this progress should not blind us to the fact that a lot still needs to be done, especially in the formulation of a philosophy of communication that will guide the building of theories that are informed by African cultural values and social structures. Then the question of appropriate methodologies also has to be addressed. There has been a great tendency to adopt without adaptation communication theories and research methodologies developed in sociopolitical and cultural contexts that are different from those prevailing in Africa. This has raised some doubts about the validity of the conclusions drawn and the relevance of the studies.

Happily, this problem is being addressed by a few scholars who see it as a challenge to make their research findings relevant to their society and also to add to the store of knowledge about the communication process in African society. Two major areas or topics that need further scholarly exploration are the exact nature and process of traditional communication or folk media, and the sociocultural impact of the new technology. The new information technology has the potential of influencing the society for good or for ill, in terms of both the distribution and the use of information within national boundaries and across them, and its sociocultural impact should be closely monitored through research. Such research will produce data that can form the basis of a carefully considered national communication policy. And this will be a major contribution by African scholars to their respective nations in the search for solutions to the problems of development.

REFERENCES

Beltran, L.R. (1976). Alien premises, objects and methods in Latin American communication research. In E. Rogers (Ed.), *Communication and development: Critical perspectives.* Beverly Hills: Sage.

Dissanayake, W., & Mohd Said, A.R.B. (Eds.). (1983). *Communication research and cultural values.* Singapore: AMIC.

Dissanayake, W. (1988). The need for Asian approaches to communication. In W. Dissanayake (Ed.), *Communication theory—The Asian perspective.* Singapore: AMIC.

Edeani, D.O. (1987). West African mass communication research at a major turning point. *Gazette, 41.*

Halloran, J.D. (1981). *The context of mass communication research* (Occasional Papers, 13). Singapore: AMIC.

Halloran, J.D. (1986). The social implications of technological innovations in Communication. In M. Traber (Ed.). *The myth of the information revolution.* London: SAGE Publications.

Halloran, J.D. (1987). The international research experience. In N. Jayaweera, & S. Amunugama (Eds.), *Rethinking development communication.* Singapore: AMIC.

Halloran, J.D., & Jones, M. (n.d.) *Media education and communication research* (Documents on Communication and Society, No. 16). Paris: UNESCO.

MacBride, S. (1980). *Many Voices, One World,* Paris: UNESCO.

M'Bayo, R., & Nwako, R.N. (1989). The political culture of mass communication research and the role of African communication scholars. *Africa Media Review, 3.*

Moemeka, A.A. (1981). *Local radio: Community education for development.* Zaria, Nigeria: Ahmadu Bello University Press.

Nwosu, I.E. (1987). *Research and training for rural development communication: Adopting the tri-modular training and sequential research methods.* Africa Media Review, 1.

Nwuneli, O. (1981). *Formal and informal channels of communication. in two African villages.* Unpublished report presented to UNESCO.

O'Barr, W.M., Spain, D.H., & Tessier, M.A. (Eds.). (1973). *Survey Research in Africa.* Evanston: Northwestern University Press.

Obeng-Quaidoo, I. (1986). A proposal for new communication methodologies in Africa. *Africa Media Review, 1.*

Obeng-Quaidoo, I. (1987). New development-oriented models for communication research for Africa: The case for focus group research in Africa. *Africa Media Review, 1.*

Ochola, F.W. (1983). *Aspects of mass communication and journalism research in Africa.* Nairobi: Africa Book Services.

Okigbo, C. (1987). American communication theories and African communication research: Need for a philosophy of African communication. *Africa Media Review, 1.*

Reddi, U.V. (1986). Communication theory: An Indian perspective. *Media Asia, 13.*

Ugboajah, F. (1985a). Media habits of rural and semi-rural (slum) Kenya. *Gazette, 36.*

Ugboajah, F. (1985b). Oramedia in Africa. In F. Ugboajah, (Ed.), *Mass communication, culture and society in West Africa.* Oxford: Hans Zell Publishers.

Ugboajah, F. (1985c). Research models and the problem of communication research in West Africa. In F. Ugboajah, (Ed.), *Mass communication, culture and society in West Africa.* Oxford: Hans Zell Publishers.

Ugboajah, F. (1987). Cultural factors in communication for rural third world development: The African case. *Communication Socialis Yearbook, 6.*

Wilson, D. (1989). Towards a diachronic-synchronic view of future communication policies in Africa. *Africa Media Review, 3.*

The "Public Sphere" As An Integrating Concept For Development Communication

ROBERT A. WHITE

In the immediate post-World War II period, the new development sciences were an attractive panacea for political leaders in the North Atlantic and in countries emerging from colonial dependence. The interdisciplinary social sciences seemed sufficiently mature to map out planned intervention to accelerate the processes of sociopolitical, economic, and cultural evolution according to the goals of the politicians. Development was hastily defined as a process of extending modern technical capacities and social organization from the industrialized countries to urban centers in developing countries, and from there into the backward rural areas (Schramm, 1964). Thus, communication was seen as a central problem. The founders of the fledgling science of communication were themselves quite anxious to prove that they had effective tools of social engineering.

In the ensuing decades vast sums of foreign aid were premised on the models put forward by communication researchers. The five-year plans and national budgets in developing countries were often designed with advice of communication experts (Narula & Pearce, 1986). Since evaluation of achievement of objectives was an integral part of planning, there was tremendous pressure on advisors to "get it right." With so little data or experience to go on, and with the demand to define central priorities, it is not surprising that there were oversimplifications and unexpected negative consequences. About every 10 or 15 years the field of development communications has been marked by agonizing reappraisals and public admissions of the inadequacy of the questions posed. Each time, the search for the "right" questions has been spurred on (Schramm & Lerner, 1976; Martin-Barbero, 1987).

In the textbook reviews that categorize approaches in terms of general paradigms,[1] a first generation of theorists defined development communication as a process of incorporating developing countries into a world communication system for the diffusion of industrial technology, modern social institutions, and a free market model of economy and society in general. The clash of this modernization paradigm with the goals of national independence led to a second generation of theorists who looked to the state, the strongest *autonomous* institution in many developing countries, as the foundation for indigenous industrialization, national planning, and cultural identity. Still another generation of theorists has argued that both the modernization and disassociation paradigms end up giving a privileged role to elites, and these theorists suggest that authentic development must be based on popular sociopolitical movements and the popular culture. Each of these three paradigms tends to legitimate a different set of political actors and reinforces profound sociopolitical conflict as well as paralyzing political stalemates. Currently, a fourth generation seeks a communication foundation for a model of political-economic and sociocultural negotiation and integration.

Obviously, to speak of paradigms and generations is a heuristic device; all of these processes have been intermixed from whatever beginning point one wants to take. Nevertheless there has been a searching conceptual dialectic in the field of development communication over the past 40 years. Nor is it surprising that, at present, many are looking for an integrating conception broad enough to encompass both the empirical research hypotheses and the normative objectives of the various paradigms.[2] What seems to be suggested is not an overarching theory but rather a point of dialogue regarding the commonalities of the paradigms.

It is the thesis of this chapter that in spite of sometimes radically conflicting priorities and partial definitions of the problem, all of the approaches to development communication have attempted to deal with a more basic question: "How can we facilitate the growth

---

[1] The contrasting typologies of communication and development appear in Hedebro (1982). The explicit terminology of *paradigms* is used in Narula and Pearce (1964).

[2] One major example of this synthesis that is producing quite an original theoretical perspective is the recent work of Jan Servaes. Cf. Servaes (1989).

of a 'public sphere' at the national and international levels?" Descriptively, the public sphere refers to that dimension of social action, cultural institutions, and collective decision making that affects *all* people in the society and engages the interests of *all* people in the national body. By contrast with this common, public sphere, the "particular" spheres are the interests of limited sectors of society: different occupational or economic groups, different social classes and statuses, religious or ethnic interests, regions, and local communities. All private and particular interests have a public dimension, and the public sphere must respect these particular interests. Each of the particularistic groupings may have its own internal public sphere, but at the level of the society these are particularistic interests.

Normatively, a public sphere requires that all social actions take into consideration the common, collective welfare, the equitable distribution of social benefits, and the equitable distribution of contribution to the common welfare (Smith, 1989).

The constitution and maintenance of a public sphere has been a perennial problem in all societies, and a nation can be said to exist insofar as it has a core of social interaction that is truly common and public. However, the creation of the institutions and culture of a public sphere has been a paramount task for the new nations. As national boundaries were drawn, people of different regional linguistic and cultural differences, divisions of caste and class, traditions of religious sectarianism, and deep familistic, tribal identities suddenly found that they had to work together as a united people. If before these societies often had been broken up into small self-subsistent economic units, each with its own corporate status and history, the challenge was to create a national economic system and a common political decision-making and service system that would incorporate and link these subsidiary units, while at the same time it respected their particularistic interests. Moreover, this common sphere was to be one of ever-improving services to an advancing quality of life requiring an equitable advance in contribution from all sectors.

This task of creating a national public sphere was double-edged in that the *internal* societal unity had to be simultaneously the public *external* international identity in the process of decolonization and entry into competitive geopolitical relations. Moreover, the national public sphere was an important point of reference in the contribution of a particular country to the creation of an international public sphere at a different level. If the national public sphere was weak, then various international networks of sectorial political, economic, cultural, and religious interests could very easily link up with sectorial interests in the country and further hamper the formation of a national public sphere. In a period when advances in the technology of international communication were rapid, people were becoming aware that they were citizens of the world with universal human rights—just at the time when creation of a national public sphere was most crucial.

The creation of a public sphere immediately posed problems of communication at different levels. The most evident level is the need for a physical structure of communication—for example, a telephone, a postal system, broadcasting equipment, a press that can print periodicals and books—and countries with advanced technology were quick to suggest this technology as an almost universal solution. There also had to be a definition of what *public* information is, that is, information that is significant for expressing the common interest and for participating in the debate about this common interest. This touched on deeper issues of common language, symbols of identification, systems of coding, and epistemologies arising from diverse philosophical and religious backgrounds. However, the most difficult question has been finding some combination of sectorial exchange networks, interests, cultures, or some entirely suprasectorial invention that subsumes most of the other communication issues and provides an acceptable common communication network. The tendency has been to seize upon one sectorial network with its infrastructure and language, and to make that the common public sphere. Theories have moved from the priority of the technical, to the economic, to the political, and to the cultural. As so happens, the "wrong" questions are at least partially right, and perhaps the wrongness comes from claiming that the part is the norm for interpreting the whole.

The objective in these few pages is modest: simply to point out the major outlines of how each of the so-called paradigms of development communication have conceived of the process of creating a public sphere. If the task of bringing these together in a more integrated conception is feasible and worthwhile, that remains a task for another day.

CONCEPTIONS OF THE PUBLIC SPHERE IN THE MODERNIZATION PARADIGM

Theorists using a modernization language to describe development, such as Lerner, Schramm, and Pye, were very much concerned with the formation of a public sphere. They saw the isolation of rural

communities, the disparate subcultures, and the lack of communication between particularistic ethnic groups as one of the most
evident characteristics of underdevelopment. Schramm especially
defined development as introducing a process of nationwide dialogue regarding national goals, national policy, and national
accomplishments. This dialogue provided the essential climate for
what Schramm (1964, p. 44) called *nation-ness.*

In this model, a first level of the public sphere was constituted by
introducing the physical infrastructure of modern communication
technology: systems of effective postal service, telephones, broadcasting, the press, satellite links, and other ever-advancing information technologies. Communication was defined very largely as
objective information, something clearly of a public nature, and the
technology was seen as essentially a common carrier to be at least
regulated in the public interest. An equally important communication infrastructure were the extension bureaucracies to diffuse
technical educational information from international sources to
national urban poles of development and then, through cadres of
change agents, out into the rural hinterlands. These ministries—of
education, health, agricultural advice, and so on—were located in
government administration, and employment in these agencies
was defined as neutral, objective, disinterested public service to all
who asked for or needed this service. All of this infrastructure was
premised on the introduction of the institutions of a modern
democratic government with its public parliamentary debate and
regulated civil service.

In the minds of many planners, the turnkey *introduction* of an
infrastructure of communication technology and extension organization in itself *automatically,* almost mechanically, constituted a
public sphere. Little thought was given to how the existing power
structure or class and caste structure, which already defined flow
of information, might influence this superimposed pattern of
communication. Once locals were technically trained, information
was expected to flow freely, with the resistance of traditionalistic
peasants as the only major obstacle. Since the emphasis was on the
quick transfer of technology, there was little analysis of the historical, endogenous process of development. As Schramm (1964, pp.
90–113) points out, the objective was to incorporate backward
rural areas into an ever-expanding urban, modernized pole within
the countries. There is little mention of how to deal with exploitive,
conflicting urban–rural relations.

The information-flow infrastructure described above rested
upon, and was expected to facilitate, a second, central level of the
public sphere: a free-market model of society that would link

individuals, isolated communities, regions, and particularistic groups into one interlocking system. This was to be essentially an economic exchange network, and all ideas, talents, styles of life, education, and so on were transformed into neutral, objective, public goods by giving them a quantified, economic market value. The exchange remained publicly available as long as there was free flow and everything retained the characteristic of an accessible commodity. It was not by accident that the keystone of modernization was the introduction of central banks, financial and credit systems, stable currencies, universal accounting systems, and linkages with international markets (Schramm, 1964, pp. 21–34). Anything that was not directly related to productivity and capital accumulation, such as the traditional wisdom of folk cultures, was of purely private value. Particularistic social relations based on ethnic or religious identifications, familistic patron–client bonds, or celebratory communal ties were judged to be of little value. For example, peasant farmers, who may have had some protected identity on the basis of these familistic, communalistic bonds, now became simply an economic object with a market value. And the characteristics of semisubsistence cultivators had little significance or value in national planning geared toward increased productivity.

At a third level, that of cultural world view and values, the modernization paradigm attempted to constitute a public sphere by stressing universalistic, value-free, rationalistic, and positivistic forms of knowledge. In this view, public knowledge is that information that can be objectively (without subjective feelings or opinion) and empirically tested and verified by anyone who is willing to use the same information-producing methods. Again, quantification is the one sure means of rendering knowledge that has been technically verified; that is, it is shown to be the single most efficient combination of actions to produce a desired result.[3] Thus, the philosophical foundation for development is the conception of all aspects of reality as part of a universal, unilinear evolution from the prescientific era dominated by subjective, particularistic (tribal) myth, ritual, providential fatalism, magical technique, and oral tradition toward ever more advanced stages of scientifically and technologically effective knowledge. The history of all cultures is to be redefined as part of this single historical process, and traditional cultures are expected to automatically wither away in

---

[3] A critical but penetrating analysis of the technological world view is found in Ellul (1967).

the face of the obvious value of rationalistic, scientific knowledge. The prescientific forms of knowledge may remain as a personal, subjective aesthetic option, but this is a private sphere of culture that is to be separate from the universalistic public sphere.

Theorists such as Lerner argued that the introduction to print media, literacy, and the mass media play a key role in developing the psychological and cultural foundations for this universalistic sharing of meaning. In Lerner's (1964) view, the empathetic, mobile personality—the person who is able to share the same public meaning of all other persons in the national or international society—is the personality capable of readily accepting the rapid changes introduced by modernization. That is, it is the personality capable of entering into this new public sphere centered on scientific and technical progress, quantified economic relations, and rationalized bureaucratic organization of information flow. In all of this, the mass media, precisely because of their massness and their guidance by change agents, are crucial for providing the cultural foundations for the new public sphere.

THE AUTONOMOUS NATIONALISTIC "STATE" AS THE PUBLIC SPHERE

For more nationalistic political leaders, especially if they were leaders of revolutionary movements to cut ties with colonial empires, the modernization conception of development clashed with their goals of political economic and cultural autonomy. The seemingly beneficial transfer of modern technology and organization was in reality an extension of institutions in the North Atlantic nations that implied a continued dependent linkage and a division of labor benefitting the industrialized nations. The definition of the public sphere as a system of international market exchange left the developing nations in a perpetually disadvantageous position, in which not only profits but the best talents and ideas were forever drained off from the periphery to the core support of the world-wide political economy. Moreover the ideal of universalistic objective values, which knew no particularistic boundaries, undermined the nationalistic ethnic and cultural identity that had fueled independence movements in the first place. Transfer often meant private linkages that reinforced the deep-seated, centrifugal, disintegrative tendencies that political leaders were trying to bring into a unified national identity. Technology and institutions that had evolved out of North Atlantic history often never really took root in the values and aspirations of the host countries, and innumerable development projects either died after the foreign money stopped or created lifeless mechanical bureaucracies that served no one but the job holders. Local people felt that their lives were split between a modern and a local world.

Political leaders could see that technology, modern forms of political and social organization, scientific competence, and even some form of market economy were important if national independence was to be sustained in the face of international competition. But leaders felt that what the modernization conceptions of the public sphere did not produce was precisely a conception of the public that built upon the history of nation-building and motivated people to work for the endogenous societal development.

For movements of political-economic independence, the institution of the state seemed to offer an organizational structure through which a sense of national identity could be developed (Ansah, 1985). In many contexts the state was virtually the only structure strong enough to counterbalance and direct the internal base of international technical-economic linkages toward national goals. The state was also the institution that would be recognized both internationally and internally as the authoritative, authentic representative of ideals of autonomy.

In the absence of a deeply rooted culture of public interest, political leaders introduced, as the most visible operative expression of the public sphere, systematic centralized planning, which would coordinate not only the many service bureaucracies, but also the more decentralized participatory regional district and village-level development organization (Narula & Pearce, 1986, pp. 64–98). And to ensure the continued mobilization of the population toward long-term planning goals, political leaders usually sought some form of one-party government or strong corporatist agreement among political leaders and parties.

To sustain political independence, leaders gave priority to establishing an increasingly autonomous industrial base, but since indigenous capital and technological capacity were scarce and entrepreneurial administrative experience was at best incipient, the state often took the initiative for industrial development, either directly through state enterprises or through close cooperative agreements with national entrepreneurial groups. Thus, international capital resources and economic advisory services were often channeled through state planning bodies. To help local entrepreneurial efforts the state would guarantee capital resources at preferential rates, provide a protected market, and build whatever communication transport or energy infrastructure was directly necessary for industrial growth. This gave the state the power to direct industrial development toward national goals and force entrepreneurs into plans for basic industries and schedules of gradual import substitution. At the same time, given such political-economic pressures as rising middle-class expectations, unemployment, and the balance of international payments, political leaders felt dependent on entrepreneurial interests, and the state was often willing to make wholesale concessions to any national entrepreneur who showed initiative. Thus, although the state defined itself as a service for the development of the whole population, the operative public sphere was a kind of political clientelism between political leaders and a new technical-economic bourgeoisie working within or in close association with state planning.

To maintain widespread popular support, political leaders had to use populist nationalistic symbols of motivation to the utmost, but given the priority of industrialization and a nationalistic mode of modernization, the rural peasantry and industrial workers were expected to sacrifice immediate improvement in standards of living. There might be extensive agrarian reform, but the major goals in this were to break the political opposition of a landed aristocracy and to rationalize agricultural production. Popular peasant or labor organizations were seen more as instruments of mobilization than as representation of grassroots interests.

Where there was a colonial legacy of state control of the print or broadcast media, these media often became instruments of mobilization and planning, with continuous educational campaigns in line with economic and political goals. Where the media were in the hands of private entrepreneurs, broadcasting especially was a means of opening up internal markets through advertising and programming displaying conspicuous consumption. There was in fact little cultural regulation as long as the media supported nationalistic political and economic goals (Fox, 1988, pp. 174–176). Political leaders were ready to give direct support to the creative community for the production of drama, film, music, imaginative fiction, or popular entertainment, especially if this formulated a national myth rooting independence movements in indigenous ethnic history. However, in the atmosphere of national mobilization and political clientelism, the media rarely developed into an open public sphere for cultural or political debate, and the creative community, especially those sympathetic to the popular classes, not infrequently developed into a core of political and cultural opposition.[4]

The media also became a problem for nationalistic cultural and political identity when the expanding middle class, often westernized in its outlook, sought an expanded range of press information and popular entertainment that could be supplied immediately only by foreign news services or imports of film and television programming. Generally, developing countries lacked the technical and capital resources for mounting more sophisticated information and cultural industries, and the New World Information and Communication Order became an important motivational symbol for mobilizing an indigenous base for national communications (White, 1988). One of the key elements in the proposals associated with the NWICO movement was precisely the kind of national communication planning that would provide a dimension of public service and public interest in the area of communications that was in fact not present in either the modernization or state-centered models of development.

POPULAR DEMOCRATIC HEGEMONY AND POPULAR CULTURE AS THE PUBLIC SPHERE

Both the modernization and national independence approaches to development have given a key role to modernizing elites and have tended to create a public sphere dominated by these elites. Although national independence movements have often begun with a wide popular base and have used populist cultural symbols, the priority given to urban-based planning service bureaucracies and industrialization generally has tended to favor the upwardly mobile individual and has tended finally to neglect the masses of semisubsistence peasants and rural migrants to the cities. The rural and urban poor generally have little independent sociopolitical organization to represent their interests in a public sphere centered around the new technical-economic classes.

This process is certainly most accentuated in the modernization model of development or in national independence approaches that have made concessions to the modernization model. With the emphasis on a competitive market concept of the public sphere, the situation of the semisubsistence cultivators and unskilled laborers

---

[4] Michael Etherton (1982). Documents both the support of dramatists by African governments and the opposition of the dramatists to one-party regimes.

deteriorates rapidly (Migdal, 1974). Establishing the transnational urban rationalized mode of life as the normative value quickly intensifies the depreciation of traditional folk cultures and the popular culture of the urban poor—a depreciation that often already exists in hierarchical peasant societies.

The increasing impoverishment of the peasantry and urban migrants in the midst of rising expectations leads to a desperation that is often ignited into spontaneous local protests and uprisings by sharp brutal injustices such as expulsion from land. These local movements are often the first step toward building an alternative horizontal communication and organizational structure among the rural and urban poor. As these groups mobilize themselves in protest, they generate a new language and culture that places a positive value on everything associated with the life of the poor, the stigmas of ethnic racial minority status, and the depreciated oral narrative history of the underclasses (White, 1969). In the face of the Herodian transnationalism of the culture of the urban middle and elite classes, the unlettered leaders of the poor are quick to perceive the popular classes as the source of the authentic culture and social energy in the interior of the nation. The popular classes are the most representative of a life adapted to the ecology, history, and indigenous tradition of the nation. In this experience there is the genesis of a conception of the public sphere centered on grassroots organizations and the popular culture.

The modernization process also creates opposition among specific sectors of the urban elites as well: intellectual leaders from a literary philosophical and sociopolitical analysis background who see the richness of the national cultural tradition destroyed by shallow, foreign-based technocracy and pop culture; religious leaders at all levels who see modernization as a process of secularization; leaders of skilled labor, who are more conscious of their exploitation for the sake of capital generation; and even the upwardly mobile, newly educated petit bourgeoisie who see that for all the rhetoric of rationalization, the best bureaucratic jobs are given on the bases of traditional personalistic ties (Wolf, 1969).

Dissident elites soon build alliances with popular mass movements and use their organizational and political skills to help mobilize spontaneous uprisings into a national popular-based movement. As dissident social scientists or educators such as Paolo Freire are driven out of universities and national planning bureaus, they bring their capacities of social and cultural articulation to the popular classes. The latter group of educated opposition is especially important in defining the popular culture as the authentic national culture and in portraying, through literature, drama, new concepts of education, and political philosophy, the popular classes as the real protagonists of national history.

These national popular alliances propose that the existing public sphere be widened to include a network of popular organization and communication and the groups proposing radical sociopolitical reform. These proposals often meet implacable opposition from modernizing elites, because the reforms imply a restructuring of social power relations, a more equitable allocation of economic resources, and a reorientation of the public services to the needs of the most disadvantaged. If the popular political movements fail to negotiate a reform of the bases of the public sphere—and failure is the most frequent result—then the movements propose the popular communication and organizational network with its quite different conception of culture and development as simply an alternative public sphere that must replace the existing organization of what is considered public (Reyes-Matta, 1982).

Creating an alternative media structure is particularly important for these popular political movements in order to weld isolated protest groups into a national alliance. These movements are generally denied access to the dominant mass media, or their information and language are so different from the standard media formats of the technical-economic modernization orientation that the translation into standard formats destroys its original meaning. The alternative popular media often develop forms of organization and formats that are quite the opposite of the dominant media, which is dedicated to imposing the urban transnational culture on the popular classes. The alternative media are participatory, nonprofessional, and openly critical; they articulate popular culture, and emphasize the indigenous national tradition. Out of these political movements come proposals for profound democratization of patterns of national communication and the institutions of the media. The popular political movements often have arisen in contexts where the state-centered national independence movements have occurred and seek a democratizing reform of these earlier movements. Thus in the NWICO proposals we find a dual emphasis: national autonomy and internal democratization of communication.

THE PUBLIC SPHERE AS A FORUM
FOR CULTURAL NEGOTIATION

The initial "era of development" from 1945 to 1975 was dominated by two great geopolitical experiences: the destructive holocaust of the two world wars and the ending of the colonial empires with the emergence of the new nations. During much of the period world politics was preoccupied with maintaining a balance of world power to avoid another world war. Policies of geopolitical development tended to treat as secondary the innumerable sociopolitical conflicts that often had a cultural base: regionalism, ethnic and religious differences, racial discrimination, and especially caste and class inequities. Although the developing countries were constantly trying to cope with these tensions, none of the major paradigms of development policy advanced a concept of the public sphere that gave priority to the negotiation of these crippling conflicts. Indeed all of the dominant policy models exacerbated these tensions in some degree. In many industrializing countries the civil strife or dictatorial suppression have been a major obstacle to equitable human social and political-economic development. In the last decade development studies have begun to focus much more on the roots of sociopolitical and cultural polarities and from this has come a conception of the public sphere where profound conflicts would be recognized and an acceptable negotiation for all parties would be found.

One of the first moves was to accept that the modernization, technology-transfer model, with its underlying premise of a "natural" unilinear path of rationalistic progress, not only failed to implant new institutions but often imposed a straitjacket that could only cause reactive explosions. Development has to be an endogenous unfolding of the history and culture of a people consonant with the ecology of the region and moving at the pace of technological adaptation set by each people. Traditional ethnic religious and philosophical roots did not just wither away but often only rose up and destroyed modernizing regimes. For many peoples the foundation for sociomoral commitment to public welfare was in their cultural history, philosophy, literature, religion, and popular narrative memory. These voices also had to be present in the sphere of public debate because they offered the only convincing moral leadership, and the differences they implied had to be dealt with. Often modernization not only did not provide a new public moral vision but destroyed the cultural resources to create a new synthesis of the modern and the traditional. Development communication theories began to speak of the *multiplicity model*, recognizing that there are many paths of development (Servaes, 1989, p. 132).

It has become increasingly difficult to justify any one "pure" political-economic model or cultural world view as a historical moral necessity or as an empirically demonstrated basis for a public sphere. Although the hypothesis of cultural imperialisms or conflicting sociocultural polarizations has heuristic value, research increasingly shows a complex process of cultural intermixture and synthesis, both within developing countries and at the international level (Wallis & Malm, 1984). In Latin America, where earlier semiological analysis seemed to demonstrate ideological domination pervading media content, the reviews of the history of media genres by the Colombian theorist J. Martin-Barbero shows that Latin American culture is a much more complex process of *mestizajes* of the indigenous and the transnational. Instead of a polarization of the mass-modern vs. folk-popular cultures, the popular culture is better described as a mass culture that has integrated the symbols of modernization as part of its more urban cultural identity and its forms of resistance to hegemonic cultural influences (Martin-Barbero, 1987, pp. 203–219). Latin America in fact has a long history of indigenous development of genres and formats of popular entertainment (the evolution of the *telenovela* is one good example) that both express the popular culture and often are one of the first forms of popular political definition.

Martin-Barbero and other Latin Americans argue that for many of the most significant new political movements organized around gender, regionalism, generational definition, and ethnic and religious identities, the most critical issues are not primarily those of control over economic production but those that involve the definition of cultural meaning (Martin-Barbero, 1987, pp. 220–228). The cultural sphere is the most active area of public conflict and negotiation. The foundations of the public sphere are not just the rights to property and productive value but also the right to authentic cultural expression and the right to participate in defining the historical development of a given culture.

In the first three paradigms of communication development the public sphere has been conceived of largely as an arena of negotiation among the *leaders* of political-economic organizations or others who have been able to gain some base of political-economic power. The new movements described above have been taken as a momentary fringe phenomenon. One response of the new movements is to define themselves as an alternative moral order, a kind of counterculture based on the grassroots feelings of people. However, on the fringes of the mass media dominated by the political-economic leadership these grassroots movements have been developing their own alternative media and building a network of communication based on the "small" and "intermediate" media (examples of the latter are people's radio stations). In some developing countries, where the dominant political-economic leadership has failed to find a way out of political clientelism and stalemating polarizations, the relatively unorganized masses working through the networks of smaller alternative forms of communication have been able to mobilize a decisive grassroots political influence (Dionisio, 1987, pp. 6–8). There is beginning to be an admission within discussions of media policy that this infrastructure of small and intermediate "alternative" media should be given greater legal and institutional recognition as an important form of public articulation. This is not a conception of democratization that seeks to give the popular classes hegemonic control of the mass media, but rather to expand the definition of what are considered the public media to include the infrastructure of the small and intermediate media and to give this infrastructure legal, financial, and policy support in a way that enables it both to continue its alternative participatory grassroots characteristics and to be recognized as a public forum. There is no utopian demand that somehow the mass professional media be done away with—the demand rather is that they increase their diversity and flexibility to encompass the broader range of cultural issues and debates that are important for negotiation of cultural conflicts (Portales, 1986).

WHERE ARE WE LIKELY TO GO FROM HERE?

This brief chapter has not attempted to classify any one of the theoretical scenarios of communication and development as definitively wrong. Rather, it is proposed that the understanding of the "public sphere" has been a central question in all of the approaches and remains an open question to be dealt with. As a form of conclusion I would like to suggest why the question of the public sphere is likely to become increasingly more central for theories of communication and development over the coming years.

1. It is obvious that after 40 years of "war among the paradigms," efforts to adopt any partial definition of the public sphere as the whole of the matter are exhausted. There are now tendencies toward a balancing synthesis. Yet it is not clear that the public sphere is to be constituted by a mechanical incorporation of the economic, the political, the popular, and the cultural. The lack of any adequate theoretical interpretation is one reason why, in regions such as Latin America, Africa, and India, there is currently a tendency to leave normative models in abeyance

and return to empirical historical analysis to understand better what forms of the public and public communication are in fact emerging.

2.   There is a widely held opinion that the definition of the state as the public sphere not only led to an overburdening of this institution with planning and executive functions, but also narrowed the public sphere to political-economic influences. At the same time there is by no means consensus that the current enthusiasm for "deregulation"—a return to the market model of society—is the answer. This has opened up a broad discussion of what is meant by the public sphere and what institutional organization of communication is an adequate foundation for the public sphere.

3.   In many developing countries the continuing civil strife based on sociocultural differences and inequities is increasingly coming to the fore as a central issue. The current major thaw in the geopolitical cold war will only serve to focus greater attention on the issue of a public sphere as the area of negotiation of these internal national conflicts.

REFERENCES

Ansah, P. (1985). The role of the state in broadcasting in Africa. *Media Development, 32,* 6–9.

Dionisio, E.R. (1986). Small media big victory. *Media Development, 33,* 6–8.

Ellul, J. (1967). *The technological society.* New York: Vintage.

Etherton, M. (1982). *The development of African drama.* London: Hutchinson.

Fox, E. (Ed.). (1988). *Media and politics in Latin America.* London: Sage.

Hedebro, G. (1982). *Communication and social change in developing nations.* Ames: Iowa State.

Lerner, D. (1964). *The passing of traditional society.* New York: Free Press.

Martin-Barbero, J. (1987). *De los medios a las mediaciones.* Mexico: Editorial Gustavo Gili.

Migdal, J.S. (1974). *Peasants, politics and revolution.* Princeton: Princeton University Press.

Narula, U., & Barnett Pearce, W. (1964). *Development as communication: A perspective on India.* Carbondale, IL: Southern Illinois University Press.

Portales, D. (1986). *La dificultad de innovar: un estudio sobre las empresas de television en America Latina.* Santiago, Chile: Instituto Latinoamericano de Estudios Transnacionales.

Reyes-Matta, F. (1982). La comunicacion alternativa como respuesta democratica. In E. Fox (Ed.), *Comunicacion y democracia en America Latina.* Lima: DESCO (pp. 245–264).

Schramm, W. (1964). *Mass media and national development.* Stanford, CA: Stanford University Press.

Schramm, W., & Lerner, D. (Eds.). (1976). *Communication and change: The last ten years—and the next.* Honolulu: The University Press of Hawaii.

Servaes, J. (1986). Communication and development paradigms: An overview. *Media Asia, 13,* 128–136.

Smith, A. (1989). The Public Interest. *Intermedia, 17,* 10–24.

Wallis, R., & Malm, K. (1984). *Big Sounds From Small Peoples: The Music Industry in Small Countries.* London: Constable.

White, R.A. (1969). Mexico: The Zapata movement and the revolution. In H.A. Landsberger (Ed.). *Latin American peasant movements.* Ithaca, NY: Cornell University Press.

White, R.A. (1988). NWICO has become a people's movement. *Media Development, 35,* 20–25.

Wolf, E.R. (1969). *Peasant wars of the twentieth century.* New York: Harper and Row.

Communication and Development The Latin American Challenge

RAFAEL RONCAGLIOLO

Research topics and methods are usually defined outside the spheres of life and the scientific communities. It is hard to find a discipline or subject in which knowledge has been accumulated in a linear way, without dialectic leaps and, above all, lacking complex and mediating interactions with legitimate and dubious demands generated by the social environs. This sort of generalization is particularly valid in the case of Latin America and for its very juvenile and uneven research on communications, within which new technologies have turned into a favorite focal point. It is hard and perhaps rather audacious to mediate on new technologies and research into their impact, even though the exercise we attempt here is a very personal one: an opportunity for a party statement that we now believe is a feasible and appropriate manner in which to start to disentangle the various forces at work.

BEFORE COMMUNICATIONISM

For more than a decade, Latin American studies on communications were characterized by copious and broad "communicationist" biases. Obviously, the threat of such an approach laid in separating communications as a landmark, only secondarily permeable to the general evolution of society. Until very recently communications were, indeed, a sort of Cinderella of the Social Sciences—particularly of politics. The unique approach to research and the lines of enquiry that gave birth to it almost 30 years ago had been overlooked. Three elements of a distinctive Latin American approach can be identified:

- In its context, the close biographical, group, and existential link between research and political life. In Latin America it seems that the roles of the politician and the academic are interchangeable according to the political circumstances and articulations of the region and of each country. Action and thought here are interchangeable.
- Because of their institutional framework, the development of new institutions outside university campuses, companies and the State, where scholars can seek refuge in times of oppression and repression. This is particularly related to social research and promotion centers, which have multiplied in Latin America in the last few years, nourishing theoretical reflection and empirical research.
- Because of its theoretical practice, the gregarious nature of regional scientific production. The isolated researcher, confined in an ivory tower and immune to outer world contamination and the wider scientific community, does not prevail. On the contrary, there is fruitful and permanent dialogue between those dedicated to these tasks that, as it were, collectivizes intellectual production. The Latin American scientific community acts more under the anticanons of anarchosyndicalism than under the individual expert model that develops its own separate school. Relations among colleagues are, hence, highly horizontal. By no means are they vertical.

THE SEARCH OF SCIENTIFIC OBJECT

The discovery of communications as a new world, open to scientific and political action, resulted in an intensive search for explanations and proposals that could explain the phenomenon and handle it with a social orientation. The relevance and charm of the topic enabled the appearance of a select group of researchers, which included Luis Ramiro Beltran, Juan Diaz Bordenave, Eleazar Diaz Rangel, Juan Gargurevich, Luis Anibal Gomez, Jose Marques de Melo, Armand Mattelart, Hector Schmucler and Eliseo Veron. In democratic governments as well as in progressive regimes, there immediately appeared the need to do something. In recent years our politician-scientists were devoted to the issue, going through four stages (more logical than chronological) that responded, as already mentioned, to the pressures of society itself. These stages were National Communication Policies (NCP), New World Information and Communication Order (NWICO), "alternative communication," and, finally, the one we are currently discussing—new communications technologies.

On a more abstract level, which is essential if we are to illuminate the general state of the art in Latin America, when we discuss new technologies we would have to speak of at least four orientations, interests, styles, or "formal objects"—technical, pure knowledge, research applied to action, and, finally , the approach motivated and addressed to policy formulation. It is a fact that we must try to reconcile these different orientations and approaches in order to speak the same language.

The most recent Latin American research on new information and communication technologies has to do with "hardware" innovations and adaptations, and it is carried out by engineers. Not less than 17 countries in the region have telecommunications research and training centers, some of which have made important advances in the subject matter. Most of these centers are grouped together in the dynamic Spanish-American Association of Telecommunications Research and Education Centers (AHCIET), of which Spain is also a member. A parallel effort in informatics (hardware' and software) is being made in some countries, especially in Brazil and Cuba.

A second tendency can be found among communication experts, social scientists, and essayists, mainly in Mexico and Argentina, who wish to address the sociological problems raised by the new technologies. Do these new technologies cause progress or do they strengthen dependence? Do they serve the cause of liberation, or do they improve the worldwide control and centralization of information and cultural flows? These queries are perfectly legitimate, especially if we consider the military and financial origin of these changes. Nevertheless, this tendency engendered the possibility of a manichean ethical approach confronting the advocates of infor-matization and telematization on the one hand, and the apocalyptics of new techniques on the other.

Almost simultaneously to those considerations, many grassroot groups in the region started to include new technologies in their own work with popular sectors. In Brazil, IBASE organized a network of computer services to be used by labor unions, church-based communities, and similar organizations to exchange information via modem. A set of centers from different countries, furnished with computers, incorporated themselves as the INTER-DOC worldwide network. Finally, in several countries in the region popular video producers, distributors, and users created associations that plan, through IPAL, to create a Latin American exchange network in order to solve the language norm and format differences that exist in Latin America.

In short, some groups started to seize new technologies, albeit marginally. This originated a third tendency, which in practical terms overcame the abstract discussion on the intrinsic good or evil of these tools. Indeed, if we refer to certain noncommercial institutions that are currently vital—including the church, labor unions, peasants, and neighborhoods—there obviously is a place left in Latin America for a valid cultural use of these innovations. Forms of popular retrieval of new technologies already exist.

Finally, the nations of the region acknowledge the political and economic problems they will have if they exclude themselves from these issues, including matters related to regional cultural sovereignty and economic security. For instance, what does the growing expansion of parabolic antennas for direct satellites reception mean for the cultural and educational policy of a country? What does the massive petty smuggling of videorecorders and videocassettes imply? What happens with an educational system that restratifies itself into "technological illiterates" and those who, because of their social origin, gain early school-age access to computer education? How can we promote the indigenous production of cultural goods, and strengthen Latin American cultural integration?

The problem of national communication policies today is more pressing than ever in Latin America, and this is so not because of the strength of the arguments or because of any theoretical discussion, but simply because the development of new technologies has created a new situation and challenge that states (and the private sectors) cannot ignore. There is no point in repeating the same speech we used ten years ago, which served as an excuse for an abusive, esoteric and super-ideological polemic. Today we have to dialogue with the states to better know and understand how research can really serve autonomous and democratic policy formulation.

We are now experiencing the omnipresence of those new information and communication technologies, capable of transforming not only economic and political life, but culture as well.

A first response to the new technologies was the establishment of national communication policies. During the first democratic government of Carlos Andres Perez, a commission was created in Venezuela to design the Venezuelan Radio Television (RATELVE) as a proposal for mass media democratization. The reform of the Peruvian press, under the progressive military regime headed by Juan Velasco Alvarado, lasted as long as the participatory impetus of the regime itself, and was limited by its very nature to being a military regime. In Mexico, too, at the end of President Echevarria's administration and during that of Lopez Portillo, an attempt was made in this direction, by writing a bylaw to an article of the Constitution that was about freedom of information. However, these were all insignificant efforts, eroded by the large private interests that control most of the mass media in Latin America. In this context, the Intergovernmental Conference on National Communication Policies in Latin America and the Caribbean, which was summoned by UNESCO and took place in Costa Rica in 1976, served more as an alarm than as a opportunity for the development of democratic and systematic communication policies.

In the same decade, at the Summit Conference of the Movement of Non-Aligned Countries, which took place in Algiers in 1973, Third World nations set forth the problem of information colonialism and international news flows.

This marked the beginning of the New World Information and Communication Order, in which researchers could find new grounds for claims and explorations. Hence, we quickly passed from the problem of news flows to the advertising flows and other cultural goods flows, similarly considered as tools of domination. By then, though, new technologies were rapidly penetrating our societies. Attention became focused on the types of message content. The new discussion caused such commotion that it finally ended in the withdrawal of the United States and other countries from UNESCO.

There were not sufficient national and international conditions to attain significant accomplishments in any of these fields. Intellectuals in general shared then a certain political myopia. The counteroffensive coming from the North and the need for efficiency pushed us into a search for new topics. Regional political thought, the product of profound defeats, privileged the ideal concept of democratization. Several journalist colleagues from the "nanica" press and the cord literature in Brazil, ranging from publications, radio stations and even clandestine news agencies, to new spaces and forms of theatrical and musical creation, turned cultural insurgency into an urgent topic. The large-scale national scenarios of NCP and the international proposal of NWICO had to be abandoned in favor of what became known as "alternative communication," with the illusion that it was possible to fight the tanks, battleships, and bombers of the big media with the small caliber bullets of a valid, meritorious, and heroic army that lacked the force to affect the ongoing third Industrial Revolution. The stage of alternative communication is, then, a much more fruitful stage in terms of political struggle than in the production of scientific knowledge.

TRANSNATIONALIZATION AND TENDENCIES

In the framework of the economics, though, during the seventies a new phenomenon began to take shape, a phenomenon which one scholar has considered "the last stage of imperialism," paraphrasing the Leninist assertion of "imperialism as the last stage of capitalism." We refer to the transnationalization process, which is the correct framework to employ to understand the field and effects of new technologies, and with which one overcomes the "communicationist" biases of the three previous stages, in which focus on communication had lacked sufficient consideration of the context.

In the political sphere, the transnationalization process is characterized by the ability of transnational enterprises to reduce the autonomy of the central and peripheral states as well. In the economic sphere, this stage is characterized by global rather than national organization of productive activities. In the cultural sphere, this same process leads to what McLuhan calls the "global village"—a global community of receptors born out of the centralized expansion of the world market of information goods and services. A unique market has been created, in which the international community is more a consumer of illusions than of goods.

Hence, research on the uses and effects of new technologies emphasized multinational research and cooperation so that Latin America could respond to the compulsive pressure of the sales campaigns of transnational corporations with real development plans on the subject.

RESEARCH TOPICS

The fragmentation of the aforementioned orientations is parallel to the proliferation of specific research topics, alongside the phenomena, variables, cases, and effects needing to be considered. The incipient idea of "new information and communication technologies" refers more to a not very precise menu of innovations, rather than denotating a systematic and exact concept. This is why it cannot suggest a first bisection between the analysis of technification processes themselves and the study of their effects. With reference to effects, the most outstanding element has been the analysis of the cultural, political and economic effects of new technologies understood in their broader sense, including employment and leisure time, family dynamics, work relations, private life, and police control.

As to the technification processes themselves, three main research topics emerge. All three have an integrational perspective and this will have important implications both for the research results and for resulting policy formulation.

A first topic has to do with the development of informatics, data bases and data banks, the problems of transborder data flows, and all the use and production of computation hardware and software in countries such as Mexico and Brazil. This line certainly prevails and includes the study of the complex process of mass media informatization.

A second topic refers to satellites, satellite broadcasting, and related national policies. The incorporation of practically all countries of the region such as the Morelos in Mexico and Brasilsat in Brazil, as well as the plans of the Andean countries (Venezuela, Colombia, Ecuador, Peru, and Bolivia) to install their Condor System, have strengthened interest and research in this field.

The videocassette topic and its relations with television, movies, and other manifestations of the cultural industry, the third topic, has gained sudden and unexpected acceptance. The new uses of cable (especially in Mexico, Argentina, and very recently in certain areas of the Peruvian jungle) has turned into an object of particular interest, mainly because of the manifold possibilities of combination and/or competition with television, satellite and videocassette.

CULTURAL INTEGRATION AND PRODUCTION

The situation is particularly serious if we consider the needs of increasing indigenous cultural production and promoting integration. The current lack of coordination between movie, television, and independent videocassette producers is difficult to accept, when they could all join together to dynamize and even substitute an important part of the programs coming from outside the region. Similarly, despite all the satellite time that countries have bought there is a surprising absence of regional exchanges that would lower intra-regional production costs in favor of an authentic and pluralist Latin American integration.

The cultural industry, propelled by its technification, has already started an integration process that eliminates the frontiers between the different media. Nowadays, movie, television, videocassettes, and cable are only instances or moments of the whole audiovisual industry complex. In this same manner, radio and disks become complementary elements of a second binary complex: the sound industry. And newspapers, magazines, and books interact, and are together dominated by the guidelines of the editorial complex. To face the technification resulting from the transnationalization of economies and cultures, the strategic task of the time is to analyze these three complexes and their interactions simultaneously, rather than setting isolated subsectorial policies. In Latin America there is the capacity, the will, and the imagination to progress in this joint, integrating and common direction. In this task, researchers have something to say and a lot to do.

REFERENCES

Beltran, L.R. (1976). Politicas nacionales de comunicacion. *America Latina*. Bogota: CIID.

Calvelo, M. (1984). *El video educativo rural*. Working paper, Lima: IPAL.

Capriles, O. El estado y los medios de comunicacion en Venezuela. *Libreria Suma*. Caracas.

Colina, C.E. "El flujo del hardware y del software de video en Venezuela". Working paper. IPAL. Lima.

Esteninou Madrid, J. (1983). *Los medios de comunicacion y la construccion de la hegemonia*. Mexico: Nueva Imagen S.A.

Fadul, A.M. (1985). *As transnacionals de informatica e a impresa de Sao Pualo: una recoilacao de datos*. Working paper, IPAL/INTERCOM, Lima.

Fernandez, F. (1980). Diagnostico sobre los medios de difusion de masas en Mexico y proposiciones para el derecho a la informacion. In *Asociacion Mexicana de Investigadores de la Comunicacion. (AMIC)*. Mexico.

Gargurevich, J. (1977). Introduccion a la historia de los medios de comunicacion en el Peru. *Editorial Horizonte*. Lima.

Mattelart, A. Multinacionales y sistemas de comunicacion. *Siglo XXI*. Mexico.

Portales, D. (1981). Poder economico y libertad de expresion. *ILET*. Santiago.

Quiroz de Tejada, M. (1984). *Recopilacion de datos sobre mensajes trans- mitidos a traves de los medios por las corporaciones transna- cionales.* Working paper, IPAL, Lima.

Roncagliolo, R. (1981). The MacBride report as a part of a process. In C. Hamelink (Ed.), *Communications in the Eighties: A reader on the MacBride report.* Rome.

Roncagliolo, R. (1982). Comunicacion y cultura transnacionales. In *Com- unicacion transnacional: Conflicto politico y cultural.* DESCO, Lima.

Roncagliolo, F. (1986). New information order in Latin America: A taxon- omy for national communication policies. In *Communication and domination (Essays to honor Herber I. Schiller).* Norwood, NJ: Ablex.

Santoro, L.R. (1985). Desenvolvimiento das novas tecnologias da com- unicacao e da microelectronica no Brasil. Working paper, IPAL, Lima.

Sauvant, K. (1976). Multinational enterprises and the transmission of culture: The international supply of advertising services and busi- ness education. In *Journal of Peace Research, 13.*

Schenkel, P. (1981). Politicas nacionales de comunicacion. *CIESPAL.* Quito.

Communication and Development: The Contribution of Research

K.E. EAPEN

From hindsight, at the dawn of the 1990s, it is intriguing that the visible holes in the dominant paradigm of the communication –development concept were not perceived and articulated earlier than they were. The myopic vision was perhaps sustained because the notions surrounding it originated in the United States and were applied elsewhere. The intended target was especially the so-called underdeveloped world, made up of the poorer nations of Africa, Asia, and South America.

Years before the upheavals in Eastern Europe, Hayeck had remarked about the "fatal conceit" consisting of the socialist assumption that "man can know enough to plan all of what has become know as the 'good life' for society." A further point of his that "developers" missed was that "any man who is only an economist is unlikely to be a good one."

In the following presentation an attempt will be made to briefly peep into "communication" and "development" aspects, and then proceed to some of the research and theoretical biases that prevailed for many decades after World War II. However, preceding this will be short discussions around a couple of studies in which this writer was involved during 1970–1972 and 1975–1976 that have direct bearing on communication and development. Following them will be other research references prior to and after the Eapen works. We end up with some of the current and unending deliberations of this much-debated topic.

The Niagara Falls of research literature related to communication and development began to descend with the late 1950s, as if communication and development were mid-twentieth century inventions. This simplistic approach, in the beginning, did not care to explicate the twin concepts. The dictionary defines the root of the word *communication* to include built-in ideas of give and take, transaction, communioning, fellowship, equity, and the like. In the early sender–receiver one-way models—bullet theory, hypodermic needle approach, the thermostat concept, etc.—many of these ideas were missing. And *development* was seen largely in terms of economic development and tended to be equated with Westernization. Improvement in the "quality of life" of both urban and rural masses was ignored.

The processes of communication and development are as old as human civilization. Darwin's notion of survival of the fittest, in a holistic sense, was not devoid of these. Philosophies about the good society were in Plato's *Republic* as well as in More's *Utopia*, which is of more recent vintage. Older civilizations such as those of India and China continued for millennia because of communication, and they also did not lack in visions of idealistic development. They were "modern" for their own times.

Goebbels's use of radio, and the success of the propaganda war of the Allies, gave the halo of power to electronic media, so much so many innocently believed that bigger media systems are better systems and that they would lead people towards change: changing for their good, in desired directions, via "social engineering." The Cold War climate in no small measure aided thinking about the opportunities (and not of media limitations), especially for the economically less developed countries, for development, modernization, Westernization, social change, or what you will. The superpowers wanted to consolidate their spheres of influence and redesign the global strategies in terms of their own interests, without appreciating national imprints.

With the failures of the U.N. Development Decades of the 1960s and 1970s, wisdom began to dawn that communication is not necessarily the missing link in development. Development, by then, had lost its lonely economic glitter. It was no more a matter of technology transfer from the arrogant developed to the supplicant less developed. Debates about the New International Economic Order (NIEO) and the New World Information and Communication Order (NWICO), to the discomfort of some of the industrialized and media-saturated societies, showed concerns about the real politik of independence, nonalignment, and the like.

Development has to be seen in terms of the totality of people and their society, and should not be limited to those social segments of poorer nations that were becoming westernized exclusively tapping the benefits technology offered.

The research in communication and development, in the meanwhile, had shifted from one of value-free neutrality to a critical one. National leadership of the South increasingly began to recognize that liberation from colonial powers, unless freed from cultural and communication dependencies, would continue to be a mirage. It was recognized that movements that cut off political umbilical chords could help achieve other goals.

A study of Zambia and Indonesia performed by this writer under the guidance of Halloran (1973) led to certain conclusions worthy of mentioning. It was argued there that in the context of development, *goals* must be locally determined with the people in the area, that existing infrastructures be involved, and that any mass media facility available must be used together with traditional indigenous communication methods. Among the guidelines the study offered were:

1.   Mass media systems in the Western sense of the world are seldom appropriate models for policy or research;
2.   Traditional channels are of utmost importance;
3.   Local knowledge is essential;
4.   Communication takes place in ongoing systems of interaction and relationships;
5.   Multimedia approaches are likely to be more successful than single medium approaches.

No "developmental absolutes," claiming universal validity, were superimposed on this exploratory work. Instead, some earthy notions such as "a square meal and fair deal for everybody" or "development as an amalgam of modernity and traditional values, built on local relevance" (dressing up new idealism in old garments) were considered helpful. Three major factors recognized were the interrelated goals of economic growth, self-reliance, and social justice.

A premise of the project was that media represent only one set of institutions among the many, and that they do not exist or operate independently of politics, economics, culture, traditions, and so on. This was willy-nilly missing in most of the communication and development research that had preceded. In the past, crude models of attitude change and behavioral formation and change had predominated; influence had gotten equated with attitude change, and effects with effectiveness.

A review of the research literature had showed an approach that had relied solely upon the experience and practices of media-developed countries. With the exception of educational TV, much of the communication research in the industrialized countries had been on the indirect impact of *mass* communication (for example, TV and violence) rather than on the deliberate use of the media, modern and traditional, for declared social transformation. Moreover, where the media had been deliberately used in the hope of producing change, there was little available evidence to offer optimism that propelled media policies and projects in developing countries.

It was observed that many vital discrepancies existed among the cultures, social structures, and media systems of Zambia, Indonesia, and developed nations. Yet both media policies and research strategies were frequently imported as though such differences did not exist. It is not entirely an idle question to ask how successful the mass media have been in Western urban societies in conveying information in changing attitudes, in influencing behavior, and in various other educative tasks. The record, on the surface, was not too impressive, but were the tasks realistic?

The stated goals of modernization are often those that appear to prevail in another culture. Values such as individualism, materialism, success, working to get on, the acceptance of deferred gratification, and the Protestant ethic are not the only criterion of success, development, or progress.

Moreover, the approaches tend to lack sociocultural sophistication. It is frequently assumed that it is change in the individual that is important (and it is this that tends to be measured), when it could be that change in the social structure and organization is something more important than the aggregate of changed individual attitudes.

In addition, many of the approaches ignore the history of developing countries: their internal ongoing process of change and conflict, external relations (often with colonial powers), traditions, and cultures. All these form a wider social context of which the modern media are only a part. The introduction of mass media is frequently neither the first nor the most important of modernizing factors. Its relevance and place in the process needs to be established empirically, not taken for granted.

Zambian and Indonesian audiences are not homogenous masses; rather, we should think of them as differentiated publics with their own idiosyncratic styles and structures. Messages are filtered. They do not drop onto an absorbent sheet but into ongoing situations, an already existing network of relationships and patterns of communication. These structures, networks, and patterns, with their gatekeepers and leaders, will be paramount in any dissemination or adoption process.

Also, there were unanswered questions: What is meant by "quality of life of the masses"? Is it the task of external elites to operate with this end in view? What right have we to change attitudes and behavior?

The other research in the domain of communication and development was done in 1975–1976 at the Satellite Instructional Television Experiment (SITE). This was the prelude to the Indian National Satellite (INSAT) system. It was confined to six widely scattered backward clusters of India and was limited to some 2,400 villages. The year-long project, which ran for $4\frac{1}{2}$ hours a day, was intended to carry developmental messages to the rural audiences. While enormous efforts had gone to maintain SITE's hardware— satellite, transmitters, receiving sets—no comparable thinking went into the final input. Evaluation by Bangalore University, where this author then worked, showed that the hardware component functioned reasonably well. What was transmitted to the South Indian viewers of the Karnataka Cluster was of only limited relevance to what turned out to be mostly the first-generation consumers of a modern medium. Both in content and in style the programs on agricultural development, family planning, health, and the like were found wanting. Many of them were not specifically produced for television; those prepared for telecasting were based on scripts written by urban scientists and put on tape by urban producers. Both had little understanding of the linguistic or cultural ethos of intended audiences. Even when some viewers became somewhat familiar with the medium and began to make sense of some of the segments, they could not often practice what was learned. There was little of the service-related structures at the village level to take advantage of.

The cultural and social distance between planners, software producers, and the ultimate audiences was too wide for the nascent technology to bridge. The present satellite-based Indian TV system continues to suffer from this gap. Its important beneficiaries have been the political bosses, the civil servants who staff it (there are repeated accusations of corruption in the selection of serials and soap operas), and the advertising world, which has a say in programming except perhaps where news and current affairs were concerned. The autonomy debate sparked around radio and TV may witness cosmetic structural changes in broadcasting without affecting its basic culture. It is unlikely to shift meaningfully the velocity of growth and utilization for what was the original and overall purpose, which was "to improve the quality of life of the masses." India is still to build up a cadre of professionals with an Indian ethos, and it is still short of scholars liberated from the grand paradigm parameters.

We may, at this stage, want to have a glance of the communication literature of the past four decades. Three principal zones emerge here: (a) modernization, (b) dependency dissociation, and (c) multiplicity or another development. The first, prevalent from the end of the World War II to the mid-1960s, pictured "traditional" societies to which the dream world of the West (technology-based democracy and accompanying culture) would be transplanted. Voices of the New International Economic Order began to be vaguely heard towards the late 1960s and were fully articulated during the 1970s. These came under the rubric of the *dependency* paradigm. Following this, the 1980s witnessed the emerging *multiplicity* (another development) pattern. Its focus is on grassroots movements for decentralization and democratization.

In the larger context of the hundred-odd poorer countries, these three change-related models have not remained mutually exclusive. In many of these nations they still co-exist. While scholars in several South American countries have postulated the multiplicity or another development approach, their counterparts in many of the others are yet to go onstream on this. Thus the cry in India, for example, for autonomy for radio and television is more political than academic. It is still the old nationalistic type elites, by and large, making new noises on issues of this nature. However, what is not visible are the vigorous grassroots movements represented through localized effect communications by isolated fisherfolk or small farmers.

Media are sometimes said to be American. Media research, especially of the communication and development brand, is no less American. Many of the early research projects in the United States were carried out for commercial purposes and government propaganda efforts. Subsequently, many of the early theories and methods used for the purpose of government propaganda efforts spilled over elsewhere, especially to the poorer nations of the world.

Irrespective of the discipline, science or social science, there exist pragmatic research relationships between American industries and academic institutions. Looking at the seminal contributions of communication researchers of the past such as Lazarsfeld, Lasswell, and others, when radio was expanding in a significant way, it is obvious that their theories were born in and influenced by the capitalist environment. Consumerism and the electoral process gave the thrust for many studies. Agricultural extension was another dimension.

With the end of the war, the slow emergence of countries from colonial shackles, and the new American global interests, the impetus for communication research beyond U.S. national boundaries seemed imperative. The triumvirate of Lerner, Rogers, and Schramm moved in. Their theories, models, and paradigms were influenced by Rostow's thoughts about the stages of economic development, which they projected into the media situation. Their notions are too well known to repeat here, but brief mentioning is unavoidable.

Daniel Lerner's *The Passing of Traditional Society* was not exactly a study of the role of communication in development. Data for it came from an extended project in the Middle East about public attitudes to the Soviet Union. It was rather an afterthought of the author to branch into a theory of the role of mass media in development. Lerner's argumentation of human rationality reflected the dominant functionalism approach of U.S. social scientists who were trying to be on a par with objective, positivistic, and empirically verifiable aspects of the natural science approach. The climate and structure in which communication happens were not enquired into so as to highlight restrictive parameters of land ownership vis-a-vis farming or the political orientation of power structures.

The functional approach was criticized by many analysts from among scholars of the less developed nations, because it prevented social scientists from critically examining how their work might serve an unjust socioeconomic and political order.

Everett Rogers' *Diffusion of Innovations* became highly influential for synthesizing the thinking about modern media and modernization based on U.S. experiences, especially from the extension front. As a rural sociologist he conceived of communication as information flowing from an expert source to the farmers in a linear mode. Here also what was missing in this effect-oriented approach was an appreciation of the social structures in nations as varied as those in Africa and Asia. He later revised the theories involved after recognizing the obvious—those with more land, political contacts, money, power, and education tend to use information better than those who lacked them.

Wilbur Schramm's *Mass Media and National Development* argued about the power of modern mass media as a cheap multiplier of information. Mass media, he said, had the capability to widen horizons, to focus attention, to raise aspirations, and to create a climate for development. He conceded, however, that "the mass media can help only indirectly to change strongly held attitudes and valued practices." His optimism, nonetheless, goaded him to say: "without mass communication probably the great freedom movements and national stirrings of the last few decades would never have come about at all."

Mass media are not a necessary condition for mass communication. Neither the violent liberation movement of the Chinese peasantry under Mao, nor the nonviolent freedom struggle under Gandhi in the Indian subcontinent, were founded on *modern* media multipliers. Kusum Singh's work on Mao and Gandhi as mass communicators reflect this in great detail.

As for the stages of development theory, it was observed during the Zambia-Indonesia study that South Africa, the most developed among African countries, had no television. While socialist Tanzania did not have TV, its island part Zanzibar had gone for color TV because the then-vice-president for that area was enamored of it. Similarly, some of the tallest antennae were seen in Madan, Sumatra, where there was no studio and no transmitter in the mid-1960s. Inquiries showed that the rich elites of Madan were trying to catch signals originating in far-away Singapore and Malaysia. Indonesian telecasting itself had begun in 1962, to coincide with the inauguration of Asiad 1962 in Jakarta. The introduction of the electronic media, and their expansion, are more determined by political decisions and status seeking than by the advent of a stage of development. Recent growth of Indian television, again, shows that there is no auspicious stage when decisions are made to have a new rural transmitter installed every day for a couple of months.

Interestingly, while *mass* media continue to be offered as the panacea for national illnesses of the poorer countries, they do not seem to solve such problems as drug use among the youth of "developed" countries.

A host of concerns led to a certain disenchantment with the dominant paradigm. Rising frustrations displaced rising expectations. Experience from countries such as China and Cuba, which had not followed the Western models, showed they attained some level of development. Critics argued that the value of the existing theory of modernization was questionable. The modern media got criticized for emphasizing consumer and materialisitc values, and for serving elites instead of stated development needs.

As an alternative to the modernization paradigm, efforts were on to seek feedback mechanisms and the impact of class on the ability of audiences to gain access to, and use, media messages. There were arguments about the need to examine normative values and ideology embedded in media contents. These were to examine also the impact of political, technological, and institutional constraints limiting media's capability to work as an agent of predetermined change. The organizational production of messages and interactions among folk, interpersonal, and mass communication were sought.

Among the issues raised at this stage were questions of power: the ability of countries to become self-reliant, the ability to make use of and control their own resources and create their own national identity. Critics pointed out that the research surrounding the old paradigm was ahistorical, and that of equal importance was change in social structures; without structural change individuals would neither have the access to the modern media nor would they be able to act upon what they are told by the media. It was contended that the role of information is limited and that those who benefit most are the ones who are not necessarily lacking information. Going for high technology in communication meant getting sucked into a spiral of development, a development that is dominated and controlled by the global capitalist system.

A variety of studies, mostly in South America, arose around this time. Paul Baran and Andre Gunder Frank outlined the earlier version of the theory of "dependency and underdevelopment." From a world system approach the dependency theorists argued that the independent state as an isolated actor was a myth. Indigenous elites were seen as belonging to a family of global elites who shared common cultural life styles and the taste of the industrialized nation. The center–periphery and the metropolis–satellite notions characterized imperialist economic relations.

In the meanwhile, the focus of structuralists such as McAnany was on the indigenous and exogenous structures inhibiting development in the poorer nations. The role of communication in development was perceived in terms of who benefits from information and what impact information has on productivity, health, and income.

Arising out of the criticism of the modernization and dependency paradigm was a group of scholars represented by Servaes, Mowlana, and others, who rejected the economism and universal relevance of earlier models. Their focus was on the social and cultural identities of nations. Each country has to define its own strategy for development in a holistic fashion, as there are no universal models of development. Development has to be need based, in the context of a particular society, and not imposed from outside. The "participatory" nature of communication and its validity were argued. Here, emphasis shifted from a nation to a community.

In this context we may cite two studies, one pertaining to a specific rural situation in the west coast of India and the other to five Asian neighboring countries. The former (Pune, 1988) has objectives focusing on three conceptual areas: (a) to explore, identify, and test team-oriented approaches for bringing about institutional change and creating new infrastructures for development communication; (b) to experiment with participatory approaches to integrated media development, which is need based and goal oriented; and (c) to validate experimentally communication strategies for delivery of development messages in villages, including effects of participatory processes on media selection and development on citizen empowerment.

The latter (Askew, 1989) states that though "community participation" is a currently popular phrase with policy makers, its operational implications of putting the idea into practice are not clearly understood. This paper presents the findings from a comparative analysis of seven case studies of community participation projects implemented by the nongovernmental Family Planning Associations of India, Bangladesh, Pakistan, Sri Lanka, and Nepal. The results suggest that, despite the policy rhetoric seeking greater community involvement and self-reliance in program implementation, FPAs most commonly use participation as a means to generate new demand for services by presenting family planning in a manner that is acceptable and appropriate to the communities involved.

The Dag Hammarskjold Foundation Report (1975), *What Now: Another Development*, dealt with "another development"/"human scale development." It argued that if people are to be main actors in human scale development, both the diversity and the autonomy of the spaces in which they act must be respected. Development has to be need-oriented, self-reliant, endogenous, ecologically sound, and based on structural transformation.

It argued that development is about people and not about objects. The GNP is an indicator only of the quantitative growth of objects. The need is for an indicator about the qualitative growth of people: on the one hand, the interaction of the needs of being, having, doing, and interacting and, on the other hand, the needs of subsistence, protection, affection, understanding, participation, idleness, creation, identity, and freedom.

These, the documents argued, cannot be structured from the top downwards, nor can they be imposed by either law or decree. Instead of being the traditional objects of development, people must take a leading role in development. Regaining diversity is the best way to encourage the creative and synergetic potential that exists in every society. "Therefore it seems advisable and consistent to accept the coexistence of different styles of regional development within the same country, instead of insisting that national styles should prevail, when these have so far proved to be instrumental in increasing the difference of some regions at the expense of the improvement of others."

Despite all these, the naive faith in the therapeutic ability of mass media to change attitudes and beliefs and to revolutionize well-established behavioral patterns in a predetermined direction continues. Investment policies in countries with scarce resources reflect this optimism. The poorer nations are not run by communication scholars and social thinkers. Many of these colonies still look westward and are fed with fresh shibboleths.

During the Zambia-Indonesian investigation it was reported that often foreign researchers arrive in a hurry with vast resources, gather data, and then vanish, never to be heard of again except via scholarly journals from abroad or through books published in the West. Many such researchers have been accused of using the host nation and providing little feedback of their findings to the countries they have studied. Now, these fly-by-night foreign researchers have given way to selected Third World individual "appropriately" trained abroad who do the selective data collection to improve old models and impose new paradigms for gullible decision makers from the poorer countries. The possibility that media messages could be dysfunctional is not traded.

In his introduction to the Zambia-Indonesia report, James Halloran made certain valuable comments on the important issue of the relationship between the sponsor and the researcher. He said that some were willing to serve in a straightforward service or administrative capacity. They appear happy to take the problem as defined for them by the sponsors and work from there on, without offering any challenge to basic values or questioning fundamental concepts. It is not that the social scientist should ignore the problem as defined by the sponsor, but that he or she should never accept such "common sense" definition at face value. One of his or her main tasks is to help the sponsor and others to redefine the problem in the appropriate wider contexts.

One of Pool's golden rules of ethics focused on seeking common ground with researchers of host countries: "a social scientist has no right to ask foreign persons to contribute time, money, cooperation or political support unless the purpose of the project is one which they see as their own.... It is not proper for us to go into the field to use fellow scientists or interview subjects solely for an advantage of our own or even for the advantage of science per se." This dictum of the early 1960s has been broken more often than it has been followed since then.

One lacuna, at least in the Indian context, has been the failure to look inward for research ideas. For example, there are scores of voluntary agencies, usually composed of committed individuals and teams, working on rural development challenges—people who live with the villagers and help them change for the better. Hardly any study has been done on the communication aspects of these not so visible endeavors.

Or take the case of Kerala Sasthra Sahitya Parishad (a community of Kerala scientists), which has been carrying the message of "science for social revolution" for over a quarter century (Eapen, 1981–1982, pp. 40–49). What has been impact of the Parishad? What lessons are there that can spill over to the rest of India? What are the theoretical notions underlying the Parishad activity? Has its communication activity suffered for ignoring the old paradigm? A host of other questions could be raised, their answers enriching the dialogue on communication and development. After all, Kerala is the success story of family planning not only in India but elsewhere also. How did it come about without *mass* communication in the accepted sense?

We may conclude this overall exercise by noting that many of the earlier ideas about the role of communication in development and their criticisms overlapped in time and across space. This narration itself, perhaps, suffers from some amount of repetition and zigzagging. For good or bad, the paradigms coexist along with their criticism, not significantly affecting their acceptance or rejection by the nonacademic communities in many parts of the world, old and new. Which leaves us with the usually unanswered question: What is the role of the social scientists in his or her own society?

REFERENCES

Askew, I. (1989). Organizing community participation in family planning projects in South Asia. *Studies in Family Planning, 20.*

Eapen, K.E. (1981). Communication, Kerala style. *Communicatio Socialio Year Book,* pp. 40–49.

Fait, J.E. (1989). 29 years of theory and research on media and development: The dominant paradigm impact. *Gazette, 44,* 129–150.

Halloran, J. (1973). *The Media and Development.*

Jayaweera, N., & Amanugama, S. (1987). *Rethinking development communication.* Singapore: AMIC.

Kumar, K.J. (1988/1989). Communication and development. *Communication Research Trends, 9.*

The Formation of Cultural Workers: Considerations on Latin American Experiences

19

NELLY DE CAMARGO

Latin America has had a long experience in the activities of cultural action, linked to the processes of development. The needs of integration of huge, poor, and unprepared migrant populations from the rural to the urban areas has been the first challenge to the institutions in the administrative, political, religious, and educational spheres.

To mention one example, in the 1940s the Basic Education Movement, working through radio forums, was launched in Brazil and reached the whole country. The program dealt with important subjects linked to social consciousness. Later, the systematic approach to the eradication of adult illiteracy, based in Paulo Freire's "Pedagogy of the Oppressed," was very successful and has been, until today, extensively used, not only in Brazil, but in Latin America in general, in alternative programs of cultural development.

These and other examples demonstrate the need for cultural action and for professionals specially prepared to perform a series of diversified duties, generally classified as cultural action or animation.

These duties and activities have a long history. Where did those persons who initially started doing such tasks come from? Research shows several academic and professional origins (Camargo, 1983). They are doctors, librarians, teachers, social assistants, nurses, housewives with some free time, artisans, and many others.

What did they have in common? Not their educational background, but an inner motivation, a desire to improve lifestyles through imparted knowledge, solidarity, action, and companionship, for those who need or seek for a "better world," by trying to organize groups to grow and to maintain their cultural gains.

Of course, this type of action was motivated by ideological and charismatic appeals. The basic element—the touchstone—was motivation. After 40 years of following several types of cultural action program, we still find that this element is responsible for the successful ones, for the creativity and alternatives in processes of decision making that such compromise seems to elicit.

It is clear that we could not recommend the development of a curriculum for the formation of professionals in cultural action only on the basis of inner motivation, but without this element any training can easily make new bureaucrats of culture, with more capacity for cultural blockage than for the sharing of its accomplishments with the population.

The cultural action programs have been ad hoc, widely divergent, and barely planned or coordinated in terms of administrative continuity, evaluation, and integration within the Latin American countries' cultural policies. Many factors can be pointed out as responsible for this: the complexity and dispersion of the units that make up the cultural sector, and their degree of specialization; the traditional administrative link between cultural programs and other sectors, mainly education; the lack of administrative experience of those who take charge of carrying programs; the disarticulation of social and cultural action at the state level, where there is a need for an intra- and extrasectorial system of coordination at different levels, in order to rationalize efforts and avoid the waste of resources.

This chapter will report, in summary, on the findings of a series of interviews, articles, results of Latin American seminars, and an extensive survey conducted by the author among the professionals of cultural animation or cultural action (as they prefer to call their task).

It is important to note that the choice and adoption of one strategy for cultural action always depends on political, financial, administrative, and technical factors, as well as on the careful formation of those people who will take over the task of cultural animation.

It is frequently stated that, first, it is necessary to create, within the parameters of the cultural policy, consciousness of the need for revision, adaptation, and flexibility within the administrative structures, in order to enhance the development of the cultural projects. This process of analytic evaluation and revision should be periodical, for it is all important:

1. to consider new and traditional ways of managing, taking in view the amplification of regional, provincial, and local power in decision making, without losing the necessary balance through a national coordination of cultural policies.
2. to establish institutional networks of cultural services, conducted by local community centers, as a measure of cultural ferment for institutional and human resources development.
3. to provide grounds for the formation of personnel, in different levels and specialties, destined to work in cultural animation and/or promotion.

WHO IS THIS PROFESSIONAL?

The aim of cultural action is to provide the community with the possibilities of access to information, of spontaneous and organized forms of expression for improvement of life style through that personal growth that reflects itself, necessarily, in the whole society.

According to the available data, the *cultural agent* (or *animator* or *cultural promotor*):

•   has the responsibility, as an agent for cultural change and community mobilization, to act as an element of facilitation for the population's active participation in cultural activities;
•   interacts and collaborates in the identification and diffusion of the local values, and in the promotion of the people's capacity for the use of their own resources, and on the other side, cooperates in the transfer of external information, and public or private cultural inputs;
•   must cooperate to encourage and to strengthen spontaneous cultural action in the communities through self-seeding processes, regarding not only artistic expression but also historic, cultural, and scientific knowledge, as well as exposing, before the users, the whole gamut of pos-

sibilities at national, regional, and international levels. For that matter, it is relevant for the cultural agent (or animator/cultural promotor) to have a clear knowledge of current national legislation and of any specific regulations concerned with cultural subjects and their processes of circulation.

Coming to the point of *who* should be selected for cultural action (or animation/cultural promotion) activities, I will use here two kinds of information: one, the papers of the Latin America meeting of experts in communication, education, and cultural animation, which took place in Lima, Peru, March 1988; and two, the results of research I carried out through the S. Paulo Association of Cultural Agents in October 1989.

First of all, every time someone speaks about "a curriculum" to form and technically prepare this kind of professional, the reaction from those already in the field is: "cultural agents are born that way"; "please, don't talk about schools forming new misfit professionals"; "don't call us professional cultural agents: we are professionals who became cultural agents," and so on.

After lengthy debate and discussion, the experts at the Lima meeting agreed on some of the characteristics to be found among the cultural agents that are necessary to their success. To be a successful cultural agent (or animator or cultural promotor) an individual must have, among other qualities, a sense of vocation, a sense of responsibility, a predisposition for community work, a capacity to develop human relations, a sense of opportunity, psychological balance, and a technical background. A training scheme could therefore be developed that built upon these qualities and amplified the operational capacities of the cultural agent (or animator or cultural promotor).

TYPES OF KNOWLEDGE NEEDED

Mention was made of some areas of knowledge that were especially pertinent: cultural policies, communication theory, audio visual techniques, elements of planning and administration, group dynamics techniques, social investigation, and community development.

Specially stressed was the notion that "the training of 'formation' of cultural agents should provide them with 'instruments' which allow them to integrate themselves in the community, enabling them to elaborate a 'realistic cultural profile' of the situation(s) found; to elaborate alternatives, taking into account the existing values of socio-cultural frames of reference, the real or potential capacity of creation, the cultural means and channels of its expression and/or inhibition, their basic organizations, the effective existing leadership, as well as the ways of expanding free time and space (UNESCO, 1988)."

From the accuracy of diagnosing the above (and other pertinent) factors or variables will depend the definition of valuable aims, the strategies of articulation among the actual forces, and the design of adequate plans and techniques to promote the real integration of the population in cultural activities.

Another emphatic point is related to actual training on field work under supervision, as a part of the cultural agent (or animator/ cultural promotor) training: candidates should be selected among the course participants, as they prove themselves apt to participate in a pilot plan, to put into practice a systematic activity of cultural development.

They should be tested in different alternatives of action, evaluated carefully in their performance and results reached, so that corrections and program amplifications and/or specializations can be tailored appropriately.

This procedure should take place at each step or level of performance. No cultural agent (or animator/cultural promotor) should, for example, proceed to a higher level of responsibility without having successfully finished the former level.

The Role of Communication

The place of communication must be stressed within the dynamic sociopolitics of Latin American societies, historically marked by cultural, economic, and technological dependency (bitter fruits of the colonial policies exerted for centuries upon the developing countries), and by deep internal inequalities in the economic, political and cultural areas, but, fortunately, also marked by the confrontations, the search for ways to transform the social environment through the removal of existing injustices, and the growth of participation of the majority of the population in social enterprise.

Within this scenario, there are dozens of projects for cultural development in all areas, at many levels, requiring the organization of the popular as well as the differentiated sectors of the many societies that coexist in the continent. Due to the different ethnic backgrounds, languages, values, religions, music, dance, and other forms of expression and ideological conception about life—individual as well as social—communication, in such a diversified society, is not only a set of channels diffusing messages. Communication is a strategic field where social means and meanings are built: a system of interactions that gives birth to processes of identification of people's characteristics, norms, and values, to the recognition and articulation of interests, accumulation and legitimation of knowledge and powers, thus contributing to the emergence of a social order.

To communication is assigned the role of promoting debate about problems, so enabling the whole society to come to grips with its value system, establish the grounds of rights and responsibilities, and the whole gamut of contents mobilized by the communication network that models and guides social behavior.

In developing societies, the voice of the common people very seldom reaches the main communication channels, and the traditional inequalities over the rights of participation in the society's dialogue generally contributes to disfavored groups continuing to be maintained as if they were constituted by second- and third-class citizens.

Group needs, however, manifest themselves through several forms of resistance, and fight to modify the exclusive communicative and social order, with peculiar dynamics of confrontation for each situation. Generally, needs and proposals are expressed in traditional ways, but also incorporate all the available means to reach their ends. These range from leaflets, newspapers, mural grafitti, theatrical representations (sociodramas), folk songs, and puppet shows, to radio, slides, and other audio-visual media, including movies, video, and TV. For the popular strata, these media represent not only the exercise of a right, but an essential instrument for mobilization and action.

However different the examples (urban and rural) that could be lined up, something remains constant: the effort of these groups in the search for adequate information, which normally is denied to them; the need for understanding and explaining the situations in which it is demonstrated the strength of the dominant groups; the need for self-recognition as social actors, identification through values; the need to become a focused group in terms of aims and interests; the need to be recognized by society as a whole, and express their ideals and projects; the need for effective participation, of handling abilities for solidary joint action; the ability to share ideas and power; and so on (Camargo, 1982).

The development of communicative practices are part of the continent's history. In Brazil, starting from the 1940s and intensifying in the 1960s and 70s, these practices became the mainstream of a large number of organizations involved with cultural development and basic educational and organizational processes.

The Process of Formation

Having in mind the above frame of reference and the peculiarity of each situation, the "formation" of the first cultural/social agents took place, not through a special curriculum, but "due to a solidary exchange of experiences, of successes and failures, empirical and critical evaluation with little systematized action, with the only purpose of creating new alternatives to enrich and offer a guiding basis for new experiences" (UNESCO, 1988).

All the processes have been originated by needs rooted in practice, be they the organization or group action itself, or the action performed by the intermediary groups of popular education. Nowadays, the systematization of knowledge deals with many subjects: some very precise, some highly inquisitive.

People working with popular groups always need to learn *operational techniques*: to better produce a paper to be edited by the group; to produce a script for sociodrama, or radio; to produce better messages; to be able to deal with different types of groups and personalities; to know how to plan, how to evaluate, and so on. The research among cultural agents in the field shows that there is always emphasis on the instrumental character of knowledge.

However, operational knowledge is not sufficient, for the cultural agent (or animator) needs to understand the *reasons behind the processes*: what are the alternative explanations? the alternatives for action? the possibilities of creating new spaces for the development of cultural and communicative practices? the different dimensions (individual, group, institution and mass) of needed and viable action?

By the same reasoning, *the organization* also needs to have clear for itself the role of media in the organizational and educational practices for the popular classes, the relationship between communication and economics/ideology/power. These are *reflexive* or *critical* needs, with strategic aims. A set of political conceptual aspects, indispensible to the arousal of such consciousness and sensitization, should be at the basis of any decision-making process of cultural action. Consequently, they should be an element of the cultural agent's formation.

Another type of need could be called *pedagogical*: concepts, attitudes, abilities, methods, and techniques scientifically recognized as relevant to trigger the multiplicative effect of the basic formation process.

There is also a type of need that fits under the title *administration*: how to plan, to set goals and divide them into phrases, so that one may be aware of the human and material resources/techniques/ etc. that are needed; how to proceed to a continuous evaluation process that should go along with action; how to plan, in different levels of action, the creation, production, dissemination, and retrieval of information; how to optimize existing resources, in terms of space–time–users–feedback; how to maintain the interflow between institutions and organizations at local/regional/international levels; how to plan and implement long-term plans and horizontal connections in a society with discontinuous policies and vertical structures.

Not least, there is the question of how to proceed to a formation of this new group of professionals without falling into the traps of "puritanism" and "populism" that have plagued many of the social and cultural programs in Latin America through the creation of illusory approaches to the questions of development, such as "the community is always right," "the popular is better," "quantity is more valuable than quality," "theory, science, and logic are enemies of participative thinking," "decision-making should be always consensual," and so forth.

The reading of reality is the most important issue in the formation of social/cultural animators, for the work roots itself in the formation, life, and future of others. From such readings—even though always incomplete—decisions are made, plans are proposed, resources and persons are mobilized, priorities are established, and processes get started in the direction of chosen aims. So, the cultural animator/agent has to be creative, for he or she is a "proposal person." Not the only one, or the most important, but a person able to build and maintain a coherent, pertinent, and resourceful capacity for sensible and appropriate proposals.

Summarizing, along with these qualities, Latin American experts on cultural action feel that four basic components should be present in the formation process (UNESCO, 1988):

1. *Conceptual framework*—the what/why of action. Knowledge about cultural environment, processes and manifestations, habits, values, and so on, that may help to define the real pertinence and the prospects of a proposal. It is the area of humanistics and social sciences, the understanding in depth of the whole, with specific attention to its variables and elements. Diagnostics.

2. *Logistical Framework*—the how and where actions are developed. Requires knowledge of organizational behavior, optimization of tasks in terms of adequacy to the environment and the proposal aims—for example, the organization of workshops, programs of diffusions, events, and so on.

3. *Structural framework*—the *who* and *with what* in the proposal: human, material, and financial resources for the whole proposal, for a clear insight of requirements is vital to the achievement of aims. This seems obvious, but most plan failures are due to the nonobservance or minimization of infrastructural inadequacies.

4. *Strategic Framework*—communication reasoning: adequacy of action to criteria such as opportunity, continuity and pertinence, in respect to institutional (federal, municipal, regional, national, etc.) policies that incorporate the cultural task to the concept and integral practice of development. Takes into consideration history and rhythm of a given group or society.

As stated before, the work of a cultural agent/animator takes place at various fields and at various levels, from directive and/or administrative tasks to the direct participation in the events. Whichever the case, and whatever its specific weight, the cultural agent needs to be able to analyze and interpret the logics of reality.

Reality interpretation implies the identification of five basic areas in the formation of a cultural agent:

1. community organization (political, economic, social, and cultural)
2. formative processes of individuals and of society
3. planning development services and processes
4. systematization of working processes
5. evaluation (of all elements and processes intervening in 1, 2, 3, and 4)

THE SEARCH FOR INNER QUALITIES
AND SELF-DEVELOPMENT

This is basic to the cultural agent's formation. He or she must compromise with his or her own growth and the amplification of his or her activity fields, and flexibility for different levels of action is vital. Directly connected with this is the area of social and behavioral sciences, which provides instruments for the growth of sensitivity and sensibility of the cultural agent.

Among others, there are some specific characteristics or attitudes that must not be lacking in the cultural agent's personality:

1. A capacity for criticism and self-criticism; honesty, respectfulness, sensibility; receptiveness, analytical capacity; capacity for dialogue; creativity.

2. Interpretation of reality, based in the progressive insight of everyday logic, enables a person with the above qualities and attitudes to face and solve intelligently those tasks linked to the cultural agent's work: organization, coordination, negotiation, management/administration, planning, field operation, evaluation, implementation, follow-up processes, and so on;

3. Translation into desirable "functions": the capacity or the ability to catalyze needs, enhance participation; program; instrumentalize actions; open alternatives for use, reflection, and enjoyment; diversify services; problematize reality; get feedback for evaluation and correction.

4. "Performances" as researcher, teacher, communicator, producer of means/carrier of cultural products, animator, and so on. In the processes of creation of those conditions and actions for development, within the group, given context and possibilities.

Of course, all these and other ideal elements are the ingredients of an ideal polyvalent professional, hard to find in practice. The processes of formation have to take into account types, levels, and extensions of cultural action. Consequently, there will be a core curriculum or set of knowledge, but for each type/level/scope of action, formation must be tailored and retailored, when the cultural agent takes or changes a given program.

An interesting exercise is to build a matrix where the types of tasks needed go in the columns, and the areas of knowledge in the rows, so that in the convergence we would discriminate the kind of tailored training for a certain cultural agent or group of cultural agents. Chanona (1988) proposed that the Cultural agents could use the same matrix for the analysis of their own specific needs in field work(see Figure 19.1):

FIGURE 19.1   Task/Knowledge Matrix

OPERATIVE AREAS	TRAINING FORMATION CAPACITATION RECYCLING	CULTURAL DIFFUSION	RESEARCH	ETC.
CULTURAL SETTING				
HISTORIC CULTURAL				
PROTECTION OF INFORMATION "PATRIMONIUM"				
SCIENCE TECHNOLOGY				
ARTISTIC CULTURE				
COMM. MEDIA CULTURE				
CULTURAL PLURALISM POPULAR CULTURE				
CULTURAL PLANNING AND ADMINISTRATION				
CREATION PRODUCTION DISSEMINATION RETRIEVAL				
LITERARY CREATION DRAMA, ETC.				
ETC.				

Chanona proposes that cultural agents should use the matrix for the planning of cultural projects dealing with:

1.   Formation, Capacitation
     —course
     —workshops
     —seminars
     —conferences

          —meetings
          —field work
          —etc.
2. Cultural diffusion
          —events, representations, shows
          —concourses
          —exhibits
          —publications
          —media production (radio; television)
          —etc.
3. Research
          —inventories, surveys
          —catalogs
          —research reports and literature
          —projects
          —etc.

To use the matrix, the cultural agent will proceed to four indispensable types of analysis:

1. Diagnostics: social/political/economic/cultural aspirations, needs and potentialities
2. Planning (including contextualization): policy/conceptual framework, socioeconomic, political and cultural reality
3. Programming: Projection of specific activities
      Budgeting
      Institutional, legal, and bureaucratic contexts
4. Evaluation: Initial/follow up/final

Every square of the matrix will provide cues for proposals that are pertinent and adequate to the community of institution needs and priorities, and can be further implemented.

Development Policy:

For the Latin American conception of self-reliant development, it is all-important that the program be guided towards the great aims of cultural development, as stated in several cultural policy documents. They are, basically:

• Self management (recognition of cultural adequacy)
    coordination of efforts/rationalization of resources

    recycling of infrastructural facilities
    avoidance of external financing, external decision taking, and adequacy to criteria external to the development processes of the community/country/region;
- Democratization
    participation and stimulation of groups, teams, individuals
    support to the existing local and autonomous initiatives
    adaptation of the cultural agent working projects to the sum of local proposals
    insertion of local groups and/or individuals in the instrumentalization of programs
- Strengthening of cultural unity and values framework
    pluralism of inputs
    alternative forms of expression
    cultural identity, in the frame of the regional and international landscape.

The reading of reality and the planning of programs are the core of further cultural activities, which should result from the open discussion of the proposals. According to the rich Mexican experience in cultural action, the best cultural agent is only a *facilitator* in the processes of cultural development.

In all countries of Latin America, the *houses of culture* and *cultural spaces* (and other denominations) do exist in great number. Maintained by their governments, by the commercial associations, religious entities, or independent foundations, these cultural centers are normally used by the population that makes use of the programs offered: movies, theater, concerts, shows, exhibits, displays, conferences, seminars and workshops, courses, meetings. In short, all sorts of events: Some are prepared by the administration; others just take place using the center's facilities.

Interviews with people working in these centers pointed up that many parameters of cultural action are set according to the source of resources: ideology, scope, duration, and budget, among others.

Other aspects are freer for the cultural agents' creation and operation, provided the main decisions on the above aspects have been respected: the choice of pedagogical techniques, information contents, program arrangements, audio-visual aids, and so on.

There are cases where the cultural agents receive training and learn to produce and implement their own programs. There are cases where the cultural agents are assigned specific tasks inside a more rigidly coordinated program. Variations can be understood within the global analysis of the institutions' aims and policies.

THE ROLE OF THE UNIVERSITY IN THE FORMATION
OF CULTURAL AGENTS (PROMOTORS/ANIMATORS)

• Cultural action is growing along with the emergence of an affluent, postindustrial information society that makes more visible—and unbearable—the inequalities between those *who have* and those *who have not*; between those who *know* and the so called *know-nothings*.

• The consciousness about the abyss-like gap established between groups inside a society, and between societies inside the international set, and its consequences for social balance, world peace, and the survival of humankind, has been stressed by thinkers, educators, governments, and also international organizations (MacBride, 1980), which created special events and study groups to help to clarify the subject, to point out its main features, and to propose policies that could minimize such inequalities and help to overcome the problems.

• Cultural action has aligned itself as one of these efforts, and the cultural agent is one of these new professionals: half educator, half communicator, with an extra and extremely important mission: to help to create favorable environments and conditions for persons, groups, and societies as a whole; to share the richness of the world's cultural, scientific, technological, and artistic production within the framework of the group's history and traditions; and to grow in self-respect and respect of other's ideas, artistic expressions, ways of solving problems, lifestyles, and so on.

• The role of the university is to prepare this background in everyone who enters it.

• The professional cultural agent cannot be prepared during the undergraduate period. The maturity, and the intra- and inter-disciplinarity, that is required of them means that any candidates coming from different academic origins, or backgrounds, and receiving the qualifications at graduate levels are suitable. (This has been the only issue that has produced a 100 percent consensus.)

Some universities in Latin American countries have already started their training for cultural agents: Mexico, Colombia, Peru, and Venezuela are among the most active. In Brazil and several other countries, there are combined efforts from the universities and the sponsoring institutions, in order to create specially tailored programs for special cultural agent groups. The majority of the Latin American universities generally run courses about the subject, laying emphasis on the critical appraisal of its features.

REFERENCES

Camargo, N. de (1974). The teaching of communication in Brazil. *Revire Comunicação e Artes*. S. Paulo.

Camargo, N. de (1982). Communication policies and perplexities of development. In Amaral (Ed.), *Comunicação de Massa, O Impasse Brasileiro*. Rio de Janeiro: Forense.

Camargo, N. de (1983). *Who are the teachers?* (Mimeo). Sao Paulo: School of Communication & Arts.

Camargo, N. de (1986). *Production and diffusion of cultural products and services: The formation of personnel*. Vienna: Mediacult.

Camargo, N. de (1989). *Cultural animation in S. Paulo - A survey*. S. Paulo.

Chanona, B.O. (1988). *Apuntes para una metodologia de la animacion cultural*. Paper given at the Regional Meeting of Animation, Communication and Education, Lima.

MacBride, S. (1980). *Many voices, one world*. Paris: Unesco.

UNESCO. (1988). *Report of a meeting Encuentro de Animacion, Comunicacion y Educacion*. Lima.

PART

VI

On Media Education

CHAPTER

Media Education and Its Future

LEN MASTERMAN

Future perspectives in media education? Given that media studies as a disciplined field of study in its own right scarcely existed in school anywhere before 1985, and given the proliferation of international developments in the field since that time, with three international conferences held in Toronto, Melbourne, and Toulouse between May and September 1990 alone, it is necessary, first of all, to catch our breath and to document where we stand in 1990 before considering what the future may hold. I will try, then, in the following pages, to trace the main movement of ideas in the field over the past five years, before offering some tentative thoughts on what may be the most fruitful lines of development in the 1990s.

DEVELOPMENT IN MEDIA EDUCATION 1985–1990

First, a caveat. Media education is always specific to the culture in which it finds a place. Existing at the interface of any society's political, socioeconomic, educational, and broadcasting systems, media education inevitably follows the unique contours of its host culture. "Follows," however, is too passive. Media education aspires to be an active force within its own culture. And its purposes and priorities will be determined by a whole range of factors, including the current consumption and use of the media by students, the potentiality (or lack of it) for democratic participation and control within existing media, and the relative autonomy of the media and educational systems from the government and the state, as well as the existence of appropriate curriculum spaces for teaching about the media. There will, in obvious ways, be major strategic differences in what media teachers are trying to achieve in, say, the very different educational and media environments of inner-city Bombay, Toronto, or Amman. We need to salute from the outset the existence of a rich and diverse range of media education practices before undertaking the task of tracing those approaches, ideas, and practices before undertaking the task of tracing those approaches, ideas, and things that do seem to have produced cross-cultural resonances. For when the differences have been acknowledged, there has been a remarkable crossfertilization of ideas across national boundaries over the past five years, while international networking is now efficient enough to ensure that ideas forged in Canadian classrooms, for example, can be made available to teachers throughout Europe, Australia, and parts of Asia in a matter of weeks rather than years.[1] In what kind of direction, then, have ideas and practices developed over the past five years?

WHY MEDIA EDUCATION? FROM PATERNALISM TO EMPOWERMENT

It would be very unusual at a meeting of media teachers anywhere in the world to find adherents of older, overtly paternalistic or protectionist approaches to media education. Though the view that the media are agents of cultural decline remains common enough among teachers generally, media educators represent an important lobby against (or at least against the central *relevances* of) such a view.

Similarly, media education practices based upon the idea that the media are most constructively thought of as popular art forms have not proved to be sustainable with any theoretical or practical rigor since Hall and Whennel's (1984) classic formulation of this position. This is not to deny or devalue the work either of those teachers who were able to integrate film and video into their teaching or who encouraged their pupils to discriminate between

---

[1] The Ontario *Media Literacy Resources Guide*, published in Canada in 1989, was already in the hands of large numbers of British and Australian teachers in its year of publication and clearly filled a gap in the international literature. The *Guide*, in its turn, had been quite strongly influenced by developments in Australia and the UK (Ministry of Education, Ontario, 1989).

"good" and "bad" films and TV programs on traditional or more progressive aesthetic grounds. But it is to suggest that, historically, media education moved on considerably when its agenda turned away from aesthetic towards more broadly culturalist concerns, and when teachers and students attempted primarily to understand rather than to appreciate the media. It was the development of a critically informed intelligence in relation to the media that was to become the key objective for most media teachers, rather than the nurturing of finely honed aesthetic judgments. If this development took an unconscionably long time to work its way through schools (as opposed to higher education, where the better ones won in the early 1970s), this was because most media teachers came to the subject via literary studies rather than the social sciences. And given the still prevalent integration of much media education work within the student's mother tongue, where it stands alongside literary studies, there remains a constant danger of the subject collapsing back to more narrowly aesthetic orthodoxies.

In spite of this, however, that notion of developing an informed understanding of the media has itself undergone a further evolution. It is now clear that successful media education has to involve an *empowerment* of learners essential to the creation and sustaining of an active democracy and of a public that is not easily manipulable but whose opinion *counts* on media issues because it is critically informed and capable of making its own independent judgments. At a time when the management and manufacture of information by governments and vested interest groups has grown apace, it is now the *liberating* potentialities of media education that perhaps provide its chief rationale across all cultures. Without retreating into mechanistic and pessimistic mass-society theories, it remains true that the early 1990s is an age in which the engineering of public consent across a wide range of issues is very big business indeed. It is the age of marketing, of public relations, of misinformation and disinformation, and of unholy convergencies between news and promotion, politics and marketing, and an age that has produced such characteristic coinings as the *advertorial* and *infotainment*.

In these circumstances it is not difficult in most cultures to see the media less as bastions of free expression than as weapons used in the service of powerful interest groups. This has given rise, even in advanced democracies, to new kinds of poverty and new kinds of inequality: between those who have easy access to the media and those who do not; between those whose world-views receive coherent expression within existing media, and those whose do not;

between those with the power to define, and those who are always only defined; between those who can speak about the world as they know and understand it, and those whose experiences are inevitably framed and interpreted for them by others; between, in short, the media rich and the media poor.

Media education is one of the few weapons any society possesses for challenging these inequalities in knowledge and power, and for closing the gap between those in whose interests media information is produced and disseminated, and those who simply consume it innocently as news or entertainment. Media education can empower its learners and greatly strengthen the democratic structures of the society that it serves by challenging the naturalness of media images, foregoing questions of representation, examining the democratic structure of broadcasting institutions, and raising questions of human rights in relation to communication.

The movements, sketched out above, from a *protectionist* through an *investigative* to an *empowerment* rationale for media education, have been accompanied by further important transformation in the concept of media education itself.

The Concept of Media Education: From School Subject to Life-long Process

In the early 1980s perhaps the most significant question facing media educators was "Is it possible to teach about the media in a coherent and disciplined way?" This remains an important question, but in the 1990s the terms of the major debates have moved on. Today it is important to see formal educational work on the media as part of a much more comprehensive and life-long process—a process that in its turn has had a profound influence on the aims and objectives of work in schools and colleges. High student motivation, for example, must now become rather more than a desirable spin-off from, or adjunct to, effective reading. It has to become a primary objective in its own right. If media education is not an enjoyable and fulfilling as well as instructive experience, then pupils will have no encouragement to continue learning about the media after they have passed beyond the gates of the school. This inevitably changes classroom objectives in fundamental ways. Media education is an education for the future as well as the present. The whole point about media education is that it should develop in children enough self-confidence and critical maturity for them to be able and willing to apply critical judgments to TV programs and newspaper articles that they will encounter in the future. The acid test of the success of any media education program lies in the extent to which pupils are critical in their own use and understanding of the media *when the teacher is not there.* The primary objective of life-long media education is not simply critical awareness and understanding but *critical autonomy.*

The importance of this objective has profound implications for course content, teaching methodology, and methods of evaluation. It is no longer good enough for pupils to process or reproduce ideas or information supplied to them by their teacher (as they do in most other subjects). Nor is it adequate for teachers to encourage pupils to develop their own critical insights in the classroom (though this is certainly important). The really important and challenging task for the media teacher is to produce in pupils both the *ability* and the *willingness* to want to go on doing this for the rest of their lives.

In the classroom this means that it is essential to teach for transfer. That is, it is always going to be necessary for teachers to move their pupils beyond an understanding of this or that particular issue or text towards an understanding of those *general principles* that will have relevance to the analysis of similar issues or texts. Evaluation will not be of what pupils know but of how they respond in situations where they *do not know the answer.* It is worth emphasizing how seldom we expect this of school pupils in our teaching of most subjects.

What Should be Taught? From Fragmentation to Coherence

To be convinced of the need for media education is one thing. To develop a successful media education practice is quite another. It is unfortunately true that much media education in the past was fragmented and chaotically divergent, depending as it often did on the enthusiasms and interests of individual teachers. In the past decade, however, widespread agreement has been reached on ways of studying and teaching about the media, and the adherents of media education would now claim that their educational practice is every bit as systematic and intellectually rigorous as those of more traditional and established subjects. It now makes sense to speak of a coherent international media education *movement.* How has this development occurred?

The major epistemological problem facing media teachers can be simply stated. It is this: How is it possible to make any kind of conceptual sense of a field that covers such a diversity of forms, practices, and products? The very object of study itself, *the media,* turns out to be, on examination, a little more than a convenient catch-all category into which many very different forms of communication can be bundled, rather than a clearly defined field. And each medium itself serves a multiplicity of functions. It was for many years far from clear how even a single medium such as television could be studied in a disciplined and rigorous way, let alone *all* of the other media and their complex interrelationships.

Up until the early 1980s the most common solution to this problem reached by schools had really been no solution at all. It was that the obvious starting point for thinking about the media lay in the uniqueness (or *specificity*) of each medium. The subject was deemed to consist of the aggregated sum of these discrete parts. So a one-year course on the media might typically consist of a term on film, half a term on television, half a term on newspapers, a few weeks on advertising, a little time on pop music, and so on. The problem here was not simply that the subject was being fragmented at the level of content. It was that different kinds of principles, concepts, and modes of inquiry were being brought into play in studying different media. Work on Hitchcock's films, for example, might be followed in the next term by the study of TV news, which in turn might be followed by work on the techniques of persuasion used in advertising or images of women in women's magazines. But what gave coherence to these very different topics? A particular mode of inquiry? The examination of important cross-media concepts? Or what?

Answers to these questions emerged slowly as media teachers began to meet and discuss their work throughout the 1980s. Continuities and correspondences began to emerge out of the most diverse range of practices and contexts. Influential too was the recognition by teachers (many of whom had had in the past a particular commitment to film studies) that if their work was to be firmly grounded in the actual media experiences of their pupils, and if they were to begin the task of responding to the significant ideological issues raised by the media, then in most societies television should play a much more dominant role in their thinking and practice than it had ever done in the past.

So it was that the principle of *nontransparency* (a principle that insisted that the media were rather more then unproblematic windows on the world, or mirrors reflecting reality, but symbolic systems requiring active reading) came to gain, from media teachers, an almost universal acceptance. It was a principle that particularly illuminated the nature of television—insisting that its meanings were actively produced, that it *represented* rather than reflected reality—but that also had a surprising degree of potency across all media. The crucial distinction drawn by all media teachers and their students between images and their referents, between representations and reality, between the signifer and the signified, produced in turn a characteristic discourse in which media teachers and students the world over spoke, not of (say) *women, poverty, prisons,* or *Africa,* but of *representations* of these things. Indeed in English that central unifying concept of representation became a kind of professional pun: the media did not present reality, they re-present it.

The principle of nontransparency, then, insisted that the media were the product of human agency. The media mediated. They were not, oppressively, the reflections of a reality that had to be accepted. They were, liberatingly, representational systems that had to be read, understood, and acted upon.

If media products were representations, then a number of other areas immediately suggested themselves for further investigation:

- *Who* is responsible for media representations? Who owns, controls, produces, and influences them? In whose interests do they work? Why are media products and representations as they are? What are the major institutional, legal, and economic influences that bear upon the production of media texts? (Media determinants)
- *How* are media representations produced? By what methods? Employing what kind of techniques and rhetorical devices? (Media rhetoric)
- *What* precisely do media representations signify? What kind of implicit and explicit values underpin them? (Media ideologies)
- *How* are media representations read and negotiated by their audiences? (Media audiences)

It is these questions that have largely constituted the framework for the development of media education practice since the mid-1980s, a development that has been accompanied by an irrevocable movement towards new dialogic ways of working with students, and towards an integration of practical criticism with a critical, rather than reproductive, practice.[2]

---

[2] Space does not permit me to consider here the development of media education practical work, but see Masterman (1985) for fuller discussions.

MEDIA EDUCATION IN THE 1990S

Spectacular though the development of media education has been over the past decade, it has scarcely managed to keep pace with the rate of change within the media themselves. The expansion of media education in the 1980s has been driven by the apparent relevance of the subject to the lives of pupils and students. But already the gap between the kind of issues discussed within the media trade press, or the media themselves, and the media studies classroom is dangerously wide; a great deal of media teaching is beginning to lose touch with the realities of the media environment of the 1990s. It is an environment of deregulated, multichannelled broadcasting, interactive cable systems, television data systems, the everyday use of videocassette and disc materials, and the general convergence of advanced media and computer technologies. But it is also an environment in which debates about the fundamental orientation of every society's culture are taking place, debates within which the role of the media themselves (as agents of cultural autonomy or dependency, enrichment or impoverishment, commercially or socially oriented) have a central importance. It is one of the crucial roles of media education in any society to prepare its present and future citizens for the fullest possible participation in such debates.

So what will be the priorities for media education over the next decade? I offer four: The strategic importance of creating and building upon international networks and national organizational infrastructures, a commitment to the creation and defense of democratically organized public information systems, the elevation of the study of marketing to a position of much greater prominence within the study of the media, and a commitment to the principle of continuous change itself in our thinking about and teaching of the media curriculum.

Building Networks

It is worth stressing from the outset that the future of media education will be shaped as much by the vigilence and organizational capabilities of media educators *now* as it will by future technological developments. Indeed, without sturdy organizational infrastructures, media education may not have a future. For many countries are now undergoing a period of profound educational conservatism and retrenchment in which even established creative arts subjects such as drama, art, and music are given low status and few resources in the face of the increasing dominance of utilitarian and instrumental philosophies of education. Fostering a critical spirit, perhaps for understandable reasons, does not seem to be high on the agenda of most governments when they consider their educational priorities. In this situation, the ability of media educators to organize themselves, and to participate in and influence public debate by putting their cases as forcibly as possible, becomes of paramount importance. The case for the future of media education is a formidable, even an overwhelming one. It can be argued, without too much exaggeration, that the very future of participatory democracies may depend upon it. But without the practice of a lively and energetic *educational politics* it is a case that is likely to go by default. What this means in practical terms is that:

- at the *school level*, media teachers have to do more than simply teach their subject; they must be *advocates* for it, advancing its cause wherever they can within their own institutions, among students, colleagues, parents, and policy makers.
- at *local and national levels*, media teachers and policy makers need to build up support networks to share ideas and resources. The most successful national media associations currently existing—in Scotland and Australia—have in common the fact that they are national networks of strongly autonomous regional and local groups. They have a federal rather than a centralized structure, and this allows a sharing of responsibilities for organizing conferences and producing journals, and ensures that the organization maintains close contact with the grassroots constituency from which it has developed.[3]
- at *international level*, the exchange of resources, ideas, and personnel between anglophone cultures is already highly efficient. Books and materials produced in the UK,

---

[3] The organizational development of media education in Scotland and Australia may be charted via the journals *The Media Education Journal* and *Metro*, respectively. *The Media Education Journal* is the journal of the Association for Media Education in Scotland (AMES), editorial address: MEJ, Department of Communication, Glasgow College, Cowcaddens Rd., Glasgow G4 OBA. *Metro* is the journal of the Australian Teachers of Media (ATOM), editorial address: P.O. Box 222, Carlton South, Victoria 3053, Australia.

Australia, or Canada have an immediate international market. European cooperation has faced greatest difficulties but has received great encouragement from a whole range of workers organized by the council of Europe,[4] while the opening up of the European Economic Community in 1992 presents great opportunities for media educators throughout the continent. Even in the most difficult yet most important field of all—collaboration between media education agencies and teachers in developed and developing countries—important progress has been made in a series of international conferences and publications organized by UNESCO (see, e.g., UNESCO, 1985, 1987). And here a tribute to the subject of this Festschrift, James Halloran, is entirely appropriate, for no one has been as selflessor as indefatigable as he in disseminating knowledge of the best ideas and practices in media research across the world. His major international overview of approaches to media education in some 15 countries, carried out with Marsha Jones for UNESCO in the mid-1980s, and his fine contributions to the two Stiftung Prix Jeunesse projects, *Young TV Viewers and their Images of Foreigners* and *Television and Family in Three Countries*, stand as testaments to a career that has had a profound and generative influence on media education practice throughout the world (see Halloran & Jones, n.d.; Halloran & Nightingale, 1982; Halloran & Linne, 1988).

The Defense and Transformation
of Public Information Systems

All teachers working within public educational systems have a de facto commitment to the principles of open and universal access to information, such access providing for their pupils the basis for their future participation in a democracy. This commitment to universal access is also, necessarily, a commitment to preserving the independence of at least some information *producers* (public service broadcasting systems, universities, research institutes) from undue commercial influence or governmental interference. For without such independence, access is of little value. Indeed, it is

---

[4] For a full list of all Council of Europe conferences and publications in media education, 1982–1987, see the Appendix to my own study (Masterman, 1988).

to drink from a contaminated well. These commitments cannot and should not be expressed as a narrow and uncritical partisanship, but rather as an open and generous allegiance to democratic values, an allegiance that is in harmony with the impulses of progressive movements everywhere, North and South, East and West. Where public service media remain, as they frequently do, under the control of narrowly based bureaucracies or social elites, it will be necessary not simply to defend but to transform them. This is now distinctly possible. Paternalistic forms of public service media are being shaken to their foundations everywhere, either by the onset of deregulation or by the forward march of democratic political movements. The sole justification of such media—that they do indeed serve the public interest—is subjected to an unprecedented degree of critical scrutiny. Under this pressure there has been a discernible movement towards greater public accountability and democratic control of public service broadcasting. At the end of the 1980s the choices for public service media systems could scarcely be starker. If they do not strengthen their democratic and representative bases, they are unlikely to survive into the 21st century.

Very large issues are at stake, then, in struggles over the future configuration of the media industries. Should information be regarded as a commodity, or does it have a social value? Is it preferable to produce information that meets general social needs, as opposed to information that makes a profit or serves the interest of political, bureaucratic, and social elites? Is access to information a right, or should it be restricted either to those who can pay or to those who can be trusted? Is information an extension of property rights or political power, or does it lie predominantly in the public domain? It is scarcely an exaggeration to say that the future shape of all cultures will lie in the ways in which they answer these questions. It is evident, too, that the effective expression of the public interest will be dependent upon the existence of an articulate and informed public. Hence the importance of the media educator's future role, and the priority that will need to be given to a consideration of public policy issues within it.

Teaching Critical Marketing

A third priority for media educators is likely to involve the elevation of the study of advertising to a much more important role within media education, as it becomes increasingly evident that advertising is perhaps the preeminent shaper of those media that survive and flourish. This will involve a fundamental shift in and expansion of our concept of advertising to include not simply "paid-for" ads, but a whole range of modern disciplines and techniques, such as public relations, the manufacture and management of information, sponsorship, product and package design, direct mailing, product placement, and the like. Advertising, that is, should be understood as a small part of the process of *marketing*, a philosophy and an industry that has a close and symbiotic relationship with the media and whose practitioners include not simply commercial organizations, but, crucially, national governments, special interest groups, and institutions of every size and shade of opinion.

The development of marketing techniques has already produced a *convergence of advertising and nonadvertising material* in the media. While television programs often contain enormous amounts of advertising (plugs for records, film and books; displays of new styles and products; the coverage of sponsored events), the ads themselves have become more product than consumer oriented and contain, in concentrated form, the kind of visual and narrative sophistication all too rarely found in the programs themselves.[5] Paradoxically, today, if one wished to study the most advanced marketing techniques, one would go to news, documentary, and fictional television *programs*. If one wished to study the most sophisticated visual and narrative forms, one would go to the advertisements.

Of fundamental importance in prioritizing the study of marketing and advertising, however, is to shift students' understanding of the role and function of the media as a whole. Up until this point media education has been largely based upon a premise of astonishing naivety and has passed on to its students a misleadingly one-dimensional view of what the media do. That premise has been that the media's primary function is to provide news, information, and entertainment for their audiences, and media education has largely consisted of the study of these media forms. Actually the chief product of the mass media are, as Dallas Smythe has pointed out, not programs or articles but *audiences*. Commercial media stand or fall by their ability to deliver desirable audiences to advertisers (and public service broadcasting systems, it could be argued, are sustained by the state because of their ability to produce audiences who are ready to support particular political, social, and economic policies). Programs are a means to an end; they constitute what Smythe (1981) has called the "free lunch," the lure by means of which the audience commodity is created.

---

[5] This point is neatly made by Dallas Smythe (1981, p. 15).

The validity of this view may easily be substantiated by reference to any of the many trade journals that circulate within the media industries. In them media teachers and their students will find audiences discussed as commercial commodities with great openness. They will find media institutions advertising not their programs, but their audiences. And they will find that media content, where it is discussed at all, only surfaces in terms of its ability to produce a particular target audience. Of consuming interest, on the other hand, are such matters as "cost per thousand," audience segmentation techniques, rate card costs, and precision "targeting."

It is a matter of some importance that pupils should have access to this kind of material and should understand the crucial function of contemporary media in segmenting and packaging audiences for sale to advertisers. This will give them a new and radically different way of conceptualizing the media and help them understand the differences that exist between the way in which the media address the public, and the way in which they speak to prospective advertisers. It will help them to understand, that is, that their own "natural" way of relating to the media is not natural at all but instead is designed to conceal from them the true nature of the audience commodity.

Commitment to the Principle of Continuous Change

While media teachers can, and ought to, make educated guesses about their current and future priorities, the precise shift of the future remains, as it must, properly enveloped in uncertainty. What is certain is that in whatever direction media and information systems develop, we, as media educators, must develop with them. This will involve not so much a commitment to this or that particular course of action, is a commitment to *the principle of continuous change itself.* It is this principle that lies at the heart of any successful media education practice, an understanding that change is not a movement from one relatively stable state to another, but an inevitable and continuing process. This then is the fundamental task with which media educators are charged: that in whatever directions media and information technologies develop and expand in the future, these changes must be matched by a commensurate expansion in the critical consciousness of their audiences.

At the end of the 1980s, media teachers can look back with some pride at their achievement in developing a critical, investigative, noninoculative practice that has operated at the leading edge of developments in the media themselves. The vital task of keeping that tradition alive, whatever the precise shape of the media in the future, is one worthy of our continuing commitment and energy into the 1990s and well beyond.

REFERENCES

Hall, S., & Whennel, P. (1964). *The popular arts*. London: Hutchinson.
Halloran, J., & Jones, M. (undated). *Learning about the media: Media education and communication research*. Documents on Communication and Society. Paris: UNESCO.
Halloran, J., & Nightingale, V. (1982). *Young tv viewers and their images of foreigners*. Munich: Stiftung Prix Jeunesse.
Halloran, J., & Linne, O. (1988). *Television and family in three countries*. Munich: Stiftung Prix Jeunesse.
Masterman, L. (1980). *Teaching about television*. London: Macmillan.
Masterman, L. (1985). *Teaching the media*. London: Routledge.
Masterman, L. (1988). *The development of media education in Europe in the 1990s*. Strasbourg: Council of Europe.
UNESCO (1985). *The UNESCO declaration on media education (The Grunwald declaration)*. Report of a UNESCO Symposium at Grunwald, FRG in 1992. Paris: UNESCO.
UNESCO (1987). *Impact of mass communication media on curriculum development and educational methods*. Report of UNESCO European Workshop held at Tutzing, FRG, November 1986. Paris: UNESCO.

Media Education in Developing Countries—The Indian Experience

21

KEVAL JOE KUMAR

Media education has yet to make its mark as a subject of learning in the formal educational systems of both the industrialized and the nonindustrialized countries. Public and private school authorities, though worried by the growth and influence of the mass media, do not see the need for burdening students with a new subject whose content and methodology do not fit into traditional educational practices. The vigorous attempts of UNESCO, for over a decade now, to promote the subjects at various levels of education have met with very little success, except in a few countries of the more affluent West (notably Australia, Great Britain, and Canada) and in Latin America.

In several Latin American countries, media education programs are organized on a regular basis at church or community levels with the specific aim of training youth, housewives, community leaders, and other social groups to exercise their right to participate in media activities and thus help democratize communications. Media education in Latin American countries has thus become an instrument for the economic and political liberation of the poor and the marginalized.

MEDIA EDUCATION IN INDIA

In most countries of Asia and Africa, however, media education has made little headway. Church organizations in India, the Philippines, Fiji, Mauritius, and parts of East Africa have been active in conducting courses in media education outside the formal curriculum. In India, media education is still at an experimental stage, kept alive by a few dedicated individuals. Though at least two of the media education projects have been regular courses (outside school hours), for the last decade or so there has been no systematic attempt made to evaluate any of the courses. Where evaluations have been carried out, they have been ad hoc and cursory in the form of assessments and comments offered by participants at the end of each course.

EXPOSURE AND REACH OF MASS MEDIA

Among Indian educationists, media education has aroused little interest. In the first place, the need for it is not felt to be so urgent, since exposure to the mass media, even in urban areas, has yet to reach the alarming level it has in the West. The mass media in India are, after all, still only minority media as far as actual access is concerned. The reach and coverage of radio and television, for instance, is no doubt extensive (94 percent and 70 percent of the population, respectively), but barely a third of that population can afford a receiver. "Community listening" and viewing are fairly popular, but both the central and state governments have dragged their feet in the allocation of funds for "community sets." The cinema continues to be the most popular mass medium, but here too access is limited because of the small number of exhibition theaters and mobile units (around 12,500 all told) across the country. In recent years, the phenomenal growth of video across the country has provided small-town and rural populations greater access to Indian films. Low literacy levels (barely 37 percent) and woefully inadequate purchasing power also limit access to the press.

OVERLOADED SYLLABI

Secondly, the syllabi in schools and colleges are so overloaded that is well-nigh impossible to introduce a new subject as part of the curriculum, or even to add a new unit to existing subjects such as English, the mother tongue, social studies, or environment studies.

What is more, teaching methods are geared to helping students pass the public examinations and then to gain admission to profession-oriented institutes, and to colleges and universities offering higher degrees in arts, commerce, and the sciences. Media education just does not fit into this state-controlled and examination-oriented system.

ROLE OF THE STATE

The Indian state plays an important part in education at all levels. The curriculum to be followed, the timetable of studies, the course to be taught, the text materials, and the appointments of teachers are prescribed by rules and regulations of the government. The National Council of Education and Research (NCERT), a body appointed by the central government on the recommendation of the General Advisory Board of Education, formulates a model syllabus in various subjects for the entire country. Each state then adapts this syllabus according to the needs of each region. In each state, educationists from various districts coordinate to formulate the state syllabus.

As a consequence, schools have hardly any choice in decision making. School authorities can only choose their own medium of instruction and introduce minor changes within the prescribed framework. Currently, the stress is on "themes" rather than on "subjects," so value education, population education, and environment education have increasingly assumed much importance. However, it has not been considered advisable to devise separate courses for these themes. Instead, they have been integrated with the subject matter of the existing areas of the curriculum.

EDUCATIONAL TECHNOLOGY

A further reason for the slow progress of media education in India is that few schools (whether public or private) have the wherewithal to be equipped with the minimum audiovisual materials or to have their staff trained in media education. Though more than 70 university departments and private institutes offer courses in journalism and communication, the attempt by and large is to turn out professionals in the media rather than media critics or media educators. Few schools of education impart any training in media pedagogy, though much is made of the importance of using audiovisual aids in the classroom. Educational Technology is taught as an optional subject in some schools of education, but its relationship to media education is rarely touched on.

Nonformal and distance learning systems have started playing an increasingly important role in promoting literacy over the last decade. It is evident that a country as large and as populous as India, with over 575,000 villages and with a student population that exceeds a hundred million, needs a multisystem and a multimedia approach to education. Since media education is by definition a threat and a challenge to communication structures (of which formal education is one) it can perhaps have a greater impact in a nonformal set-up.

FOUR EXPERIMENTS IN MEDIA EDUCATION

Media education has been taught since the late seventies in classes in a few high schools in Bombay, Hyderabad, Secunderabad, Calcutta, and Madras, but as a subject outside the formal school curriculum. The initiative in all these cities has been taken mostly by enthusiastic individuals after their return from communication studies abroad. The response of educational authorities to this essentially private enterprise has been rather lukewarm.

Media Utilization Course

The first Indian program in media education was launched in the mid-seventies by the Amruthavani Communication Centre at Secunderabad. It was called a *Media Utilization Course* (MUC) and was primarily directed at students at convent high schools in the cities of Hyderabad and Secunderabad. It was (and after more than a decade still continues to be) a voluntary, fee-paying course held once a week outside school hours. It meets at the center, rather than in any school environment. It has published booklets and textbooks that set out the subject matter of the two-year course, along with the questions it seeks to raise. A close examination of the syllabus and the booklets on each of the mass media (newspapers, radio, television, and the cinema) suggests that the history, language, technical aspects of production, and types of programs in each medium are the topics accorded priority. The social, political, and economic dimensions do not find any mention. A scrutiny of the MUC's aims reveals that the Center's approach is moralistic and protectionist.

The *Mediaworld* Project

The Xavier Institute of Communications, Bombay, has since the mid-sixties been teaching part-time evening professional courses in journalism, advertising and marketing, public relations, photography, audiovisuals, and film production, and in recent years television production, too. In 1979 the institute started a program of media education for high school students in Bombay. Like the Amruthavani venture, this too is a voluntary, fee-paying course, taught outside the formal school system. Known as *Mediaworld*, the course is run on school premises by a team of practicing primary and secondary school teachers.

The main objective of the course, as detailed in course literature, is "to develop a critical attitude towards the media, to foster the creative imagination with regard to the media and to develop a critical attitude to its values." The hope is that "this course completes what the student learns in school, and widens his perception of the audiovisual culture in which we are all immersed."

The course seeks to achieve its objectives in 12 two-hour sessions spread over 2½ months. Three of the sessions deal with advertising, the next three with newspapers, and then four with the cinema. The final two sessions are devoted to practical projects, such as putting together an advertisement, a chart, a poster, a newspaper, or a scrapbook, and to guided visits to film and communication institutes.

Unlike the Amruthavani course, Mediaworld does not have course books or texts but uses worksheets and printed handouts for discussion and analysis. Some of the questions raised during the sessions are:

- How deeply have the media affected you?
- What kind of films do you see?
- Are they all fantasies, or are they based on reality?
- In whose hands is the control of the media?
- Is this control commercial, or political, or ideological?
- Why are advertisements called "hidden persuaders"? Are all advertisements varnished lies?

Educommunication Project in Tamilnadu

The Culture and Communication Institute at Loyola College, Madras, has conducted a media education program for high schools and higher secondary schools in Tamilnadu since 1983, the International Year of Communication. Known as an *educommunication* program (after the UNDA term for media education) it was started in response to the Vatican II decree, *Inter Mirifica*, and to the Pastoral Instruction, *Communio et Progressio*, of Pope Paul VI.

The program has two main objectives:

1. To impart media awareness and help students develop a critical appreciation of the media;
2. To teach students some skills in mass media and group media.

The syllabus of the course was formulated in consultation with the Xavier Institute of Communications, Bombay. The emphasis in the Tamilnadu experiment is on practical exercises.

The Chitrabani Experiment

An equally significant, albeit short-lived, experiment in media education was carried out in the early eighties by Gaston Roberge at the Chitrabani Communication Centre, Calcutta. It was essentially an attempt to get a group of young people to explore the popular cinema as a form of entertainment, through informal discussion and reflection. Roberge describes his method as "the method of discovery which is determined in pace and content by the students of a particular group and by the film available at the time." The method, he observes, is *synthetic* (many subjects are dealt with simultaneously), *organic* (it involved all the student's faculties), and *cyclic* (the same subjects are dealt with several times at various levels). For Roberge it matters little whether you start with film, advertising or any medium; what is required is to probe into the media environment. The media, therefore, are not art first and foremost; rather they are always commodities, experiences, and environments.

CONCLUSION

Some broad principles and concepts can be garnered from the four experimental ventures in media education in different parts of the country. The common approach is underscored by a definite "provalues" rather than a "value-neutral" orientation. The values to be promoted are Christian, or at least broadly humanistic. Further, the approach to the technological media, such as the cinema or the press, is critical but not entirely negative. The tendency, though, is to look at media products as art forms rather than as popular cultural forms, with an aesthetic very different from that of traditional art or literature. Further, the media are for the most part considered in isolation, rarely in relation to each other and hardly ever in a sociocultural or socioeconomic context. This is characteristic in particular of the Amruthavani approach. Where the analysis of the media is concerned, there are few principles that are enunciated to guide students and teachers. Most analyses stop at the content, instead of moving on to probe questions such as those related to authorship and production, or to the media as institutions and industries. In sum, the media-centered approach of the Indian projects (like many of the projects worldwide) leaves little time for the large social context in which students and teachers experience the media.

The pedagogy adopted in the media education projects is fairly open and loosely structured because of their nonformal setting. No course admits more than 30 students, thus making it possible to have group discussions and practical work in small teams. In the formal school setting, classes often have up to 60 students in small classrooms where only the talk-and-chalk or lecture system makes sense. This is the greatest advantage of teaching the media away from the formal school environment—it allows for an openness and a flexibility in curriculum and pedagogy. At the same time, without the support of the school system, media education projects tend to be ad hoc, taking place only occasionally, without any systematic organized study over time. In fact, they tend frequently to be one-shot affairs with little or not follow-up. In the Indian context, media education can become a serious subject of study only as part of formal education; otherwise, it will remain at the project or experimental level, and of little significance. However, it is highly unlikely that the state (which controls the media as well as the education system) will accede to the demand of a small band of teachers and parents lobbying for integrating media education into the formal curriculum.

On Communication
Technology

Communication, Technology, and Ecology

22

HERBERT I. SCHILLER

Though often referred to as such, the mass media do not constitute a universal, generic category. The mass media are not exclusively technological instrumentation, performing identical functions wherever they operate. The mass media are an integral part of the social system and cannot be isolated from that system. It follows that the media display different characteristics, depending on the historico-economic conditions in each national space where they are located. The media at work in the contemporary world, therefore, would include locales where they are privately owned and managed, as in the dominant world powers, the United States and Japan. There are also the dozen or so highly industrialized market economies that are autonomous in varying degree from the United States and Japan. These would include most of the countries in Western Europe and a few others elsewhere. Then there are the media, privately owned, or in some instances state supported, in countries that once were colonies, and that remain heavily dependent, economically and culturally. Finally, there are those societies that have been organized with state ownership of basic industries, media included. This group of countries is in the midst of radical change, and their media institutions also are being fundamentally restructured. There are other defining characteristics as well, which affect, directly or indirectly, media performance. Some would be: the historical experience and sophistication of a state's dominating stratum; the presence or absence of large oppositional parties that affect the political tone of the country and condition, to a degree, the structure and performance of the media. In industrialized market economies, the existence of strong social democratic parties would be such a factor. In this overall schema, the United States is in a class by itself. There are reasons for this. The entire post-World War II era has witnessed the global circulation and predominance of American media products and services. This dominance has not receded, though general American systemic power definitely has begun to wane.

Partly as a result of the forty-year-long saturation of the world with U.S. media, English has become the lingua franca of the international community. It now serves to deepen and perpetuate Anglo-American ideological influence. It occurs alongside the continuing growth and expansion of American media companies and Anglo-American advertising agencies. In certain fields, television news for example, a significant part of the world's information diet is supplied by Anglo-U.S. agencies and services. Working with this global topography of cultural production, and the exceedingly prominent role exercised by U.S. mass media and related informational services, brings into serious question some of the ideas that currently are fashionable. For example, what is now standard terminology in describing the world scene—interdependency—may not represent an accurate condition. If the views, values, and cultural outputs of the (relatively) few enjoy preponderant influence over those of the many, is it not also likely that what is of concern to, and serves the interest of, the few is imposed on the many? And if this is the case, are not the interests of the many likely to receive very short shrift in the opinion agendas that are constructed daily in the dominant world media? A case in point is the definition of *terrorism*. The massive amount of coverage terrorism receives in the Western mass media can only be understood in relation to the still very privileged position of American and Western power and the benefits that derive from its exercise in global affairs. Two American writers observe that "the discourse of terrorism has been specifically designed to maintain repression within countries or communities whose labor, resources and ideological alignment have sustained the wealth and privilege of the 'Free World.' In other words, we see the discourse emanating from the advanced capitalist countries (led by the United States), that use as their object the Third World" (Goldson & Bratton, 1988, p. 148).

Terrorism, however, is only one of a great many concepts shaped by the dominant definition makers. It is actually a subset of a more inclusive category which can be labeled *crisis*. Undeniably, there are crises in the world, many crises. There are also some places arbitrarily designated as *trouble spots*, another nicely created construct suggesting that some locations carry a trouble virus.

The crisis that most people become aware of, inevitably, is given its identity, and receives its priority status, from those defining interests located in and around the powerful Western media systems. Once a crisis has been identified by these interests, there usually is some space for other national and local interpretations of the crisis, depending on variables such as the proximity of the problem and the degree of autonomy of national media reporting the situation.

But whatever the variability in the different accounts, the essential contours of what is brought to audiences around most of the world are formed and shaped in a few highly concentrated informational-image-making centers. In these sites, the interests defining the parameters of the bulk of the reportage or narrative are those of the dominant groups and classes, the main beneficiaries of existing power relations.

When this condition is understood, the basis for discovering and spotlighting a crisis usually is quite predictable. If phenomena of the natural world—earthquakes, storms, floods, and so on—are excluded, crisis generally is found to exist in any development or substantial effort to change radically—or even threaten to change radically—some significant prerogative of the privileged groups.

This might be a big strike or large demonstrations by dissatisfied individuals. It could also be unexpected electoral victories by radical parties, or unified actions by poor and largely powerless states, for example, the Non-Aligned Movement's call for a new, international information order. It could be a coup by left-leaning rather than rightist military leaders, or any of innumerable lurking threats to the established order.

The passive, but no less important, part of the definitional control process is the routine disregard of the long-maturing social origins of seemingly sudden and unexpected crisis developments. The many structural misfortunes that afflict working people, for example—unemployment, sudden job loss, work-related injuries and illnesses from unsafe work conditions, general speed-up of work processes and consequent emotional and physical strain, the examples are endless—rarely receive even passing regard, much less sustained attention, in general media coverage.

These routine social disasters generally do not qualify as crises, at least not in the news judgments of the authorities making such decisions. So, for example, the precipitous decline in the living standards of most Mexican people in the 1980s is a story that, if it is mentioned at all in the Western media, receives at most a casual reference. Let the leaders of Mexico, however, so much as hint at repudiating the huge debt owed to the transnational bank corporations—the service charges that have been the cause of the collapse of the people's living standard—and there is the making of a full-blown crisis.

Crisis generates conflict or arises out of it. Conflict also is rich soil for media interpretation, though here the practice can be tricky and sometimes threatening to privileged interests. Yet conflict reporting is the meal ticket of profit-turning media corporations. The supply of events that may offer exciting imagery, violence if possible, and scenes of disorder and carnage, agitated or disconsolate people; these are the bread and butter of commercial television news and the raw material for TV drama. (To be sure, the print media have no less enthusiasm for the same kind of material.) Eye-catching visual material, TV action footage, photos, and hyper-charged text are proven audience catchers.

The reason for the media's eagerness to report conflict is well known. Commercial television and a good part of the print media derive the bulk of their revenues from advertising. Advertisers make their expenditures on what they trust are reliable statistics of audience size and composition; that is, income, age, gender, race, and so on. To achieve the size and type of audience most desired by the sponsors and their advertisers, the commercial media rely on the tried and tested formula of heavy doses of sex and violence. This is regarded as good business practice, at least for the media industry.

For those who benefit from this formula, however, there is one complication. Media programming that regularly broadcasts images and prints accounts of social breakdown and physical mayhem hardly contributes to social stabilization. And social stability, above all else, is what investors crave for their capital.

Even a limited representation of the conflicts that rend the social fabric—gender, race, class, and the destruction of the earth—can excited potentially unmanageable popular reactions. These can have unpredictable consequences for the prevailing institutions and those who manage them. This dilemma is never fully resolved.

In the late twentieth century, the commercial media have at their disposal an abundance of situations and conditions replete with violence, imminent disaster, and fierce conflict. The supply of this kind of material increases exponentially as the governing institutions in growing numbers of countries fail to satisfy the most elemental needs of huge numbers of people. Simultaneously, extravagant consumption is promoted wherever advertising penetrates across the globe.

The availability and ever-widening use of new, powerful information technologies, capable of transmitting electronic messages and images instantaneously and universally, magnifies for audiences everywhere existing instabilities and steadily more explosive conditions. There now exists a highly combustible combination of excitement-seeking commercial media and an advanced information technology to spread the word of deepening social and political problems, and, most inflammatory of all, of consumer artifacts that are widely beyond the reach of the majority of the world's population.

No one is more aware of this volatile environment than the state and corporate elites, expecially those in the most industrialized countries, who sit at the apex of the national social pyramids. In the United States, a couple of basic formulas are applied with considerable success, not for solving the central dilemma of media-publicized crisis, but for limiting the potential for such information for social enlightenment, awareness and resistance.

United States practices merit attention because American media products, including sports, advertising, public relations, theme parks, and tourism, not only continue to dominate world culture spaces and markets but are in the process of expanding their international influence still further. This is all the more remarkable because it occurs alongside a weakening American economic and financial base (Schiller, 1989). Two closely related techniques are widely used in U.S. media practice in the representation of conflict and crisis: personalization and ahistoricism.

In American media entertainment, especially in film and dramatic TV series, there is no lack of conflict. It is pervasive. Also, it is often abrasive, violent, and bloody. But it is almost always personalized. The conflict situations generally depict enraged, bitter, crazed, vengeful, or emotionally disturbed people. The source of their grievances, however, is mainly individualized circumstances abstracted from the social totality. Social class, gender, or race may be discernible as a background feature. It is rarely brought into focus as a determining factor.

And so, the world, the nation, and the local community appear as threatening places, filled with violence-prone and excitable human beings colliding in highly specific circumstances with frightening consequences. What is absent from this stream of media-represented conflict is the social origin of the individual behavior.

There is one exception to this customary pattern. It occurs when the Other is being depicted. Who or what is the Other? It is readily identifiable as different from us, not like us. For 70 years, and up until Gorbachev, the political Other for the West generally has been the Soviet Union. In certain periods, the Chinese communists, or Libyan or Iranian "terrorists," have been found to qualify.

When the Other is presented, personal motivation and behavior invariably are the outcomes of a malignant social system. But this connection is made only in the media's presentation of the Other. It is conveniently dropped as an explanation for domestic episodes of aggressive and antisocial behavior.

A second means by which social understanding is badly impaired—especially observable in the presentation of "news"—is the excision of history and the narrowing of context. Events are reported, for the most part, as free-standing episodes. There is a carousel of items; fresh ones are added, stale ones dropped. The flow never stops, and it is never depleted. There is always a supply on the shelf, as it were.

The events are unrelated, appear to be selected at random, and float into view without a past. There may be nothing objectionable about this style when the account concerns a "natural" occurrence: an earthquake, a flood, an erupting volcano. It is another matter when social situations receive the same treatment. A social occurrence by its very nature has to have a history, a pattern of development and unfolding, a maturation and an aftermath, that can be examined.

The prevailing practice of covering an event in a thirty-second, or at most, a two-minute bite, is a device that almost guarantees the deprivation of context. As one event follows the next, each devoid of context, the viewer can only struggle to make sense of the "news."

Yet social issues, political questions, and economic policy are the main constitutive elements in what gets reported as news. For this reportage to be minimally useful, context, historical or comparative, is essential. Without it, news is a meaningless construct and often a misleading exercise. Still commercial television thrives on discrete episodic events, especially if they are action oriented. Taken together with the commercial imperative to attract large numbers of viewers in order to maximize advertising revenues, the character of prevailing Western-style news reporting is understandable.

Not to be overlooked in this scenario is the never-absent ideological factor in media presentation, which may on occasion conflict with the strictly for-profit drive. In such an eventuality, the ideological factor usually is given primacy. Ideology does not have to be inserted into each segment of the programming. It is already deeply embedded in the selection process and training practices of media personnel. The professionals of the print and broadcast fields have full recognition of what is expected of them. If not, they learn rapidly if they expect to retain their jobs. There is little uncertainty about what is not acceptable to the management. This well-understood condition neatly obviates the need for direct censorship.

THE TIME AHEAD

Given the commercial, technological, and ideological imperatives of the television and print media, deeply structured into most Western institutional arrangements, is there any way, short of social catastrophe, to achieve measurable improvement? Or, to put it differently, can the present awesome control of information be brought under some form of public accountability? (Here it may be noted that the public accountability, limited as it was, in many Western European broadcasting systems is well on the way to abandonment, succumbing to fierce transnational corporate pressures.)

The task is daunting because the customary means by which an urgent problem can be ventilated by its publication in the mass media is unavailable. The media, in most instances, are fully committed to keeping the issue of their own authority off the public agenda and out of sight. James Halloran's valiant efforts to produce and make available basic research about the communication process often ran up against this institutional roadblock.

Of necessity, therefore, an agent external to the media is required to bring public attention to the subject. Where to look for it? Routinely, technology is offered as the solution to inadequate or deficient information. Such a prescription ignores the near-total absorption of new technologies by old institutional interests. But a new source has come on the scene. The environmental movement is gaining adherents everywhere. It is a very logical site for assuming the responsibility for critiquing the informational sector, although up to this point the movement has been largely disinterested.

As people become increasingly concerned with their deteriorating living space, one vital component of this menaced space has escaped serious attention. This is the cultural sphere, and its informational/entertainment component in particular.

Sooner or later, it will be recognized by environmental forces that one of the most insidious forms of pollution, no less and perhaps more destructive than physical waste and toxic chemicals, is commercial domination of the meida.

Let it be understood that this is not a matter of personal taste and preference, of outraged elite sentiments. The issue is not whether one likes the tone of this or that commercial or is disturbed by the interruption of programs. The underlying and basic point is the role of commercial television as the most powerful instrument for creating and channeling consumer demand to fulfill corporate marketing needs and objectives. The utilization of the informational apparatus for transnational (and national) corporate aims is the root issue.

All else follows from this increasingly globalized institutional pattern. It is this structured arrangement that enables giant private firms to create people's tastes and expectations and that allows them to be transformed into consumers before anything else. It is the corporate quest for markets that now shapes the contours of TV "news" and programming in general. Consequently, a way out of the deepening environmental impasse is unrealizeable unless the cultural-informational component of Western market economies is made the focus for corrective action.

It has to be expected that if recognition of this relationship does develop and remedial changes are proposed, the systemic response will be to accuse the challengers of seeking to infringe on freedom of expression. But freedom of expression and personal liberty are *human* rights and enjoyments. Corporations exercise these rights to an ever-increasing extent only because their enormous influence has enabled them to shape the legal system to their benefit and to the disadvantage of the bulk of the population.

Individual rights and freedom will be immeasurably extended, and the despoliation of nature lessened, if the freedom of big businesses to control international and national public opinion and cultural values is reduced.

In my view, this is the overriding priority in the time ahead.

REFERENCES

Goldson, A., & Bratton, C. (1988). Counterterror. In C. Schneider & B. Wallis (Eds.), *Global television*. New York: Wedge Press.

Schiller, H.I. (1989, August) Faut-il dire adieu á la soverainete culturelle? *Le Monde Diplomatique*, pp. 10–11.

CHAPTER

23

Communication Technology: Researchers and Practitioners in Confrontation

OLOF HULTÉN

What kind of research do practitioners want?

This was the question invited representatives of the media industries addressed at a plenary session of the 9th Nordic Conference on Mass Communication Research in the summer of 1989. Their talks, and the ensuing discussion, revealed a major gap between the research community and practitioners, a failure of communication between the two groups that is not simply explained.

What it all boils down to, though, is an apparently mutual lack of interest in one another's roles and circumstances. An essentially careless disregard, perhaps, but one that tends to take on an edge in plenary debates at gatherings of the clans like this one, where role expectations and peer allegiances naturally come to the fore. Whatever the motives, the Nordic researchers gathered in Borgholm received a tongue-lashing they will not soon forget. Sadly, the abuse the media spokesmen piled on their heads revealed a surprising degree of ignorance of what the research community has to offer.

The interchange at Borgholm reminded me of a confrontation that had taken place some 20 years earlier, at a conference hosted by James Halloran and the Centre for Mass Communication Research in Leicester in 1970 on the theme "Broadcaster/Researcher Cooperation in Mass Communication Research." Clearly, mass communication research has made great strides since 1970—although there is still a tendency to resort to in-group jargon that effectively restricts the currency of what we have learned. It was therefore especially sad to hear uninformed, seemingly uninterested, but highly placed media practitioners complain that researchers had nothing to offer them. One would think that 20 years of research and public debate of media issues, not to mention the collaboration between media and researchers that has developed in some sectors, would have brought the two groups closer.

Karl Erik Rosengren summarized the practitioners' part of the discussion in Borgholm, pointing out that they demand two things of the research community: "Help us, tell us what we should do. But don't go telling us we're not doing a good job!"

The questions they wanted answered were, for example: Should my newspaper invest in a new press for X million pounds, or not? How should I go about launching my new community tabloid? How can I develop the visual language in my programs to win over viewers from competing stations? These are all interesting questions of obvious importance to the practitioner. But to demand that scientific research provide unequivocal answers to them—"It's rubbish if it can't!"—is unreasonable. If researchers had all the answers, they would be making the decisions themselves!

The second demand in Rosengren's rendition is, of course, irrelevant. It can hardly be the duty of scientifically trained students of the media to humor media professionals.

It lies near to hand for me to discuss this confrontation between media research and the media in relation to communication technologies and technological innovation in the media. For nearly 20 years now I have been working with new technologies—some of which, obviously, are no longer new—both as a researcher and above all as a consumer of others' research. Secondly, the contradiction in roles is so very salient in this economically and politically volatile area.

A little less than a decade ago I addressed the same subject before the 5th Nordic Conference in Reykjavik. The theme there was "Can Research Influence the Media?" to which I posed the counterquestion: "Why Should It?" Why should we expect research, of all things, to have an influence on the media? As I saw things then, and still do, research can of course influence the media, but does so to only a limited extent. Without having thoroughly studied the record, I would say that media research findings have decisively informed few decisions in the realm of media policy these past couple of decades—in the Nordic countries, at least.

The volume of mass communication research has mushroomed during the past decade, particularly if we include policy research commissioned of academically trained researchers by private enterprise, public authorities, or political bodies. Not all academic researchers are prepared to accord policy research full value as scientific inquiry, however. In his introductory chapter to *Broadcaster/Researcher Cooperation in Mass Communication Research* (Halloran & Gurevitch, 1971) published after the Leicester conference, James Halloran effectively rebuts the concept of utility as a fault: "There is no reason why a piece of research which aims to facilitate a better understanding of the workings of the media should be scholastically trivial, or why a well constructed intellectual tool should inevitably have a blunt practical cutting edge" (pp. 14ff). I find this attitude far more constructive—for all parties concerned.

But mass communication research has other, more important *raisons d'être* than bread-and-butter utility. It is valuable in its own right, in the realm of communications as well as in the academic fields of social science and the humanities. Research generates knowledge and presents conceptions of reality that make up our collective memory and nourish our sense of identity. The vigor with which research fulfills these functions is particularly important in an area such as media technology, so often touted as crucial to the further development of our societies: the dawning of the Information Society! Without a firm grasp of the what, how, and why of the present, it will be impossible to influence our future course, or even to formulate viable alternatives. The democratic process cannot do without a vigorous, independent research community. Research is needed to assess and critique prevailing conditions, and, where needed, to propose remedies. Democratic principles assign the privilege of making policy to popularly elected politicians; were scientists to decide, it would be technocracy. Scientifically founded critique and political judgements are mutually interdependent; they are in fact so intimately intertwined that neither is actually pursued to the full. A true will to reform means publicly admitting the need for critical, disinterested analysis. Even this is more than many policy makers are able to do. Critical, disinterested analysis, on the other hand, presumes that information can be gathered and knowledge generated without political or other constraints. Halloran put the case for the independence of the social sciences most eloquently, I think, in his keynote address to the abovementioned Leicester conference;

> We are interested in broadcasting institutions and in communication processes. Broadcasting institutions which are involved in these processes have policies, and within the institution decisions are

made at several levels with regard to both the formulation and execution of these policies. These decisions and policies are based on a variety of assumptions—and these include assumptions, not all of them articulated, about the process of communications, the composition of the audience, the nature and type of impact and effect, the availability of resources, the possibility of alternative policies or sources of action, the structure of the organization, professional ethics, and so on....All these questions are important, but it is particularly important for the researcher to look at the question of alternatives, especially where the broadcasting institution has a long established tradition. One of the main tasks of the social scientist is to try to expand the range of choice by drawing attention to alternative policies, methods and solutions. (Halloran & Gurevitch, 1971, p. 21)

Informing opinion and supporting democratic decision making are thus central functions research performs. In effect, they increase our accumulated knowledge concerning possible, desired, and lamented choices and decisions. That practitioners may find such perspectives irrelevant and meddlesome at best, and threatening at worst, is not surprising. Decision makers who are charged to administer enormous sums of money and other resources profitably naturally feel a need to reduce their uncertainty. In some cases their uncertainty may be due to lack of knowledge, and in such cases research offers a remedy. But new knowledge can also challenge old assumptions and thereby *produce* uncertainty. Decision makers—entrprises, bureaucrats, and controlling authorities— seek to reduce uncertainty their own way: they establish certainties of their own. They systematize and categorize; make rules; impose standards, norms, and guidelines; and gradually create a separate, predictable, and controllable universe—a surrogate reality, in which most uncertainity has been reduced to sets of options.

In his fascinating book, *The Control Revolution: Technological and Economic Origins of the Information Society,* James Beniger (1986) shows, starting with examples from the infancy of the industrial era and carrying through to the present day, how the struggle *against uncertainty* and *for control* has been waged. It is in this struggle, he asserts, that we find the dynamic forces that have led us to the Information Society. These forces are not the products of computers and innovations in electronics—it is the other way around. Mass communication and marketing in a broad sense, with the technology and practices that go along with them, have become increasingly important strategic factors in the struggle.

As citizens we are all anxious to form some idea of what is to come; as scientists and scholars it is our mission to try to make the future visible, while pointing out options and alternative courses along the way. Science should seek to maximize the freedom of choice available to us. Those in charge of new technology, who make their livings on the front lines of innovation, so to speak, are equally anxious to form images of the future, but they also feel a need to *reduce* the degrees of freedom in favor of their own preferred course of development.

The best vision of the future is that which clarifies the present, imbues it with meaning. The future creates order in the present. The risks at stake, and the scale on which modern technology and our economies operate, are of such magnitude that visions of the future, and the order they impose on the present, assume national strategic importance.

The manner in which the concept of the Information Society entered into European social and political thought is illustrative. One of the most well-known concrete examples is Simon Nora and Alain Minc's (1978) *L'Informatisation de la société*, the cabinet-level report that gave us the concept of *télématique*. Commissioned by President Valery Giscard d'Estaing, Nora and Minc projected the future of France in the light of modern information technologies that were seen to revolutionize not only economic life and technology, but social relations and societal processes, as well.

Nora and Minc's treatise reads much like the Psalms of David. The very first sentence in the book sets the tone: "If France does not respond effectively to the serious new challenges she faces, her internal tensions will deprive her of the ability to control her fate."

Here, Nora and Minc are referring to a more general malaise that French society has suffered in recent decades. But the authors leave no doubt that technology, and telematics in particular, is the key to the future of the nation: Each technological revolution has brought about far-reaching economic and social reorganization. A technological revolution may simultaneously create a crisis and the means to overcome it, as was the case with the coming of the steam engine, the railroads, and electricity.

The "computer revolution" will have wider consequences. The computer is not the only technological innovation of recent years, but it does constitute the common factor that speeds the development of all the others. Above all, insofar as it is responsible for an upheaval in the processing and storage of data, it will alter the entire nervous system of social organization. (Nora & Minc, 1978, p. 4)

As computers become more and more widely accessible, they will become "as indispensable to society as electricity." Seen to open "entirely new horizons," telematics (that is the interlinking of computers and telecommunication) also carries an implicit threat: "Unlike electricity, 'telematics' will not transmit an inert current, but will convey information, i.e. power" (Nora & Minc, 1978, p. 5). And throughout the book, the authors oscillate, like David, between perceived threats—personified in *le défi de l'IBM*—and affirmations of faith—faith that "telematization" will save France by solving the three main threats to its future by increasing productivity, stimulating internal demand, and (thereby) reducing poverty. "Plan Cable," one of the fruits of this dualistic, strategic thinking, envisaged the establishment of a fiber-optical broad-band network throughout France to accommodate sophisticated information services to both households and commercial subscribers. The plan is more than an expression of French electronic firms' desire to sell media-technological gadgetry. Plan Cable also reflects the anxiety of a national, a major power, in the face of uncertainty about the future, anxiety that the traditional authority of the state might be undermined or supplanted.

Popular demand for cable services was not as had been anticipated. This, together with high costs, had caused Plan Cable to be shelved, for the time being at any rate. Other countries, too, have conceived more or less ambitious plans of this kind, especially in the fields of aeronautics and telecommunications. Most such projects originate in anxiety concerning the competitive strength of domestic high tech industry. This industrial political concern is then translated into projects, some of which have had ostensibly inadvertent but nonetheless far-reaching effects on national cultural policy and the media sector.

The Swedish parliament authorized cabling because everyone was convinced that otherwise Sweden would be left standing alongside the tracks as the locomotive of informatics technology sped past. A broad consensus prevailed around the idea that Sweden should go in for hi-tech industrial production; a modern national telecommunications infrastructure was seen to be a vital prerequisite to the nation's entry into the Information Society. Further, Parliament ruled that the cable network should be established on a commercial basis; unlike Swedish policy vis-a-vis other areas of the communications and media sectors, regulation was to be kept to a minimum (Hultén, 1986).

This is not the place to catalogue the innovations in media and information technology that have aroused our curiosity and influenced political agendas in Europe these past couple of decades. We are all familiar with the stirs created by video, satellites, cable networks, computers, PC networks such as Minitel, and, at this writing, the prospect of HDTV. Common to all these phenomena is a powerful thrust toward internationalization and integration of technologies, services, actors on the market, and legislation. These trends are, yes, the products of technological advances, but they are also in great part the result of political, administrative, and economic policy decisions. Technology is not an autonomous force; its "imperative" derives from judgments in the socioeconomic system that surrounds it.

The interplay of technique (machines, equipment, tools) and technology (the surrounding cultural and organizational framework) is, in my estimation, a crucially important focus of research. Arnold Pacy, whose definitions these are, discusses the great variety of human experience—technical, organizational and cultural—encompassed by what he calls *technology-practice:* "Many different clusters of values are associated with this range of experiences, not all of them compatible. Thus individuals feel conflict, and society as a whole is periodically divided by controversy about issues relating to technology" (Pacey, 1983, p. 122).

Why, one may well ask, did Europe opt to acquire satellite capacity of its own? Under what premises was this capacity then made available for the privatization and internationalization of traditional European television? May cabling be said unequivocally to have strengthened the national information and cultural systems of European countries? What are the social implications of technical innovations like these and the institutional changes they give rise to? I find it easy to join Halloran in asking: Information is the answer, but what is the question?

It surprises me that the Nordic (which I know best) and the European research communities have not thrown themselves into developments in the field of communications technology with greater curiosity and perseverance. Obviously, the field is immensely complex and volatile, and keeping abreast of it, surveying and analyzing it, is demanding of resources. But, while industrial and media interests as well as national and international policy makers are fusing and integrating, researchers still find it difficult to transcend the bounds of their respective nations and institutions.

All too much of the research being done is fractionalized—divided among isolated individuals, carved up between academic specialities, and atomized on the temporal plane by the short-sightedness of its motives. The lack of perseverance in academic inquiry in this field is a severe handicap, as the record in my own Nordic region, for example, shows. When satellite and cable came on the scene in the 1970s and early 1980s, with preliminary fact finding followed by massive investment programs on the part of private enterprise and public agencies, numerous research projects and project groups were initiated, some of them even on an interdisciplinary basis. As we enter a new decade and projects lists are updated, we find that most such projects have disappeared, evaporated.

Obviously, individual researchers may have had perfectly legitimate reasons to move on to other subjects, but judged collectively, from the point of view of media research per se, it is a sad state of affairs. It means lapses in our collective memory.

Our failure to follow up and evaluate innovations in a systematic fashion means that our memory tends to contain only the bright prospects the policies and innovations were seen to promise. This prevents our learning from past mistakes, and registering the unintended effects policies may have had.

Knowledge is made up of the information stored in our memory. If knowledge is power, we are powerless to the extent that our memory fails us.

Part of the reason why research interest in the field was so keen a decade ago has to do with policy makers' and investors' desire to reduce their uncertainty. This anxiety meant a generous climate for research funding. As projects were implemented, some researchers were recruited to industry and attendant regulatory agencies. When the projects were completed and summary reports written, funding dried up and researchers were obliged to seek out other patrons. In most cases, this entailed a shift of focus.

Developments in the field of satellites and cable have exerted a palpable influence on a second set of issues that are crying for scientific analysis on a broad front—the politico-ideological and economic foundations of traditional European public service broadcasting. What is happening to such revered ideals as pluralism, competition, and dedication to quality? Before Europe had experienced satellite and cable distribution, and before television and radio began to be commercialized in the mid-1970s, these concepts were considered so self-evident that few people paid them any attention. Today, public service broadcasters are in the throes of an identity crisis, and policy makers are asking what *public service* is all about and wondering how they can harness market forces to achieve quality, pluralism, and productive competition.

Unfortunately, I don't think European media research as it stands today is mature enough—well enough developed, if you will—to be able to contribute as much as it might to these policy discussions. There *is* no particular reason why media researchers should be better equipped than, say, journalists, politicians, or cultural commentators to answer these questions, but no one can doubt the benefit had the research community been able to offer input in the form of empirically founded definitions and economic theories developed especially for the media and communications technology sectors.

Public policy vis-à-vis media research, furthermore, is complicated by its political sensitivity. For reasons relating to freedom of expression and intellectual freedom as such, the powers of state do not wish to—or, at any rate, do not wish *to be seen* to—steer media research. Governments are therefore chary of financing such inquiry and refer instead to private interests. Industry, on the other hand, has little in the way of altruistic motives for supporting independent, stringent, and possibly critical research. Consequently, too little such research is done.

The prevailing attitude among media practitioners and industrial interests is pragmatic: "If society needs research, then let society pay for it." James Halloran, writing in 1970, saw a graver dimension to the problem, however: "The question who should pay for research, important though it is, is not the main point. Let us first have it accepted that the research must be done" (Halloran, 1970, p. 177). As I see it, today there is no doubt that the research must be done, nor do I personally have any doubts as to who should bear the lion's share of what it costs. It is the responsibility of government to ensure that qualified research can be conducted on a continuous basis. How government may choose to finance such research is another question.

Unfortunately, the outlook in Europe today is not particularly bright. Most European universities are in such dire economic straits that they find it difficult to maintain past levels of activity, let alone start new and costly research programs. Any and all expansion requires extraordinary powers of persuasion and an indomitable will. The Centre for Mass Communication Research at Leicester is, to my mind, one of all too few European academic institutions with the necessary perseverance and perspective.

Lacking permanent institutions and research groups that span more than the personal experience of individual scholars, no long-term solution presents itself. Depending on national traditions, efforts to bolster research in the area may come on the initiative of central authorities or on that of universities given the freedom to set their own priorities.

Having the freedom—the duty!—to question prevailing views and conceptions of reality without, what is more, having to suffer the consequences of one's critique, is an enviable position, indeed. But it is also one that exacts obligations, makes demands of both the maturity of individual researchers and of how research is organized. Systematic investigation on broad fronts needs to replace the discrete and random inquiries of today. We need to fill out our knowledge of telecommunications history and mount interdisciplinary studies of media and information, fields that themselves span so many and various aspects of human activity. Only by gaining a better understanding of media technologies and their ramifications can we improve our methods and refine our theories.

REFERENCES

Beniger, J.C. (1986). *The control revolution: Technological and economic origins of the information society.* Cambridge, MA: Harvard University Press.

Halloran, J.D., & Gurevitch, M. (Eds.). (1971). *Broadcaster/researcher cooperation in mass communication research.* Leicester, UK: University of Leicester.

Hulten, O. (1986). Current Developments in the Electronic Media in Sweden. In Carlsson, L.I. (Ed.) *Media in transition.* Göteborg: NORDICOM.

Nora, S., & Minc, A. (1978). *The computerization of society.* MIT Press.

Pacey, A. (1983). *The cuture of technology.* Cambridge, MA: MIT Press.

PART

VIII

On International Issues

International Communication Research in the 21st Century: From Functionalism to Postmodernism and Beyond

HAMID MOWLANA

As we enter the last decade of the twentieth century, there seems to be growing interest in two fundamental areas of communication arts and sciences: a resurgence in the study of the philosophy of communication as evidenced by the number of publications and conference panels in this area; and a keen interest in new epistemological schools of thought and research methodologies beyond the "Ferment in the Field" (Miller, 1983) in which positive empiricism and critical theory were the only positions debated among the students of communication studies. Whereas the philosophy of communication is replacing transcendental philosophy as the prime concern of philosophical reflection, there is also a new interest in exploring new conduits of inquiries and fresh approaches to methodologies (Rajchman, 1985; Hayles, 1983, Foucault, 1979; Hassam, 1987; Wilbur, 1983; Jantsch, 1980; Grossberg, 1982; Mowlana & Kotz, 1988).

INTERNATIONAL COMMUNICATION AS A FIELD OF STUDY AND RESEARCH

Elsewhere, I have defined *international communication* as a field of inquiry and research that consists of the transfer of values, attitudes, opinion, and information through individuals, groups, governments, and technologies, as well as the study of the structure of institutions responsible for promoting or inhibiting such messages among and between nations and cultures. It is a field of study and research that entails an analysis of the channels and institutions of communication. More importantly, it involves examination of the mutually shared meanings that make communication possible (Mowlana, 1986, p. 216).

In an attempt to discern the substance of international communication as a field of inquiry, many controversial theoretical questions are raised. Both explicitly and implicitly, the new literature portrays the quest for a substantial and more elaborated theory, one that will take into account the "high stakes" enterprise of communication in an era of technological and industrial change. Communication research, like any scientific study, depends essentially on the quality of theory or conceptualization to give it direction and focus. Specifying the conditions under which predictions can be hypothesized is the function of a well-integrated theory of communication research. The basis for achieving this is still an unresolved issue of debate among communication researchers.

This question is not merely a scholarly controversy, but also a highly politicized debate that is fundamentally based on the notion of power and its implications for communication. The fact that communication research does not function in a political vacuum makes the concept of power a very relevant issue indeed. Hence, many of the scholarly debates in the social sciences are, in fact, political controversies, poorly disguised.

The role of theory and the areas of research priority need to be clarified. To know the important questions, they way they should be approached, and the scholar's role in society are issues of crucial importance. The crux of the matter is whether theory should emanate out of reality to explicate it, or whether it should construct another vision of reality. In short, should it perpetuate, modify, or eradicate the existing order? Assuming that a universal paradigm of communication behavior is attainable, the political biases hinder the prospect of achieving this hypothetical endeavor. Perhaps the reason is that much of what passes for metatheoretical debate in actuality fixates on pseudo problems instead of illuminating substantive issues. In other words, the current disputes within the realm of communication research are often fueled by ideological preferences and not by substantive intellectual issues.

TRANSITION TO A NEW PARADIGM

In general, there seem to be four kinds of communication models underpinning the research carried out during the last four decades: (a) mathematical, (b) social psychological, (c) linguistic, and (d) politico-economic and culturally analytical. The mathematical models of information and communication seem to be a growing field, and the low-level mathematical theories have come from empirical and theoretical research done on information flow, military strategy, and even politics and nationalism. The social psychological tradition has had tremendous influence on politics and mass media research, with the linguistic tradition leading to such areas as symbol analysis. Political economy and cultural analysis have often been alternative and challenging perspectives to the first three.

Can communication research attain the knowledge needed through which to understand and to change social reality? This is the persistent and troublesome question for international communication research in the 21st century. This question presumes the necessity and feasibility of social change: the evolutionary or revolutionary—relative to historical circumstances—transition from a present society to a projected society. Yet the prevalent theoretical monomania and methodology exclusivity of communication research cannot meet the challenge of designing concrete images of situations that can be made into reality. Comprehending the reasons for the failure to meet this "normative" challenge is a very bewildering task. It has been said that work by communication researchers, particularly within the domain of mass communication, demonstrates a heightened concern for the practical implications and social relevance of communication issues. Although the tightly controlled laboratory study that dominated early research efforts is still much employed, a heartening move toward naturalistic studies and more reliance on field experimentation has considerably evolved. Diversity in research strategies is the order of the day, and the restless urge for social relevance has served as one powerful stimulus for such diversity (Miller, 1983, pp. 31–42).

A new outlook for the effects of media has emerged when the notion of the "unlimited capacity" of media to directly affect behavior in itself proved invalid. It has been argued that media have come to be viewed not as an active agent of change in isolation, but as having influence through a complex set of cultural, economic, and sociopolitical factors (White, 1983, pp. 31–42). Thus, there is a need for a radical departure from the premises of the old perspective about the role and effect of media. A review of the work of key theorists concerned with the relation of media and culture suggests that a more elaborate theory for the interaction of change in social structure, change in communication patterns, and change in culture is needed in communication research. Implied in this assertion is a new research perspective in which the focus is shifted from communication as social control to communication as integral to sociocultural change. Therefore, a different set of disciplinary methodologies must be formulated to operationalize this type of research.

The old framework was challenged on the basis of its preoccupation with effects of mass media messages on audiences perceived as potential consumers. This type of research displaced the focus of inquiry away from the media (the object) to the audience (the subject). In addition, the methodology adopted revealed its pro-status-quo bias in that it never considered the alternative of creating a new system but rather presented a functional adjustment of the old. A transition towards a new paradigm is evident, but there is no general unanimity on the direction of the paradigmatic shift.

The new rhetoric for a more comprehensive theory was stipulated by the realization of the ever-increasing importance of research in the high-stakes enterprise of communication for an era of "information production." The significance of studying communications is becoming a self-evident fact, more obvious every day. The long-term, deep structural forces and the dynamics of the power relations are making communication the central process in global, national, and local social organizations. The most powerful national and transnational decision-making groups are employing compelling new information technologies to consolidate and extend their positions. The maintenance of power systems nationally and transnationally is in the balance. Thus, communication study is largely the outcome of global and national forces that have propelled the communication process and information to the center of domestic as well as international attention and concern (Schiller, 1983, p. 256).

The emerging crisis within the philosophy of science, and the growing political cynicism among the general public, have given rise to a widespread questioning of the prevalent modes behind the established legitimacy of both knowledge and power. This questioning, within communication studies, has generated an interest in the critical social theory initially advocated by Max Horkheimer, Friedrick Pollock, Theodor Adorno, and their associates at the Institut Fuer Sozial Forschung (The Frankfurt School) in the 1930s. The critical approach to communication research has subsequently been articulated and enriched by Herbert Marcuse and Jurgen Habermas in their respective endeavors to secure a basis for emancipating communication in industrial societies (Slack, 1983).

The preoccupation of researchers with the power structure came as a result of this realization. Hence, there is no safe harbor in which researchers can avoid the established power relations, even if they declare their neutrality. Neutrality itself is not apolitical because of the unavoidable alignment of the research process with economic and political factors.

The central characteristic of this historical era makes international communication a significant field of inquiry. Five major factors contribute to this phenomenon. First, the transformation of the world political scene from a handful of commanding states to the threshold of a potentially genuine international community promotes the vitality of international communication as an area of study. Second, the reactions of 160 or more nations to their preindependence and postliberation communication experiences have crystallized the particular importance of this field. The once seemingly silenced periphery is now a multitude of independent actors voicing their own interests and reflecting their own creativeness. The other side of the coin is the importance of international communication to the system maintenance of the superpowers, a third critical element. The fourth contributing factor to the prevalent significance of international communication is the gigantic expansion of the transnational corporations. Indeed, the most revolutionary dimension of these corporations is not their size, but their worldview. Fifth, and finally, the concept of the sovereign nation-state as a force to control the economic life of the citizens has been eroded, and the role of international communication has become central to this process.

CHALLENGE TO THEORETICAL ORTHODOXY

Communication research has been based upon the conceptual and methodological orientations established by researchers in the West and particularly in the United States. This fact has led to the inappropriate application of culture-bound research methods to survey studies in less developed countries. That communication studies have subscribed indiscriminately and markedly to theoretical models mostly imported from the United States is not the main issue. The crucial matter is that the "made-in-the-U.S.A." type of communication research suffers from insensitivity to contextual and social-structure factors in different societies. Thus, the style of communication research appropriate for U.S. conditions has proved to be quite inappropriate in other socioeconomic and political contexts. The failure of the so-called "development-oriented communication campaigns" has become self-evident when applied to the Third World countries.

Review of the communication literature reveals that the most serious theoretical problem stems from the premise that communication plays an independent role in affecting social changes and behavior. Consequently, two preoccupations have become paramount since the early days of Harold Lasswell and Robert Merton: one preoccupation was with the effects of mass media on the individual's behavior, and the other with the function of these media in society. Stated differently, researchers examined what media do to people and how messages can use people, rather than studying ways in which people use or can use messages. The joint and systemic comprehension of channel-message capabilities and audience-response mechanics was to produce a behavior-controlling rhetoric serving the interest of the communicator. Accordingly, research methods appropriate to these main conceptual requirements were devised whereby content analysis and the sample survey through structured interviews came to form the basic methodological arsenal of most communicologists (Beltran, 1976). This method restricted the researcher's attention to the receiver's possible reactions to specific manifest contents of communications, while keeping covert the motivations and intentions of the communicator. Emphasis has been placed on the development of increasingly formal theory and methodology in the hope that a body of scientific rules will provide the key to conduct future research. Unfortunately, this process has resulted in models that are hardly recognizable as representations of behavior in the real world. Furthermore, if ideally there is no bias inherent in the scientific method, such a bias exists in practice, for results clearly find their way into ideological, economic, and political practice. The abstract analytical categories of idealist thought have become substantive descriptions and have taken habitual priority over the whole social process to which, as analytical categories, they were attempting to speak.

The belief in one-way mechanistic causation rather than mutual causation is the underlying epistemological error that characterizes the linear models. The basic problems with the linear models emanate from the epistemological assumptions about the nature of human beings and the nature of information, how we seek it, and what kind of quality it is. Information is treated as if it were purely a physical entity that could be moved around like billiard balls on a table (Kincaid, 1979, p. 4). Hence, mainstream communication researchers perceive the concept of causality in simple linear terms, in which the sender, message, and receiver are isolated as terms in an unmediated simple causal chain. Often what have been proposed as alternatives to the hypodermic model have been merely elaborations.

In the final analysis, all empirical results are conditioned by a theoretical base, even when that base remains unexposed. It has been asserted that the epistemological differences besetting the world of communications scholars lie in the notion of science as emancipation or as domestication, that underlying this dichotomy is the ontological definition of reality, either as including yet to be realized potentialities or as confined to factual manifestations (Hamelink, 1983).

The definition of reality as potentiality is fundamental to the choice of science as a tool of emancipation. Therefore, science on the one hand can be a tool for the liberation of people from those forces that keep them from being free to think about what they want to do. On the other hand, science can be a tool for the overt or subtle domestication of people into a dependency upon those forces that prescribe social reality as an objective part to which they must adapt.

The ever-increasing production of communication technologies stipulates a new wave of exciting research on communications. Communication research will most likely be directed toward new questions made salient by drastic changes in the communications situations. New technologies raise different questions than do the mass media. An information retrieval system is not the sole format for the coming age, yet it is the prototype of what is becoming increasingly important. The chief characteristic of the new electronic media is that they provide diverse material on demand to individuals (Pool, 1983). They also allow for fragmentation of the mass audience and even for quite individualized communication. In this case, the relevant research question will focus on the way the new media are institutionalized and modified to meet what society demands rather than what the electronic media are technically capable of delivering.

In an effort to critically assess the contributions and limitations of critical theory, one can ask whether the emancipatory project of critical theorists have offered any practical plan for resistance or a program for translating criticism into action. Thus, much critical analysis tends simply to assume that existing institutional structures are the problem and must be changed. Unfortunately it usually does not provide a clear idea of how these structures

behavioralism and empiricism that dominated the social sciences. In Europe there was evidence of other social movements in the 1968 student rebellion in France and the liberalization movement in Prague. In the non-West, which was ignored by the West, there was evidence of the roots of the Islamic movement in Iran and elsewhere professing a different epistemological view.

In developing a history of the development of communication discourse, the omissions in the field of inquiry and research can be of great import. The lack of inclusion of other perspectives, except those of positivism and critical theories, into the literature of communication of the early post-World War II period falls in this category. It was only in the late 1970s and the 1980s that students of communication and of the other social sciences slowly became interested in the study of contemporary social phenomena, employing different typology and world views beyond that of empirical positivism and critical perspectives.

Attempts were being made to develop a different approach to communication in which linearity is replaced by circularity, causality by catalysis, syntax for semantic-pragmatics, the rationality of Western norms for the arationality of desiring production, hierarchical relations for heterarchical relations, and the centered subject for the decentered web of relations and difference.

For example, one perspective outlined viewed communication on the principle of connection, heterogeneity, and multiplicity. There are no discrete boxes of sender, receiver, media, and message, no homogeneous set of ready-made signifying messages as in information theory, no subjective linear choices that may prevent the entry of heterogeneous substances of expression into the process. As noted by Deleuze and Guattari (1987, p. 23), "There is no longer a tripartite division between a field of reality (the world) and a field of representation (the book) and a field of subjectivity."

In the linear sender—receiver model of communication, and in the tradition of Western social, cultural, and political discourse, the component of the media took a royal if not a despotic position. With the rise of mass media theory and urban sociology, coupled with the tremendous attention paid to industrial and technological growth, communication research in both empirical/administrative and critical/dialectic circles was transformed into the royal position of media status. This media-centered research, ranging from the studies of popular culture (cultural identity in terms of the Frankfurt School) to audience analysis and totalitarianism, culminated in the work of Marshall McLuhan—"the medium is the message."

If the deterministic image of society that the triple-M (mass society, mass media, mass culture) theorists portray is drawn from the laissez-faire doctrine of economics (if not totally from the Protestant view of society), the political economy theorists and the critical theorists draw most of their ideas from the Marxist view of production.

By and large the triple-M theory of the media and culture is a theory of social control from above, even though it is premised on the necessity for making concessions to mass tastes in order that the masses be controlled most effectively. The political economy theorists view the process from below where, through an elaborate feedback of political and economic machinery, the masses can participate in the production and distribution of cultural messages. Both theories of social communication, however, tend to be media-centered, linear, and structural.

The process of deconstruction or restructuring begins when the black box of the media is removed from the communication model and discourse, all the while recognizing media's traces everywhere and in every point in the process. *This is communication without media.* We are watching television as much as it watches us. Instead of focusing our attention on a single element, we pay attention to an assemblage in its multiplicities.

Here we can think of communication not as a tree with roots and branches, but as rhizome, a network, where any point can be connected to any other with roots everyplace. As Deleuze and Guattari (1987, p. 7) point out: "A rhizome ceaselessly establishes connections between semiotic chains. Organization of power, and circumstances relative to the arts, sciences, and social struggle. ...There is no ideal speaker-listener, any more than there is a homogeneous linguistic community."

RESEARCH QUESTIONS FOR THE 21ST CENTURY

The international communication critiques of the last decade or so, noble and persuasive as they were in their presentation, did not go beyond political and economic debates. Whose version of the New World Information and Communication Order are we supposed to construct? Should there be a new *single* world structure based on a nation-state system as we have now? Or would that constitute too many orders in the field of free play? Can we equate universal agreement with universal good? Whose ideal of international peace and world community are we talking about? In the tree-shaped and linear model of communication, we have examined ground, roots, and branches, and we have analyzed the gatekeepers through channels; but have we located the gate makers and gate producers whose roots cannot be detected from our model? Will the progressive replacement of mechanical and energy-based mode by yet more powerful linear models, inspired by current information/communication paradigms, serve to transform rational self-perception and to give individuals a new image of themselves? Would a new rationalism created as a result of the modern technologies be likely to impose a policy of radical instrumentalism, under which social problems would be treated as technical problems? These questions and the many others that inevitably will follow are pressing international communication research into new, uncharted territories in the 21st century. And this will be for the better.

As we approach the 21st century, I believe that the most wide-ranging questions regarding communication research will be seen at the international level. The increasing internationalization of domestic policies and its domestication of international politics should provide new challenges for international communication scholars. Here are examples of the main problem areas and themes as well as a few research questions raised by the new communication technologies and new development in international and intercultural communication:

1. In what ways are relationships between modern nation-states likely to be affected during emerging communication technologies and their political, economic, and cultural impacts? At the center of this question are the economic and strategic aspects of international communication for the wealthy and powerful states as well as the inevitability of technological dependency for the so-called developing countries and the Third World. The fact that existing instructional and regulatory structures of international systems have proven incapable of dealing with all the technological and political questions make the international legal regime somewhat problematic at the present time. This also raises further questions as to whether past and present strategies of self-reliance and self-sufficiency handled by a few developing countries wil be applicable to new realities in the 21st century. The question remains: How possible will it be in the future for developing countries to maintain a capacity for independent technology assessment? To what degree will the declining power of the superpowers make them abandon the strategy of status quo and help lure some fundamental changes into

the structure of international communication as we know it?

2. To what extent do the new international communication technologies increase the erosion of cultural vitality and how will the modern nation-state systems, with their secular-oriented national sovereign signifier, cope with emerging religiopolitical ideologies such as Islam, which is based on universal community or *ummah*? This will require a thorough examination and understanding of communication systems of non-Western societies in both their traditional and modern forms as well as research into the world-reviews, theories, and assumptions underlying the modes of both interpersonal and social communication in most geographical areas of the world. Especially important is the question of whether our orthodox and traditional methods of research will be enlisted to reinforce obstacles to our understanding of intercultural communication, or if will we be able to improve and create methodologies that may assist us to expand our knowledge in understanding and respecting other forms of communication.

3. How much do we really know about the relationships between international communication and international peace and conflict resolutions? At the core of this question is the growing importance of modern communication technologies for the expansion and maintenance of the existing military-industrial complex of modern states, especially the great powers. At the same time, the last part of the 20th century has seen nationalism, anti-imperialism, and revolution in many parts of the world and diverse nations and cultures in quest for self-determination and a new world order, as militarily weak powers confront the major powers with increasing success. Will the new century bring about a new course of action for reconciliation and cooperation, or will it increase the amount of disinformation and deception through modern channels of communication, thus leading the world into a greater state of entropy?

4. What should (or would be) the role of mass media in helping to articulate and give identity to the various biological (age-group), psychological, and aesthetic groupings that have begun to emerge as a result of the decline of

traditional groupings and the increase of the so-called postmodern or hypermodern environments? Traditional communication research, especially in the field of mass media, emphasized the flow of information and content analysis, gate-keeper process, and audience investigation, but paid little attention to the sources generating information as well the ultimate utilizers who absorbed the information for a variety of decision-making purposes. Consequently, our knowledge about the role of communicators, political leaders, economic elites, religious and spiritual personalities, and new actors who have gained legitimacy remains sketchy. We also know so little about how information is handled by those who are exposed to it. Communication research in the 21st century must go beyond the simple production and distribution states and direct its attention to both the initial sources of the message as well as to its absorption and utilization. To do this, international communication research needs to go beyond the existing political, economic, and sociological models to incorporate anthropological, linguistic, and sociocultural frameworks into its well-established domain.

5. What is the evolution of linguistic form and specialized languages under the impact of modern international communication technologies and the development of science and arts? The relationship between language and international communication, though very obvious to any student in the field, has been very much neglected in both textbooks and research journals. The relationships between world languages and international flow of goods and services as well as cultural industries will, in my estimation, be of even greater importance in the future as we move toward adopting a single language as a means of technical and instrumental transfer of know-how and at the same time are faced with the ever-growing interests in national languages and educational policies.

6. What about the role of communication research in understanding the dynamics of modern world systems in terms of studying the transnational actors, international division of labor, immigrants, refugees, and individual economic, political, cultural, and military elites whose actions and reactions bypass the national boundaries and in themselves formally and informally constitute new leases of power, bargaining, and negotiations?

7. What role can communication research play in the ecological and environmental issues of the 21st century? What about the impact of communication technologies in such areas as disaster prevention, public health, hunger, and other international, regional, and national disaster issues?

8. And last but not least, will the information society of the 21st century also be primarily a material society, as was the case with the Industrial Revolution? Where are the spiritual and ethical and moral sources of the new area we are talking about? What will be the role of communication researchers in handling these critical questions?

REFERENCES

Baudrillard, J. (1980). The implosion of meaning in the media and the implosion of the social in the masses. In K. Woodward (Ed.), *The myths of information: Technology and postindustrial culture.* Madison, WI: Coda Press.

Beltran, L.R. (1976). Alien promises, objects, and methods in Latin American communication research. In E.M. Rogers (Ed.), *Communication and development: Critical perspective.* Beverly Hills, CA: Sage.

Deleuze, G., & Guattari, F. (1987). *A thousand plateaus: Capitalism and schizophrenia.* Minneapolis: University of Minnesota Press.

Foster, H. (1983) (Ed.). *The anti-aesthetic: Essays on postmodernism culture.* Port Townsend, WA: Bay Press.

Foucault, M. (1979). *Discipline & punish: The birth of the prison.* New York: Vintage Books.

Grossberg, L. (1982). Does communication theory need intersubjectivity? Toward an immanent philosophy of interpersonal relations. In M. Burgoon (Ed.), *Communication Yearbook, 6,* 171–205.

Habermas, J. (1983). Modernity—An incomplete project. In H. Foster (Ed.), *The anti-aesthetic. Essays on postmodern culture,* Port Townsend, WA: Bay Press.

Hamelink, C.J. (1983). Emancipation or domestication: Toward a utopian science of domestication. *Journal of Communication, 33,* 74–80.

Hassam, I. (1987). *The postmodern turn: Essays in postmodern theory and culture.* Columbus, OH: Ohio University Press.

Hayles, A.K.N. (1983). *The cosmic web: Scientific field models and literary strategies in the 20th century.* Ithaca, NY: Cornell University Press.

Jantsch, E. (1980). *The self-organization universe.* New York: Perryman Press.

Kincaid, L.D. (1979). *The convergence model of communication.* Honolulu, HI: East-West Communication Institute.

Lyotard, J.F. (1984). *The postmodern condition: A report on knowledge.* Minneapolis: University of Minnesota Press.

Miller, G.R. (1983). Taking stock of a discipline, *Journal of Communication.* Ferment in the Field (Special Issue), *33.*

Mowlana, H. (1986). *Global information and world communication: New frontiers in international communication.* White Plains, NY: Longman.

Mowlana, H., & Kotz, B. (1988). The implosion of communicative rationality: From the hegemonic battleground of political identity to the molecular force-field of becoming minor. In B. Dervin & J. Wosko (Eds.), *Beyond ferment.* Norwood, NJ: Ablex.

Nelson, C., & Grossberg, L. (1987). *Marxism and interpretation of culture.* Urbana, IL: University of Illinois Press.

Pool, I. de Sola (1983). What ferment. *Journal of Communication, 33,* 260–261.

Rajchman, J. (1985), *Michel Foucault: The freedom of philosophy.* New York: Columbia University Press.

Schiller, H.I. (1983). Critical research in the information age. *Journal of Communication, 33,* 249–257.

Slack, J.D. (1983). The political and epistemological constituents of critical communication research. *Journal of Communications, 33,* 208–219.

White, R.A. (1983). Mass communication and culture: Transition to a new paradigm. *Journal of Communication, 33,* 279–302.

Wilbur, K. (1983). *Up from Eden: A transpersonal view of human evolution,* Boulder, CO: Shamlhala.

CHAPTER

25

Journalistic Practices and Television Coverage of the Environment: An International Comparison

ANDERS HANSEN
OLGA LINNÉ

Mass media interest in the environment, and environmental issues and their coverage of them, has fluctuated considerably during the last 20 to 30 years since environmentalism first became established as a public concept during the 1960s.

It would be tempting to assume that media coverage of the environment, both in the present and over a longer historical period, reflects, if only in very general terms, not only the seriousness, importance, and social significance of environmental issues as a whole, but also the seriousness and importance of individual environmental issues relative to other such issues.

Needless to say, such a view would be simplistic and run contrary both to evidence produced by communication research on mass media coverage of environmental issues specifically (Schoenfeld, Meier, & Griffin, 1979; Lowe & Morrison, 1984; Strodthoff, Hawkins, & Schoenfeld, 1985) and to our knowledge of the highly selective nature of media representations generally.

However, while there is a now a relatively large body of research evidence on aspects of the mass media and the environment (see Hansen, 1990 for a review), little progress has been made in terms of understanding the media construction of environmental issues. Much of this can, as Halloran (1991; 1970) and others (e.g., Schlesinger, 1990) have often reminded us, be explained in terms of the reluctance of communication research to move away from mediacentrism.

Drawing on recent critiques of news production research and on advances in constructivist approaches to the media and social problems, we argue in this article for the importance of larger cultural climates in understanding how environmental issues are covered. We argue here as well for an expanded understanding of primary definers that takes into consideration the news scenarios or fora by which primary definition in the mass media is circumscribed.

In expanding this argument with particular reference to the television news construction of environmental issues, we intend to focus, quite selectively, on a recently completed international comparative study of television news coverage of environmental issues in Britain and Denmark.[1]

CULTURAL RESONANCES AND THE PRODUCTION OF NEWS

In his elegant review of three prominent perspectives in the sociology of news production, Schudson (1989) criticizes all three perspectives (the political economy perspective, the social organization perspective, and the culturological perspective) for falling short in terms of their attention to the cultural givens that circumscribe the production of news:

> Molotch and Lester, Tuchman and other who emphasize the "production of culture" do not focus on the "cultural givens" within which everyday interaction happens in the first place. These cultural givens, while they may be uncovered by detailed historical analysis, cannot be linked to features of social organization at the moment of study. They are a part of culture—a given symbolic system, within which and in relation to which reporters and officials go about their duties.
> (Schudson, 1989, p. 275)

From the perspectives of constructivist and social problems theory, attention has similarly been drawn to the importance of cultural givens or cultural resonances in understanding how claims-making activities in certain areas are more successful than in other areas, and how certain problems gain prominence in the

[1] The study, which was funded jointly by Danmark's Radio and Statens Samfundsvidenskabelige Forskningsraad (The Danish Social Science Research Council), was carried out by the authors in collaboration with Kim Minke, Danmarks Journalisthøjskole, Aarhus, Denmark.

public sphere while others do not. Gamson and Modigliani (1989) argue that three broad classes of determinants combine to influence the success or failure of particular issues in the public sphere—cultural resonances, sponsor activities, and media practices. Briefly, to gain prominence in the public sphere, an issue has to be cast in terms that resonate with existing and widely held cultural concepts. Gamson and Modigliani use the themes of "technological progress" and "mastery over nature as the way to progress" as examples of such deep-seated cultural assumptions in Western industrialized societies.

Hilgartner and Bosk (1988), in developing their public arenas model to explain the rise and fall of social problems, similarly point out that selection principles of all institutional arenas, including the mass media, are "influenced by widely shared cultural preoccupations and political biases. Certain problem definitions fit closely with broad cultural concerns, and they benefit from this fact in competition" (p. 64).

A problem in invoking cultural givens as a way of explaining intercultural differences in media coverage of environmental issues is, of course, that the media themselves are inseparable from broader social and cultural climates. The media at once both articulate and help set cultural climates. Bearing this in mind, it is perhaps little wonder that studies of media coverage of environmental issues have rarely referred to general cultural climates in their explanations of how and to what extent different environmental concerns come to be represented in the media. To do this, it is necessary to make cross-cultural comparisons or to examine the development of social issues, including environmental issues, in a longitudinal, historical perspective, rather than to perform a snapshot analysis of how the media cover this or that issue.

The advantage of carrying out an international comparative study, comparing the news coverage of environmental or other issues in countries whose public service broadcast institutions differ relatively little from each other, is that differences in the coverage between two countries force us to go beyond the more conventional concerns of news production studies (such as professional values, news values, and organizational constraints). It forces us to call, also, upon wider notions of the general cultural climate framing media coverage of particular issues.

In a recent study, we chose to compare journalistic practices and television news coverage of environmental issues in the main evening news programs of the British Broadcasting Corporation and the Danish Broadcasting Corporation (Danmarks Radio) over a two-month period.[2] A systematic analysis of television news coverage was combined with a series of interviews with environmental journalists, editors, and producers in the two countries.

Despite the many similarities between the public service broadcasting systems of the two countries, as well as similarities in the types of environmental problems that face Britain and Denmark, and, perhaps most significantly for the purposes of the present argument, a great degree of uniformity in the attitudes, values, new-gathering practices, and perceptions of news values among the journalists and media professionals interviewed in the two countries, the analysis of news coverage uncovered marked differences in both the extent and the nature of environmental issues coverage.

While there was considerably less coverage of environmental issues in *The 9 O'Clock News* (BBC1) than in *TV-Avisen* (DR), the coverage was also thematically much more restricted. Thus, certain types of issues that appeared prominently in *TV-Avisen* received no coverage at all in *The 9 O'Clock News*. Differences in three particular types of coverage point to the need to call upon the notion of wider cultural resonances as an important factor in the news construction of certain environmental problems. The three types of coverage, discussed below, are "Nuclear and radiation-related issues," "Waste problems/sea pollution," and "Harmful substances in the workplace."

Environmental issues on *The 9 O'Clock News* were defined, in the period analyzed, primarily as "nuclear and radiation-related" issues.[3] That this should be the case is not in itself particularly startling. Britain has a comparatively large nuclear industry (Denmark has no nuclear industry), which has been the subject of public controversy since the early to mid 1970s (Delaney, 1985; Hall, 1986; Heald & Wybrow, 1986). Nor is it particularly surprising, against the background of a series of nuclear power plant accidents (from Windscale in 1957, through Browns Ferry and Three Mile Island in the 1970s, to Chernobyl in 1986), that nuclear/radiation-related issues should receive some news coverage.

----

[2] The two months analyzed were October and November of 1987. Full details of sampling, coding, interviews, and results are available in Linne and Hansen (1990).

[3] The single most prominent type of environmental coverage on *The 9 O'Clock News* during the sample period was 'Natural Disaster' coverage. We are disregarding this category in the present argument, as it is perhaps the only type of environmental coverage that calls attention to itself and is, by virtue of its unpredictable and sudden event nature, newsworthy par excellence.

An indication of the much greater degree to which nuclear issues have become established as issues for public anxiety and concern in Britain than in Denmark, comes, however, from the finding that *The 9 O'Clock News*, in its already thematically and quantitatively restricted coverage of environmental issues, should devote a third of its coverage of nuclear issues to a comparatively small event, involving radioactive contamination in Brazil—a country that, like most developing countries, does not normally command much news interest in the British media. By contrast, this incident received no coverage in *TV-Avisen*. We see this, then, as an example of how a cultural environment already tuned to concern about nuclear and radiation-related issues leads to the privileging (within environmental issues coverage) of such coverage in television news.

Environmental issues on Danish television news were defined primarily, although in no way exclusively, as problems concerning waste disposal and waste management, particularly concerning the pollution of the seas around Denmark. In contrast, there was no coverage of waste problems and sea pollution (other than as a subcategory of coverage of nuclear and radiation-related issues) in *The 9 O'Clock News* in the period analyzed, despite the importance attached to these problems by the British journalists in interviews.

The prominence of this type of coverage in the Danish television news was due in large part to comprehensive coverage of one particular story: protest actions by Greenpeace and Danish (and some English) fishers against the incineration of toxic waste in the North Sea. This story started with the attempts made by Greenpeace to stop one particular incineration ship, the *Vulcanus II*, first through legal action and then with a physical blockade, from incinerating its load of toxic chemicals in the North Sea. (Henceforth we shall refer to this story as the Vulcanus story.) The event's momentum as a news story accelerated dramatically as a fleet of Danish fishing boats joined Greenpeace in their blockade action, and as the owners of the incineration ship quickly turned to the courts to prevent further obstruction of their activity.

Starting initially as a demonstration/protest-action story involving the environmental pressure group Greenpeace, this story, which accounted for 18 percent of the environment news stories on Danish television, very quickly developed into the news fora[4] of the courts, government and parliamentary politics, and science. The

---

[4] We define *forum* simply as the setting or scenario, geographical or institutional, through which an event or an issue is articulated and becomes the subject of news coverage.

elaboration and comprehensive coverage of this story on Danish television is then less surprising, in terms of conventional news production values, once the issue becomes part of the routine news fora of the courts, government/politics, and science. An explanation for the extent of elaboration and coverage of the story, as well as the fact that it became a news story in the first place, however, must be sought in a framework that goes beyond an understanding of the routine orientations and quarries of news-journalists.

This is particularly necessary because the story started as an essentially staged event orchestrated by Greenpeace in order to attract public attention to the larger problem of waste and pollution in the North Sea. The Danish journalists interviewed in the study (while acknowledging, as did their British counterparts, the importance of environmental groups as news sources generally) unlike their British counterparts, expressed a great deal of skepticism and reluctance concerning the use of Greenpeace as a news source.

The extent and elaboration of this story, then, was in part due to the way in which they story very quickly moved from the initial Greenpeace-initiated dramatic events into established routine news scenarios involving "legitimate" and "credible" social actors (politicians, the judiciary, scientists, Danish fisher, industry management representatives—here all opposed to Greenpeace as a group whose activities and strategies extend to the margins of social legitimacy). However, another explanation for the story's prominence can be found in its cultural resonances.

First, the event and the subsequent story development fit well with an already existing category of coverage: even within the relatively short sample period of two months, this particular story, which broke in the second week of the period, had already been preceded by two separate stories about the problems and implications of sea pollution and unrestrained industrial fishing practices. Both of these stories were science-forum stories in the sense that their appearance could be ascribed not to sudden events or political developments, but to claims making by scientists.

Second, the Vulcanus story enabled cultural resonance at the crucial level of a chain of culturally deep-seated oppositions, including the following: us versus them; Danish fishers versus multinational large industrial companies (the company owning the Vulcanus incineration ship was a large U.S.-based company); and a view (partly promoted in the coverage through the prominence of the Danish government as a primary definer) of the Danish government as being anxious to control and minimize pollution versus foreign governments and industries seen as reluctant to act on pollution.

The ability to activate and play up culturally deep-seated notions organized around the basic value dichotomy of us = good versus them (foreign countries) = bad can equally be invoked as a partial explanation for the continued prominence of waste/sea pollution as an environmental issue in *TV-Avisen after* the Vulcanus story. The end of the sample period coincided with a key news diary event, a conference of North Sea countries on North Sea pollution. Unlike its British counterpart, *TV-Avisen* ran three preparatory stories[5] on North Sea pollution, in addition to giving comprehensive coverage to the conference itself.

Journalists and editors involved in the production of environmental coverage in both countries put pollution of the seas in general, and pollution of the North Sea in particular, as key problems facing the environment in Britain and Denmark. Yet, despite this similarity in journalistic views, and despite the conference that was held in London during this period, which drew together all the North Sea countries to discuss pollution in the sea, the key television news programs of the two countries differed radically in the extent to which they portrayed waste problems/sea pollution as an environmental problem. We suggest that in some part the differences are due to cultural resonance differences, but it is also clear that such an explanation should not be taken too far; the deep-seated cultural oppositions—with which themes in the Danish waste problems/Sea pollution stories resonated—can also be found, possibly no less strongly, in British culture (see for example Hansen & Murdock, 1985).

The second most prominent category of environmental issues coverage on *TV-Avisen* was Harmful substances in the work-place and/or associated with the production process. As with waste problems/sea pollution, there was no coverage of this type on *The 9 O'Clock News*. Before invoking cultural differences as an explanatory framework, however, it is worth noting not just the difference in subject matter between *The 9 O'Clock News* and *TV-Avisen*, but also associated differences in the primary news fora through which these issues become articulated and the subject of news coverage. Thus, the issue of Harmful substances in the work-place was

---

[5] Two of these preparatory stories were feature stories by *TV-Avisen*'s foreign correspondents (not environment correspondents) in England and West Germany.

covered as a result primarily of its appearance in two news scenarios or fora: one, industrial action or equivalent worker/union protest against the use of certain substances in the production process, and, two, court cases involving worker compensation claims against employers in relation to exposure (and subsequent adverse health implications) to harmful substances in the production process.

Neither Harmful substances in the workplace or any other environmental issues did appear in *The 9 O'Clock News* articulated through the news forum of industrial action. This may seem surprising, given that industrial action is generally considered to be a newsworthy scenario by *The 9 O'Clock News*, and one that figures in *The 9 O'Clock News* with some regularity (Hartmann, 1976; Glasgow University Media Group, 1976; Cumberbatch, McGregor, Brown, & Morrison, 1986). It does so, however, primarily in terms of wage, productivity, and closure-related conflicts, and as this analysis shows, not in terms of industrial conflict concerning workers' protection against environmental hazards at work. The size of the industry/occupation involved is another factor that distinguishes coverage on *The 9 O'Clock News* from coverage on *TV-Avisen*. Industrial conflict is covered on *The 9 O'Clock News* primarily when big industries or key occupations are involved—for example, miners, workers in the automobile industry, nurses, teachers, or doctors. In contrast, *TV-Avisen* regularly covers industrial conflict in relatively small types of industry,[6] including, as in this sample, coverage of industrial conflict related to environmental issues.

The prominence of worker compensation-related court cases as a forum, of industrial action as a forum, and of the coverage of harmful substances in the work-place as a type of coverage (which is completely absent from *The 9 O'Clock News*) on *TV-Avisen* is, then, indicative of some considerable differences in what the two news programs define as newsworthy and suitable for coverage, and in a wider sense, of how deep-rooted cultural differences circumscribe such definitions.

In this case it would seem that the explanation for the comparative prominence of worker/workplace-related environmental issues on *TV-Avisen* must be sought in the strong Social Democratic tradition characteristic of labor/industry relations in Denmark for most of this century. While the differences in coverage may thus, in

---

[6] We recognize that this difference is in part a reflection of differences between the nature of the industrial/business structures of Denmark and Britain.

part, be seen as stemming from the fact that the two countries are at different stages in their development from industrial to postindustrial societies, and from associated differences in democratic and political traditions, the point here is that in Denmark not only is the work environment seen as an important aspect of the wider spectrum of environmental problems, but it serves also as a legitimate news context for the articulation of environmental issues.

PRIMARY DEFINERS AND FORA

In the first part of this chapter we have attempted to use examples from an international comparative study of the coverage of environmental issues to show the need to call upon cultural differences and cultural resonances in an attempt to account for the marked differences in coverage of environmental issues by two very similar news programs. In the remaining part, we expand further on a constructivist perspective on the processes by which environmental issues become news, and on the way in which these processes help determine the inflection of environmental issues in television news.

In Hilgartner and Bosk's terminology, an examination of the rise and fall of particular social problems must address itself to the social arenas in which such problems become articulated:

> If a situation becomes defined as a social problem, it does not necessarily mean that objective conditions have worsened. Similarly, if a problem disappears from public discourse, it does not necessarily imply that the situation has improved. Instead, the outcome of this process is governed by a complex organizational and cultural competition. To understand this competition, it is necessary to examine the social arenas in which it takes place. The collective definition of social problems occurs not in some vague location such as society or public opinion but in particular public arenas in which social problems are framed and grow.
>
> (Hilgartner & Bosk, 1988, p. 58)

This view is fundamental to an understanding not only of how and why certain issues become elaborated and defined as social problems by the media, but also of how the forum through which an issue becomes defined contributes to the setting of boundaries, or the terms of reference, for public discussion of that issue. Above, we argued that the elaboration of the Vulcanus story on Danish television news was due in large part to the fact that the story very quickly moved into established news fora, which in turn contributed to the framing of the problem, pollution of the North Sea, as a problem of legal matters, political initiative, and scientific evidence.

Hilgartner and Bosk's formulation resonates well with one of Hall's earlier analyses of the place of the media in the social structure:

> Many institutions contribute to the development and maintenance of hegemonic domination: but, of these, the mass media systems are probably (along with the schools) the critical ones.... They "connect" the centers of power with the dispersed publics: they mediate the public discourse between elites and the governed. Thus they become, pivotally, the site and terrain on which the making and shaping of consent is exercised, and, to some degree, contested. They are key institutions in the operation of cultural hegemony....
>
> (Hall, 1975, p. 142)

> Political and economic power is shadowed by what we may call the unequal distribution of cultural power. Cultural power consists, essentially, of the command over certain crucial processes: (a) the power to define which issues will enter the circuit of public communications; (b) the power to define the terms in which the issue will be debated; (c) the power to define who will speak to the issues and the items; (d) the power to manage the debate itself in the media.
>
> (Hall, 1975, pp. 142–143)

While clearly recognizing the importance of "institutional contexts" in the above quote, Hall and his colleagues (e.g. Hall, Critcher, Jefferson, Clarke, & Roberts, 1978) and others focusing on the analysis of primary definers have, however, tended to assume that the analysis of primary definers or actors in media coverage would by itself show the institutional contexts by which issues are framed and defined. As Schlesinger (1990) has pointed out, such a view of primary definition is too narrow, and it ignores the possibility of disagreement within groups of primary definers and elites. It is also a view of primary definition that does not allow for the framing that the arena or social scenario itself imposes on the activity of various primary definers, and on the inflection of such issues in news coverage.

The importance of distinguishing between actors/primary definers on the one hand, and, on the other, the fora, arenas, or scenarios through which issues are articulated, is apparent particularly in relation to an understanding of the role of environmental pressure groups as agenda-builders and claims-makers on environmental issues.

While, as Lowe and Morrison correctly argue, "environmental disasters automatically command media attention as dramatic events" (Lowe & Morrison, 1984), dramatic and/or spectacular environmental disasters constitute only a small part of what environmentalists would define as environmental problems or issues. The depletion of the ozone layer, and associated global warming and greenhouse effects, is a classic example of an environmental issue that enjoys a great deal of media coverage despite the absence of dramatic visual events. It is equally notable for its history as a public arena problem, in terms of its emergence and considerable news play in the early to mid 1970s, followed by a decade of virtual exile from the media agenda, only to emerge during the mid to late 1980s as perhaps *the* environmental issue (see also Nelkin, 1987).

One of the reasons given for the difficulties of the mass media in covering environmental issues is that most environmental problems simply do not fit the temporal imperative in the production of news, the focus on events and the 24-hour cycle that characterizes mass media news production (Schoenfeld, Meier, & Griffin, 1979). Environmental problems by and large take a long time (in television news terms) to develop and become evident or visible, their definition is circumscribed by scientific uncertainty, and their complexity may make it difficult to place them in one of the established scenarios commanding news attention.

Several studies (Schoenfeld, Meier, & Griffin, 1979: Lowe & Morrison, 1984) have indicated that one of the initial major obstacles to environment and environmental issues becoming newsworthy was the act that few papers and television organizations had an environment news beat covered by an environmental reporter. While this may have been an obstacle in the early days of environmental claims-making, this situation no longer holds true. Most of the major "quality" media now have environment correspondents—indeed, some have several.

Some researchers have gone further to argue that environmental reporting in the mass media constitutes a special case in the sense that environmental journalists are more positively tuned to their subject matter than for example political reporters or crime reporters. Lowe and Morrison (1984) for example point out:

In interviews, environmental journalists expressed undisguised sympathy for many of the issues raised by environmental groups....Though retaining a critical attitude towards pressure groups and their information, the journalists confirmed that the existence of environmental pressure groups greatly aided their work, and not just as source contacts. Without the groups, it was agreed, the environment would be a more difficult "story" to place, because their activities had put the environment on the political map and continued to generate issues, and thus created the demand for coverage.

(Lowe & Morrison, 1984, p. 82)

While journalistic and editorial sympathy towards environmental issues promoted by environmental interest groups has similarly been documented elsewhere (Schoenfeld, 1980; Porritt & Winner, 1988; Linne & Hansen, 1990), the evidence from analyses of media coverage of environmental issues paints a contrasting picture, indicating that the positive attitudes of media professionals toward environmental pressure groups do not manifest themselves as an increased presence of presence groups as primary definers in media coverage.

Virtually without exception such analyses have shown that media coverage of environmental issues is essentially no different from media coverage of other types of issues or problems in terms of source orientation and primary definitions.

In her analysis of environmental coverage in the Canadian press, Einsiedel (1988) found interest group representatives greatly outnumbered by government officials, scientists, and private industry as sources used in coverage of environmental issues. Greenberg and his colleagues (1989), in their analysis of television coverage of environmental risk, found that government and industry accounted for 28 percent and 13.2 percent of sources respectively, while advocacy groups were only 6.8 percent of sources. Similar patterns have been found in analyses of coverage of specific environmental disasters or events (Molotch & Lester, 1975; Wilkins, 1987; Westerstaahl & Johansson, 1987).

In our own comparative study of news coverage of environmental issues on British and Danish television we found that despite the generally positive, albeit cautious, attitude of journalists towards certain environmental groups, these groups were notable chiefly for their relative absence as primary definers in the actual coverage. Environmental groups appeared as primary definers in only 6 percent of stories, compared with 23 percent for public body or authority representatives, 21 percent for government, and 17 percent independent scientists or experts.

It is evidence such as this which leads us to question whether the environment is any different, as argued by some researchers (e.g. Lowe & Morrison, 1984) from other types of news subjects in terms of media coverage, and in terms of the elaboration of environmental issues as issues for public and political concern.

We are not here questioning the validity of research findings taken from studies of journalists and their attitudes to environmental groups as sources that show that journalists see environmental groups as important sources and claims-makers. We are, however, suggesting that the evidence from studies of actors and primary definers appearing in actual media coverage indicate that (particularly in hard news coverage, as opposed to features, documentaries, and magazine formats) while environmental groups may be important as initiators or catalysts of public debate or controversy and subsequent media coverage, they do not, on the whole, command a prominent role in terms of the definitions that are elaborated and contested in the media arena.

Moreover, there was some indication from the study of British and Danish television news that when spokespersons for environmental pressure groups *do* appear as primary definers, they do so through the forum or news scenario of public demonstration or protest action rather than as a legitimate or authoritative news forum in their own right. Not only, then, do environmental pressure groups appear to have limited access to "the power to define the terms in which the issue will be debated" and "the power to manage the debate itself in the media" (Hall, 1975, as quoted above), but when they do gain access to television news as primary definers, their primary definition is articulated through, and circumscribed by, a forum that carries connotations of activity on the margins of the socially legitimate.

The distinction, then, between primary definers and news fora or news arenas serves at least two purposes in an attempt to understand the news construction of environmental issues: (a) it highlights the rather restricted way in which environmental pressure groups (representing a radical perspective on environmental issues) gain access to news coverage; and (b) it indicates how the environment, very much like most other social issues, depends for its elaboration in the media arena on becoming part of and being articulated through the established and legitimate news fora of government and parliamentary politics, science, the courts, and so on. However, an understanding of the news construction of environmental issues will also need to draw on the notion of cultural resonances, as we have sought to demonstrate. The radical differences between two very comparable and similar news programs in their coverage of environmental issues are differences that can only be explained and understood by going beyond the conventional concerns of news studies and by invoking differences in the cultural climates in which particular issues are rooted and with which they resonate.

REFERENCES

Cumberbatch, G., McGregor, R., Brown, J., & Morrison, D. (1986). *Television and the miners' strike*. London: BFI Broadcasting Research Unit.

Delaney, J. (1985). Energy and the politics of nuclear power. In B. Jones (Eds.), *Political Issues in Britain today* (pp. 117–131). Manchester: Manchester University Press.

Einsiedel, E. (1988). The Canadian press and the environment. Paper presented at the XVIth Conference of The International Association for Mass Communication Research, Barcelona, Spain, 24th-29th July.

Gamson, W.A., & Modigliani, A. (1989). Media discourse and public opinion on nuclear power: a constructionist approach. *American Journal of Sociology, 95*, 1–37.

Glasgow University Media Group (1976). *Bad news*. London: Routledge & Kegan Paul.

Greenberg, M.R., Sachsman, D.B., Sandman, P.M., & Salomone, K.L. (1989). Network evening news coverage of environmental risk. *Risk Analysis, 9*, 119–126.

Hall, S. (1975). The "structured communication" of events. In Unesco (Eds.), *Getting the message across* (pp. 115–145). Paris: The Unesco Press.

Hall, S., Critcher, C., Jefferson, T., Clarke, J., & Roberts, B. (1978). *Policing the crisis*. London: Macmillan.

Hall, T. (1986). *Nuclear politics: the history of nuclear power in Britain*. Harmondsworth: Penguin.

Halloran, J.D. (Ed.). (1970). *The effects of television*. London: Grenada.

Halloran, J.D. (1991). *A quarter of a century of Prix Jeunesse research*. Munich: Prix Jeunesse.

Hansen, A. (1990). Socio-political values underlying media coverage of the environment. *Media Development, 37*, 4–6.

Hansen, A., & Murdock, G. (1985). Constructing the crowd: populist discourse and press presentation. In V. Mosco & J. Wasko (Eds.), *Popular culture and media events* (pp. 227–257). Norwood, NJ: Ablex.

Hartmann, P. (1976). Industrial relations in the news media. *Industrial Relations Journal, 6*, 4–18.

Heald, G., & Wybrow, R.J. (1986). *The Gallup survey of Britain*. London: Croom Helm.

Hilgartner, S., & Bosk, C.L. (1988). The rise and fall of social problems: A public arenas model. *American Journal of Sociology, 94*, 53–78.

Linné, O., & Hansen, A. (1990). *News coverage of the environment: A comparative study of journalistic practices and television presentation in Danmarks Radio and the BBC*. Copenhagen: Danmarks Radio Forlaget.

Lowe, P., & Morrison, D. (1984). Bad news or good news: Environmental politics and the mass media. *The Sociological Review, 32*, 75–90.

Molotch, H., & Lester, M. (1975). Accidental news: The great oil spill. *American Journal of Sociology, 81*, 235-260.

Nelkin, D. (1987). *Selling science: How the press covers science and technology*. New York: W H Freeman & Company.

Porritt, J., & Winner, D. (1988). *The coming of the greens*. London: Fontana.

Schlesinger, P. (1990). Rethinking the sociology of journalism: source strategies and the limits of media centrism. In M. Ferguson (Eds.), *Public communication: The new imperatives* (pp. 61–83). London: Sage.

Schoenfeld, A.C. (1980). Newspersons and the environment today. *Journalism Quarterly, 57*, 456–462.

Schoenfeld, A.C., Meier, R.F. & Griffin, R.J. (1979). Constructing a social problem—The press and the environment. *Social Problems, 27*, 38–61.

Schudson, M. (1989). The sociology of news production. *Media, Culture & Society, 11*, 263-282.

Strodthoff, G.G., Hawkins, R.P., & Schoenfeld, A.C. (1985). Media roles in a social movement. *Journal of Communication, 35*, 134–153.

Westerstaahl, J., & Johansson, F. (1987). *Tjernobylnedfallet och myndighetsbeskeden (The Chernobyl fall-out and the advice from public authorities)*. Stockholm: SPF.

Wilkins, L. (1987). *Shared vulnerability*. New York: Greenwood.

Communication Research and the New International Information Order: An Essay on a Delicate Alliance

26

CEES J. HAMELINK

Those of us in the communication research community who have in the past decade indulged in the vicissitudes of the N.I.I.O. debate were to our detriment not always guided by some of Jim Halloran's adagia. Among them the most salient ones are:

- the need to ask the right questions ("If you ask silly questions, you get bloody silly answers");
- the need to be engaged ("You cannot study social problems with the face towards the shelves and the back to the world");
- the need to be critical, in particular with regard to our own presupposition ("We need a sociology about sociologists").

If we were not at all times guided by these concerns, we can at least use them as a frame of reference in the assessment of a decade of research on that most engaging question of the reordering of the world's communication structure.

THE DEBATE ON THE NEW INTERNATIONAL
INFORMATION ORDER

In other texts the N.I.I.O. debate has been reviewed rather extensively. Therefore, it suffices for the present purpose to sum up the main issues at stake. Taking its departure a decade ago from a meeting of the heads of state of the nonaligned countries (in Algiers), the debate has had a predominantly political character, its key agenda item being the problem of the redistribution of one of the world's increasingly important resources: information.

It all started with the recognition that, despite the formal liberation from military occupation and political patronizing, developing countries in the early 1970s were still for the most part economically and culturally colonized. The former was in most cases abundantly manifest, the latter tended to be far less clear. This was due to a number of factors. There was the prevailing acceptance of such concepts as the free international flow of information, the largely unrecognized hidden agenda of most cultural traffic, and the identification of cultural imports as indicators of development.

In 1973 the powerful cultural legitimation of the metropolis—satellite structure was discovered and publicly debated, and proposals for counteraction were proffered. From this point the debate moved towards the recognition that the need to reorder cultural—information relations in the world was intrinsically linked to the need to restructure the international economy. Around 1975 the pace of the debate stepped up. More actors became involved. Controversies heated up. Resolutions, counterproposals, conference reports followed upon each other with remarkable speed. The issue has attained international stature. So much so that, by 1978, most members of the international community admitted that something was wrong and that something ought to be done about that!

The 1978 UNESCO General Conference in Paris provided the forum. In great unanimity the UNESCO member states articulated the need for a new order in the field of international information, albeit in sufficiently ambivalent semantics to make some of the observers of the debate suspicious. The original phrase, a "new international information order," was coined anew and turned into a "new more just and more effective world information and communication order" (NWICO from then on).

The world embraced a new order, but darkness prevailed for those inquiring whose order this was supposed to be.

In the 1980s the contours a new world order became clearer. They were not the ones the originals protagonists had in mind.

It seemed as if the new world order shaped in this decade was primarily intended to meet the needs and purposes of the global transnational industrial and financial networks. This was aided by the emphasis in the international political debate on the expansion of North—South transfers of resources and the implicit legitimation of export markets this entails for the transnational corporations. In general, it transpired that the main beneficiaries of the new order would be found in the North. The description of the new order as one of integration and interdependence could only mean that the most powerful participants were to benefit most.

Since with the increasing number of interactions among parties of unequal strength the advantages are primarily for the stronger party, a further widening of existing North–South disparities was the likely outcome.

Indeed, drawing up the balance sheet today, the perspective is bleak. The dependence in the South is not less, the discrepancies have not decreased, and in the rapidly moving field of advanced information technology the Southern catching-up has become sheer illusion.

RESEARCHERS AND THEIR CONTRIBUTIONS.

The N.I.I.O. debate did attract a relatively large crowd of contributions. Among them were many more than the representatives from academia. There were the representatives of international governmental organizations (such as various UN bodies), regional governmental organizations (such as ASEAN), and the professional organizations (such as I.O.J. and I.F.J.). Then there were the voices of prominent international civil servants (such as UNESCO Director-General A. M'Bow) or of such government officials as M. Masmoudi.

Several practitioners of the information trade joined in the debate, such as Reuters's Gerald Long, Inter Press Service Director General Robert Savio, IPI President Max Snijders, and journalists such as Rosemary Righter, Mart Rosenblum, Claude Julien, D.R. Mankekar, and C. Raghavan. All these contributors, however valuable or questionable, are not the focus of this chapter. This is the small group of academicians who participated in the debate. They distinguished themselves from the others not by virtue of university positions, but largely by such criteria as the systematic use of references, the efforts to locate issues in a theoretical perspective, and the attempts to construct hypotheses that could be tested. That group, although it excited disproportionately large audiences, was very small indeed. To be precise, the group would have to be divided into those who directly and internationally gave input to the political debate, and those who contributed rather more indirectly, because their writings took on extra significance when studied in the N.I.I.O. context. Among the latter category most prominent are Dallas Smythe, William Melody, Peter Golding, Rita Cruise O'Brien, Elihu Katz, Jeremy Tunstall, Oliver Boyd-Barret, and Thomas Guback.

Related to this category are those authors who made in passim reference to the new international information order, such as Glen Robinson and Glen Fisher. There is today very little comprehensive work on the N.I.I.O. issues. Closest to this type of study would be the contributions of Anthony Smith, Thomas McPhail, and the present author.

The less comprehensive contributions can be divided into the following six categories.

1. General contributions. Important names in this category are Jörg Becker, Luis Ramiro Beltrán, Osvaldo Capriles, Neville Jayaweera, Enrique G. Manet, Tomo Martelanc, Jose A. Mayobre, Kaarle Nordenstreng, Ithiel de Sola Pool, Rafael Roncagliolo, and Raquel Salinas.

2. Contributions on the transnational structure of international information. In particular these writers include Cees J. Hamelink, Noreene Janus, Armand Mattelart, Herbert Schiller, and Juan Somavia.

3. Contributions on cultural dependence/cultural imperialism. In this category the names of some writers whose indirect contributions have been very significant have to be mentioned. Their work on the thesis of imperialism in the field of information and culture is certainly part of the wider N.I.I.O. debate. Relevant names are Tran van Dinh, Oliver Boyd Barret, C.C. Lee, Evelina Dagnino, and Karl Sauvant.

4. Contributions on information flows and their patterns. Here should be mentioned Phil Harris, Wilbur Schramm, and Tapio Varis.

5. Contributions on alternative communication, in particular the studies by the ILET staff (Mexico) and the research unit of Inter Press Service.

6. Contributions on the relationship between the N.I.I.I. and the new international economic order. This work was done by Meheroo Jussawalla and Breda Pavlic.[1]

---

[1] The pertinent works by these authors are listed in the references.

MODALITIES OF RESEARCH

Evidently—as with the politicians—the academic contributors were divided into pro and contra writers on various N.I.I.O.-related topics.

As in all other areas of communication research such distinctions could be made as conservative versus progressive, positivistic versus hermeneutic, repressive versus emancipatory.

Given the issue at stake, it is not very surprising that a majority of writers are of a predominantly progressive orientation. However, even among them there are considerable divisions about degrees of ideological affiliation, inclination towards political action, and technological fixation. One way of achieving some order (evidently at the loss of much detail) is to roughly distinguish between those researchers who approach the international information system with a rather more synthetic view—oriented towards concepts as interdependence, global order, and world—and those with a rather more conflictual view—geared more towards thinking in terms of North–South contradictions, conflicts, and delinking. Further, a division could be made between those who concentrate on a holistic approach—studying the totality of the information system—and those who take a more particularist approach because of their specific interest in only parts of the system (such as the news agencies). Putting these four categories together, a matrix emerges that provides a minimal amount of ordering of the work done on N.I.I.I. topics.

THE MAIN CONCEPTS

	particularistic	holistic
synthetic	A	B
conflictual	D	C

At the risk of indignant contestation I would propose to put (by way of an example) the work of Wilbur Schramm in A, the work of Ithiel de Sola Pool or Jeremy Tunstall in B, the work by Herbert Schiller in C, and the TV flow study of Tapio Varis in D.

These different approaches yielded a number of concepts that were meant to provide an understanding of the existing information structure in the world and to explore alternative structures. The most important concepts in the N.I.I.O. debate can be listed as follows.

- Alternative communication/Access/Participation
- Another development/Another news/Contextual information.
- Cultural autonomy/Cultural imperialism/Media imperialism/Cultural synchronization/National culture.
- Democratization of communication.
- Dissociation/Delinking/Self-reliance.
- Imbalance.
- Information as a commodity/Information as a social good/Information as a resource.
- Interdependence/Integration.
- One-way flow of information
- National policy/National sovereignty.

At some time in the future someone with more distance from the scenery than the present author could take a good look at these concepts and precisely analyze their strengths and weaknesses. For this chapter I would prefer putting them in some order and commenting on some of their shortcomings.

Basically there were three types of concepts used—descriptive, analytical, and programmatic. The descriptive category was meant to assist the understanding of the existing structure of international information and put it into a broader historical, politico-economic context. Examples include such concepts as dependence, imbalance, and one-way flow. The analytical category was meant to explain why the structure is as it is. Examples include the transnational structure and cultural synchronization. The third category, programmatic concepts, was meant to guide towards strategies, action, and models of resistance. Examples include alternative communication, democratization, and dissociation. All these concepts have at times contributed to the N.I.I.O. debate and have provided both intellectual and political guidance. However, rather than unduly enjoying a self-congratulatory tone, it seems pertinent to highlight the shortcomings of a few of them. In the descriptive category the concepts *imbalance* and *one-way flow* certainly dominated the debate. To some extent they helped in understanding what developing countries were complaining about, and they were undoubtedly of great political assistance in raising the consciousness of government administrators and the public at large for the inequities in the international information structure. At the same time, they were very misleading, and it remains a question whether the short-term asset they represented will not be lost against the liability they may turn out to be in the long term.

Imbalance presupposes that balance is the key indicator of a structure that would do justice to all its participants. The new international information order (in its original intention) stood for an information exchange in which all parties participate with inputs and outputs that are appropriate to their particular situations and not necessarily balanced in quantity or quality with the inputs and outputs of the others. The new international information order stood for a system of nonhierarchical relations between the participating nation-states, whereas a balanced system is not necessarily nonhierarchical. Balance can easily imply continued dependence. It assumes that imbalances can be overcome by catching up—which has to take place through such increased transfers from the North to the South that will further dependencies.

One-way flow is a seemingly correct and attractive concept, since the international information traffic indeed runs overwhelmingly from the North to the South. Yet the concept tends to obscure a characteristic of this traffic that is more important. The basic feature of the international information system is its bureaucratic nature. The information flows go two ways. There is information flowing from the top to the bottom, and the other way round. However, the nature and the significance of the information varies greatly with its direction. One-way flow tends to ignore this. It is important to recognize the bottom-top flows, since they feed the top-bottom flows (for example, through raw data to be packaged in the North into functional information) and they facilitate the top-bottom flows (through assembling parts of information technology that in the North will be integrated into functional information equipment) through legitimizing them (through alliances between local capital and foreign information sources). In the category of analytical concepts the most convincing work has been done on the transnational structure. Particularly in this area a relatively large amount of empirical data have been collected and processed. Yet this provided only the beginning. More insights are definitely needed in at least the following fields: the internal contradictions of the transnational industrial and financial structure, the impact of industrial concentration upon the diversity of products and services delivered, and the psychological determinants of the transnational effects upon local culture.

We need also more insight into the intrinsic nature of the transnational corporation. Are its inherent features sufficiently neutral as to make its operations mainly dependent upon the operators, or are they destined to lead to damage no matter who manages them?

In the category of programmatic concepts the debate certainly could not be said to suffer from a want of well-intended guides. The problem with most of them, though, is their immaturity and—by definition—their speculative character. Since the debate of the 1970s was necessarily concentrated mainly on description and analysis, with the 1980s the time for strategic implementation had come. Work was now to shift towards the serious exploration of the programmatic concepts. Many of them had a strong appeal, but even so very little thorough theoretical thinking was dedicated to them.

An example is provided by the concept of democratization. Connected with the democratization of communication there are at least three complex problems worth in-depth investigation.

In the first place the concept of democracy has that peculiar problem so adroitly expressed by Bernard Smith: "It has to come to mean whatever anyone wants it to mean."

In the second place proposals for the democratization of communication are haunted by that unresolved tension dating back to the early days of North American democracy: the Jefferson versus Madison controversy about the conflicting demands of majority rule and individual freedom. In the third place there is the following complexity. The formal democratic system—as we know it today—has very specific communication needs. The problem, however, is that meeting these needs does not contribute to the democratization of communication. Basic to bourgeois democracy is the necessity to legitimize an inegalitarian social order.

In its actual operation most democratic systems are highly exclusive: their executive power is very unevenly distributed, while they formally carry the pretense of political participation.

The implicit contradiction is that if the participatory dimension is not met, the legitimacy of the system is undermined. If, on the other hand, all parties in the system can participate equally, then the overall stability is endangered. Communication has the capacity to manufacture the sensation of participation and thus to legitimize the existing political order. Since political legitimation no longer emanates from evident higher principles and has to be produced, constrained rather than open communications may be needed. The complexity ensuing is that if communications are further democratized, the formal democratic system is undermined. At the same time, if the formal democratic system is further strengthened, the democratization of communications is effectively undermined.

RESEARCH AND THE POLITICAL DEBATE

In the N.I.I.O. debate communication researchers certainly played a significant role. They assisted in creating awareness of the issue at stake, they helped to broaden the general political attention, and they contributed to at least a partial understanding of the complexities involved. Yet it must be realized that the alliance between research and the political debate was and continues to be a delicate one.

This delicacy is as much caused by the researchers as by the politicians. In this respect three points are worth mentioning.

1.   What needs to be kept in mind—and was sometimes lost in the encounter—is the need for researchers and politicians to see themselves as distinct from one another. They are different actors with different responsibilities. The researcher is not necessarily antagonistic vis-à-vis the politician, but at all times he or she needs to be sufficiently critical and independent. This does not exclude political engagement. However, even when they are part of the same process, the researcher and the politician have different angles from which they approach the issues, and they may easily be at odds while fighting for the same cause.

2.   The expectations about the researcher–politician relationship in the N.I.I.O. debate need to be tempered by the general experience that research has only limited influence on political measures. The alliance is almost without exception a very unhappy one, suffering under limitless lists of mutual complaints. Most of the studies done on the impact of social research on public policy are rather discouraging. A constant finding of such studies is that

some 50 percent of senior civil servants totally ignore all research, and a good 40 percent, if hard pressed, cannot identify any piece of useful social research. If findings of social research are used, they tend to serve the following purposes: to improve bureaucratic efficiency, to delay action, to avoid responsibility, to discredit opponents, to maintain prestige, and to ask for more research.

3. The contribution of research to the political debate has suffered most from research's own inadequacy. Most communication research exercises today—whether conservative or progressive—are haunted by the shortcomings of its basic nonemancipatory paradigm. The demand for a new international information order was a demand for liberation/emancipation. Eventually, only when science is perceived as a tool for emancipation can it meaningfully contribute to such a demand. This perception, however, is fundamentally hampered by the mode of knowledge generation that dominates the work of positivists, and of a whole range of critical sociologists, neo-marxist political economists, and development theorists alike. They all prefer the discursive over the intuitive. They are all bound to the scientific methods and techniques based on the rational-empirical consciousness that has pervaded Western science since Descartes and Newton. This mode of thought has undoubtedly yielded impressive intellectual and technical achievements; it has also created problems (such as they very real threat of the world's annihilation) that it cannot solve. The rational-empirical mode is extremely well versed in controlling its environment—it is not at all suited or its liberation.

Therefore, we are in need of new approaches. We need a radical departure from the prevailing paradigm and have to explore alternative modes of knowledge generation.

We are in need of new theories, but they should not be the mechanistic constructs of a logical sequential discourse, but true to their (Greek) semantic root they should be visions. Such visions would need to combine in complementary ways inputs from both rational knowledge and intuitive sources of knowledge. This could constitute the departure from a paradigm that has mainly obstructed the understanding of realty and that is certainly incapable of its emancipation.

RESEARCHERS' RE-ASSESSMENT

On balance there may be no reason for overwhelming dissatisfaction, but researchers need to face the observation that now, in the 1990s, we confront an agenda that is in many respects different from that of the 1970s.

Although it is never possible to erect sharp borderlines between successive decades, it must be realized that the debate on the international information order confronts in the 1990s an environment with features distinctly different from those of the 1970s and the 1980s.

At the beginning of a new decade it is possible to look back both in anger and with encouragement. On the one hand many expectations have not been fulfilled, and on the other it can not be mistaken that the issues brought forward inter alia by social scientists are increasingly recognized as among the leading concerns of the latter part of the 20th century.

In order to be well equipped to address the concerns of a new decade:

1. Social scientists need to contribute to a broadening of the debate; at times it has been too much restricted to small experts' circles, and a larger awareness and participation is necessary.

2. The analysis of problems on the national level needs to be initiated more vigorously. Unless national equivalents to a new international order are created all proposals will remain diplomatic phrases.

3. Particularly in the national context the role of the state needs careful study. Critical questions relating to the margins of state intervention, the delineation of state, government, and party, as well as the public sphere—private sphere dialectics, remain unresolved.

4. The 1970 introduced the notion of the need for policy making and strategic and operational planning. In the 1990s the skills in policy formation, and the techniques of planning needed to implement them, have still to be developed.

5. Particular emphasis has to be given to the improvement of access to technical knowledge. The capacity to critically assess technological offers and selectively integrate and

innovate technologies will be a decisive factor in the years ahead.

6. The single most important concept that was not sufficiently explored, and that was at the core of the N.I.I.O. debate, is *power*. All the topics involved in the debate were related to this concept. Neither did we analytically define it, nor did we elaborate its programmatic significance. The study of the execution and distribution of social power— in which information plays an increasingly large role— must have high priority. We need to know how power emerges, how it operates,and how it can be contained.

EPILOGUE

In another decade, in another Festschrift for another esteemed colleague, again an assessment might be made that wonders whether we asked the right questions, and whether we were committed while remaining independent. A positive finding of that assessment can be made more probable if we dare to take our shortcomings seriously and if we commit ourselves to new routes towards an emancipatory mode of communication research. I am aware of the fact that this is not so easy, since communication researchers—and Jim Halloran especially will know this—are devout adherents to these words of Hamlet: "We rather bear those ills we have than fly to others we know not of."

REFERENCES

Becker, J. (Ed.). (1979). *Free flow of information: Informationen zur neuen internationalen informationsordnung.* Frankfurt: Gemeinschaftswerk der Evangelischen Publizistik.

Beltrán, L.R., & Fox de Cardona, E. (1977). Latin America and the United States flaws in the free flow of information. In J. Richstad (Ed.), *New perspectives in international communication.* Honolulu: East-West Communication Institute.

Beltrán, L.R. (1978). TV etchings in the minds of Latin Americans: Conservatism, materialism and conformism. *Gazette,* 24(1), 61–65.

Boyd Barrett, O. (1977). Media imperialism: Towards an international framework of the analysis of media systems. In J. Curran, M. Gurevitch, & J. Woollacott (Eds), *Mass communication and society.* (pp. 116–141) London: Edward Arnold.

Capriles, O. (1979). Acciones by reacciones en San Jose: el debate de las comunicaciones en la UNESCO. In A.R. Eldredge (Ed.), *El desafío de la comunicación internacional* (pp. 81–124). Mexico City: Neuva Imagen.

Capriles, O. (1980, August). *From national communication policies to the new international information order.* Paper presented at the 12th Scientific Conference of the IAMCR, Caracas.

Cruise O'Brien, R. (1976). *Professionalism in broadcasting.* Sussex: IDS paper 100.

Cruise O'Brien, R., & Helleiner, G.K. (1982). The political economy of information in a changing international economic order. In M. Jussawalla * D.M. Lamberton, (Eds) *Communication, economics and development* (pp. 100–132). New York: Pergamon.

Dagnino, E. (1980). Cultural and ideological dependence: Building a theoretical framework. In K. Kumar, (Ed.), *Transnational enterprises: Their impact on Third World societies and cultures* (pp. 297–332). Boulder, CO Westview Press.

Fisher, G. (1979). *American communications in a global society.* Norwood: Ablex.

Golding, P. (1977). Media professionalism. In J. Curran, M. Gurevitch, & J. Woollacott. *Mass communication and society* (pp. 241–308). London: Edward Arnold.

Guback, T. (1978). *Notes on imperialism and the film industry.* Unpublished paper, University of Illinois.

Guback, T. (1984). International circulation of theatrical motion pictures and television programming. In G. Gerbner & M. Siefert (Eds.), *World communications* (pp. 153–163). New York: Longman.

Hamelink, C.J. (Ed.). (1980). *Communication in the Eighties.* Rome: IDOC.

Hamelink, C.J. (1983). *Cultural autonomy in global communications.* New York: Longman.

Harris, P. (1977). *News dependence: The case for a new world information order.* Report to UNESCO, unpublished.

Harris, P. (1979). *Putting the NIIO into practice: The role of Inter Press Service.* Rome: Inter Press Service.

Hedebrö, G. (1979). *Communication and social change in developing countries.* Stockholm: School of Journalism, Stockholm University.

Janus, N.Z. (1981). Advertising and the mass media in the era of the global corporation. In E. McAnany, J. Schnitman & N.Z. Janus (Eds), *Communication and social structure* (p. 287–316). New York: Praeger.

Katz, E., & Wedell, G. (1977). *Broadcasting in the Third World.* Cambridge, MA: Harvard University Press.

Lee, C.C. (1980). *Media imperialism reconsidered.* Beverly Hills, CA: Sage.

Manet, E.G. (1979). *Descolonización de la información.* Prague: I.O.J.

Mankekar, D.R. (1981). *Whose freedom, whose order?* New Delhi: Clarion.

Mattelart, A. (1979). *The multinational corporations and the control of culture.* Atlantic Highlands, NJ: Harvester Press.

Mayobre, J.A. (1976). *Información, dependencia y desarrollo.* Caracas: Monte Avila.

McPhail, T. (1981). *Electronic colonialism.* Beverly Hills, CA: Sage.

Nordenstreng, K., & Schiller, H.I. (Eds). (1976). *National sovereignty and international communication.* Norwood, NJ: Ablex Publishing corp.

Nordenstreng, K. (1979). *Struggle around the new international information order.* Unpublished paper Tampere University.

Pavlic, B., & Hamelink, C.J. (1985). *Interlocks between the economic and the information order.* Paris: UNESCO.

Pool, I. de S. (1980, August). *The new structure of international communication.* Paper presented to the 12THE Scientific Conference of the IAMCR, Caracas.

Robinson, G. (Ed.). (1978). *Communications for tomorrow.* New York: Praeger.

Reyes Matta, F. (Ed.). (1978). *La información en el neuvo orden internacional.*

Salinas, R., & Paldan, L. (1976). Culture in the process of dependent development. In K. Nordenstreng & H.I. Schiller (Eds.), *National sovereignty and international communication* (pp. 82–98). Norwood, NJ: Ablex.

Sauvant, K. (1980). Socio-cultural investments and the political economy of North-South relations: The role of transnational enterprises. In K. Kumar, *Transnational enterprises: Their impact on Third Word Societies and Cultures* (pp. 275–296). Boulder, Co: Westview Press.

Schiller, H.I. (1976). *Communication and cultural domination.* New York: International Arts and Sciences Press.

Schiller, H.I. (1981). *Who knows: Information in the age of the Fortune 500.* Norwood, NJ: Ablex.

Schramm, W. (Ed.). (1978). *International news wires and Third World news.* Hawaii: East-West Center.

Smith, A. (1980). *The geo-politics of information.* London: Faber & Faber.

Van Dinh, T. (1979). Nonalignment and cultural imperialism. In K. Nordenstreng & H.I. Schiller, (Eds.), *National sovereignty and international communication* (pp. 261–275) Norwood, NJ: Ablex.

Varis, T. (1973). *Television traffic: A one-way street?* Paris: UNESCO.

Varis, T., Salinas, R., & Jokelin, R. (1977). *International news and the new information order.* Report 39, Institute of Journalism and Mass Communication, Tampere University.

Publications

BY JAMES D. HALLORAN

Control or Consent: A Study of the Challenge of Mass Communication. Sheed and Ward, 1963.

Television and Violence. *Twentieth Century*, Vol. 173, No. 1024, 1965, pp. 61–72.

Mass Media and the Family. In *The Family*, Proceedings of The Social Studies Conference, Republic of Ireland, 1965, pp. 47–55.

Wirkungen des Fernsehens. Studien zur Massenkommunikation 3. Verlag Hans Bredow-Institut, 1966.

Difficulties in Communication Research. *Educational Television and Radio in Britain: A New Phase in Education.* BBC Publications, 1966, pp. 237–50.

Television Violence. *Censorship*, Vol. 8, Autumn 1966, pp. 15–21.

Probleme der Fernsehforschung. *Rundfunk und Fernsehen.* Jahrgang 1966, Heft 1, pp. 6–24.

Communications and Social Science. *The Month*, Vol. 35, No. 3, March 1966, pp. 167–76.

Studie o pusobeni hromadych sdelovacich prostrekku. Praha: CS. Televize, 1966.

The Fifteen to Sixteen Year Old as a Television Viewer. In *Report on ITA Consultation on Schools Programmes*, November 1967, pp. 5–7.

Violence and Mass Media, *The Guardian*, 18th November, 1967, p. 7.

The Contribution of Research to the Use of Mass Media in Adult Education. In *Report on Prague Seminar-Mass Media and Adult Education.* Czechoslovakian Unesco Commission and International Central Institute for Youth and Educational Television, August, 1967, p. 39.

Television and Attitude Formation and Change—A Social Scientific Perspective. Report of the First International Seminar on Television and the Formation of Social Attitudes, Madrid, December 1967.

On the Impact of Television. *The Advertising Quarterly*, Vol. 14, Winter 1967–68, pp. 56–62.

Television and Violence. In O.N. Larsen, Ed., *Violence and the Mass Media.* New York: Harper and Row, 1968, pp. 139–51.

Los Efectos de la Presentacion por los Medios, de la Violencia y de las Agresion. *Revista Española de la Opinion Publica*, Vol. 13, July–September 1968.

Mass Communication Research and Adult Education. Vaughan College Paper, No. 12, 1968 (Out of print).

The Communicator in Mass Communication Research. In P. Halmos, ed., *The Sociological Review Monograph,* No. 13. University of Keele, 1969, pp. 5–21.

Mass Media Research. *The Listener,* 27th March, 1969, pp. 407–8.

Producer/Researcher Co-operation in Mass Media Studies. In P. Taff, ed., *Report on the First EBU Workshop for Producers of Children's Television Programmes.* European Broadcasting Union, Geneva, 1969, pp. 31–41.

Introduction to *Reports on International Evaluation of Children's Reactions to the Swedish Television Programme "Patrik und Putrik."* J.D. Halloran, ed. Internationales Zentralinstitut für das Jugend-und Bildungsfernsehen Bayerischer Rundfunk, Munich, March 1969. pp. 7–13.

Studying the effects of television. In Halloran, J.D., Ed., *The Effects of Television.* Panther Books Ltd., 1970, pp. 9–23.

The social effects of television. Ibid., pp. 25–68.

The effects of the media portrayal of violence and aggression. In Tunstall, J., ed., *Media Sociology.* London: Constable, 1970, pp. 314–21.

Attitude Formation and Change. Leicester: Leicester University Press. For the Television Research Committee, 2nd Impression, 1970.

The Theme of the Seminar. In J.D. Halloran and M. Curevitch, eds., *Broadcaster/Research Co-operation in Mass Communication Research.* A Report on an International Seminar held at the University of Leicester, England, December 17th-21st, 1970, pp. 9–27.

Some Concluding Remarks. Ibid, pp. 170–9.

Does TV violence matter? *The Guardian,* 25th March, 1970, p. 12.

Mass Communication in Society. *Educational Broadcasting Review,* Vol. 4, No. 6, 1970, pp. 17–33.

Mass Media in Society: the need of research. *Unesco Reports and Papers on Mass Communication,* No. 59, 1970.

The Effects of Mass Communication, with Special Reference to Television. Leicester: Leicester University Press. For the Television Research Committee, 5th Impression, 1971.

Joukkoticdotusvalineiden Vaikutusta Tutlrimassa. In *Tiedotuspin Laitos Opetus-moniste.* Tiedotustutkimuksen Näköaloja, Tampereen Yliopisto, Kesäkuu 1972, No. 2.

Communication, Churches and Development. In Hans-Wolfgang Hessler, ed., *WACC Journal* No. 2/72: Satellites, Cassettes, Cable/Part 11. Eckart-Verlag, Witten/Ruhr, Germany, pp. 12–16.

The Mass Media and Violence. In Hans-Wolfgang Hessler, ed., *WACC Journal* No. 3/72: Violence. Eckart-Verlag, Witten/Ruhr, Germany, pp. 12–26.

Die massenmedien und die Gewalt. In M. Löffler, ed., *Die Darstellung der Gewalt in den Massenmedien.* C.H. Beck, Munich, 1973, pp. 8–15.

Massekommunikasjonens virkninger. In H.F. Dahl, ed., *Masse-kom-munikasjon*. Gyldendal Norsk Forlag, Oslo, 1973, pp. 172–202.

Fernsehen, gesellschaftliche Anpassung und Kriminalität. In *Medien-forschung: Colloquium Verlag Berlin*. Berlin: Otto H. Hess, 1974, pp. 122–29.

Mass Media and Society: The Challenge of Research. *Inaugural Lecture* delivered in the University of Leicester, 25 October 1973. Leicester: Leicester University Press, 1974.

Hochschulausbildung und Massenkommunikation. In *Kommunikations-Medien und die Zukunft der Hochschul-Ausbildung: Dokumentation zu einem internationalen Symposium in Stuttgart*, November 1973. Bild der Wissenschaft, Stuttgart, 1974, pp. 18–22.

Research in Forbidden Territory. In G. Gerbner, L.P. Gross, and W.H. Melody, eds., *Communications Technology and Social Policy: Understanding the New "Cultural Revolution."* John Wiley and Sons Inc., 1973, pp. 547–53.

The Media and Communication in a Developing Country. In *Mass Media Research: Report on International Workshop in Hilversum*, November 1973. Geneva: Lutheran World Federation, 1974, pp. 63–70.

Visual Language. In *Intermedia*, Vol. 2, No. 1. London: International Broadcast Institute, 1974, p. 3.

Training in the Critical Reading of Television Language. Report on an International Colloquy in Leicester, September, 1973. Strasbourg: Council of Europe, 1974.

Understanding Television. In *Education and Culture*, No. 25, Summer 1974. Strasbourg: Council of Europe, 1974, pp. 15–20.

Communication and Change. In Hans-Wolfgang Hessler, ed., *WACC Journal* No. 4/74: Political Access to the Media (1). Eckart-Verlag, Witten/Ruhr, Germany, pp. 34–44.

Mass Media and Race: a Research Approach. Introduction to *Race as News*. Paris: The Unesco Press, 1974, pp. 9–34.

Mass Media and Socialization. In *Der Anteil der Massenmedien bei der Herausbildung des Bewussteins in der sich wandelnden Welt*. Sektion Journalistik. Karl-MarxUniversität, Leipzig, 1974, pp. 39–43.

Über die Ansatze zur Erforschung der Sozialisation in der Familie: Ein Uberblick aus Grossbritannien. In *Fernsehen und Bildung*. Verlag Dokumentation Munchen, 9, 1975, 2/3, pp. 98–110.

On the Research Approaches for Studying Socialization in the Family: An outline from Great Britain. In *Fernsehen und Bildung/Special English Issue*. Verlag Dokumentation Munchen, 9, 1975, 2/3, pp. 15–25.

The Mass Media and Leisure Provision and Use. In *La Revista del Instituto de Ciencias sociales*. Diputacion Provincial de Barcelona, 1975, pp. 29–37.

Communication and Community. Strasbourg: Council of Europe, June 1975.

The Development of Cable Television in the United Kingdom: Problems and Possibilities. Strasbourg: Council of Europe, August 1975.

The Mass Media and Violence. *Forensic Science*, vol. 5, no. 3, 1975, pp. 209–7.

Need for Independent Research. In *View*, Independent Television Publications Limited, No. 2, November 1975, pp. 79–93.

Mass Media in Society—the Need of Research. Arab States Broadcasting Union. *Broadcasting Report No. 3*, 1975.

The Problems We Face. In *Journal of Communication*, vol. 25, no. 1, Winter 1975, pp. 15–25.

Attitude Formation and Change. Originally published in 1967 by Leicester University Press. Reprinted by permission of LUP, by Greenwood Press, Connecticut, 1976.

Leisure and Society. In Lionel Salter, ed., *Third International Forum of Light Music in Radio.* Munich, 2-6 June, 1975. Geneva: European Broadcasting Union, English and French editions, 1976, pp. 13–25.

Mass Media and Society. In *Juklaviikon Yleisöluennot.* University of Tampere, Finland, 1976, pp. 52–59.

(Ed) *Mass Media and Socialization.* International Association for Mass Communication Research, 1976.

Introduction. Ibid, pp. 10–12.

Die Berichterstattung in den Massenmedien über kriminelles Verhalten. In *Universitas.* Wissenschaftliche Verlagsgesellschaft m.b.H., Stuttgart, August 1976, pp. 819–26.

An Explanatory Study of Some of the Factors that Influence the Production of Drama in an Independent Television Company in the United Kingdom. In *Organization and Structure of Fiction Production in Television.* Torino: Editizione RAI. 1077. pp. 9–50. Italian and French translations, pp. 51–140.

Broadcasting and Continuing Education. In *The Japan Prize Symposium.* Supplement to the Report of the 11th Japan Prize Contest. NHK, Tokyo, 1077, pp. 7–18.

Understanding Television: Research and the Broadcaster-Cooperation-Conflict—Compromise. Council for Cultural Cooperation. Council of Europe. Strasbourg, 1977.

Introduction. In *Ethnicity and the Media.* Paris: UNESCO. 1977, pp. 9–24.

Television y Violencia Mensaje y Medios. *Revista de los Profesionales de la Comunicacion.* Instituto Oficial de Radiodifusion y Television, No. I, October 1977, pp. 80–83.

Social Research in Broadcasting: Further Development—or Turning the Clock Back? *Journal of Communication*, vol. 28, no. 2, Spring 1978, pp. 120–132.

Mass Communication: Symptom or Cause of Violence. In *International Social Science Journal.* Vol. XXX, No. 4, 1978, pp. 816–833. Pp. 865–82 in French edition, pp. 886–904 in Spanish edition.

Introduction. In *Mass Media and Man's View of Society, A Conference Report and International Bibliography.* International Association for Mass Communication Research. Leicester. 1978, pp. 5, 6.

Mass Communication Research: State of the Art—Where We Are and Where We Should be Going. Report on the First Session of the IAMCR Conference 1976. In *Mass Media and Man's View of Society. A Conference Report and International Bibliography*. Leicester. 1978, pp. 7–21.

Studying Violence and the Mass Media: A Sociological Approach. In Charles Winick, ed., *Deviance and Mass Media*. Sage Annual Reviews of Studies in Deviance, vol. 2, 1978, pp. 287–305.

(With Brown J.D. & Chaney, D.C.) A Mass Media Delinquency Project. In *Television Research Committee: Second Progress Report and Recommendations*. Leicester: Leicester University Press, 1969, Appendix A, pp. 50–4.

Television and Delinquency. Leicester: Leicester University Press. For the Television Research Committee.

Fernsehen und Krimnaliktät. Verlag Volker Spiess, 1972.

(With Croll, P.) Television programs in Great Britain: content and control. In G.A. Comstock and E.A. Rubenstein, eds., *Television and Social Behavior, Vol. 1*. Government Printing Office. Washington. 1971. pp. 41–92.

Research Findings on Broadcasting, Appendix F. In *Report of the Committee on the Future of Broadcasting*. HMSO. London. August 1977, pp. 29–73.

(With Elliott, P.) Television for Children and Young People: A Summary of a Survey Carried out for the European Broadcasting Union. In *Television Research Committee: Second Progress Report and Recommendations*. leicester: Leicester University Press, 1969, Appendix E, pp. 95–106.

Television for Children and Young People. European Broadcasting Union. Geneva. 1970.

(With Elliott, P. & Murdock, G.) *Demonstrations and Communications: A Case Study*. Harmondsworth: Penguin Books Ltd, 1970.

Konkluziok: A tuntetesek mint hirek. In *A Televizios Jelenseg*. Ed Tamas Szecskö. Gondolat. Budapest. 1976, pp. 321–40.

(With EyreBrook, E.) *Children and Television News*. Danish Radio, Copehagen, 1970.

(With Gurevitch, M., eds.) *Broadcaster/Researcher Co-operation in Mass Communication Research*. A report on an international seminar held at the University of Leicester. England. December 1970.

(With Noble, G.) A Report on Several Evaluations of Children's Reactions to a Prize-Winning Film for Young Children (ages 5 to 8 years). From the Second Prix Jeunesse Competition, Munich, 1966: and a summary of the English contribution to this report. In *Television Research Committee Second Progress Report and Recommendations* Leicester: Leicester University Press. 1969. Appendix D, pp. 77–94.

Researcher/Producer Co-operation. Ibid, Appendix C. pp. 64–76.

Information and Communication. *Aslib Proceedings*, vol. 31, no. 1, January, 1979, pp. 21–8.

Television in Focus. *The Unesco Courier*. March 1979, pp. 4–9.

New Information and Economic Orders: Need for Research-Based Information. *Communicator*, vol. XIV, no. 4. October 1979, pp. 13–14.

Introduction to *What do TV Producers Know About Their Young Viewers?* Stiftung Prix Jeunesse, Munich, 1979, pp. 7–29.

Mass Communication: Symptom or Cause of Violence? *Mass Communication Review Yearbook*, vol. 1, Sage Publications, 1980, pp. 432–449.

Communication Needs and Communication Policies. *Massa Communicatie*, VIII/3-4, 1980, pp. 152–157.

The context of mass communication research. *Papers for the International Commission for the Study of Communication Problems*. No. 78. Paris: Unesco, 1980.

Introduction to *Mass Media and National Cultures*. International Association for Mass Communication Research, 1980, pp. 5–7.

The Need for Communication Research in Developing Countries, *Media Asia*, vol. 7, no. 3, 1980, pp. 137–144.

Mass Communication: Symptom or Cause of Violence? *Violence and its Causes*. Paris: Unesco, 1981, pp. 125–140.

The Context of Mass Communication Research. In McAnany, E., Schnitmann, J. & Janus, N.Z., eds., *Communication and Social Structure: critical studies in mass media research*. New York: Praeger, 1981, pp. 21–57.

The Context of Mass Communication Research. Occasional Papers 13. Asian Mass Communication Resarch and Information Centre, Singapore, January 1981.

I Bambini e la Televisione. *Documenti*. Anno IV, N.22/23 Mass Media e Famiglia. Maggio-Agosto, 981. pp. 7–13.

Mass Media Involvement and Social Action. In *Proceedings of Symposium* 2-3 September, 1981, Leiden. The Netherlands. pp. 41–55.

Introduction and Background in *Communication in the Community—An International Study on the Role of the Mass Media in Seven Communities*. Paris: Unesco, 1982, pp. 5–14.

Young TV Viewers and Their Images of Foreigners—a summary and interpretation or a four-national study. Stiftung Prix Jeunesse, Munich, 1982, pp. 1–22. Introduction to *New Structures of International Communication? The Role of Research*. International Association for Mass Communication Research, 1982, pp. 7–8.

Introduction to The Mass Media and Village Life: an Indian Study. Leicester: Centre for Mass Communication Research, University of Leicester, 1983, pp. i–iv.

Research Considerations, Possibilities and Proposals. Introduction to *The Media Coverage of Disarmament and Related Issues*. Report to Unesco, International Association for Mass Communication Research, 1983, pp. i–vi.

A Case for Critical Eclecticism. In Ferment in the Field, *Journal of Communication*, vol. 33, no. 3, 1983, pp. 270–278.

Information and Communication: Information is the Answer, But What is the Question? *Journal of Information Science* 7, 1983, pp. 158–167.

Foreword in *Communication and Democracy: Directions in Research*. Leicester: International Association for Mass Communication Research, 1983, pp. iii–iv.

Foreword in *History in Black and White: An Analysis of South African School History Textbooks*. Paris: Unesco, 1983, p. 9.

Sobre Comunicacion y Democracia. In *CHASQUI*. Revista Latinoamericana de Comunicacion. CIESPAL. July/Sept 1983, pp. 6–11.

Introduction in *Television and the Images of the Family*. Stiftung Prix Jeunesse, Munich, 1984, pp. vii–xiii.

The New Communication Technologies and Research. In *Communication Manual*. Bonn: Friedrich-Ebert-Stiftung, 1982, pp. 50–58.

Sobre Communication y Democracia. *CHASQUI*. REvista Lationamericana de Comunicacion. Quito: CIESPAL. July/Sept 1983, pp. 6–11.

Freeing the Media from Market Forces. *UNESCO Features*, No. 783, 1983, pp. 6–9.

Introduction. In *Social Communication and Global Problems*. Leicester: International Association for Mass Communication Research, 1984, pp. 7–9.

(With Jones, M.) La famille a la télévision: Le poertrait de la famille a la télévision Britannique. *Les enfants et la télé vision—Études de radio-télévision*. Brussels: RTBF, 1985, pp. 151–177.

Information and Communication: Information is the Answer, But What is the Question/ In B.D. Ruben, ed., *Information and Behavior*, vol. 1, Transaction Books, 1985, pp. 27–39.

What Can Research Tell Us? Paper presented to the Australian Children's Television Foundation, International Conference on "The Challenge of Kids' TV," Melbourne, Australia, Conference Paper No. 9, 1985.

Trendsettrs or Trendfollowers, the Contribution of Research. *Massa Communicatie*, August 1985, pp. 157–165.

Coping with Information. In E. Denig and A. Van der Meiden, eds., *A Geography of Public Relations Trends*. Dordrecht: Martinus Nijhoff Publishers, 1985, pp. 23–36.

International Democratization or Communication: The Challenges of Research. In J. Becker, G. Hedebro and L. Paldan, eds., *Communication and Domination*. Norwood: Ablex Publishing Corp., 1986, pp. 241–248.

The Social Implications of Technological Innovations in Communication. In M. Traber, ed. *The Myth of the Information Revolution*. London: Sage Publications, 1986, pp. 46–63.

Spoteczne implikacje innowacji w technice komunikowania. *Zeszyty Prasoznawcze*, 1986, R. XXVII, Nr. 4 (110).

The International Research Experience. In N. Jayaweera and S. Amunugama, eds., *Rethinking Development Communication*. Asian Mass Communication Research and Information Centre (AMIC), 1987, pp. 129–148.

(With Jones, M.) Learning About the Media: Media Education and Communication Research, *Communication and Society*, 16, UNESCO, 1987.

(With Linné, O.) Das Fernsehen und die Familie. Zusammenfassende darstellung und interpretation. In: *Fernsehen und Familie in drei Landern*, stiftung Prix Jeunesse, 1988, pp. 7–33.

(With Linné, O.) Television and the Family: A Summary and Interpretation. In *Television and the family in three countries*, Stiftung Prix Jeunesse, 1988, pp. 5–30.

Asking the Right Questions. *Airwaves*. Independent Broadcasting Authority, Winter 1988/89, pp. 15–16.

Ethnics and Broadcasting. Monograph *Foundation for Broadcast Culture*. eoul, December 1989, pp. 11–21. Korean language version, pp. 23–33.

Mass and Violence. In R. Bluglass and P. Bowden, eds., *Principles and Practice of Forensic Psychiatry*. Churchill Livingston, 1990, pp. 571–575.

A Quarter of a Century of Prix Jeunesse. Munich: Prix Jeunesse, 1991.

Author Index

Subject Index

413